Harmony and the Balance

Harmony and the Balance

An Intellectual History of Seventeenth-Century English Economic Thought

Andrea Finkelstein

Ann Arbor

THE UNIVERSITY OF MICHIGAN PRESS

Copyright © by the University of Michigan 2000
All rights reserved
Published in the United States of America by
The University of Michigan Press
Manufactured in the United States of America
♾ Printed on acid-free paper

2003   2002   2001   2000   4   3   2   1

A CIP catalog record for this book is available from the British Library.

Library of Congress Cataloging-in-Publication Data

Finkelstein, Andrea, 1949–
    Harmony and the balance : an intellectual history of
seventeenth-century English economic thought / Andrea Finkelstein.
        p.   cm.
    Includes bibliographical references and index.
    ISBN 0-472-11143-4
    1. Economics—England—History—17th century.   I. Title.
HB103 b.F56   2000
330'.0942'09032—dc21   99-050841

For David

Contents

Acknowledgments

The genealogy of a first book is complex and thus the list of those to be thanked long: the family and friends who ran our errands when we disappeared into the stacks for weeks on end, the colleagues who covered our classes, the professors who inspired, corrected, and cajoled, and the departmental secretary who got our committees to the defense on time. To my parents, then, because they were my first teachers of bookkeeping and budgeting. To Messrs. Bass, Friedman, Allen, Monaghan, Seiden, and Stempel who taught me the ins and outs of business, and to the gentlemen at Rosenfeld, Hauptman and Shields, who were never too busy to teach a bookkeeper just a little more accounting. To Professors Trainor, Harris, and Greene at New York University (SCE) who believed economics was essential. To Professor Rogers who taught me to look beyond disciplinary boundaries. To Professors James R. Jacob, Bernard Semmel, and Stuart E. Prall at the Graduate Center (CUNY), who made a historian out of me, sometimes even against my will. To Mrs. Betty Einerman, for treating graduate students with tender, loving care. To Ms. Francine Kapchan, Ms. Marilyn Harris, and Professors Frank Warren and Martin Pine at Queens College (CUNY) who also believed adjuncts were human beings. To all my colleagues at Bronx Community College (CUNY), but especially to Professor James D. Ryan, Professor Jacqueline Gutwirth, Mrs. Paulette Randall, and Mrs. Regine Cajuste for seeing me through. To my family, my friends, my students, and Miss Edelman who began it all, I say, with thanks, the mistakes are mine, the credit is thine.

Introduction

The importance of the work done in seventeenth-century England to the development of modern economic thought has long been acknowledged, but studies of this work invariably end in verdicts of "confusion" and "inconsistency." To take but one example: John Maynard Keynes credited John Locke (1632–1704) with "twin" quantity theories of money but concluded that Locke had confused the "relation" between them.[1] Sir Eric Roll accused Locke of confusing money with capital.[2] Douglas Vickers defended this "confusion" as a "central part" of the period's achievement in monetary theory, but insisted that Locke "clearly missed the logic of his own [recoinage] argument."[3] The works of the other leading economic writers of the day—Gerard de Malynes (fl. 1586–1626), Edward Misselden (fl. 1608–1654), Thomas Mun (1571–1641), Sir William Petty (1623–1687), Sir Josiah Child (1630–1699), Nicholas Barbon (1637–1698), Sir Dudley North (1641–1691), and Charles Davenant (1656–1714)—are full of similar puzzles. We are always faced with the paradox of why men with such seemingly clear insights into specific features of the marketplace failed to apply those insights across the full spectrum of economic activity.

This study attempts to find an answer to that paradox by putting these writers back into their century—politically, economically, and especially intellectually. It looks at these nine writers through the lens of the philosophical models offered by that century rather than through analytical models constructed afterward by economists, historians, and sociologists. Even such a familiar label as *mercantilism* has been avoided until it can be reconstructed from the evidence offered by the nine writers discussed herein.

Questions of economic and political history form the foundation of this work, but adding a detailed intellectual approach may reveal not only an underlying unity to those persistent inconsistencies, but also the depth of interaction between intellectual and economic thought. The resolution toward which this study points is that the economic concepts under consideration were intended to "save" their writers' visions of a moral or essential universe, not to construct our vision of the observed regularities of an existential one. Thus the verdict of this author, briefly speaking, is that the century's major "economic" writers were as ambivalent about market values and their power to transform society as were their contemporaries in religion, politics, and natural philosophy, and for the same reason: they were afraid that there was something inherently chaotic in a market society. One might even say they forged their economic laws in order to rein in that chaos.

In the cosmology inherited by the seventeenth century "all things in heaven and earth" were governed "by one perpetual order," and that order was hierarchical: trees had a higher place than grass, birds higher than trees, lions higher than birds, humans higher than lions, angels higher than humans, and so forth.[4] Ordained of God it could not be otherwise: without degree there could be no order, only chaos, but the perfect mind of God could only create reason and order, thus His creation could not be chaotic, and, therefore, not without hierarchy.[5] Ordained of God, the values embedded in this cosmos were both quintessentially objective (in the thing and not the observer) and intrinsically moral. These values could not be reduced to merely quantitative units without destroying their very nature.

Thomas Milles, a customs official at the turn of the century, believed "limitation" was "both the Perfection and Preservation" of all things.[6] In Genesis, *logos* (order) was created from *chaos* by the *differentiation* of light from dark and land from sea and by the *boundaries* set to each. The Ptolemaic cosmography saw the universe as a series of nested crystalline spheres with the earth at its immobile center and the stars embedded in a final, cosmos-enclosing sphere. Since Ptolemy's second-century compilation, astronomers had known that numerous mathematical adjustments were required to make the spherical model fit observed planetary positions, but the "perfect" spherical shape remained in the model as the manifestation of the perfection of the universe's creator: the constraints of a value orientation overrode the empirical data. Copernicus and Galileo moved the sun to the center but kept the basic model.

An integral part of the evolution of modern science was the swing away from metaphorical models to mathematical ones. In form, at least, Kepler's was a mathematical universe rather than a qualitative one. His Laws of Planetary Motion state, after all, that (1) the orbit of each planet is an ellipse, of which the sun's center is one of the foci, (2) the radius vector (a straight line drawn from the planet's center to the sun's) of each planet moves over equal areas in equal times, and (3) the square of the period of each planet's revolution around the sun is proportional to the cube of its mean distance from the sun. But Kepler refused to abandon the idea that the stars were embedded in one final sphere marking the boundary of a finite universe fashioned for a particular purpose by an infinite, eternal God. Even the hundreds of previously unknown stars revealed by the newly invented telescope failed to shake Kepler's certainty in that boundary. Rather than admit the stars might be farther away, Kepler insisted they were merely too small to be seen with the unaided eye. A more-distant-stars theory opened up the possibility that the universe had no limits, and such a universe had no predetermined, particular structure: no order, no harmony.[7]

Intellectual developments over the course of the century—the rise of millenarian social thought, the emergence of the mechanical philosophy and the development of modern scientific method, the increasing use of natural law, and the continuing influence of both Christian and civic humanism—had a powerful but complex effect on the ongoing development of economic thought. The power of that effect lies in the ultimate result, for without these intellectual currents economics as we know it could not have arisen, but the complexity lies in the fact that the ultimate result was far from the intended one: the economic writers who were influenced by these intellectual schools tried to use them to support their original assumptions of intrinsic value.

The threat the seventeenth century felt when links between the political, economic, philosophical, social, and religious theories grounded on its logos were challenged has been either the main theme or a persistent subtext of many treatments of the age: Popkin's *History of Scepticism,* Rabb's *Struggle for Stability,* Collins's *Divine Cosmos,* Shapiro's *Probability and Certainty,* Krailsheimer's *Studies in Self-Interest,* Keohane's *Philosophy and the State in France,* and Toulmin's *Cosmopolis* among them.[8] But intellectual historians have proved extremely reluctant to test their conclusions on the full range of the century's economic thought. J. G. A. Pocock's *Machiavellian Moment* asserted that "the first chapter in the history of political economy" was "a further chapter in the continuing history of civic humanism" without citing one economic writer earlier than Charles Davenant. Albert Hirschman's *Passions and the Interests* looked for the genesis of Adam Smith's "invisible hand" in the work of Montesquieu, but, except for one brief mention of Josiah Child, avoided getting any closer to seventeenth-century economic theory than the work of Thomas Hobbes. There are no French economic writers in Krailsheimer's study despite its title nor in Keohane's monumental survey of three centuries of French thought despite its extended treatment of *l'amour-propre.*

The failure to include this economic material seems unfortunate, especially the failure to use the material coming out of England. The sixteenth and seventeenth centuries were, together, a period of profound religious, political, economic, social, and intellectual upheaval across much of the continent of Europe. Spain, France, England, the Netherlands, and the lands of the Empire faced a common set of problems (demographic revolutions, price revolutions, political revolutions, the forever splintering Reformation, the Catholic Counter-Reformation, the assault of Pyrrhonism, etc.) with a common pool of ideas (Aristotelianism, neo-Platonism, hermeticism, humanism, neo-Stoicism, etc.). Each nation produced a body of economic writings addressing those problems: the School of Salamanca in sixteenth-century Spain was followed by the works of Pedro Fernández Navarrete (fl. 1621) and Francisco Martinez de la Mata (fl. 1650), the works of Jean Bodin (1529/30–1596) and Antoine de Montchrétien (ca. 1575–1621) in France and Giovanni Botero (1544–1617) in Italy, of Jacob Bornitz (fl. 1625) and Christoph Besold (1577–1638) in Germany, of Dirck Graswinckel (1600–1666) and Pieter de la Cout (1618–1685) in the Netherlands, and yet others. But nowhere did the seventeenth century see anything like the flood of economic literature produced in England.

There are numerous reasons for that inundation, but the central one seems to be the intersection of a swiftly changing economy with England's unique political situation. The seventeenth century (1604–1714) was the first great age of English economic expansion. While ongoing enclosure and increasing agricultural innovation brought capitalist organization to an ever increasing number of estates, national banks and their forerunners revolutionized the financial center. At the century's dawning, Bills of Exchange were specialized instruments familiar only to a narrow circle of merchants, while at its evening, paper money was common throughout the land. Global expansion and internal innovation went hand in hand. The East India Company, the greatest of the joint-stock trading companies, was chartered in 1600; by 1700 the price of stocks on the exchange was a regular feature of the periodical press.

On the political side, the increasing importance of Parliament forged by its ongoing battle with the Crown provided an open forum for the formation of economic policy while making it necessary for the merchant elite to influence that forum. There was neither such a national forum nor such an opportunity to influence it anywhere else among the major powers on the Continent—except in the United Netherlands. But in the Netherlands, the merchant elite already had a much greater role within the provincial seats of power: they had less need of the public press when they could win their points inside the council rooms.

England is also of particular interest because of its traditional characterization as the birthplace of economic (as well as political) liberalism, which is generally held to rest on the acceptance of a self-regulating (self-maximizing) economy. If we have to reexamine our ideas about the source, growth, or nature of economic liberalism in England, we may have to adjust those ideas overall.

Gerard de Malynes, Edward Misselden, Thomas Mun, Sir William Petty, Sir Josiah Child, John Locke, Sir Dudley North, Nicholas Barbon, and Charles Davenant have been chosen for this study primarily because they appear more frequently than their peers in histories of economic thought. No group of nine individuals can literally represent an entire century, but it seems not unreasonable to ask if the "best" the century had to offer were comfortable with the marketplace. Their working lives span the economic and political crises of the century so well that it is possible to recreate that century through their careers. They can also, rather like the century itself, be divided into thirds, allowing us to explore the influences of three different intellectual models: the organic body-political, the mechanical universe, and the balance (of power, of interests, or of elements in a constitution).

Gerard de Malynes, Edward Misselden, and Thomas Mun were the best known and most influential of the writers struggling to explain (and find a way out of) an economic crisis that hit England in 1620. They were also the men who codified the balance of trade theory that was to become the century's most universally held economic model. As Malynes actually belonged to the generation prior to that of his opponents, he also acts as a baseline for the century as a whole.

Petty, Child, and Locke belong to the generation that came of age during the Commonwealth, though the bulk of their work came before the public during the Exclusion Crisis and after the Glorious Revolution. They were also the first generation of economic writers for whom the new mechanical philosophy was a major influence. The old model of the body economic (derived from the body politic) underwent a significant shift in their hands that can be traced back to William Harvey's work on the circulation of the blood (though Harvey was not a mechanist) as well as to the mechanical universe of matter in motion as it was applied by Thomas Hobbes to the human mind. In Petty's work, in particular, we can see all this merge with a millenarian-tinged program of social reform, a Baconian authoritarianism, and a method composed of Baconian induction with a Cartesian emphasis on mathematics. In this group also, Statistical Man and Economic Man get their first tryouts with a significant nod to Thomas Hobbes.

North, Barbon, and Davenant represent the variety of end-of-century responses to the rapidly changing political and economic climate in England. North brings what might be called an outsider's eye to the mounting problems of the coin supply during the last years of Charles II and James II by virtue of his twenty years' stay in Turkey. The survival of his ledgers also allows us to compare his economic writings with his business practices and explore the intersection of theory and practice. Barbon, who abandoned his medical training for a career in construction and real estate, provides a perspective on England's economic life outside the usual bounds of the import-export house or the government bureaucracy. Charles Davenant lived through the Continental wars of the last Stuarts and the great series of financial experiments they engendered, and he had a lot to say about all of them. The England he lived to see was, in many respects, one Gerard de Malynes would scarcely have recognized.

As a group, these nine men also possessed as much practical financial expertise as the century would see. Malynes, Misselden, Mun, and Child were merchants proper (import-export traders) and "mere" (i.e., active traders from trading families). The gentry family that apprenticed North to a Turkey merchant had its roots in that class as well. Barbon and Petty were physicians turned businessmen whose roots were in the lesser business classes (Petty's father was a minor clothier and Barbon's a tanner turned preacher). Also from a mercantile family that rose into the gentry, Locke managed his estates, trained as a physician, and served on Trade and Colonial Boards after putting in his apprenticeship under Shaftesbury in the Exchequer. Davenant, playwright and son of a playwright, had been a Commissioner of Excise and Inspector-General of Exports and Imports. If any men in England should have understood the concepts and categories of a market society, it was this group of nine.

Historians of economic thought, whether working in the disciplines of history or economics, do, of course, discuss these economic writers, with varying degrees of attention to the enveloping intellectual milieu. Our nine subjects have their place in massive historical surveys and in more specialized studies of monetary, trade, or value theory. But despite the great variety of these works, their authors utilize fewer approaches to their material than might first be supposed. In fact, there seem to be only six, although they do cut across disciplinary lines: (1) the paradigmatic, (2) the mathematical, (3) the ideological, (4) the historically determined, (5) the methodological, and (6) the Geist models. Some will prove more pertinent to this study than will others.

1. *The paradigmatic approach.* This model owes its genesis to Thomas S. Kuhn's *Structure of Scientific Revolutions.* Kuhn claimed the course of scientific knowledge was not a stately, incremental march but a series of shift-

ing *paradigms* (underlying attitudes determining problems investigated and acceptable methodology) elaborated by their practitioners until accumulating anomalies forced the abandonment of that paradigm for another (the revolution).[9] Applied to economics, this internalist approach becomes a debate over whose work deserves to be called revolutionary. Terence Wilmot Hutchison (*On Revolutions and Progress in Economic Knowledge*) proposed three revolutions: Smith's (the systematization of the self-adjusting market), a Jevonian (marginal utility), and a Keynesian (macroeconomics), while rejecting a mercantilist (because it coexisted with Scholastic thought "for centuries"), a physiocratic (as "subsidiary" to Smith), a Ricardian (merely a "methodological" change), a Marxian (because his ideas dominated only where supported by "propaganda ministries and police terror"), and both neo-Keynesian and monetarist (neither adds "significant" empirical content).[10] On the other hand, Guy Routh (*The Origin of Economic Ideas*) argued that the paradigm has not actually changed since it was established in the seventeenth century by Sir William Petty.[11] Ranging over the entire economic corpus, this approach far exceeds the scope of this study, but one question might be asked of it for the seventeenth century. That question concerns the often overlooked Kuhn corollary. According to Kuhn, the normal-revolutionary alternation was the inevitable result of the way in which scientists were trained (in the existing paradigm) and worked out their professional careers (doing "normal science" until the paradigm broke down).[12] The lack of an institutionalized, professional training program and career track caused Kuhn to conclude that before Newton's work, "normal science" could not appear: all was simply a welter of competing views.[13] The question to be posed then is whether or not the Kuhn thesis should be applied to the preprofessional period.

2. *The mathematical approach.* Seventeenth-century economic writing lacks our specialized vocabulary. Instead, it abounds in metaphor and analogy. To surmount this language barrier, Robert V. Eagly (*The Structure of Classical Economic Theory*) devised a mathematical model of mercantilist analysis, with particular emphasis on its "absence of *market* mechanisms."[14] A much more market-oriented set of formulas was devised by Hans Brems (*Pioneering Economic Theory, 1639–1980: A Mathematical Restatement*).[15] If such restatements make it easier for the contemporary student to compare particular elements of modern and premodern economic thought, they do so at the cost of masking the historical reality. Malynes and company did not, after all, think in formulas.

3. *The ideological approach.* Historians and economists alike have been guilty of being led by their politics. One might argue that Hutchison's beliefs have colored his judgment of Marx, while, if we continue reading

Guy Routh's book, we will find that his sympathies lie with the "heretics" who used "the labour theory of value to demonstrate that the whole of the product of industry should belong to those by whose labour it was produced."[16] Defending his theory (in *Possessive Individualism*) against Jacob Viner's critical review, C. B. Macpherson bridled at the suggestion that his Marxism colored his interpretation of Locke, but proffered that he had not bothered to make the claimed attack on "ethical foundations of liberal democracy" because their "weakness" was "now acknowledged on all sides."[17] A distaste for a particular belief or system may not be the best guide to it. We might actually be better off when the shoemaker sticks to his last. Ronald L. Meek's *Studies in the Labour Theory of Value* proclaimed from the first that labor theories of value were "good sense and good science."[18] The treatment of the main subject matter was at least sympathetic, even if Meek passed over in silence almost every seventeenth-century attempt to tie utility value (and price) to the "Humour of the Buyers."[19]

The ease with which political bias can be detected limits its harm, but there is a narrower bias, less easily detectable by and thus more dangerous to the student-reader. Basic economics courses rarely cover the depth of disagreement between competing economic schools, but a writer's allegiance can have a tremendous impact on the evaluation of the material covered. Even when this allegiance is clearly stated, the damage is not entirely avoided. Murray N. Rothbard wasted no time informing the reader of his *Economic Thought before Adam Smith* that he was "an adherent" of the "praxeologic" variant of the "Austrian School" of economics,[20] though nonspecialists would have to read all the way up to page 325 to find that praxeology "is economic theory resting a few broad, self-evident axioms grounded in apprehension of reality, then logically deducing the implications of these emphatically true axioms."[21] By then his readers might be better able to judge references to North's (deductive) "brilliance" and Petty's (empirical) "jejune" mercantilism, though they might have to work a little harder to understand why Rothbard praised the "hard-money, metallist, anti-inflationist" Locke while denouncing Barbon and other "inflationist schemers,"[22] as Rothbard has neglected to explain the libertarian *positions* of his Austrian school. Joseph A. Schumpeter's *History of Economic Analysis* presents a much more modulated account of the same material, but could still pose a problem for those unaware of his *unstated* econometric bias. For Schumpeter, North did no more than "sum up, incompletely but effectively, the contribution of the 'mercantilist' writings to 1691,"[23] while Petty was praised as "first and last a theorist" for whom "generalizations are the joint products of figures and reasoning that are never allowed to part company."[24]

For the purposes of this study, both the broader and narrower ideological approaches seem deficient in their tendency to substitute blame for explanation in handling inconsistencies in seventeenth-century economic thought. This tendency compounds itself when transferred to the broader intellectual ground. How does it help Rothbard's readers understand Malynes et al. to find the "flimsy organicist analogy" "dominant in English political thought from the early sixteenth to the early seventeenth century" dismissed as "a form of simplistic and militant" absolutism?[25]

4. *The historically determined approach.* This approach stresses the sociology of economic knowledge, viewing it as a reaction to the conditions of economic and political life in which it grew. The link proposed may be very event-specific, job-specific, or more generally tied to the technological realities of the day. Event-specific studies like B. E. Supple's *Commercial Crisis and Change in England* insist that it is "almost impossible fully to understand the ideas of Misselden, Malynes and Mun apart from the depression of the early 1620s."[26] The strength of such works is the specificity of the historical context they provide, but it can also be their weakness. Supple has no explanation for why the books Malynes published in 1622 and 1623 repeat arguments he first devised in 1600 and 1601.

Job-specific approaches such as E. A. J. Johnson's pioneering *Predecessors of Adam Smith* present us with a Gerard de Malynes who "could not see his economic world except through the tangled web of foreign exchange operations," in contrast to a Thomas Mun who "peered out of his counting house and complacently assured the world that the merchants were the saviors of economic well-being."[27] But this offers little insight into why Mun and fellow East India merchant Sir Josiah Child worked from a parallel attack on bullion regulation to divergent positions on balance of trade theory—Mun helping to codify and Child leading the attack against it.

The technological general variant sees the whole cluster of economic constraints—supply of the money commodity, customary payment periods, transportation risks, government policies, means and mode of production—as shaping period thought. In his *History of Economic Thought,* Sir Eric Roll contended that "the mercantilist attack on high interest rates was natural in an age of great scarcity of liquid funds" and "underdeveloped banking facilities."[28] Some of what Roll saw as "confused" but "natural" John Maynard Keynes saw as eminently sensible. Keynes went quite a distance toward rehabilitating seventeenth-century economic thought in the "Notes on Mercantilism" appended to his *General Theory.* He believed the constraints of the seventeenth-century economy dictated and demonstrated the considerable "elements of truth" in mercantilist thought.[29] D. C. Coleman took a similarly determinist line in his introduction to *Revisions in Mercantilism.*[30] But because Keynes and Coleman emphasized different determining variables, full employment appeared as a major goal in Keynes's seventeenth century but only "a minor current" in Coleman's.[31] Seventeenth-century theory could not fail to be affected by the age's economic constraints, but it is dangerous to assume a priori that these were a *sufficient* cause. After all, present-day economists sent back into the seventeenth century would not suddenly adopt a metallist definition of money, because they would look at the seventeenth-century world through the lens of twentieth-century economic thought. The limiting factor here derives not from Marxist materialism but from a key foundation of economics itself. Modern economics deals with interdependent variables that appear alternately as causes and effects in the formulas and models constructed of them, but these variables—interest rates, consumption-savings ratios, money supply, and so on—are invariably economic. Economists are trained to work from economic effects back to economic causes. What this study attempts to do is combine insights gained from the politicoeconomic context with those gained from the intellectual.

5. *The methodological approach.* This view seeks to plot the development of economics as a method of analysis rather than to construct a chronology of particular economic insights. Schumpeter set the parameters: "Economic Analysis" was "the result of scientific endeavor"; "Economic Thought" merely denoted the dominant "opinions on economic matters" prevailing at any given time.[32] In a much earlier work, *Economic Doctrine and Method,* Schumpeter had suggested that the "science of economics" had two distinct "roots" (despite their occasional historical overlap), one being "the study of the philosophers" and the other "accumulated by people of various types whose primary motive had been their interest in practical problems of the day."[33] This assumption of a sharp divide between theory and practice makes it difficult to see the one in the other.

One of the better known works using the methodological approach is William Letwin's *Origins of Scientific Economics,* which explored the competition between Baconian empiricism and Cartesian deduction in forging economic science, although its main theme was the role played by the need to convince the political elite of the writers' objectivity. For Letwin, who wished to draw a hard and fast line between practical and theoretical knowledge, the works of Malynes, Misselden, and Mun "were to economic theory as an engineer's manual is to theoretical mechanics," but this approach left Letwin having to characterize their fellow merchant North's superior analytical skills as an "irreducible" mystery.[34] Given Letwin's characterization of one methodology as devolving from another (and a not very well hidden deductive bias), the intellectual context was both too broadly and too narrowly drawn by him to solve that mystery.

A more recent, and broader, survey, Karl Pribham's *History of Economic Reasoning*, also links a change in English economic thought in the seventeenth century to a change in philosophical thought. Pribham explained the increasing use of "nominalistic principles" and "mechanical conceptions, especially the equilibrium concept" as a form of economic Baconianism.[35] French thought he saw as mired in a static Cartesianism.[36] This is a divide proposed by Letwin, except that Letwin found both Baconian and Cartesian strains in English thought. Pribham's intellectual models are as schematic as Letwin's. Pribham seems to have concluded that Hobbes was a Baconian because he rejected Scholastic methods and "made sense impressions produced by outside sources the primary agents to initiate all intellectual processes."[37] This not only distorts Bacon's thought, but also ignores the vital influence on Hobbes of Cartesian deduction, natural law tradition, mechanical philosophy, and the rhetorical tradition. William Harvey's influence on the century's thought has been ignored. Even when dealing with a trained physician such as William Petty, Pribham easily comes to the conclusion that the numerous anatomical analogies in his work were "only incidental and not significant for his methodology."[38]

The classic treatment, however, remains that of Schumpeter, who set out to separate "the intellectual efforts that men have made in order to *understand* economic phenomena" from the "economic sociology" that dealt with "the question how they came to behave as they do."[39] But his explanation of seventeenth-century economic thought relied on the overweening importance of "the particular mental habits generated by the work in the business office" and the lesser but still important influence of the "growth of capitalist enterprise."[40] These leave us asking why, given the chaotic state of seventeenth-century business practice, the seventeenth-century business mentality should be twinned with the twentieth, which takes us into the problems of the approach most directly connected to this study.

6. *The Geist approach.* This perspective looks to the development of capitalism or the intrusion into the traditional social order of a capitalist or business mentality to explain the strengths and weaknesses of seventeenth-century economic thought. It is both the oldest and newest approach, because, as seen above, it tends to contaminate the others. Historians and sociologists have been even more energetic than economists in pursuing this approach. What Schumpeter called "the particular mental habits" of the businessman was itself a restatement of Richard Henry Tawney's contention (in his *Religion and the Rise of Capitalism*) that the "spirit of modern

business" had modernized Calvinism rather than the reverse as earlier claimed by Max Weber.[41] Much more recently, the merchant-writers in Joyce Oldham Appleby's *Economic Thought and Ideology in Seventeenth-Century England* were (with the exception of Malynes, her Scholastic touchstone) treated as somehow *necessarily* comfortable with the "workings of the market" on whatever level they happened to understand them.[42] Based on a survey of the century's voluminous pamphlet literature, Appleby depicted an era comfortable with market mechanisms and the importance of demand caught, at its end, in an ideological conflict in which this comfort was turned into a class-based weapon for a resurgent oligarchy.[43] That these pamphlets contain plentiful praises of "infinite wants" and "the natural freedom of trade" cannot be denied, but the *depth* of the century's acceptance of a market economy is less certain. Appleby paid less attention than was warranted both to the contemporaneous *usage* of these phrases and to the measures these pamphlets actually supported.[44]

The difference between the modern analytical model of the capitalist *Geist* and the organic analytic model of the seventeenth century is the subject of the next chapter.

I

Geist vs. *Weltanschauung*

CHAPTER 1

Merchants and
the Body Politic

The spirit, or *Geist*, presumed to animate the marketplace has long had a bad press. The citizens of ancient Athens feared its contagion so much they banned its practitioners from setting foot in the Agora (the square where the political assembly was held) unless summoned by the magistrate.[1] When Cato recommended disposing of elderly slaves as one did worn-out oxen,[2] Plutarch took him to task for "thinking there ought to be no further commerce between man and man, than whilst there arises some profit by it."[3] Christian theologians were equally disdainful. Gratian would have all buyers and sellers "cast forth from God's temple."[4] And, while Aquinas admitted that gain was not altogether evil if used to feed one's family or for charitable ends, he just could not rid himself of the feeling that there was "something shameful" about commerce.[5]

In Britain, the cradle of laissez-faire, the critique of market values has been as deep and long-lasting as the advance of that market itself. By the 1530s, anonymous pamphleteers, alarmed over the conversion of farmland to pasturage, blamed the resulting social dislocation on the values of the *commercial* classes:

> all their labour, stody and policy is be [by] bying and selling to gete sin-gler richis frome the communaltie, and never workith to gete their lyv-ing nother by workes of husbandry nor artificialite, but lyveth by other menes workes and of naught risith to grete richis, entending nothing ellse but only tò gete riches, which knoweth no common weale.[6]

Clergymen did not appreciate commerce. Thomas Lever's sermon of December 14, 1550, took on the "marchaunts of mischiefe" who came "betwixte the barke and the tree," making "all thinges dere to the byers; and yet wonderfull vyle and of small pryce to many, that must nedes sett or sell that whyche is their owne honestlye come bye."[7] The humanists mistrusted it. Sir Thomas More sought to banish commerce as far as humanly possi-ble from his *Utopia* (1516) by reworking Plato's idea of holding all posses-sions in common.[8] The civilians despaired over the imbalance it created in

God's ordained order. Thomas Wilson's *Discourse uppon Usurye* (1572) asked, "what is hee nowe a dayes that is of anye estymacion, if he want wealth? Who maketh anye accompte of him, bee hee never so learned, never so vertuous, or never so worthy, that hath no the goods of this world?"[9]

The more necessary to the health of the state that commerce became, the higher up went the voices of protest. James I was not about to put up with any bourgeois cheek. "The Merchants," he said,

> thinke the whole common-weale ordeined for making them up; and accounting it their lawfull gaine and trade, to enrich themselves upon the losse of all the rest of the people. . . . They buy for us the worst wares and sell them at the dearest prices . . . being as constant in their evill custome, as if it were settled Law for them.[10]

The Stuarts were soon to have more pressing problems, but antimerchant sentiment easily crossed the divide between Parliamentarian and Royalist. Archbishop Laud believed that there was "no private end, but in something or other it will be led to run cross the public; and, if gain come in, though it be by 'making shrines for Diana,' it is no matter with them though Ephesus be in an uproar for it";[11] while James Harrington restricted the influence of the merchants, shopkeepers, and artisans of *Oceana* (1656) to (and by) a self-censoring ward and guild system.[12]

By the end of the century the battle against the merchant seemed already to be lost. In 1698, Andrew Fletcher bemoaned "the luxury of Asia and America" that sunk all "Europe into an abyss of pleasures," changing that society's "frugal and military way of living" without a thought for the "unspeakable evils" that were "altogether inseparable from an expensive" one.[13]

Two years before James Watt patented his improved steam engine, Adam Ferguson complained of the "detached and solitary being" of commercial society so set "in competition with his fellow-creatures" that "he deals with them" only "as he does with his cattle and his soil, for the sake of the profits they bring."[14] Watt, Ferguson, and Fletcher were compatriots of Adam Smith; Ferguson and Smith were friends. Clearly not all Scotland was equally sanguine about the new order, and even Adam Smith was far from being a thoughtless booster of "the lust for gain."[15]

The new world order that Smith's *Wealth of Nations* was thought to advocate came in for sharp criticism south of the Tweed as well. In William Godwin's *Poetical Justice* (1798) the "division of labor" employed in the famous pin factory was condemned as "the offspring of avarice," a means "to gild over the indolent and the proud" at the expense of the laborer on whose efforts all wealth rested.[16]

After the Romantics brought an impossibly sanitized Middle Ages back into fashion, Thomas Carlyle could look back to a "perfect Feudal time" when "*Cash Payment* had not then grown to be the universal sole nexus of man to man."[17] But intellectuals were not the only ones in opposition: the Luddites earned themselves a place in history by smashing the new order's machines.

As the factories and railroads marched across Europe, a small army of historians, economists, and sociologists followed behind searching for the origins of capitalism, as though they could find there the weapon to bring it down; in the process, they shaped the lens through which we look at the past. But capitalism and its *Geist* are especially problematic concepts for anyone doing research in the history of the seventeenth century. Our analytical models work backward: we scour the past for the onset of key features of some "present" system without agreeing amongst ourselves on which features are actually "key," or even working from the same "present."

For Karl Marx, the free market in labor was the defining "matrix" of *capitalism*. "Capital" itself could not be created unless "the owner of money" met "in the market" with

> the free labourer, free in the double sense, that as a free man he can dispose of his labour-power as his own commodity, and that on the other hand he has no other commodity for sale, is short of everything necessary for the realisation of his labour-power.[18]

Slaves were commodities, not sellers of commodities. Thus it was "nonsense" to speak of "capital" as "fully developed" in the ancient world "except that the free labourer and a system of credit was wanting."[19]

Post-Comte and post-Darwin, Émile Durkheim saw society's increasing economic and social division of labor as a "particular form" of a "general process" of biological evolution.[20] In this evolution, the "organic solidarity" of traditional society was transformed into a less binding "mechanical solidarity" that grew "ever slacker" as social specialization advanced.[21] The end result was paradoxical. On the plus side the process had created the true "individual" (civilization minimized differences between "collective types" while maximizing differences between "individual types" within the collective unit).[22] On the negative side, it had stripped that individual of his/her moral staple, for thanks to unregulated capitalism, modern society was in the same state of "juridical and moral anomie" as its market.[23] Unless something was done, the future was likely to be a Hobbesian state of nature redivivus, for "Human passions stop only before a moral power they respect. If all authority of this kind is wanting, the state of war is necessarily chronic."[24] What Durkheim proposed was the transformation of corporate capitalism into a modified guild system.[25] Durkheim's anomie seems not all that far from the seventeenth century's fear of chaos. But there still is more deductive archetype here than historical specificity.

His contemporary, Max Weber, explored the mind-set he believed had created the economic system:

> Unlimited greed for gain is not in the least identical with capitalism, and is still less its spirit. Capitalism *may* even be identical with the restraint, or at least a rational tempering, of this irrational impulse. But capitalism is identical with the pursuit of profit, and forever *renewed* profit, by means of continuous, rational, capitalistic enterprise [defined as one] adapted to a systematic utilization of goods or personal services as means of acquisition in such a way that, at the close of a business period, the balance of the enterprise in money assets . . . exceeds the capital.[26]

In sorting out the origins of a uniquely Western "sober bourgeois capitalism" from the "adventurer type" found in all continents and ages, Weber looked to a Protestant ethic he saw as ascetic, utilitarian, "completely devoid of any eudaemonistic, not to say hedonistic, admixture," and "dominated by the making of money, by acquisition as the ultimate purpose" of life.[27] For the historian of seventeenth-century economic thought, the problems in applying Weber's thesis range from his slighting Italian contributions to accounting to the fact that so many of his characterizations are based on examples from the eighteenth century.[28]

An acquisitive *Geist* stripped of its asceticism but not its rationality (and renamed *possessive individualism*) underlay C. B. Macpherson's vision of "bourgeois society":

> By bourgeois society I mean a society in which the relations between men are dominated by the market; in which, that is to say, land and labour, as well as moveable wealth and goods made for consumption, are treated as commodities to be bought and sold and contracted for with a view to profit and accumulation, and where men's relations to others are set largely by their ownership of these commodities and the success with which they utilize that ownership to their own profit. Alternatively, bourgeois society may be defined in terms of prevalent moral values, for a society cannot be dominated by the market unless the appropriate moral values are widely accepted. So defined, bourgeois society is one in which accumulation of wealth through the market (in the broad sense, including the market for land and labour) is regarded as honourable or even natural, and in which justice is the performance of contract rather than commutative or distributive justice.[29]

Macpherson was certain he had found such a society in the writings of Thomas Hobbes (1588–1679) and, in this regard, placed a particular emphasis on the following passage from Hobbes's *Leviathan* (1651):

The *Value*, or WORTH of a man, is as of all other things, his Price; that is to say, so much as would be given for the use of his power: and therefore is not absolute, but a thing dependent on the need and judgement of another. An able conductor of Souldiers, is of great Price in time of War present, or imminent; but in Peace not so. A learned and uncorrupt Judge, is much Worth in time of Peace; but not so much in War. And as in other things, so in men, not the seller, but the buyer determines the price. For let a man (as most men do,) rate themselves as the highest Value they can; yet their true Value is no more than it is esteemed by others.[30]

Macpherson claimed this represented a society in which

Transfers of power are assumed to be so usual that there is a market in power. A man's power is treated as a commodity, regular dealings in which establish market prices. . . . The degree of honour accorded to a man thus measures his actual value in comparison with the value he sets on himself. But the actual power is determined by what others would give for the use of his power. . . . We have here the essential characteristics of the competitive market.[31]

Keith Thomas has pointed out the parallels between Hobbes's terminology, medieval courtly literature (e.g., the equation of *Pris* with *Wirde* by German poets), and sixteenth-century aristocratic literature. In both traditions, one's honor (reputation) was a valuation placed on you by others: to each tradition its particular competitive spirit. Thomas concludes that Hobbes's ethical ideal (and orientation) was, in fact, an *aristocratic* one: no *bourgeois* spirit or market was involved.[32] Certainly Macpherson would not suggest that the medieval Holy Roman Empire was the embodiment of a "possessive market society." In English *value* has been a synonym for *status* since at least 1330.[33] Status, being a legal or at least a customary rank, was always ultimately set upon you rather than self-determined. Macpherson would not have considered fourteenth-century England to be a "possessive market society" either.

Whether Hobbes was describing a society well on its way to marketization or was dressing up one tradition in the rhetoric of another, the relativism (or subjectivity) in the pricing mechanism still applied. One might even go so far as to say that it was subjectivity that lay at the heart of Hobbes's concept of the state of nature as one ultimately of the war of all against all: men's estimations of their needs were as subjective as the prices they put on everything else.

But if this is the case, one must look at the lengths to which Hobbes went in *Leviathan* to rein in that subjectivity: the surrender of the individual to the sovereign, the patriarchal mediate-cosm supporting the authority of the state, and state control of alternative sources of values such as religion and education, among other measures. Hobbes clearly did not accept the "moral values" Macpherson saw as "appropriate" to a bourgeois society.[34]

Ahistorical models of capitalism share what Maurice Dobb deemed a tendency "to lead inexorably to the conclusion that nearly all periods of history have been capitalist."[35] In an article felicitously entitled "Capitalism— What's in a Name?" R. H. Hilton provided a few pointed examples of the discovery by modern historians of "capitalist revolution[s]" ranging backward in time from the thirteenth century to the Carolingian era.[36] Alan Macfarlane built an argument for a thirteenth-century capitalist England based on individualized ownership of land, absence of restrictions on testamentary disposition of land, the degree of rationality in fourteenth-century account books, the "extensive evidence" of a cash economy to be found in thirteenth-century works on estate management, and evidence of the penetration of wage labor into fourteenth-century society drawn from the occupations listed in the poll tax records.[37] But his de jure emphasis left him wide open to the criticism that, as the English did not generally make use of their freedom to will property away from their families during this period, it was highly questionable to characterize them by this privilege.[38]

The assumption of an ahistorical business mentality is especially problematic when focused on the contribution of accounting theory to economic thought. Weber stressed the *rationality* of modern capitalism: the "separation of business from the household" and the development of "rational book-keeping."[39] Double-entry bookkeeping had been codified as early as 1494 in the "*De Computis et Scripturis*" section of Luca Pacioli's *Arithmetica, Geometria, Proportioni et Proportionalita*. It had been translated into English (and Dutch and French) by 1543, starting off a long line of bookkeeping manuals. Pacioli's work is rarely discussed without some comment on how little the mechanics of bookkeeping have changed since its day. In his introduction to a 1963 translation of the work, Alvin R. Jennings, C.P.A., remarked that

> Although we have now abandoned the Memorandum as the book in which business transactions should be recorded chronologically, the overall process described by Paciolo [*sic*] is otherwise precisely the same as is now performed.[40]

But there is a vast difference between the mechanics of bookkeeping and the comprehension of profit. Pacioli believed it "absolutely necessary" to include "ordinary household expenses" such as money spent at the barber's or on food for the table (and even "extraordinary" personal expenses such as gambling losses) in the same set of books as one's business concerns. This was a reasonable arrangement for a system designed to tell you "the entire value of your property,"[41] but this same arrangement precluded your *rationally* pursuing profit in your business since it failed to distinguish the profits your business earned from your spending of them.

Rather than work backward from our models of the marketplace, this study suggests that we work forward from the societal model inherited by the seventeenth century in order to discover what in market behavior disturbed it and where the merchants themselves stood on this issue. The model in question is the "body politic."

The body was the oldest sociological model European civilization possessed. In all likelihood, it was ancient long before Aristotle marked out his six essential concerns of the body politic—food, tool-making skills, arms, money, religion, and a method of decision making or rule—and assigned them to six classes of men: agricultural laborers, skilled artisans, soldiers, wealthy men, priests, and judges.[42] Though this described a social division of labor rather than a productive one, there was nothing in the idea of the body itself that prevented it from accommodating the concept of an economic system. Bodies are capable of doing eloquent duty in economics. Whenever we talk of the *organs*—the banks, the Fed, and so forth—of the financial *system* we are, in fact, borrowing from biology. There were, however, considerable impediments to such an accommodation in the way that biological model was understood in the first half of the seventeenth century.

In the first place, its "organs" were considered almost exclusively in relation to the functions they performed for the whole body and only accidentally as they affected each other. Since the cardinal assumption of organicism is the primacy of the whole[43] it is not surprising that the most frequent exhortation to the members of the body politic was that they work for the whole. With that nesting urge so deeply rooted in the age's *Weltanschauung* as to be almost a mania, Richard Hooker (1554–1600) saw the whole world as a body politic with commonwealths for its component parts:

> For as civil law, being the act of a whole body politic, doth therefore overrule each several part of the same body; so there is no reason that any one commonwealth of itself should to the prejudice of another annihilate that whereupon the whole world hath agreed.[44]

His contemporary and fellow divine William Perkins (1558–1602) worked on a somewhat smaller scale but still drew the same lessons for members of bodies as small as families and as large as states:

every member in the family according to their ability, [must] employ themselves in some honest and profitable business to maintain the temporal estate and life of the whole.[45]

In man's body there be sundry parts and members and every one hath its several use and office, which it performeth not for itself but for the good of the whole body; as the office of the eye is to see, of the ear to hear and the foot to go. Now all societies of men are bodies. A family is a body and so is every particular church a body and the commonwealth also: and in these bodies there be several members which are men walking in several callings and offices, the execution whereof must tend to the happy and good estate of the rest.[46]

Both these merchants and these ministers were only following in the footsteps of the humanists. Thomas Starkey (ca. 1495?–1538), chaplain to Margaret Pole, Countess of Salisbury, had earlier maintained that

to this all men are born and of nature brought forth: to commune such gifts as be to them given, each one to the profit of others, in perfit civility, and not to live to their own pleasure and profit, without regard of the weal of their country, forgetting all justice and equity.[47]

Not surprisingly, the most frequent complaint was that against any member seen to be feathering his or her nest at the expense of that whole. William Perkins called it a "sin of injustice" when men abused "their callings to the hurt and hindrance of others," castigating the sharp practices of the merchant and the rent-racking of the landlord.[48] The merchant, as we have amply seen, came in for more than his share of the blame, though never so vehemently as when Robert Burton (1577–1639) condemned the whole world, in his *Anatomy of Melancholy* (1621), as a marketplace in which "every man is for himself, his private ends, and stands upon his own guard."[49]

Second, even the functions the "organs" performed for the whole tended to be viewed indirectly through the mediation of the head that was simultaneously the depository for the benefits provided by the "organs" and the "organ" that directed the redistribution of those benefits throughout the body. Edward Forset (1553?–1630), a divine-right royalist, insisted that

as in every man there is both a quickning & ruling soule, and a living and ruled bodie; so in every civill state, there is a directing & commaunding power, & an obeying and subjected alleageance. . . . Where all will rule, there is no rule, and where none doeth rule, there is all misrule: but to rule well, and to bee well-ruled, is the surest bond of humane societie.[50]

William Perkins would have agreed with him:

Christ alone is the head of the catholic church and . . . he neither hath nor can have any creature in heaven or earth to be fellow herein. For the church is his body and none but he can perform the duty of a head unto it, which duty stands in two things: the first is to govern the church by such power and authority whereby he can and doth prescribe laws properly binding the conscience of all his members; the second is by grace to quicken and put spiritual life into them.[51]

In a less peaceful time, the hierarchical understanding of the body made it a useful political tool. Richard Baxter (1615–1691), a Presbyterian divine who re-conformed after the Restoration, was urging his fellow countrymen in 1659 to "Look but to the Sun and Moon, and Stars, and see their inequality and Order," for there could be only "one Head to every Civil governed body."[52] In the same year, the anonymous author of a republican pamphlet entitled *Chaos* complained that "the Tail commands the Head, and all things are out of course; insomuch as a Solon was never any where more needful."[53]

The ranking impulse went much deeper than the simple idea of a gulf between head/soul and body; there were marked inequalities between the worth and hence the rewarding of the other organs. It was but a step from Aristotle's idea of justice as equal treatment of equals and unequal treatment of unequals to Forset's view that

> In the bodie naturall, the sustenance is not all carried to one side, or to one part, to the pining and beguiling of the rest: So in the state, the nobilitie is so to bee maintayned, as that the Commons bee not wronged, and the clergie so to be cherished, as the laytie be not overlayd. . . . Neither yet must wee hereuppon induce any paritie or equallitie, which nature herselfe abandoneth. . . . Not so much as our garments but must be fitted to our bignesse or smallnesse . . . when then should it be grudged at, if the nobilitie and gentrie of the land (in whom the dignitie and the well-shewing countenance of the state consisteth) be better stored and furnished than the meaner of the people?[54]

The tailor's measure was a common metaphor for the need to keep each rank in its place; William Perkins had used it earlier:

> our rule must be the common judgment and practice of the most godly, frugal and wise men with whom we live: and that which they in good conscience judge sufficient and necessary for every man, according to his place and calling, that is to be esteemed sufficient. And here we must remember not to make one rule for all men, that things sufficient for one should be sufficient for all, but every man must be measured according to his condition and degree.[55]

Equality in Christ did not translate into equality in society; Richard Hooker insisted that

> although the nature of the mystical body of the church be such, that it suffereth no distinction in the invisible member . . . all are equally

Christ's, and Christ is equally theirs: yet in the external administration
of the church of God, because God is not the author of confusion, but of
peace, it is necessary that in every congregation there should be a distinction, if not of inward dignity, yet of outward degree.[56]

This hierarchical disposition did more than unconsciously work
against understanding interorgan functions: it deliberately fought against
the organs gaining such knowledge. Forset was convinced that

[in] the bodie politique each part is to know and administer his owne
proper works, without entermixing or entermedling in the office of any
other. Shall the foot be permitted to partake in the point of pre-emi-
nence with the head?[57]

Hooker warned against private men dabbling in either civic or ecclesiastical policy:

If it be granted a thing unlawful for private men, not called unto public
consultation, to dispute which is the best state of civil polity . . . is there
any reason in the world, why they should better judge what kind of reg-
iment ecclesiastical is the fittest? For in the civil state more insight, and
in those affairs more experience a great deal must needs be granted
them, than in this they can possibly have.[58]

Sir Francis Bacon (1561–1626), in a book devoted to the *Advancement of
Learning,* supported similar barriers:

Duty is subdivided into two parts; the common duty of every man, as a
man or member of a state; the other, the respective or special duty of
every man, in his profession, vocation, and place.[59]
Concerning government, it is a part of knowledge secret and retired, in
both those respects in which things are deemed secret; for some things
are secret because they are hard to know, and some because they are not
fit to utter.[60]

Bacon was equally concerned that humans did "not presume by the con-
templation of nature to attain to the mysteries of God."[61]

What drove these men was a fear of the absolute chaos they thought
would result if even the smallest "cell" in this "body" was disturbed. As
Hooker so succinctly put it:

For as in a chain, which is made of many links, if you pull the first, you
draw the rest; and as in a ladder of many staves, if you take away the lowest, all hope of ascending to the highest will be removed.[62]

But so deep a fear was a powerful deterrent to any analytic effort.

What then was the threat this world saw in merchants? One problem
was that the merchant stood outside the land-based status hierarchy inherited from the Middle Ages.[63] Neither lord nor vassal, he was bound in

homage to no one and served no one's ends but his own. In a sense, he also stood outside the polis itself, for the word *merchant* was reserved for the import-export trader, the individual whose commerce depended upon and fed foreign markets in goods and money. But more generally it was the trader's self-direction that society found both revolting and rebellious. We have only to go back through the litany of complaints at the beginning of this chapter to see the depths of that revulsion. For a nation to be increasingly dependent on a class whose efforts were aimed at their own welfare rather than that of the whole was intolerable, but was it actually the case?

This study argues that while Gerard de Malynes, Edward Misselden, and Thomas Mun may have created a new model (balance of trade) for the market, they sought (in so doing) to preserve the value-mentality of the old. Their mental universe was not, as Schumpeter claimed, dominated by the "particular mental habits" of "the business office,"[64] but by the very same organicism that defined the world of Johannes Kepler, Richard Hooker, or William Perkins.

CHAPTER 2

Gerard de Malynes: *Institutio Mercatoris Christiani*

Gerard de Malynes (fl. 1586–1626) was a slightly older contemporary of Sir Francis Bacon (1561–1626) and William Shakespeare (1564–1616). A merchant, an autodidact, and a part-time spy, his was a mercantile career shaped by the cutthroat nature of Elizabethan commerce. But when his first two books, *A Treatise of the Canker of England's Commonwealth* and *St. George for England, allegorically described,* appeared on the scene in 1601, they bemoaned the ruinous effects of usury and the international money-market on England's moral fiber and socioeconomic fabric. A voracious reader who sampled every school of thought his age had to offer, he remained at heart an Aristotelian in spite of his real attraction to elements of both Baconian and Paracelsian thought. His work provides a baseline both for seventeenth-century economic thinking and for those conflicts within its intellectual inheritance that forged a new social as well as a new physical science.

Malynes tells us that his family originally came from Lancashire, though he himself was born in Antwerp.[1] Exactly when he was born is not known. Referring to a commission on which he served in 1600–1601, Malynes remarked on his "owne knowledge concerning assayes . . . observed and knowne above fortie yeares, my father also having beene a Mint-master."[2] Taking this to mean knowledge he had picked up growing up in such a household, we would arrive at a birth year around 1560, but if the "above fortie yeares" experience dates from his apprenticeship (perhaps under his own father), a birth year closer to the midcentury mark emerges. The earliest extant references to his presence in England concern his membership in the Dutch Church in London, where, in 1586, one "Geraertt de Malines" promised twenty shillings per year to a Church fund "for the support of selected students of their congregation at Cambridge University and elsewhere."[3] But his family may have returned to England as early as 1561, when his father's profession would have made him in demand during a major recoinage effort undertaken in that year.[4]

Following in his father's professional footsteps, Gerard de Malynes the assay master served on a government commission on foreign exchange in 1600.[5] His first book (*A Canker of England's Commonwealth*) may have been, in essence, that commission's report.[6] If so, Malynes was distinctly disappointed with its results as "there ensued but an alteration in the valuation of gold concerning the proportion, with some small reformation concerning the Standard: but in Exchanges nothing was effected."[7] His private affairs were equally unsuccessful.

At one point in his *Lex Mercatoria,* Malynes commented on the dangers of partnership by agency (or acting as a "factor" for another).[8] This was the closest he came to describing a tangled case in which he himself was involved in 1592. Three Amsterdam merchants, Hans Hongar, Pieter van Moucheron, and Filippo Georgio (originally a Portuguese), gave Gerard de Malynes and Guillam Vermuyden £28,065 to bid on the cargo of the *Madre de Dios,* a captured Spanish ship. Since Malynes was competing with a group led by Alderman Garroway of London, he thought it wise to enlist the aid of Sir Horatio Palavicino (whose court connections were far better than those of Malynes) in securing the deal. When Hongar claimed to have received goods worth only £20,000, the resulting lawsuits went as high as the Lord Treasurer, the Privy Council, and the Barons of the Exchequer before their final dismissal in 1610. After trying every legal trick he could, Malynes ended up spending a total of about three years in prison (while he carried on his affairs by proxy).[9]

Malynes also occasionally took on diplomatic work that might more properly be characterized as espionage. A letter of October 26, 1596, survives from "Garrett de Malynes" to Robert Cecil about the extraction of some diplomatic letters sent to the governor of "Calis" and the possibility of a peace treaty, although nothing seems to have come of the scheme.[10]

Early in 1598, "Gherard de Malines" and Robert Bromley chartered a ship called the *Experience* from John Basadonna for a voyage that ended in recriminations: the English crew members were taken off in Naples and sent to forced labor in the galleys, Malynes and Bromley claimed the goods already purchased as Spanish spoils, and Basadonna complained to Essex that the voyage should be resumed and the goods given to him.[11]

One way or another, Malynes's luck continued to be bad. In 1613, John, Lord Harrington obtained a patent for minting lead farthings that he assigned to Malynes and William Cockayne (later replaced by John Couchman). But the coins were unpopular, the patent was infringed, and it was Malynes who ended up in Fleet Prison in 1619, addressing a petition to the king (on February 16) blaming his misfortunes on the partners who had insisted on paying him in his own farthings.[12]

Even his semiofficial standing was eventually lost. In 1622, Malynes appeared before the standing commission on trade to give evidence on the state of the coinage,[13] but it would be his younger rivals, Thomas Mun and Edward Misselden, who were honored with official places on that commission. Malynes was either too old, too old-fashioned, or too disgraced to win another appointment.

His date of death remains as much a mystery as his date of birth. An undated petition addressed by Malynes to the House of Commons has been assigned to 1641 by the editors of the *Calendar of State Papers,* but Lynn Muchmore has pointed out that the petition contains no mention of the Patent for a Royal Exchanger issued in 1627, a fact that, given Malynes's long campaign for its reestablishment, he would hardly have forgotten to mention.[14]

In all, Gerard Malynes published six books. *A Treatise of the Canker of England's Commonwealth* and *St. George for England, allegorically described,* both appearing in 1601, attacked the international money-market. *England's View in the Unmasking of two Paradoxes* (1603) contested the debasement and treasure explanations for the price revolution advanced respectively by M. de Malestroit and Jean Bodin. *The Maintenance of Free Trade* (1622) and *The Center of the Circle of Commerce* (1623) responded to criticisms of his theories by Edward Misselden. Malynes's magnum opus, the *Consuetudo vel Lex Mercatoria, or the Ancient Law Merchant* (1622), was meant to be both a blueprint for a new code of mercantile law and a general handbook of international trade.

Of his importance in seventeenth-century circles there can be no doubt. Malynes was cited approvingly in Thomas Milles's *Customer's Replie* (1604), Lewes Roberts's *Merchants Mappe of Commerce* (1638), and William Lowndes's *Further Essay for the Amendment of the Gold and Silver Coins* (1695).[15] Even Thomas Mun (who lambasted the idea of an exchange fixed at *par pro pari*) acknowledged that Malynes was "skilful in many things which he hath both written and collected concerning th' affairs of Merchants."[16] The *Lex Mercatoria* remained a standard merchants' guide, reprinted in 1629, 1636, 1656, and 1686, either by itself or with similar handbooks. Malynes was also well-known outside of strictly economic circles. Book Two, Chapter Two of the *Lex Mercatoria* was also reprinted in *A Figure of the True and Spiritual Tabernacle* (1655), while a section on beekeeping was reprinted in Samuel Hartlib's *Reformed Commonwealth of the Bees* (1655).

Malynes's works fell out of the public eye in the eighteenth century, although a chapter from the *Lex Mercatoria* on the fishing industry was privately reprinted in 1720,[17] and of all the "economic" treatises produced in the seventeenth century only the *Maintenance of Free Trade* seems to have struck Sir William Oldys as worthy enough to abstract in his *British Librarian* in 1737.[18]

Modern opinion, both of his place in the history of economic theory and in the march of possessive individualism, varies wildly. For his *Religion and the Rise of Capitalism* (1926), R. H. Tawney looked at a passage by Malynes on the sequence of wheels in a clock and decided that "the spirit of modern business could hardly be more aptly described."[19] But by 1933, E. A. J. Johnson dismissed him as "a pathetic advocate of medieval justice who could not understand the amorality of the modern market."[20] In 1947, the Marxist economist Maurice Dobb transformed Malynes into a pro-toimperialist.[21] Before the free-marketeer William Dyer Grampp was through with Malynes in 1952, he had remade him into a pioneer of "the idea that individuals are the best judges of their own welfare," anticipating "the conception of natural law held by the classical economists . . . the touchstone of political and economical liberalism."[22] In 1955, Raymond de Roover knocked him back to a plagiarizing "link" between the Scholastic and mercantile schools of thought without a thought in his head that had not been cribbed from someone else's text.[23] By 1978, Joyce Appleby was more interested in his "static and authoritarian" patrimonialism than in the fact that "given the validity" of his "assumptions, his remedies might have worked."[24]

Back in 1938, Max Beer had credited him with "the first empirical and tentative expression of the quantity theory of money" (in British economic thought).[25] Joseph Schumpeter considered (in 1954) that "during the whole of the century no other writer surpassed him in clear and full understanding of the international mechanism of foreign exchanges that works through price levels and gold and silver movements."[26] In 1963, however, William Letwin reduced that verdict to one of a merely mechanical understanding.[27] But the 1991 edition of a standard textbook, *The Growth of Economic Thought* by Henry William Spiegel, gives us a Malynes who comes closer than anyone before David Hume to solving the problem of "the automatic flow of specie and attending changes in prices" that was "to bring the curtain down on mercantilist thought."[28]

What Gerard de Malynes thought of his world and his place in it was something entirely different.

Of his formal education there is no record, but what can be gleaned from his works is quite revealing, thanks to the seventeenth century's penchant for never using only one analogy when ten were available. Of the special skills required by a merchant, Malynes was quite the master. Rooves and pipes of sherry and muddles and scheppels of salt appear among the nearly forty pages on ancient and modern weights and measures. Tables of the "monies" of countries ancient and modern, both actual and "of account"—their divisions, weights, alloys, silver-gold pars, and exchange rates in various markets—intermingle with discourses on mining and metallurgy. The principal commodities of the countries within and outside of European Christendom roll off his pen. There are enough praises to and examples from arithmetic and geometry to prove the sincerity of his worship at the "Fountaine of Numbers," and there is enough on the newly imported Italian invention of double-entry bookkeeping to prove him thoroughly familiar with that "noble order of Debtor and Creditor." He treated the reader to proverbs in Spanish, Dutch, and Portuguese and refuted a book by Jean Bodin on the price revolution long before it had been translated from French into English. And he could cite medieval maritime laws from Genoa (1186), Marseilles (1162), Venice (1262), and Aragon (1270 and 1340) as easily as he could those of Antoninus or the latest change in the "Sea-Lawes of the Haunce Townes, made in the year 1614."[29]

But the chapters in the *Lex Mercatoria* devoted to elaborating these qualities veer off in directions we might never expect of a "mere Merchant." His treatment of the merchant's need to understand fabric dyes was prefaced by a small essay on color theory. A discussion of the merchant's need for mathematics led up to a Pythagorean encomium to the "great mysteries and vertues . . . contained in numbers," as Malynes waxed euphoric over the unity of one, the holiness of three, and the harmony of ten. In a world split between the Gregorian and Julian calendars, practical instructions for setting deadlines moved from a placement of the Earth in its proper astronomical position based on the relative length of its annual revolution through a brief survey of the current theories of its age before advancing to a final recommendation of the Gregorian calendar as the more accurate of the two.[30]

Malynes's biblical references (emphasis on the Old Testament) were numerous, but classical to biblical his citations ran at about 5:3. He had no Greek, and was sensitive about it,[31] but went through as much of the Greek canon as was available in Latin. He was a devoted student of Aristotle's *Politics, Ethics, Physics,* and *Metaphysics;* he knew enough of Plato's *Republic* and *Laws* to discuss their differing takes on communal property; and he had at least a passing acquaintance with Euclid.[32] Ancient Greeks and Romans seem to have been his daily companions. He knew his Cato and his Cicero, of course, and could always find just the right verse from Horace (or rewrite one from Virgil) to skewer an opponent.[33] He mined the works of Strabo, Pliny, Suetonius, and Procopius as much for moral exempla as for evidence of ancient commercial practice, and he retold Plutarch's story of

Sertorius and the pulling out of the horse's tail, hair by hair, with obvious relish.[34] There is no doubt that Malynes was intensely proud of the scope of his learning. When he apologized to his readers for a digression on the Lapis philosophorum as "being farre from Merchants profession," it was in the nature of a boast rather than a proposed limitation on studies appropriate for merchants.[35]

But Aesop and Ovid were by far his favorite authors from the ancient world, and tellingly so.[36] Whether his sources were high literary or low, the wisdom gleaned was, in fact, decidedly moral. He belonged to a moment in time in which there was a growing attempt to discipline popular culture, and elements of that change could be seen in his condemnations of those who

> live licenciously, following whores, harlots, wine-tavernes, and many other unlawfull games, to their utter destruction. . . . [or] spend their stockes by prodigall riot, sumptuous fare, and strange and proud new fangles in their apparell . . . spending their time and dulling their wits, with the use of dicing and carding.[37]

These were sins to which the rich might be as prone as the poor, but the transgressions of the two groups had different consequences. When the poor were idle, peace itself was threatened, therefore "all other artificers and workemen shall be set on worke, to avoid idlenesse which is the root of all mischief."[38] Idleness being "most dangerous in countries which are populous," Malynes recommended following the Roman example of planting colonies to prevent the idle many from stirring up "more commotions."[39] The sin of the rich about which he worried most was their tendency to enclose lands and switch from tillage to pasturage. Such men "maketh sheepe to become devourers of men, destroying the lustie husbandmen which are alwaies the best souldiers."[40]

A search for moral exempla and commercial history drove Malynes forward through the centuries. He could cite Aquinas and Scotus on the five ways of transferring things (donation, permutation, buying, selling, and lending of money), and "Doctor Rabanus" (on numerology).[41] He steeped himself in the treatises of Civilians as well as the works of those Common Law partisans Sir John Fortescue and Christopher St. German.[42] He consulted English histories closely and often, plucking the text of a letter patent to Cardinal Wolsey from Grafton's *Chronicle,* or picking up Edward III's commercial policy from Malmesbury and Henry VII's from Holinshed.[43]

But Malynes also loved certain authors so greatly for their literary skill that he borrowed great chunks of their work without attribution. His *St. George for England* virtually reproduced the "General Prologue" to

Chaucer's *Canterbury Tales,* while phrase after phrase from Thomas More's
Utopia filled the rest of the piece.[44]

Malynes lived in a world in which a new learning was competing with the
old. If Aristotle's empiricist thrust had been reduced to dogmatism by the
Scholastics, a new empiricism had arisen in Europe, and Malynes devoured
it eagerly, if not always uncritically. This was, after all, the heyday of
Paracelsianism in England: Thomas Muffet, originally trained in Galenic
medicine at Cambridge, brought it back to England from his trip to Basel;
Sir Theodore de Mayerne brought it from France to his patron James I; and
Robert Fludd, one of the most radical of Paracelsian mystics, was accepted
as a Fellow of the Royal College of Physicians under James.[45] Malynes had
read John Dee's work, which was full of neohermetic and Paracelsian ideas,
but Malynes had also "read all the bookes of Paracelsus" that he "could find"
and compared his alchemical treatises with those of Ripley, Roger Bacon,
and Norton of Bristol.[46]

Malynes believed humans must "obey the knowne will of God" and
"reverence (with admiration) his secret will not declared unto us."[47] He
damned the mercantile exchange because, the valuation of the coin being a
matter of "the soveraignty and dignity of the Prince," it was a matter "of too
high presumption for subjects to step into."[48] The royal prerogative was, in
many respects, the legal embodiment of the concept of *noli altium sapere,*
which Carlo Ginzburg characterized as "a separate sphere of 'highness'
(cosmic, religious, political) which was forbidden to human knowledge."[49]
Ginzburg used a change in the depiction of Icarus in emblem books from
the incarnation of intellectual hubris to "a winged man, quietly swimming
in the air" above the caption "dare everything" to trace changes in seventeenth-century attitudes toward science. Soaring on "Icarian" wings was the
epitome of folly in Malynes's estimation; he cut an opponent down to size
by tarring him as Horace had an imitator of Pindar:

> Iulus who strives, Pinder to emulate
> With waxen wings, which Dedals Art did make:
> He flies in vaine, to give by haplesse fate
> Names to the Icarian glassie blewish lake.[50]

But Malynes actually belonged to that transitional point in Ginzburg's
thesis in which science, although not yet politics or religion, was no longer
forbidden knowledge. Malynes kept abreast of the voyages of Drake and
Cavendish, and the discovery of "*Terra Australis incognita*" by Ferdinand de
Quir in 1615. He made more than a hobby of cartography, arguing over the
correct representation of meridians of longitude and organizing the entire

text of his last treatise (*The Center of the Circle of Commerce*) around the climate zones formed by the Arctic and Antarctic Circles and the two Tropics.[51] He was fascinated by the very size of the earth ("5400 Geometricall Miles, or 21600 ordinarie Miles") and his country's portion of it ("29 million, 568 thousand acres"). And, counting by parishes, he optimistically estimated that there were 16.8 million people in England.[52]

He shared both an interest in all aspects of agricultural and commercial improvement and a preference for state-managed development with Sir Francis Bacon (1561–1626). In his writings were schemes for transnational trade councils, mining improvements, new coinages, regulated loans for the working class, arguments for patent protection, and endorsements for new plantations, fishing, and navigation improvements.[53]

But there were places where the nascent new science went that Gerard de Malynes would not follow:

> The Pithagorians doctrine lately revived by *Copernicus*, touching the scituation and moving of the bodies Coelestiall, denying the stabilitie of the earth, may in some measure be admitted *argumentandi gratia;* for they set forth some Astronomicall demonstration, albeit imaginarie. . . . But Aristotle his reasons are generally approved, to prove the earths stabilitie in the middle or lower part of the world, because of gravitie and levitie, the earth being (of all other Elements) most heavie, and all ponderous things are carried unto it.[54]

He would admit only those elements of the new science that did not threaten the order supported by the old.

Gerard de Malynes could not have been much more than a child when the works of Sextus Empiricus first saw print in 1562. How Malynes came across them is unclear. But however Malynes became exposed to Pyrrhonic Skepticism, he stood steadfast against it:

> For some men (upon private respects) will cast doubts beyond the Moone. . . . And to the other I may say, Know you not that the skeptike Doctrine of Pyrrho, Aristen, and Herillus, hath been long agoe hist out of the Schooles, or rather banisht and confined amongst the Barbarians? Will you cause us to doubt of all things: then shall wee doubt whether you doubt or no.[55]

Malynes linked the just distribution of property to Cicero's definition of law as right reason in this fashion:

> True Law, is a right reason of nature agreeing therewith in all points, diffused and spread in all Nations consisting perpetually, whereby Meum and Tuum is distinguished and distributed by Number, Weight and Measure.[56]

The original of "Number, Weight and Measure" occurs in the Wisdom of Solomon as "For thy almighty hand, which created the world out of formless matter . . . thou hast ordered all things by measure and number and weight" (11:17–21). Later in the century, "Number, Weight and Measure" would become Sir William Petty's favorite shorthand for his Baconian-influenced inductive method. But, for Malynes, "Number, Weight and Measure" stood for the idea that order inevitably entailed hierarchy, and, consequently, that equity or justice was invariably proportional to one's place in that hierarchy.

The *Zeitgeist* inherited by the early modern world from the medieval was not only that of that single hierarchy of the Great Chain of Being but one of hierarchies nested within hierarchies, like the nested spheres of both the Ptolemaic and Copernican Universes, each linked to the other by correspondences: the essential qualities of the macrocosm (the Universe) being reproduced not only in the microcosm (man), but in all the intermediate spheres of the family, the social or professional group, the community, the country, and Christendom. The Cosmos was composed of four elements: fire, air, water, and earth. Each had a corresponding "humour" (a psychological trait as well as a bodily fluid) in the human body, created by the liver out of the food consumed by the individual: fire corresponded to choler (temperamental), air to blood (sanguine), water to phlegm (phlegmatic), and earth to the melancholy humor (melancholic).[57] Each "cosm" survived only as long as the mixture of those elements remained harmonious. Every society remained in harmony only as long as its members kept to their ordained places. Even the relationship between domestic currencies and the international monetary exchanges could be so explained:

> as the Elements are joyned by Symbolization, the Ayre to the Fire by warmenesse; the Water to the Ayre, by moisture; the Earth to the Water, by coldnesse: So is exchange joyned to monyes, and monyes to commodities, by their proper qualities and effects.[58]

The idea of man as a "Little World" or microcosmic mirror of the "Great World" (or Cosmos) and society as a mediating cosm partaking of the two has a long and complicated origin. Greek social thought had aggregate as well as organic elements. The belief, shared by both Plato and Aristotle, that society was analytically an aggregate of individuals (or heads of families)[59] allowed Plato to propose that such qualities as justice (which belonged to the individual) might be more conveniently studied in that aggregate.[60] This aggregate concept favored the development of an outward-directed correspondence between the human body and the "body politic" (with certain elements in the polis seen as functionally analogous to human organs) that, ironically, fostered a change from the aggregate orientation to an organic one.

Plato's concept of the "forms" provided the nucleus for an inward-directed correspondence (from the greater to the lesser) with its idea that all things in the universe were imperfect reflections of eternal "Ideas" (or "Forms").[61] Ptolemaic cosmology presented the universe as a cosmos of concentric circles, each enclosed within a greater. Christianity's concept of a creator God as a final encompassing and infinite sphere who had made humanity in His own image further reinforced inward-directed analogies. In the second to fourth centuries, a series of pseudo-Egyptian writings (collectively known as the *Hermetica* from their ascription of the philosophy contained therein to Hermes) mixed neo-Platonic epistemology, Stoic cosmology, and assorted Eastern influences into what we might call the *efficient* source of early modern microcosmic theory. That they were mistakenly believed to be more ancient in origin than either Plato or Moses only added to their luster. According to these works,

> The Kosmos is made by God, and is contained in God; man is made by the Kosmos, and is contained in the Kosmos.[62]
> And rightly has it been said of him [the Creator] that he is all things; for all things are parts of him.[63]
> The individual is a part of the kind . . . and must necessarily agree in quality with the kind of which it is a part.[64]
> [God] has made man as a composite being to govern in conjunction with him. And if man takes upon him in all its fullness [this function] . . . he becomes the means of right order to the Kosmos, and the Kosmos to him; so that it seems the Kosmos (that is, the ordered universe) has been rightly so named, because man's composite structure has been thus ordered by God.[65]

The editions of these works published by Marsilio Ficino (1433–1499) ushered in a new wave of hermetic neo-Platonism that challenged the more traditional philosophies of the Italian Renaissance. But the analogy had also played an important part in the *Docta Ignorantia* of Cardinal Nicholas of Cusa (1401–1464), which held that:

> [Human nature] enfolds intellectual and sensible nature and encloses all things within itself, so that the ancients were right in calling it a microcosm, or a small world.[66]

A similar idea that "man sums up in himself the total faculties of earthly phenomena" could be found in the *Natural Theology* of a fifteenth-century Spanish philosopher, Raymond de Sebonde, whose ideas gained greater currency through their treatment in the *Apology for Raymond Sebond* of Michel de Montaigne (1533–1592).[67] In addition, the work of Paracelsus

(1493–1541) was shot through with the analogy "man is a child of the cosmos, and is himself the microcosm" so "the physician must have exact knowledge of man and recognize in him the mirror of the four elements in which the whole microcosm reveals itself."[68]

By the beginning of the seventeenth century it was difficult to find a strain of philosophy that did not incorporate the macro/mediate/microcosmic analogy in some fashion, so we should not be surprised to find it turning up in Malynes's very first book, *The Canker of Englands Commonwealth*, when he set out to show that a "Marchandizing Exchange" was the hitherto "unknown disease" debilitating "the politicke body of our weale publicke."[69]

As he explored the parallels between the body natural and the body politic in his later works, Malynes began to push them into a new direction, however:

> so Exchange for moneys by Bills of Exchanges (being seated everywhere) corroborateth the Vitall Spirit of Trafficke, directing and controlling (by just proportions) the prices and values of commodities and money. For albeit the Spirit of man, is rightly termed to bee the Facultie of the Soule; yet the parts of the Soule concerning Understanding and Will, have their proper relation; for that part called Understanding, is seated chiefly in the Soule, as Will is in the Spirit, both to be accompanied with Knowledge. The Phylosophers have made this distinction by the Chimiricall observation: and such as place the Soule in the bloud (dispersed through all the veynes of the bodie) do also place the Will of man in the spirit, residing in the heart of man, which the anatomists demonstrateth to be a little concavitie, where the drops of the vitall bloud are placed in the heart, which are seared up, and the place is shrunke in bodies which have been poisoned.[70]
> And then he shall finde, that as the Liver (Money) doth minister Spirits to the heart (Commodities,) and the heart to the Braine (Exchange:) so doth the brayne exchange minister to the whole Microcosm or the whole body of Traffique. Let the heart therefore by the liver receive his Tinctured Chilus by his owne mouth and stomacke, and the bloud full of Spirits, shall fill all the Veines, and supply the want of monyes.[71]

This is Galen's medical universe, not yet William Harvey's,[72] but of all of the analogies used by Gerard de Malynes in describing trade (whether clocks, climate zone circles, or ship's rudders), this one would prove to be the most influential model the century would know. Malynes did not invent the link between the blood/veins/spirit and trade/circulation/money, but the widespread influence of his *Lex Mercatoria* helped to popularize it. In Malynes's own case, the most likely source for all of this was a friend described as an unfortunate physician who succumbed "to a burning

ague after a long sickness,"[73] most likely the same friend who had introduced Malynes to the work of Paracelsus.

The body politic constructed by Malynes, however, still relied heavily
on Aristotle. Malynes claimed:

> Our society and weale publicke is furnished with sixe necessary things,
> namely divine service, judgement, armes, riches, arts and sustenance . . .
> and those that have the managing thereof as Clergy men, Magistrates,
> Noblemen, Merchants, Artificers and Husbandmen . . . execute their
> charge according to their profession.[74]

Of which professions:

> the Clergie-men did say, we instruct; the Noblemen, we fight; the Mag-
> istrates we defend; the Merchants, we inrich; the Artificers, we furnish;
> and the Husband-men, we feed.[75]

This was almost straight out of Aristotle's *Politics*.[76] Malynes's only real
change, which he felt his century's increased experience with trade justified,
was to substitute merchants (who brought bullion into a realm when they
traded correctly) for Aristotle's reliance on landed wealth.[77] But neither
Aristotle nor William Perkins nor Richard Hooker had less sympathy than
did Gerard de Malynes for men who overreached their ordained places:
Malynes believed apprentices who sought "untimely" to become masters
not only drowned themselves, but "spoile[d] their maisters occupation and
their owne."[78]

For Malynes, laws designed to keep all men in their place were not a
true restriction but a positive good:

> The Statutes of the Kingdome restraining from the exercise of sundrie
> Crafts all such as have not served an Apprentishood unto the Art which
> they would exercise, doe it to no other end but that those Arts might bee
> brought to better perfection, and the things made, might be good and
> serviceable for those that buy and use them.[79]

Nor would Malynes's belief that "office of a king towards his subjects,
doth very well agree with the office of the head"[80] have given Aristotle
much pause, for it, like Malynes's own primitive version of the social contract, preserved the fundamental Aristotelian divide between the work of
the head and the work of the hand:

> When Almightie God had created man, good and a sociable creature,
> who could not live so well alone, as other creatures sufficiently provided
> (by nature) for their sustenance . . . necessitie did require a concourse of
> men helping one another to supplie (with a common strength) the said
> weaknesses. . . . Then it came to passe, that by mutuall contribution of

offices, everie man did afford the means according to his abilitie for the common good, so that those who which were of a strong bodie did emploie their labour to get living and maintenance for themselves and others: And those which were endued with the best part of the soule, as Understanding and Reason, did undertake the most important matters, teaching men how to live well, and informing them of their felicitie (which they judged chiefly to consist in vertuous actions).[81]

Aristotle himself had noted that the rule of intelligence over desire was like the rule of a statesman or king over the body politic.[82]

Malynes had, however, also moved beyond Aristotle's preference for monarchy[83] in his elevation of the king:

The state of Monarchie must needes be the Supreamest thing under the cope of Heaven, when Kings are not only Gods Lieutenants upon the earth, and sit upon his throne; but also are called Gods, by God himselfe, in regard of their Transcendent Preheminences and Prerogatives, whereby they maintaine Religion and Justice, which are the onely true supporters and fundamentall stayes of all Kingdomes and Common-weales.[84]

In English thought, the difference between king and subject had been moving from a quantitative to a qualitative one for at least a century. Sir Thomas Elyot's *Book Named the Governor* (1531) transformed the king from princeps (first among equals) to a sun that "ruleth over the day" and a "shepherd" ruling over a flock.[85] We can find a turn-of-the-century equivalent in Thomas Milles's *Customers Replie* (1604) with its king characterized as the "Day-Starre."[86] And, since 1606, Bodin's *Six Books of the Republic* had been available in English, where anyone could read that "Soveraigntie" was the "most high, absolute, and perpetuall power."[87] But a suspiciously similar sentiment had already been uttered by James I, king of England, in his speech of March 1, 1609 (o.s.), to the assembled Parliament. Here James took the position:

The State of Monarchie is the supremest thing upon earth: For Kings are not onely Gods Lieutenants upon earth, and sit upon Gods throne, but even by God himselfe they are called Gods.[88]

In 1598, James published a book entitled *The Trew Law of Free Monarchies* in which he elaborated on the divinity of a king's office, placing it under the heads of ministering justice and maintaining religion.[89] In this same book appeared the sentence "And the proper office of a King towards his Subjects agrees very wel with the office of the head towards the body."[90] Both the *Trew Law of Free Monarchies* and the *Speech of 1609* were included in a collection, *The Political Works of James I,* published in 1616. Malynes dedicated his *Lex Mercatoria* to James I; did it require all that subtle a flattery to include his king's own words in that dedication?

Such imitation, however, does not detract from the genuineness of Malynes's absolutist leanings. For Malynes, as for James I, the king's prerogative was expressly designed to leaven the limitation of the law with "the Mercy of God" and thus stood above it.[91] This was definitely a head in full control of its body.

The harmony that produced concord in this body was a hierarchical but moderating mean. The "Dragon" of usury destroyed that harmony "by too much enriching some, and by oppressing and impoverishing some others."[92] But while Malynes disliked both extremes, he was far more exercised by any prospect of absolute equality. His one mention of "Puritans" condemned what he erroneously believed to be their practice of taking equal shares of the profits of ventures in which they had not equally invested.[93]

Plato and Sir Thomas More were scolded on the same head:

> Plato the Philosopher perceiving that equality would be the cause that every man should have enough, was of opinion and willed all things in a common wealth to be common, whom sir Thomas Moore in his Utopian common weale seemeth to imitate. But this equality cannot be established, neither was there any such ever used in any age or commaunded by the word of God, but that possessing these worldly goods, we should so use them with charity towards others, as though we did not possesse them at all.[94]

Plato came out ahead of More in Malynes's estimation, because, in his *Laws,* he repented of the stand he had taken in the *Republic* and revoked "his former opinion" as absurd, as there could be no "Commonwealth without a private wealth."[95]

The recognition that there could be no "Commonwealth without a private wealth" did not signal an attempt on the part of Gerard de Malynes to substitute an aggregate social model for the standard organic one, but served only to defend the idea of private property in the context of proportional justice.

What could never be tolerated in such a worldview was reform originating from below; that would be, horror of horrors, a leveling innovation—something as dangerous as removing "the corner stones of a building."[96] If rank was equivalent to order, democracy, in commerce as well as in politics, was equivalent to chaos. Sir Francis Bacon, as we will see, would have heartily agreed.

For Gerard de Malynes the body commercial was a deductive construction. He invariably began with the definition of the "three simples" of commerce: (1) commodities, (2) money, and (3) bills of exchange.[97] To these we will add (4) merchants and (5) banks, the two other keys to his economic worldview. His choice of the term *simples* reveals yet another link in the chain the century would forge between medicine and the development of economic thought: "So hath the Physition finite simples, though he doe make infinite compounds."[98]

Commodities

Malynes often repeated the standard Scholastic division of commodities into Natural (agricultural) and Artificial (mined or manufactured):

> *Aristotle* saith, that riches is either naturall or artificiall. The naturall riches as lands, vines, forrests, meddowes, and such like. The artificiall, as money, gold, silver, wooles cloth, and all other moveables and household stuff. Nowe as this artificiall riches is proceeding of the natural riches, and that both these doe receive their price and estimation by money . . . so reason requireth a certaine equality betweene the naturall riches of lands, and the artificiall riches of commodities proceeding of the same.[99]

But Malynes was merely using the distinction as another example of the importance of an Aristotelian balance ("a certaine equality") in maintaining a just social concord. To Malynes, the key problem of maintaining a socio-politico-economic structure was maintaining order within that structure, not making certain it could reproduce itself economically. In his *St. George for England*, Malynes had laid out the far-reaching disruptions of allowing commercial lending, pawnbroking, and a "marchandizing exchange" free rein in society: men and women refusing to live "contented" in their "vocation[s]," abandoning the Christian virtues of "hospitality" and "charity" in their zeal for a return on their money or the easier profit to be made on sheep-raising than on farming, beggaring their offspring by wasting their estates in "outward shew," gluttony, whoring, drinking, and dicing, or turning themselves into litigious misers without respect for any "science or learning" that did not lead to gain.[100] For Malynes, self-interest was quintessentially irrational and dysfunctional: rather than functioning to insure a society's economic survival, it was forever threatening to rip asunder its social (read *moral*) fabric.

Thus a more important distinction for Malynes (than that between natural and artificial) was that between the necessary and the superfluous. Necessities were limited to houses and things "*ad victum & vestium*" (for the back and for the belly), but even within this group Malynes made some rather revealing distinctions. One should neither "pay to much" for foodstuffs nor sell clothing "too good cheape," although such luxury as got into clothing by way of "civility" must itself be subordinated to "the good of the common-weale."[101] The restraints proposed for spending on food were simultaneously a warning against the profits forestallers reaped when prices were high and a warning against gluttony. The purpose of high prices for clothing was to prevent the common folk from copying the "outward shew" of their superiors.[102] Every private impulse had to be subordinated to the harmony of the whole because every private impulse threatened that whole and the value system that upheld it.[103]

Money

Any college student exposed to Economics 101 learns a definition of money—a medium of exchange, a unit of account, a store of purchasing power, a standard of deferred payment—specifically intended to separate the idea of the measure (money) from the thing measured (purchasing power/wealth). Seventeenth-century systems builders had yet to create the technical vocabulary such a distinction requires: in their texts *money* might mean any or all of the above.[104] Malynes, for example, understood the fictitious ("imaginery") nature of coins "of account,"[105] but he also suffered from the common confusion between money (as a function) and currency (one physical form that function can take). He lived in an age when currency was coined of gold and silver bullion that had market prices independent of the government stamps they bore. Malynes understood that there was a conventional aspect to the stamp:

> if any Prince wold call in al the good mony, and deliver base money for it, which by his authority should be valued and proclaimed at such rates as the good mony was, the matter wold be of small importance, for so much as concerneth the course of things amongst his subjects . . . and that the Prince were sure that other nations should not draw that good money from him, or deceive him with the like base money.[106]

But he also knew that taken abroad, that stamp had less weight than the goldsmith's scale: it was not the king's mark that made the "Pound" good in the United Provinces, but the sterling therein,[107] which also set its price against the guilder. There was a nascent system of paper money in the Bills of Exchanges and primitive deposit banking, but the paper was accepted because it could be, and in the end would be, turned into coin.

This was a process that required some sophisticated arithmetic. The system in use was that of Troy weight: a "pound" divisible into twelve ounces each further divisible into 20 pennyweights each of 24 grains, (except in countries that counted 32 "azes" per pennyweight and called those "graines").[108] When Malynes first wrote of the matter in 1601, a restored standard "pound sterling" consisted of eleven ounces, two pennyweights of pure silver and eighteen pennyweights of copper or some other metal.[109] The currency was often manipulated. Debasements reduced the proportion of this alloy used in the actual coins without changing their stamped value. Governments might also depreciate their currency by keeping the bullion content (and the weight) of coin the same, but stamping a higher value on it.[110]

Debasement had been rife in the centuries preceding the 1560–61 recoinage: during the reign of Henry IV enough base metal was added to yield 360 pennies, during the reign of Henry VI enough to yield 450 pennies, and during the reign of Henry VIII enough to yield 576 pennies to the true Troy pound.[111] With the 1560–61 recoinage, only the pre-1544 standard was restored, but from then on the coinage remained reasonably stable (at least through Elizabeth's reign).[112] Complicating the problem of older coins remaining in circulation was that of coins of several states circulating within the same country. The English tried to avoid this by restricting currency to their own coin, but this put an added strain on the currency supply as English coins drawn abroad in trade could not be replaced by foreign coins as was the case in France or the Netherlands.[113]

To avoid errors in "cashing in" Bills of Exchange, one also had to know the *Par* between the gold and silver coins of account. In Malynes's day, the *par* or ratio of silver to gold was set at 11:1 in England;[114] that is to say, one pound of Crown gold could get you eleven pounds of sterling silver.[115] But none of these standards was universal. In France the par between gold and silver was most often 12:1.[116] Governments might also seek to influence bullion flow by altering these ratios. The actual trading pars that Malynes recorded for July 21, 1622, ranged from 13.2 in England, 12:1 in Rome, and 11.66:1 in Germany to as low as 9.33:1 in Milan because of a high demand there for silver gilt thread.[117] The pound Troy weight could differ as well: France's standard was three pennyweights lighter than that used in England, Holland's was two and a half pennyweights lighter, while Scotland's was four pennyweights and nine grains heavier. In an age without calculators it is a wonder anyone ever got this arithmetic right.[118]

The practical problems of a currency that was both real and conventional were not the only reasons the seventeenth century tended to think of money differently than do we. The relationship of the measure to the thing measured was different. The natural laws of their world were not yet exclusively those of simple mechanical causation but often moral laws whose nature was preeminently prescriptive rather than descriptive. Malynes wrote of "the law of God, whereupon all humane laws *ought* to be grounded."[119]

Law itself was not a single concept with a single meaning in the seventeenth century, but an ever evolving hierarchy charged with different degrees of inevitability as can be seen in Richard Hooker's *Laws of Ecclesiastical Polity*. Descending from the absolute eternal immutability of God's own Being (that "is a kind of law to his working") was the "Celestial" law observed by Angels, "Nature's Law" as it applied involuntarily to the unthinking beast, "the law of Reason" that was Natural Law for the "Voluntary agents" that were human beings, and the "Divine Law" of "Revelation."[120] But even Revelation (Scripture) required "Tradition" to be properly comprehended,[121] and the "Law of Reason" was eminently capable of being overthrown by the "Appetites."[122] What humans should do according to these "Natural" laws was far from being synonymous with what they could do, even if that doing resulted in a "singular disgrace of Nature."[123]

Law may have functioned as a balancer or equalizer in Malynes's worldview, simultaneously defending "the feeble from the mightie" and "rendering everie man his due,"[124] but it was as hierarchical as it had been for Hooker. If every individual had a different "due," every law did as well:

> even as wils, contracts or testaments of particular men cannot derogate the ordinances of the Magistrates, and the order of the Magistrates cannot abolish customes, nor the customes can abridge the generall lawes of an absolute Prince: no more can the lawes of Princes alter or change the lawe of God and Nature."[125]

According to Malynes, the king's divine office (as we have seen) was to uphold justice (the moral order). If he did nothing to prevent his coin from being traded abroad at market rates, he was like a draper who "suffered the buyer to measure out" the cloth "by the buyers owne false yeard."[126] This was a violation of a moral world-order in which "the yard doth measure the Cloth, but the Cloth doth not measure the yard."[127] Money's *moral* role was to stand as *publica mensura*, "the measure and rule to set a price to everie thing," maintaining a balance between the value of land, its products, and manufactured goods; hence its overruling of (i.e., determining) the course of commodities, as it was overruled in its turn by the exchanges, which were meant to act as "the rule & square" in the international sphere as money did in the domestic.[128] Gold was not used for exchange merely because it was more convenient than bulk barter, it was special in and of itself. The four elements had "such an equall proportion" in gold that "all corruption" was thereby "excluded."[129] Malynes's ideas about money were as much conditioned by his intellectual understanding of "value" as a function of intrinsic qualities as by the fact that the currency had both a "real" and a "conventional" worth.[130]

Bills of Exchange

Bills of Exchange were used to move money from country to country without moving coin. For Malynes, their ordained role was to act as a moral balancer between monies:

> the right exchange is most commendable, necessarie, and convenient for
> the maintenance and traffick of entercourse betwixt merchant and merchant, or countrie and countrie.[131]
> The true royall Exchange for Moneys (by Bills of Exchanges) is
> grounded upon the weight, finenesse, and valuation of the Money of
> each countrie, according to the Par, which is, value for value . . . and if we
> differ not with them in the proportion betweene the gold and silver, then
> may our Exchanges run at one price both for gold and silver.[132]

This was known as *par pro pari*, or value for value. But the greed of merchants and bankers had turned this Exchange into an international money-market "rising and falling in price, according to plentie and scarcitie of Money, and in regard of discrepaunce and distance of time and place."[133] "Discrepaunce and distance" were allowable factors to accommodate the difficulties of merchants,[134] but making a commodity of coined money (letting plenty or scarcity set its price) was an unforgivable sin.[135] In fact, it was two sins, for it violated the laws of both (1) the mediate-cosm or the state and (2) the macrocosm ordained by God.

1. The "Marchandising Exchange" was a sin against the state because it usurped its authority: the "valuation or alteration of money" was a "thing peculiar" to princes,[136] for they were "the warrant of the monies unto their subjects."[137] That valuation was "of too high presumption for subjects to step into" as well as being "against reason, to change the course of nature in the coin, as though a pound weight should be more weighty then a pound."[138] Because the greater always commanded the lesser, the international exchange overruled "our particular exchange of England."[139] That the right exchange should predominate over merely national policies was natural, but the overruling under discussion was not innocent, because private bankers (or even the heads of municipal banks) "commonly in league" with each other set the rates at their convenience, rather than with an eye toward the common good.[140] Malynes believed English coin was being undervalued on the exchange, causing its exportation. This in turn caused the price level of domestic commodities to drop and those of foreign imports to

increase.[141] Whereas, if the exchange were held to *par pro pari,* "neither difference of weight, finenesse of standard, or valuation of monies" could cause its exportation, because "if you inhaunce the Coyne," the exchange would "rise accordingly" and if you "undervalue the same" the exchange fell.[142] Because merchants could make greater profits in these money markets than in mere trade, "money which should be employed upon the commodities of the realme" was diverted to currency speculation.[143] Alternatively, unbalanced rates would incline merchants to favor foreign commodities over domestic, causing both domestic employment and the balance of trade to suffer.[144]

2. The second sin was against the macrocosm of society itself, for money's main function as *publica mensura* was to "infuse life to traffique by the meanes of Equality and Equity, preventing advantage betweene Buyers and Sellers."[145] Those who claimed making a gain on money was as lawful as making a profit on "the rents of their houses, revenues of lands, or gaines of corne and cattell, or wares and merchandizes," were ignoring money's special role as "a pledge or right betwixt man and man."[146] Without a sure standard there could be no certain justice between buyers and sellers, and without that justice there could be no trust, and without that trust there could be no commerce: commercial, political, or human.

Malynes was hardly alone in this view. A very similar analysis can be found in Thomas Milles's *Customers Replie* (1604) in which the "Merchandising Exchange" was excoriated for usurping the authority of princes and turning a public convenience into an engine for private profit.[147] Milles also explained what he considered to be the fraud underlying the discounts in these Bills for "Usance" (money to be delivered in thirty days) and "Double Usance" (money to be delivered in sixty days) that created a different price for the same currency than when it was deliverable "at Sight."[148]

Malynes's problems with the role price played in the marketplace were not limited to its influence over international currency flows. He understood its conventional nature and dependance on demand:

> Plentie or scarcitie of Commodities doth also alter the price of the things wanting or abounding to the use thereof, which is grounded upon estimation by consent, after the pleasure and sensualtie of man.[149]

But this understanding was precisely the reason he wished to limit its role in the marketplace.

A perfect example of this can be found in Malynes's response to a depression affecting England's woolen industry in the years between the publication of his first three and his last three books. Partially finished woolen cloth (neither dyed nor dressed) made up the largest portion of

England's export trade.[150] But most of the profit went to dealers in Holland where the dyeing and finishing were carried out. Alderman Cockayne put forward a scheme to turn the trade over to a new company that would secure native finishing for the cloth and keep that profit in England. There was trouble from the start. An insufficiently skilled work force meant the goods were never up to the quality of those produced in Holland, and when the Dutch retaliated by forbidding the import of the finished cloth, the scheme fell through entirely. Exports dropped sharply enough by 1617 that Cockayne's patent was revoked and the trade returned to the status quo ante. But the damage was done: by 1622 exports were down to less than half of the 1614 high, a slump that continued into the 1640s.[151]

The first years of the slump were marked by considerable discussion in England over what had gone wrong. When voices were raised suggesting that the finished goods had to be sold at too high a price (native labor being better paid than foreign) to compete abroad, Malynes retorted that "other Nations . . . did never complaine that the Clothes were sold too deere, but they did alwaies complaine of the false making of our Cloth."[152] He went on to endorse the statutory restrictions on "exportation of Wools, Wool fells, Wool-yearne, Fullers earth, and Wood ashes" used in the production of finished cloth.[153]

By keeping the exchange fixed at *par pro pari* (fixed at the respective metallic contents of the coins), Malynes would ensure that supply and demand never affected the exchange-price of money. The laws of the market would have no effect on the value of the *publica mensura*.[154]

Since there was no effective international agency, the only mechanism available for reforming the international exchange was the individual state, though that could only act to protect its own coin. In his first book, *A Canker of Englands Commonwealth*, Malynes discussed two possible ways to do this. Both began with publication of the approved rates of exchange. The first, and rejected, solution involved binding brokers by oath "to deal honestly betweene partie and partie," and merchants "upon a penalty" not to make any exchanges independently of these brokers.[155] This was not sufficiently binding for Malynes. He preferred the restoration of the medieval office of the Royal Exchanger, under whose auspices all merchants would be required by law to settle their Bills.[156]

His advocacy of the re-creation of the Royal Exchanger has caused Malynes to be subject to abuse in the twentieth century as well as in the seventeenth. Raymond de Roover (like Edward Misselden) dismissed Malynes as "a perennial office-seeker who advocated exchange control in the hope that he himself would be appointed the controller."[157] Lynn Muchmore looked to Malynes's lack of prominence at Court to conclude that there could be no truth to such an allegation.[158] Whether or not Malynes hoped to hold the office, a Royal Exchanger was internally consistent with the rest of his deductive system.

Merchants

For Malynes, anyone who "continually dealeth in buying and selling of commodities, or by way of permutation of wares both at home and abroad in forreine parts" was a "Merchant."[159] The key word was *both*—the merchants in question were overseas traders, not domestic wholesalers or retail shopkeepers (neither of whom contributed to bullion flow).

It is easy to find passages in the writings of seventeenth-century merchants that look like paeans to those soldiers of capitalism. Included in Malynes's dedication of his *Lex Mercatoria* to James I was this extravaganza:

> because riches is the bright Starre, whose hight Trafficke takes to direct it selfe by, whereby Kingdomes and Commonweales doe flourish, Merchants being the meanes and instruments to performe the same, to the Glorie, Illustration, and Benefit of their Monarchies and States. Questionlesse therefore, the State of a Merchant is of great dignitie and to bee cherished; for by them Countreys are discovered, Familiaritie betweene Nations is procured, and politike Experience is attained.[160]

But there was a distinct difference between the good a merchant could do for his country if he fulfilled his proper function and what merchants actually did in the real world.

Keeping to his division of "Traffique" into "three simples," Malynes used a parallel classification of merchants: those who dealt exclusively in commodities, those in money, those in exchanges, or "for all three or any of them."[161] He was, however, far less interested in their choice of "simple" than in the principles guiding their trading in or choice between the three. Their actions were routinely determined by whichever

> yieldeth them most benefit and gaine; and herein is their particular profit, or Privatum Commodum, more respected than the generall good of the common-wealth, whereby corruptible and unnecessarie commodities are given for Staple wares and durable commodities, to the impoverishing of kingdomes and common-weales.[162]

Malynes wanted "Princes and Governours . . . to sit at the sterne of the course of Trade and Commerce,"[163] because merchants were inherently untrustworthy. They beat down the price of the cloth they bought from the clothier in order to sell it "good cheape" abroad, but did not share the resulting profit with the clothier, so the hard-pressed clothier was forced to put the squeeze on the wool-grower, "which disimproveth the Revenue of lands." And all the while merchants connived to evade customs impositions and "winke at the false making of Cloth."[164] The issue of the middleman would be explored in much greater detail toward the end of the century by John Locke, but both men shared the same belief that eliminating the middleman would result in a much more equitable flow of profit.

As a class, merchants were as unfit to be consulted in the reformation of trade as "the Vintner to the consultation of lawes to bee made against drunkards."[165] And all because "Nothing doeth force trade but Gaine."[166] Could any minister come up with a harsher denunciation of market morality?

Banks

Gerard de Malynes had nothing but praise for those monarchs who, like Louis IX, Philip the Fair, and Philip de Valois of France, confiscated bankers' goods and sent them packing.[167] We can actually construct a functional definition of an early-seventeenth-century bank (private or municipal) by compiling a list of the sins Malynes thought they committed. We have already seen him condemn them for manipulating exchange rates to the harm of one or another country's trade. He dismissed their unsecured bridge loans to merchants with good credit records as fictions because the banks did not really pay out any money to the merchant's creditor, but only transferred debits and credits from Peter to pay John on Peter's behalf.[168] That banks would use Bills of Exchange to do this for Peter's international accounts was but the same flummery writ large.[169] Even worse, they only gave 3 to 5 percent interest on deposits (although the depositor might draw it "into his owne hands . . . once but in twentie yeares" and even if the depositor was a widow or an orphan) while lending those same funds out at 25, 30, or even 50 percent to impecunious monarchs.[170] The rate given the depositor was unjust and uncharitable, but that charged princes approached the usury of pawnbrokers who

> feede upon the sweate and labour of the poore, by taking (and that upon pawne, whereby many times their meanes of living are hindred) twelve pence for the lending of 20 shillings for one moneth, which is above 60 pro 100 . . . a most pernicious and damnable dealing, not to be suffered amongst Christians. . . . this biting usury.[171]

The struggles of Christian Europe to find a way alternately to rid itself of a condemned practice or accommodate a necessity of commerce had produced a monumental number of texts long before Malynes ever entered the fray. The condemnations went all the way back to the Bible. Exodus 22:25 forbade making a profit on money lent to the poor: "If thou lend money to *any of* my people *that is* poor by thee, thou shalt not be to him as an usurer, neither shalt thou lay upon him usury."[172] This kind of usury (or consumer lending) was both an offense against charity and a violation of the harmony that was justice, for justice was "a measure ordained by God amongst men, to defend the feeble from the mightie."[173]

Like most men of his age, Malynes condemned this outright. To eliminate it, he proposed adopting the Italian institution of the *Mons pietatis,* a government regulated though privately funded institution that lent to the working poor at a rate (3 percent) low enough to avoid beggaring them (and thus making them a charge on the parish) but strict enough to encourage their industry in paying it back.[174] Thus the householder who "liveth honestly by his handie worke and labour" would not be "destroyed" when, "being visited by sicknesse," he was "constrained to pawne his goods or substance" unto "uncharitable people."[175] When Malynes chided an opponent to this scheme with the retort that

> Poverty and want is not without feeling, neither ourt to be without commiseration. For the transportation of moneys to heaven is lawfull, by charitable giving to the poore, which God himselfe hath promised to reward, although men were never so unthankfull[176]

he was making the age's classic distinction between the working poor and the idle.

The more problematic issue for the sixteenth and seventeenth centuries was that of commercial lending: how much, if any, interest might be charged the merchant expecting to profit from the goods he purchased with the loan? Here, the search *ad fontes* led back as much to Aristotle as to the Bible. For Aristotle, all commerce was "justly discredited" as not being "in accordance with nature" because it involved "men's taking things from one another." But usury was even more contemptible in that making a gain from "money itself" was not even the natural use of money: "money was brought into existence" solely "for the purpose of exchange." Wealth gained through the charging of interest was "of all forms [of wealth] the most contrary to nature."[177]

In Malynes's day, the classic treatment of the subject was still that to be found in the *Discourse uppon Usurye* (1572) by Thomas Wilson (1525?–1581). Wilson's book took the form of a dialogue between a merchant, a student of the law, a civilian, and a preacher, in which the preacher (representing Wilson's own view) eventually won his opponents over to his own condemnation of the myriad forms of usury. Malynes not only referred favorably to the book several times,[178] he borrowed great chunks of it, such as the use of the metaphor of a pound somehow weighing more than a pound to describe the injustice of private men overriding the prince's valuation through such an exchange.[179] The issue here is not one of originality—some of these ideas were commonplaces before Wilson ever wrote of them—but of judging the difference between agreement and influence. For the differences between the two are more important than the borrowings. Before he was converted by Wilson's preacher, Wilson's lawyer suggested that beggars, householders, and rich merchants or gentlemen should be dealt with differently—the first given money, the second lent freely or "mercifully," and the third lent at gain—only to be struck down by the preacher's response that it was as great a sin to take interest from the rich as from the poor.[180] Malynes not only sided with the lawyer, but plagiarized the *Discourse* to do so, by copying the passage on the three sorts of men and the different types of dealings commendable with them.[181] And Wilson's *Discourse* only took up the "bankes of charitye" to condemn them as equally usurious, albeit considering them less harmful than "excessiyve" usury in which money was "lent onely for greedye lucre and private gaine."[182]

For Malynes the distinction between consumer and commercial loans was a crucial one:

> Usury is greater therefore to take but two or three upon the hundreth of one that maketh no benefit of the money, than to take tenne or twelve upon the hundreth of a Merchant, who maketh a greater gaine thereby.[183]

As long as Malynes drew a line between commercial and consumer lending, he could not be said to be attacking the spirit of self-interest per se (although he was attacking its excesses). It was, after all, the magnitude of the banker's spread (rather than the spread itself) that he had attacked. But when he tried to trace the causes of the "incertaine" price of money that he found so disruptive to trade, he did take aim at the heart of the market, for

> The price of money becommeth incertaine in particular, when private men will give or receive any money in specie above the price of their valuation imposed by the authoritie of the Prince. . . . [But] The price of mony in generall becommeth incertaine, when usury is tollerated, whereby one hundreth pounds are esteemed and valued (in regard of time) to be worth one hundreth and ten pounds, and in some other countries more.[184]

This was the intolerable case of the cloth measuring the yardstick.

He remained in this, as in many other things, a man straddling two worlds, unable to commit wholeheartedly to the new but accepting that the old ways would no longer work unaltered. The taking of interest on commercial loans could not be legislated away; it could only be eased by increasing the money supply (and thus decreasing its price):

> Albeit in some respects, Trade is increased by monyes delivered at use or interest upon occasions, when the Usurer is glad to find a taker up of his monyes, and doth pray him to doe the same, by reason of the abundance of money; which maketh the price of Usury to fall, more then any Law or Proclamation can ever doe.[185]

But the welfare of the poor could not be left to the mercies of the market:

> The biting usury & intolerable extortion committed by certain unchari-table men, common called Brokers for pawnes, is not to bee touched in a word, for this is the only the remarkable sin, (I mean extortion & oppression:) for which the first world was drowned.[186]

Like any good deductive thinker, Gerard de Malynes built up a set of ordering theorems from his "simples." The most important of these, drawn primarily from money's role as *publica mensura*, was no less than the root of the quantity theory of money and formed the basis of sixteenth- and seventeenth-century explanations of the price revolution long before Hamilton devised his American treasure thesis:

> plentie of Money maketh generally all things deere, and scarcitie of Money maketh generally things good cheape: whereas particular com-modities are also deere or good cheape, according to plentie or scarcitie of the commodities themselves, and the use of them. . . . if Money be wanting, Trafficke doth decrease, although commodities be aboundant and good cheape: and on the contrarie, if Moneys be plentifull, Com-merce increaseth, although commodities be scarce, and the price thereof is thereby more advanced. . . . everie thing is inhaunced in price by the aboundance of Bullion and Moneys (which came from the West-Indies into Europe) which like unto an Ocean, hath divided her course into severall branches through all countries. . . . So that plentie of Money concurring herein made verie thing deerer, and especially the forreine commodities.[187]

It is the "root" of the quantity theory and not the theory itself for two rea-sons. It asserts that the quantity of money and the price level move in the same direction, but it does not quantify the dimensions of the change in the one that the other produces. Nor does it address the relationship between the quantity of money in and the velocity of circulation. The usual model is Fisher's (1911): $MV = PT$, where M = money in circulation, V = velocity, P = price level, and T = volume of transactions (normally now Y as used in GDP calculations).

For an explanation of the price revolution, Malynes borrowed directly from Jean Bodin's 1568 *Response* to a 1566 pamphlet (*Les paradoxes . . . sur le faict des Monoyes*) by the Sieur de Malestroit, controller of the Royal Mint in

Paris. Malestroit blamed the century's intractable inflation on successive devaluations of the French coinage. Bodin rejected devaluation as the sole cause of the price revolution because the magnitude of the inflation was far greater than the extent of the devaluation.[188] Instead Bodin opted for multiple causes: a treasure influx (first and foremost), the monopolistic practices of both merchants and labor, a scarcity "caused as much by the export as by the waste," the bad example of the extravagant dress and tastes of "kings and great lords," a population increase, and that coinage debasement.[189] Malynes accepted Bodin's causes as part of the problem, but he remained certain the *key* position in the causal chain was the "marchandizing exchange."[190] In this universe the greater was always logically prior to the lesser: the international "public measure" must "overrule" the merely domestic measure. When his opponents argued otherwise, he complained that their reason was drawn "from a particular to an universall," which was "preposterous and retrograde."[191] Turning this greater standard into a money market upset the balance upon which all lesser standards should rest.

A key problem in evaluating sixteenth- or seventeenth-century responses to England's (or, for that matter, Europe's) economic situation is determining the accuracy of those responses. Attempts to nail down the magnitude of the changes in population, prices, and quantity of coin in circulation during the sixteenth and seventeenth centuries has resulted in a blizzard of statistical analyses that stand on rather shaky ground: national averages have been built up on partial data from scattered localities, conclusions reached about economic pressures from monetary records in an economy that still relied on both money and payment in kind, price levels on "consumables" compared to daily wage rates to determine the extent to which wages kept pace with inflation when we are uncertain how many days per year the wage earners in question worked. But accepting that the numbers present only the roughest of estimates, we are still presented with a country undergoing some startling changes.

The most widely quoted population figures remain those published in 1981 by E. A. Wrigley and R. S. Schofield. According to their data, the population of England grew from just under 3 million in 1561 to just over 4.1 million in 1601 and just under 5.1 million in 1641.[192] Calculations of national income range as high as 13.5 million for 1561, 22 million for 1600, and 35 million for 1643.[193] The most commonly used consumables "index" (using 1491–1500 as 100) would give us an erratic but definitely inflationary economy:

1540 = 147	1600 = 459 (+34%)
1560 = 265 (+80%)	1620 = 485 (but 1610 = 503; +10%)
1580 = 342 (+29%)	1640 = 546 (+13%)[194]

Immediately after the recoinage of 1561, there appears to have been about 1.45 million pounds sterling in circulation; by 1603 this number had more than doubled to 3.5 million; by 1643 it would hit 10 million, yet the economy was still strained by a supply of coin insufficient for its volume of trade.[195] And the merchant was not the only one feeling the strain.

Malynes noted over and over that money was universally held to be *Nervi bellorum* (the sinews of war).[196] The sentiment was not entirely universal. Machiavelli had devoted an entire chapter of his *Discourses* to proving that characterization rightly applied to good soldiers and not treasure.[197] But Francis Bacon, who was just enough of a Machiavellian to agree that money would not suffice "where the sinews of men's arms" were "failing," still counted "treasure" as among the "four pillars of government" (the other three being religion, justice, and counsel).[198] James I, who spoke of trade as "a maine pillar of this Kingdome" in that already cited speech of 1609, had called money "Nervus belli" all the way back in 1599 in *Basilikon Doron,* a book of instructions in kingship written for his son.[199] For Malynes, money linked the functions of princes in the "two seasons" of rule: "the time of warre when arms are necessarie, and the time of peace more fitting wholesome laws."[200]

Money was a problem for the Crown throughout the years covered by Malynes's published writings. The Earl of Essex had spent enough to ensure a victory in Ireland without getting one. In the wake of his failure, a Spanish army had been put ashore in Ireland in 1601, leaving Elizabeth to deal with it as well as with the Earl's own rebellion. With all her economy, the Crown was still £350,000 in debt at her death.[201] Her successor managed to ring up a cool million in debt by 1608.[202] James came hat in hand to Parliament in March 1609, stretched between sending "a Supply of forces to Cleves," and keeping up forts in Flushing and Brill in the Netherlands besides the standing army in Ireland.[203] James evidently felt compelled to have his treasurer lay out some of his accounts for the Parliament in substantiation of his claim, reminding them that this accounting was a "favour" kings "seldome" bestowed upon their subjects.[204]

Something had to be done about the money supply, but letting it be regulated solely by the forces of the marketplace was not any kind of a solution in the mind of Gerard de Malynes. The idea of a "floating" *publica mensura* would have struck him as more than passing strange: if commodities overruled money, then the cloth was measuring the yardstick. Was this not the same complaint as that of the anonymous author of *Chaos* that "the Tail commands the Head, and all things are out of course"?[205]

CHAPTER 3

Edward Misselden and the "Natural Freedom" of Trade

Edward Misselden (fl. 1608–1654) is known to posterity for two books, *Free Trade, or the Means to Make Trade Flourish* (1622) and *The Circle of Commerce* (1623), in which he crossed metaphors with Gerard de Malynes over the true cause of England's trade "crisis" and took up arms for the "Balance of Trade" and against the *par pro pari* as the First Commandment of commerce. Scattered praises of the "natural freedom" of trade found in his books have caused some historians of economic thought to label him a pioneer of the modern conception of economic life as an autonomous system.[1] But advocates of this position have failed to resolve the opposing stands on key issues such as bullion exportation taken in Misselden's first and second volumes or to consider to what extent his more modern-sounding positions were nothing more than special pleading on behalf of the East India Company (as his more traditional-sounding positions supported his earlier association with the Merchant Adventurers). But, then, Misselden's life, like his thought, suffered from his trying simultaneously to serve two masters.

Of Edward Misselden's date of birth we have no record, though he appears to have been slightly the junior of Thomas Mun, his onetime neighbor in Hackney and eventual fellow in the East India Company. Misselden originally came up through the ranks in the Merchant Adventurers' Company. In 1615, he was sent to Amsterdam to negotiate on their behalf as England teetered on the brink of a major economic depression fueled by wartime international currency manipulation, war, and the ill-advised attempts of Alderman Cockayne (already described) to grab a greater market share of the wool trade.[2]

The European conflict eventually called the Thirty Years' War began in 1618. But 1617 to 1623 were also the years of the *Kipper- und Wipper-Zeit*, a series of currency manipulations in Poland, Germany, and the Baltics that raised the cost of English imports and made it more profitable for English merchants to bring in foreign goods (and to export bullion).[3] As B. E. Supple pointed out, the early-seventeenth-century English economy was "sufficiently 'sticky' to throw large sectors of the economy out of gear if the circulating medium were suddenly diminished."[4] Thus, though their analyses begged the question of the side effects of a long-term positive trade balance, Malynes, Misselden, and Mun were wise to address themselves to the immediate problems of a negative balance.[5]

When they were not arguing over the king's seeming lack of interest in the Protestant cause, Parliament and the Privy Council spent a good portion of 1620 and 1621 in debates that resulted in the calling (in April 1622) of a formal commission of inquiry into the cloth trade and the issuing of the *Proclamatio contra Exportationem Bullionis.*[6] On the Commission sat persons "of quality and experience"—Members of Parliament, gentry, and merchants alike, including Thomas Mun and Dudley Digges, and to which Gerard de Malynes and Edward Misselden addressed their testimony and their respective volumes in the policy wars, although only Edward Misselden made it onto the Commission as a result.

Misselden fired the first shot when his *Free Trade* (1622) dismissed the idea of reestablishing a *par pro pari* monetary exchange as useless. Although not mentioned by name in Misselden's book, Gerard de Malynes took the attack personally and responded with his own version, *The Maintenance of Free Trade,* in which he made a line-by-line attempt to destroy Misselden's position and rehabilitate his own. Before a year had passed, Misselden countered with *The Circle of Commerce* (finished June 1623) and Malynes returned fire with *The Center of the Circle.*

By then Misselden was too preoccupied with his own affairs to respond further; from 1623 to 1633 he served as deputy-governor of the Merchant Adventurers' branch at Delft, while negotiating with the Hague on behalf of the East India Company.[7] With the increasing success of the English East India Company, a once simmering rivalry between Dutch and English traders had begun to boil over. At the Dutch settlement of Amboyna, ten English East India Company traders were executed while still others were imprisoned by their hosts. The negotiations to get some satisfaction for the English East India merchants, like those to gain import concessions on English cloth for the Merchant Adventurers, dragged on for years without success, while both sides engaged in a small propaganda war to win approval for their version of the incident.[8]

In the infancy of bureaucratization, governments gathered their foreign intelligence from whatever sources were to hand, and merchants were likely informants, but serving two masters is never easy: in 1628, Edward Misselden was accused by the States-General of spying for England and by Carleton, the English ambassador at the Hague, of working for the Dutch against the interests of the English.[9] Letters to and from Carleton over the

summer and fall of 1624 make it clear that Misselden, as the representative
of the East India Company, was demanding more from Carleton than the
ambassador, given his instructions, was able to perform.[10] As the representative of a less than first-rank power unwilling to become embroiled in an
ongoing European war, there was really very little Carleton could do.[11]

In any case, Carleton appears to have been persuaded to hold his temper, and Misselden, feathers smoothed by the Privy Council, returned to
the Netherlands to throw himself into the thick of Archbishop Laud's
attempts to bring the practices of English congregations abroad into line
with the uniformity being imposed at home.[12] As his fellow company
members in Delft were "strongly presbyterian," Misselden's Laudian stand
on the imposition of the *Prayer Book* cost him his post at Delft and the
chance to become deputy-governor at Rotterdam in 1635 (by which time
the king's efforts on his behalf likely did him more harm than good).[13] Yet
he was still running interference between Charles I and the Merchant
Adventurers in Rotterdam in 1640.[14]

Not surprisingly, Misselden did not fare as well under the Commonwealth or Protectorate as he had under the monarchy. Letters to
Cromwell's advisers went unanswered,[15] and Edward Misselden died, forgotten, in 1654. Even his balance of trade theory would be remembered as
the work of Thomas Mun.

As rivals for the hearts and minds of Parliament, Misselden and Malynes
were well matched. Misselden could match Malynes Dutch proverb for
Dutch proverb, Italian for Italian, and damn *le par* in his own French
coinage.[16] He advised all merchants to be well "acquainted with the Manners, Customes, Languages, Lawes of forraine Nations" and their "Religion, Revenue, Strength, and Policy."[17] And he was just as quick as his foe
in insisting that they had better keep a knowledgeable eye on shifts in the
"Intrinsique" and "Extrinsique" of monies in their accustomed markets: any
merchant foolish enough not to adjust the selling price of his goods "in due
proportion" would "come home by weeping crosses" whether he returned
with "Money, Bullion, or Wares."[18]

But Edward Misselden was as enamored of the world outside the
countinghouse as was Gerard de Malynes. There was nearly as much of art
history (Giotto's ability to draw a perfect circle freehand), geometry (doubling cubes and "the Quadrature" of circles), chemistry (whether there were
four elements or ten and which philosopher espoused which system),
mythology (Cadmus's serpent's teeth), or legal and constitutional theory
(the difference between *jus* and *consuetudo*, *malum prohibitum* and *malum in*

se, or the proper uses of the dispensing power)[19] in Misselden's work as there was of exchange rates or bookkeeping.

If anything, Misselden's learning was rather more deep than that of Malynes. Where Malynes had Latin, Misselden also had the Hebrew and Greek needed to complete the trilingual program of Catholic and Calvinist humanists. And Misselden was as emphatic as Malynes in insisting that "learning and languages" were "an Appendix not unnecessary to the facultie of a Merchant."[20] Where he acquired his erudition has not been discovered. We know he believed in higher education enough to send his son Samuel to Emmanuel College, Cambridge,[21] but Edward Misselden's mercantile apprenticeship would have provided a different form of education. He would have been given training in bookkeeping and arithmetic, penmanship, and the art of business correspondence, as well as some exposure to cosmography, navigation, and modern languages.[22] Before apprenticeship (which usually began in the middle of one's teens) would have come grammar school, possibly even one sponsored by the apprenticing field. The Merchant Taylors had endowed a school in 1561 that offered Greek and Hebrew as well as Latin, though that was more the exception than the rule.[23]

From whatever source, Misselden certainly drank deep. Searching through the sources on whose works he depended for his causes immediate and remote, primary and secondary, particular and general, active and passive, we will find Aristotle and his Categories, Pacius and his *Commentaries on Aristotle,* Aquinas, Bartolus, Straccia, and a host of other Civilians paraded before our eyes in digressions whose primary purpose was to prove that Malynes could not even distinguish "the Principles of natural things from their Essence" or matter from "Forme" and the "Privation" thereof.[24] The Scholastic strain ran as deep in Misselden's mind as in his adversary's.

But jumbled amidst the Scholastic sources were Virgil and Columella, Cato and Tacitus, Cicero and Seneca, Horace and Ovid, Homer, Pliny, Plato, and from a later day Ramus, Bodin, Althusius, Joseph Scaliger, Grotius, and Sir Thomas More. Competing with Scholasticism and the old curriculum for the mantle of orthodoxy in the intellectual world were various strains of Humanism sharing an ideological and methodological cry of *ad fontes* that fed into a new exactitude made possible by the use of print. In Misselden's heavy use of citations we can trace the development of both "footnotes" and the concept of plagiarism as he accused Malynes of piecing his pamphlets together with "with stollen stuffe."[25]

But as avant garde as Misselden might have been on the subject of literary property, his was a modernism more apparent than real.[26] We may begin to reconstruct both his physics and his metaphysics from remarks such as "Everything moves it selfe to its Center" or "the other Great Lights in the Spheares [of the Cosmos]."[27] Thus the "ballance of trade" was introduced as the "Center" to which the "Circle of Commerce" must "contract,"[28] and "the finenes of monies" was "that Cynosure or Center, whereunto all Exchanges" had "their natural propension."[29] We can begin to deduce a fixed economic worldview in which one nation's gain must come at another's loss from the finiteness of this Aristotelian-Ptolemaic universe, or work backward toward that universe from a tirade against the incursions into English waters of Dutch fishermen (revealing the finite value assigned even to the word *infinite*):

> [the] Encroaching of Strangers, in Fishing upon our Coasts: whereby not onely the bread is taken out of the subjects Mouth, but that infinite Wealth, which God hath made Proper and Peculiar unto us, is become Common unto them. Whereby also, their Navigation is wonderfully encreased, their Marriners are multiplied.[30]

Here again is that anthropomorphic universe of nested "cosms" with its authoritarian hierarchy:

> Neverthelesse when I looke upon the Face of the Great body politique of this Weale publicke, and therein consider the High wisdome of His sacred Majesty, as the intellectual part of this Microcosme, or alter orbis as Caesar calles it: the Prudence & Providence of His Nobles, as the Eyes thereof; the great decay of Trade, the Nerves thereof.[31]

Here "Government" was a representation of the "Majestie and Authoritie of the King," and fearing God and honoring the king were two sides of the same coin,[32] so the idea of a *loyal dissent*, whether in terms of religious practice or commercial policy, was a dangerous oxymoron:

> It [trade policy] is subject, as all great Actions are, to Faction abroad, to Faction at home. Both and either are evill Engines, to subvert Companies, yea, Kingdomes also.[33]

Or, as Sir Francis Bacon had it: "disputing, excusing, cavilling upon mandates and directions, is a kinde of shaking off the yoke, and assay of disobedience."[34]

There was, in Misselden, a classically Aristotelian sense of outrage over violations of the naturally hierarchical equity of distributive justice, audible when he bemoaned the fact that

> now a dayes most men live above their callings, and promiscuously step forth Vice versa, into one anothers Rankes. The Countrey mans Eie is upon the Citizen: the Citizen upon the Gentleman: the Gentleman upon the Nobleman.[35]

His proposed cure for this ailment was not market-based, however, but governmental: "lawes Vestiary and Sumptuary" such as he had seen working in Germany.[36]

Worse than this social promiscuity or any prodigal excess of the rich was the sinful idleness of the poor who would "never fall to working" as long as they could "live by begging."[37] In Misselden's proposals for poor relief, a privately funded *Mons pietatis* substituted for the government-funded model proposed by Malynes, but in which public control created something very like a workhouse.[38] The current forms of "charity" did nothing but make the City "swarm" with idle beggars, while the orderly use of funds for their employment would be the "more charitable" for serving both individual and "publique good."[39]

Economics was simultaneously a moral and a political science. We can see this equally as clearly in Misselden's condemnation of tobacco. It might first appear that he had a "puritanical" aversion to its use, coming down even harder on it than on silk or sugar,[40] but he accepted as a lesser sin restricting its import to the produce of England's Virginia and Bermuda colonies, keeping the coin used to pay for the tobacco in English rather than in Spanish hands.[41]

When it came to defining that science of trade, we find in Misselden the same medical analogy that saw money supply as the determining and trade as the determined variable

> For Money is the vitall spirit of trade, and if the Spirits faile, needes must the Body faint. As the Body of Trade seemeth to be Dead without the Life on Mony: so do also the Members of the Commonwealth without their Meanes of Trade. We say, that an Artizan or Workeman, cannot Worke without Tooles or Instruments: no more can a Merchant Trade without Money or meanes.[42]
> For although by the Placcaets or Proclamations of those parts [Holland], the Iacobus pieces, & and other Species of gold and silver, are there set at indifferent rates answerable to their valuation heere with us respectively . . . [yet they have many means to circumvent it] by the Connivence of the Magistrate. . . . [and thus] the Hepatites, or Liver veine of this Great Body of ours being opened, & such profusions of the Life bloud let out: & the Liver or fountain obstructed, & weakned, which shuld succour the same; needs must this Great body languish, and at length fal into a Marasmus, or Hectike Fever.[43]

Since his societal model was organic, Misselden's solution relied on the same medical analogy: the state was his chosen physician. In addition to the sumptuary laws already mentioned, Misselden supported imposing tolls on foreigners fishing in native waters, organizing trade with Spain into regulated companies, and possibly even adopting the Dutch custom of taxing any foreign imports competing with native goods.[44] He also praised the "Statute for Employments" as one of the two ways in which coin might be kept within the realm.[45] This act had nothing to do with *employment* as we know the word, but required that foreign merchants use the money they made selling their goods in England to buy English goods for resale abroad. The second way to prop up the money supply was "Princely and Prudent Negotiation, with the Princes of our Neighbour Countries . . . to keep a more constant course in the values of their Coines."[46] The first was a blatant attempt to force "the course and use" of trade, and the second attested to the success of the similarly aimed policies of the Dutch. In the very next breath, Misselden asserted that neither policy could be affected by the "Par of Exchange" because it was "not the rate of Exchanges, but the value of monies, here lowe, elsewhere high" that caused "their Exportation" as it did the value of "the Exchanges."[47]

Those values, however, could easily be manipulated by the Dutch:

> As either by their Banckes, when the Banckiers will for their occasions give a greater price for money then the Proclamation suffereth, and then it is called Banck gelt: or else by slacke paymasters, that for their owne advantage in the raising of Money, will pretend not to make present payment of their debts, unless you take their Money at a higher rate, then either the Proclamation, or the Banck money. Which being paid and received, produceth a third kind, which they call Current gelt.[48]

Misselden was not arguing modern supply and demand against a medieval order represented by Gerard de Malynes; Edward Misselden was simply arguing over which policy would successfully manipulate supply. He was certain that there were ways to use legislation to create or undo that "scarcity" which determined the market "value" of money.

Nor did Misselden's spirited defense of his profession necessarily imply partisanship of a society dominated by the values of the marketplace. Certainly he could, and often did, wax eloquent in defense of a rightly ordered commerce:

> when Trade flourisheth, the Kings revenue is augmented, Lands and Rents improved, Navigation is encreased, the poore employed. But if Trade decay, All these decline with it.[49]

And thus the decay of trade not only reduced the king's customs revenues, but also his subsidies, for

> the subjects beeing impoverished through want of Money and decay of Trade, are disabled to doe that service to His Majesty, which otherwise they would be willing, and heretofore have beene able to performe, in flourishing times of Trade.[50]

When Misselden claimed that allowing the Dutch to fish in English waters strengthened Dutch navigation, he was reminding policymakers of a service English commercial companies rendered the English state in their turn.[51] His conclusion certainly reads like an endorsement of a "Possessive Market Society":

> And is it not lawfull for Merchants to seeke their Privatum Commodum in the exercise of their calling? Is not gaine the end of trade? Is not the publique involved in the private, and the private in the publique? What else makes a Common-wealth, but the private-wealth, is I may so say, of the members thereof in the exercise of Commerce amongst themselves, and with forraine Nations?[52]

But what we forget when we take this display of panache for such an endorsement is that it also fits right in with a worldview in which monks pray for, nobles defend, peasants till for, and merchants enrich the whole (and thus private and public involve each other). Read it in the context of the century's merchant-bashing and its advocacy is reduced to a plea for social toleration. Misselden might claim that merchants were "of high account in all parts of the world,"[53] but whereas

> the States and States-men, Governours, Counsellors, and Magistrates of Venice, Luca, Genoa, Florence, the United Provinces of the Low Countries, and many other well governed Commonwealths, are by education Merchants[54]

this was not the case in England, where the opposition, as we have seen, was led by the Crown. One had to remember the centuries of blaming the merchant for every economic ill when one hears Misselden arguing that

> all the Causes of our Under-ballance of Trade might be contracted into two words. . . . Poverty alas, and Prodigality. The Poore sterve [starve] in our streets for want of labour: the Prodigall excell in excesses.[55]
> Also the want of restraint of the Excesse of the Kingdome, in Usury and Prodigality: the one being a Viper in a Kingdome that gnaweth through the bowels thereof: the other a Canker that fretteth and wasteth the stocke, in spending the forreine wares, more then it vendeth of our owne.[56]

Thus the Low Countries were an example for England, not only because they valued merchants and did not restrict the flow of bullion, but also and ultimately because there you saw neither "Excesse in superfluous consumptions of forraine Commodities" nor "Projects nor Projectors, but for the Common-good."[57] This was as much an attack on the unfettered self-interest of any sector of society as it was a defense of a properly (read socially) harnessed self-interest on the part of the merchant. Misselden was a man who truly believed it was his duty as a merchant to work for that common good and not to take his profit at its expense.

In his first book, Misselden wrote of the "Publicke Liberty of Commerce" whose just (and monopolistic) ordering by "the Wisdom of the State" was "both Lawefull and Beneficiall to the Common-wealth,"[58] but in his second he claimed that trade "hath in it suche a kinde of naturall liberty in the course and use thereof, as it will not indure to be fors't by any."[59] But in what sense did he believe in or advocate allowing such freedom? There are three concepts interwoven here—(1) free trade, (2) natural liberty, and (3) the state of nature—whose seventeenth-century meanings have to be uncovered before that question can be answered.

"Free Trade"

Complicating the problem of discovering what Edward Misselden felt could or could not be "fors't" with respect to trade was the fact that he advocated policies in his second book (favoring the East India Company) that he had earlier condemned in his first book (favoring the rival Merchant Adventurers), leaving him open to the charge of believing in nothing more than whatever favored his current association. Some explanation of why the two companies favored opposing policies seems in order.

The East India Company was organized as a joint-stock company: although its active members were merchants, any individual could, and many of the gentry did, buy shares of stock in the firm that yielded them proportionate shares of the profits earned by the Company trading as a whole. The Merchant Adventurers were organized as a "regulated" company: only qualified "Merchants" who had been passed by their peers after serving an apprenticeship and/or paying a suitable "fine" could trade under their protection. Members of regulated companies traded as individuals, keeping their own profits or absorbing their own losses, although bound by the terms of trade set by the company (as on the maximum yardage each member could export annually).[60] Both joint-stock and regulated companies were forms of government-sponsored monopoly: either might have the sole right to trade in a particular commodity in a set region, or the sole right to all trade with that region, or something in between the two.

The Merchant Adventurers, the earliest of the regulated companies, had been set up to handle England's wool and cloth exports in the days when England's direct foreign trade was only with the rest of Europe. Their privileges were confirmed in charters reaching as far back as 1505, but they were still reeling from the damage to their profits caused by the finishing patent granted Cockayne. The East India Company had been created to garner for England the full benefit of the trade with the East Indies by cutting out the Turk as a middleman. Founded by royal charter in 1600, the East India Company may have been the new kid on the block, but it was increasingly able to flex its muscle. The separately undertaken voyages of 1601 through 1612 had yielded an average profit of 155 percent; those under the aegis of the first joint-stock issue of 1613 through 1623 had done almost as well at 87 percent; and its shipyards at Deptford and Blackwall were turning out ships as fast as the company could absorb them.[61] By reexporting to Europe whatever East Indian goods they could not sell in England, they were also competing in the same markets (though not necessarily in the same products) as the older firms. Classics of their type, the differing organizations of the Merchant Adventurers and the East India Company point up an accident of time that turned into a successful and consciously pursued policy: the greater capital demands of the longer-distance trades making the joint-stock choice a more efficient engine of success, one can divide the various trading companies into regulated or joint-stock roughly on the same basis as one can divide them into intra- or intercontinental trade.[62]

Either kind of company could hold its privileges by Royal Patent or by Statute. As the Crown found it easier to keep them on a short lease, privilege by Patent became the policy of royal choice as the century wore on.[63] Thus the companies were doomed to become another battleground between king and Parliament in their struggle for control of the government. Civil wars or revolutions aside, attacks on the trading companies ebbed and flowed in inverse proportion to the health of the economy. In the trade depression of the 1620s the attack must have been particularly furious, if only to judge from the volume of defense propaganda hitting the presses from merchants who had to justify their privileges to the great trade commissions of the government as well as to the "public" whose good they purported to serve.

To us, perhaps, the great irony is that all the attention was being focused on the tail and not the dog. A common thread in all the early-seventeenth-century treatises defending the practices of the East India Company was their authors' ignorance of how much of that firm's prosperity was being fueled by a growing domestic market: hence the surge not only in luxury goods imports (silks), but also in less class-bound items such as currants and tobacco.[64]

We do not, of course, have accurate statistics on what portion of the nation's total trade was foreign. W. G. Hoskins put it at a maximum of 10 percent and possibly as little as 5 for much of the Tudor Age.[65] Gregory King's 1688 estimate was probably less accurate at 4:1 (domestic:foreign) but still reflective of some real growth in the sector.[66] But a number of factors, many of them only contingently economic, conspired to keep foreign trade in public view out of all proportion to its contribution to England's overall economy. For one thing, these trades provided the bulk of England's naval power; though pre-1649 England might be said to have a "standing" navy even though it did not yet have a standing army, royal shipbuilding and supplying paled before that undertaken by the East India Company.[67] For another, control of trade in any product or to and from any region was a direct component of the "balance" of power as well as of trade: the East India Company's capture of Ormuz from the Portuguese in 1622 simultaneously redounded to the benefit of the English Crown and threatened to entangle it in a trade war.[68] For a third, James I was always short of money,[69] and the movement of bullion in response to foreign trade was clear enough for any seventeenth-century theorist to follow even if the real effect of domestic demand was not.

For a fourth, a large group of England's ruling class had invested in these trades. On the one hand, the "nearly 5,000 investors" in these companies not only constituted "a group of unprecedented size" in this country of less than 5,000,000 people but one in which most of their working capital came from the small investor.[70] On the other hand, some 23 percent of the classifiable investors (3,800 out of 5,000) came from the gentry or the nobility, almost half of whom sat in Parliament.[71] To put an even finer point on it, investors in the East India Company's second joint-stock issue (1617–32) eventually included

> Sir Thomas Merrye, the Clerk Comptroller of the royal household, Sir Thomas Lake, the Secretary, Lord Chief Justices Hobart and Montague, Sir Henry Yelverton, the Attorney General, Sir Ralph Freeman, Master of Request, and Sir Julius Caesar, Master of Rolls . . . Francis Bacon, the Lord Chancellor . . . [and] Prince Charles.[72]

General interest in foreign trade did not translate to uniformity of interest in the various divisions within that trade. Not surprisingly, gentry investment appeared overwhelmingly concentrated in joint-stock enterprises, while merchants were active in all kinds of concerns.[73] What type of policy the government should follow to rectify the economy was thus complicated by constituency issues. In both regulated and joint-stock companies, the branches organized in the outports chafed under London's tendency to dominate trade, but when it came to legislation making it easier for individuals who were not "mere Merchants" to enter into foreign trade,

East India Company stockholders were more likely to stand for and members of the Merchant Adventurers to stand against. In addition, the mercers wanted a greater say in a cloth trade they saw as dominated by the import-export companies, while producers and consumers wanted relief from prices they considered too low or too high. It is no wonder that the Crown supported what might seem to us to be conflicting policies.

It is difficult to find a single session of Parliament or a single volume of *State Papers* from the 1590s[74] to the outbreak of war in 1642 in which there was no complaint of monopoly or call for "free trade." But these turn out to be nothing more than demands for a greater say for the outport members in the company's activities or for making it easier for nonmerchants to garner their share of these monopolistic profits. *Free trade* (or even a domestic *free market*) as we understand it was never on the line: whether we look at the "Free Trade" Bill of 1604 that excluded "clothiers, retailers, innholders, farmers, mariners and handicraftsmen" from its benefits or the provincial "free-traders" who ignored the grievances of London interlopers.[75] Of course, this does not mean that the propaganda of these decidedly nonliberal skirmishes was not transformed into something quite different in a later century. The evolution of "free trade" would be rather the same as that of "toleration"—a movement from demands for particular inclusion in a restricted *privilege* (and the word was synonymous with *liberty* in that sense) to a general and natural right—but in 1622 that transformation had yet to begin. Calls for the abolition of all types of trading companies as restraining freedom of trade would have to await the advent of the Levellers.[76] In strictly economic terms, the best description of the propaganda wars of the 1620s may be that characterizing them as an attempt by the merchants to save their "monopolistic rents."[77] When Misselden supported the Statute of Employments in his first book, he was fighting just such a political battle.

Misselden's main explanation for the want of coin in England was an "undervaluing" of that coin in foreign markets even when official exchange rates were set at Malynes's ultimate remedy of *par pro pari.*

In a universe in which money supply was thought to rule trade (rather than the volume of trade calling forth the necessary money supply), pinning down the value of money was of vital importance:

> and when I say, that the plenty or scarcity of monies, causeth their Values: would any man but Malynes have thought I spake of their Finenes? By Price in the one, is ment Valuation: by Value in the other, is ment Denomination or account. . . . It is true, the name of a thing doth not alter it really, but nominally: and denomination of money, doth alter it in

name, though not in substance. The cloth doth not measure the yard, but the yard the cloth: but the greater the measure is, the fewer yards the cloth containeth, and the lesse the measure, the more yards: and so is the denomination of money, the measure thereof to him that receiveth it, whereby it is more or lesse in account.[78]

Underlying this distinction between money's market price and value was the assumption that there was at base an *intrinsic* value in the money (its precious metal content or "finenes") independent of its denomination and independent of Misselden's own law of "plenty and scarcity." Misselden would prove to be as anxious as was Malynes that the foreign exchange reflect that *intrinsic* value (and not its relative purchasing power). Malynes concentrated on ways rates might be officially manipulated, while Misselden concentrated on the ways official rates were got round, but their basic assumptions were the same: human action/greed was the sole explanation of any seeming imbalance in the natural order.

And, given their essentially negative view of human nature and their belief in the wisdom of God's ordered universe, we should not be surprised to find Edward Misselden, like Malynes before him, calling for government supervision of trade, for

> Those that Trade without Order and Government, are like unto men, that make Holes in the bottome of that Ship, wherein themselves are Passengers. For want of Government in Trade, openeth a gap and letteth in all sorts of unskilfull and disorderly persons. . . . [and] also Marre the Merchandize of the land, both in estimation and goodnesse: then which there can bee nothing in Trade more prejudiciall to the Publique Utility. . . . And how can the Merchant, that hath no skill in his Commodity, looke to it, that the Maker performe his part.[79]

Misselden was actually addressing the desire of members of regulated companies such the Merchant Adventurers to avoid having their trades opened up to men not of their profession: it was a decrease rather than an increase in the competitiveness of the market that was being sought. In fact, one never comes across a condemnation of monopoly in Misselden's *Free Trade* in which in almost the same breath he calls for the reorganization of the trade with Spain into a regulated company.[80] It is fair to say that Edward Misselden was putting forward a policy that would be of benefit to himself, but it is no more fair to dismiss his first book as concocted solely of self-serving platitudes than it was for him to lay such a charge at the volumes produced by Malynes:[81] both were the logical result of a particular set of ordering assumptions.

The primary assumption here was a harmonic social division of labor derived from the hierarchical nature of order itself, which "good Lawes" ought to reflect, as can be seen in Misselden's rejection of Monopolies:

Monopoly is a kind of Commerce, in buying, selling, changing, or bartering, usurped by a few, and sometimes but one person, and forestalled from all others, to the Gaine of the Monopolist, and to the Detriment of other men. The parts of a Monopoly are twaine. The restraint of the libertie of Commerce to some one or few: and the setting of the price at the pleasure of the Monopolian to his private benefit, and the prejudice of the publique. . . . And these two parts are respectively repugnant to the two fundamental requisites of all good Lawes: to wit, Equity, and Utility, For it is against Equity, that one Member of a Common-wealth should bee more free then another of equall ranke and condition. And what can be more contrary to Publique Utility, then that some one or few persons, should sway the price or any thing usefull to the Common-wealth, to their owne Enriching, and the Common losse of other men?[82]

Though Misselden's attack on monopolies can been seen as informed by Aristotle's notion of reciprocity, that notion was itself informed by a hierarchical concept of justice, hence the emphasize on "equall ranke."[83]

The key distinction between a monopoly and a properly governed commerce was not the degree or absence of restraint but the extent to which the restraint benefited the public good. This was exactly the ground on which Misselden asserted that the special freedoms/privileges granted the Merchant Adventurers did not fall under the category of monopolistic practice:

And although all other men stood lyable to the Statute [*28 Henry VIII* against exporting undyed cloth] still, and were restrained, yet the Utilitie that hereby arose to the Common-wealth, did farre exceede the restraint of the Publique Libertie.[84]

Thus Misselden found "no good Equality" in the arguments for unrestricted entry into trade, for

it were very unequal, that one man should serve for his freedome, or buy the same: and another man should have it for nothing. . . . [For] there cannot bee any greater Bane to a Well-governed Common-wealth, then Ill governed and Disorderly Trade. . . . So that in this case the general rule must be this; that such a Restraint of the Publique Liberty, as is before mentioned, is alwayes to be allowed, when the same is recompenced with a Publique Utility.[85]

He stood firmly in favor of the Statutes of Apprentices, patent protection for new "inventions," and "Suit of Mill" (requiring residents to have their grain ground at particular mills).[86] In fact, Edward Misselden knew of only one result that could come from the institution of ungoverned trade, and he learned it from an adage that cast a shadow as far forward in time as the American Civil War. Misselden believed that "where Trade is disordered, and the traders ungoverned, there they are like a house divided, which cannot long subsist."[87]

Edward Misselden was supporting a commercial system coming closest to that described today as *oligopoly:* a market dominated by a small number of sellers, some of whom are large enough relative to the size of the total market to influence that market price. While a modern firm in such a position might choose between strategies intended to maximize overall sales volume or per-unit profit, the great trading companies of Misselden's day seem to have been trying to do both simultaneously. *Oligopoly* itself was a newly coined term Edward Misselden would have come across in More's *Utopia,* although Misselden, like the rest of his contemporaries, did not adopt More's linguistic innovation, either because they did not understand it, or thought it made the policies they favored sound too much like those they condemned.[88]

"Natural Liberty"

To the eighteenth century "natural" might mean "mechanical" (standing for forces independent of and unalterable by the human will), but our writers were struggling with two competing meanings of the term *natural:* that emerging mechanical view and the older meaning attached to the anthropomorphic analogy in which harmonic imbalances were naturally righted by human action. If "Remedies ill applyed" worsened the disorder, application of the correct remedy removed it. It is true that this interference with the Body Human/Politic was a restoration rather than an innovation (just as law was still primarily seen as a clarification rather than as legislation), but it was understood as a beneficial manipulation.[89]

The casting of money as the "Artificiall matter of commerce" in contrast to the "Natural matter" (commodities themselves)[90] made human regulation even more appropriate to it: the product of artifice could not be beyond the control of the artificer.[91] The example already given of the way in which the Dutch manipulated exchange rates put the lie in advance, as it were, to everything Misselden would say in his second book about the "Natural freedom" of trade defying the attempts of princes or merchants to manipulate it in their favor, for none of the adverse reactions he then predicted defeated the policies of the Dutch; they had been forcing trade to their profit all along.

This is not to say that in his first book Misselden never considered any way in which the political might be overridden by the natural. Discussing a general price rise that might accompany a correction in the valuation of the coinage, he was not unaware that the "raising also of the Coine, would raise the price of Plate," bringing more out "to be molten into Coine"; but without an alteration in the spending habits of the English (or without the prodding of sumptuary laws) this added money supply would be wasted "in consuming the Commodities of forreine Countries in such abundance, to our owne losse."[92] But, again, he assumed state action (sumptuary laws) could force the current of this "natural" law of trade from a harmful channel to a profitable one.

The effect of foreign trade on England's coin supply was a rather delicate issue, and here also the East India Company and the Merchant Adventurers parted company. It was easy enough for the Merchant Adventurers to claim they really traded goods for goods, even if it was wholesome necessities such as wool and tin to France in return for sinful frivolities such as wine and silk. But the peoples of the East Indies having little use for English goods, the East India Company had to "pay" for its pepper with cold, hard cash. The general perception was that the East India Company exported bullion, draining Christendom in general and England in particular of that "sinews of war" and "vitall spirit" of trade that was silver coin. Defenders of the East India Company claimed that it did not export English bullion, but took whatever East Indian imports the English would not buy and reexported them to Europe for the Spanish bullion it used to purchase new supplies of East Indian goods to import. It was for this foreign coin, then, that the East India Company needed those constant exemptions it received from the Crown from the laws against the export of bullion. The cumulative bullion exports of the company stood at £753,336 in 1624 as against £351,236 of commodities originally or reexported. What the East India Company got out of all of this was the opportunity to buy cheap (silver being worth so much more in India) and sell dear.[93] But the English public remained unconvinced that the silver taken to India could not be somehow diverted to England.

The "State of Nature"

Like Gerard de Malynes before him, Edward Misselden could use the century's evolving social contract theory to explain how the *political* state corrected the deficiencies of the *natural*. This version of his argument began with what he saw as two different kinds of exchanges. The first or "Natural Exchange" occurred when money was "exchanged Value for Value, according to the Intrinsique or inward finenes, or true value thereof."[94] This was natural as physical in the Aristotelian sense, for "the finenes of monies" was "that Cynosure or Center, whereunto all Exchanges" had "their natural propension."[95] Thus, though Misselden had already defined Bills of Exchange as essentially credit instruments, he would not allow interest (discounted, charged, or even disguised as exchange fees) in a natural exchange.[96]

But for Misselden, such a natural exchange was ultimately *unnatural,* because

> if you should so limit or restraine Exchanges, that no man should take or deliver any mony, but according to the just finenes: then the use of exchanges in all places would bee taken away. For then there would be no advantage left neither to him that delivereth, nor him that taketh, when mony must bee answered with money in the same Intrinsique value.[97]

In this instance, society had the remedy for what nature lacked, a second kind of exchange: a "Politique Exchange" of money for money based on "the extrinsique or outward valuation." Herein was taken into account the uncertainties "of time, and place, and persons," or the length of time before the money would be called for, its price in a particular location, and the needs of the parties to the contract (it being "a common thing amongst men, to sell one & the same commodity, to divers men at divers prices").[98]

In his first book Edward Misselden had proclaimed money "the rule and square whereby things might receive estimation and value."[99] In his second book, he sought to restrict that proposition to the domestic sphere, claiming, "the Reddition is false, that the exchange is the publique measure betweene us and forraine nations,"[100] because he wanted to use a different measure—the balance of trade—as that international "rule and square."

A "Politique Exchange" was now universally advantageous: it gave the Crown access to ready money in foreign parts (presumably to supply its troops or diplomats) as it did for young gentlemen traveling abroad, and all without the inconvenience of having to carry coin. Young merchants might thereby gain access to the credit they needed to supplement their as yet meager capital, and older merchants might find it eased the wheels of commerce in times of dead trade or gave them liquidity when their stocks were tied up in inventory. That the Dutch and the Germans had been manipulating these money markets to the detriment of England's economic health has been forgotten: here only the good they could do was rehearsed for the reader. And this was propped up by all the authority Misselden could find for the justice of the voluntary contract.[101]

Although the *political* exchange (that for profit) had just been shown as efficaciously altering the natural (*par pro pari*), Edward Misselden concluded that the attempt to use the *political* to alter the *natural* must rebound to the injury of the one who made the attempt:

> trade hath in it such a kinde of natural liberty in the course and use thereof, as it will not indure to be fors't by any. If you attempt it, it is a thousand to one, that you leave it not worse then you found it. And therefore Bodin saith excellently, *Est enim libertas naturalis huiusmodi, ut voluntas bene a natura informata, imperium alterius pst Deum Immortalem*

reiiciat. Natural liberty is such a thing, as the will being by nature rightly informed, will not endure the command of any, but of God alone. Which must be understood of natural liberty in the use of things indifferent; and not of Regall authority in the exercise of government. And hence it is gone into a Proverbe, *Quod natura dedit, tollere nemo potest,* That which nature giveth, no man can take away.[102]

This seems to imply that the *political* (profit-seeking) exchange is actually the *natural* one that cannot be altered by any government except to its detriment (though Misselden has been at great pains to show how the Dutch did just that). Is Misselden attempting to build a case for what Adam Smith would later call the "invisible hand"? Then why was the profit-seeking of coin cullers, the profligate rich, and the idle poor not to be tolerated while the profit-seeking of the merchant was? Why complain of Dutch manipulation of the exchange if it was part of an unalterable natural course of trade? Because, for Misselden, profit-seeking in and of itself was not really the thing "indifferent."

Nor was it any adumbration of the international version of laissez-faire. We must go back to Misselden's admiration for and fear of Dutch economic policy. The Dutch may have had a more liberal attitude toward the immigration of skilled labor and entrepreneurial expertise, and may have been more concerned with the overall volume of trade than with amassing bullion, but they were not "free traders." Misselden spent years of his life trying to convince the Dutch authorities to remove their restrictive tariffs on goods brought in by foreign traders or foreign manufacture, when those same goods came and went duty-free if brought in or made by the Dutch. If trade truly "hath in it such a kinde of liberty" that it would "not indure to be fors't," such a policy should have wreaked havoc with the Dutch economy.

If we are to accept that Misselden came to a new understanding of the market in his second book,[103] the strangest suggestion in Misselden's *Circle of Commerce* remains the last—that removing the causes he listed in his earlier work was the proper remedy of the trade decay.[104] A summary of those causes as he categorized them in *Free Trade* follows:

I. Immediate reasons
   A. Primarily, the undervaluation of His Majesty's Coin relative to that of neighboring countries hinders the importation and causes the exportation of money.
   B. To a lesser extent:
      1. Coin culling
      2. Money hoarding (the great superfluity of plate)

II. Mediate or remote reasons
    A. Domestic
        1. General: imports in excess of exports because people live above
           their callings
        2. Special: the detaining of the East India Company's ships by the
           Dutch
    B. Foreign
        1. Wars between Christian nations waste their resources
        2. Trade between Christendom and the East drains silver
III. Efficient causes
    A. Usury
        1. Commercial interest rates being too high
        2. Pawnbrokers preying on the poor
    B. Lawsuits keep merchants from their proper work, wasting
       resources
IV. Inconveniences as causes
    A. Foreigners fishing our coasts and strengthening their navigation,
       taking our wealth without paying us for it
V. Causes not specifically categorized
    A. False labeling of cloth
    B. Monopolies (with joint-stock firms being under the greatest suspi-
       cion of monopolistic practice)
    C. Interlopers (unrestricted entry into trade)

This mix of economic, social, strategic (or political), and moral factors
in every subhead should recall to mind the similarly broad set of ill effects
Malynes believed were the results of letting loose the dragon of greed.
Equally broad were the solutions Misselden proposed in *Free Trade* to
change the natural course of this Western-Oriental trade imbalance: end-
ing the "war" between England and Holland, cutting out the Turkish middleman, pushing the Persians to buy English cloth and tin, being especially
cautious about exporting "Ordinance and Munition" (though this last
applied as much within Europe as without), encouraging vigilant enforcement of the law against bullion export, and being wary of "Trade in Joint
Stockes."[105] His proposals show him to be a man who put national security
and well-being over any individual merchant's desire for profit. Even in
Circle of Commerce, when he would have to backtrack on the issue of bullion
movement, he maintained a desire to promote the welfare of Christendom
over that of its "rivals," prompting the Crown to encourage those who
would take the Persian trade away from Turkey and thus weaken its
"tyranny over the Christian world."[106]

What, then, did he mean by the "natural freedom" of trade that he so wished to channel to England's advantage? Nothing more than what we might call cultural trade patterns:

> For although the trades within Christendome are driven with ready Monies, yet those Monies are still Contained and Continued within the Bounds of Christendome. There is indeed a Fluxus and refluxus, a Floode and Ebbe of the monies of Christendome traded within it selfe. . . . [but] It commeth and goeth, and whirleth about the Circle of Christendome, but it is still contained with the Compasse thereof. But the money that is traded out of Christendome into the parts aforesaid, is continually issued out and never returneth againe.[107]

Compare this to the mechanics of the price equilibrium argument that underpins laissez-faire critiques of trade balance models: if England exports more goods than it imports, the resulting inflow of money will (if not offset by a greater production) create a price rise in English goods (factor and finished) making them less competitive abroad. The relative cheapness of imported goods will help reverse the trade balance and, thus, the monetary flow. The domestic price level will fall, making English exports more competitive abroad. This is a very different "fluxus and refluxus" than the one Edward Misselden described.

But, then, he was trying to get his countrymen to remove the restrictions on bullion flow precisely because there was no "fluxus and refluxus" between England and India similar to that between England and its continental neighbors. The inability of the Europeans to sell their wares to the Indians created two different patterns of trade, two patterns that might be called "natural" either in the sense of "customary" or of being beyond mere statutory control in the sense that Natural Law superseded Statute Law. In his first book, Misselden had railed against the Eastern trade pattern, claiming wares brought in from "Turkey, Persia, and the East Indies" did not add to the total "stock" of Christendom because they could not be purchased without depleting its "stock" of silver:[108] the "true nature" of commerce was "a change of wares for wares, not money for wares."[109] In his second book, he accepted the silver outflow. Whether or not this policy change was caused by his move to the East India Company or not, it was still just a policy change and not a change in his basic understanding of the different trade patterns of Continental and Eastern trade. Of course, no law passed by an English parliament could, by itself, alter the cultural preferences of the rulers or inhabitants of India. And, of course, laws forbidding bullion export hindered England's ability to prosper from that trade. But what has any of that to do with an equilibrium argument?

CHAPTER 4

Thomas Mun and the
Finite *Zeitgeist*

Thomas Mun (1571–1641), like his associate Edward Misselden, is known to posterity for two books, *A Discourse of Trade, from England unto the East Indies* (1621) and *Englands Treasure by Forraign Trade* (posthumously published in 1664), in which seemingly opposing economic views are espoused. While the first book was simply too much like the common run of pro–East India Company propaganda to make a lasting impression,[1] the second became a classic almost overnight. The second edition of *Englands Treasure* hit the stalls in 1669, the third in 1698, the fourth in 1700 (packaged with Lewes Roberts's *Merchants Map of Commerce*), the fifth in 1713, and the sixth in 1755. Adam Smith even referred to it by name.[2] Mun was often cited by fellow seventeenth-century writers: approvingly by Roger Coke, Nicholas Barbon, and the two anonymous treatises known as *Englands Great Happiness* (1677) and *Britannia Languens* (1680).[3] Modern commentators, impressed by what they see as marked differences between the *Discourse* and *Englands Treasure*, often speak of the latter as if it were Mun's only work and take him for a champion of the free play of market forces.[4] But that was not the way in which the first generation to read *Englands Treasure* understood its author. Among leading members of the Royal Society such as Robert Boyle and John Beale, the signal importance of Thomas Mun was the *way* in which he proposed that England achieve the minimization of imports and maximization of exports needed to create a positive trade balance. As James Jacob put it,

> Mun's insistence on hard work and plain living and his attack on luxury, especially imported luxury goods, as ruinous to prosperity chimed with their own views on the desirability of reconciling wealth and virtue.[5]

Boyle and Beale belonged to a group of "social Baconians" (as Mayling Stubbs put it) who aimed "to transform England into an island utopia by means of technology and reason, ingenuity and industry," but always with a moral weather-eye on the dangers of unleashed economic forces—a vision for which they were convinced they found substantial support in

Mun's treatise.[6] Beale, for example, specifically proposed to use Mun's ideas to combat John Houghton's acceptance of "prodigality" as a foundation of prosperity.[7]

While the twentieth-century analyst may better understand the implications of Mun's arguments, the seventeenth-century reader was the more accurate interpreter of their grounds. Mun's case parallels that of Edward Misselden: the policies he supported did not logically derive from the assumptions upon which he wished to ground them (even in *Englands Treasure*), and his attempts to make them fit within the bounds of the universe of value created logical gaps in his argument that could not be bridged.[8]

The families of Thomas Mun and Gerard de Malynes may have crossed paths long before these two men did, for Thomas's grandfather, John Mun of Hackney, held the office of provost of moneyers at the Royal Mint from 1553 to 1561,[9] while an uncle, William, was also a moneyer at the mint. If Malynes senior did bring his family over during the great recoinage of 1560–61, he might have worked directly under "John Monnes." Thomas Mun's father and elder brother were mercers. Only brother Edward broke the family mold by joining the church and rising to the position of subalmoner to Queen Elizabeth. Thomas was not quite two years old when his father died in 1673, and not quite three when his mother's remarriage gave Thomas and his brothers yet another mercer, Thomas Cordell, for a stepfather. It was in Cordell's footsteps as a director of the East India Company that Thomas Mun would eventually follow.

Thomas Mun spent a great part of his early career in Italy, where, by his own account, he became close enough to Ferdinand I, Grand Duke of Tuscany (1587–1609), to be lent 40,000 crowns interest-free for transmission to Turkey to purchase merchandise for Italy.[10] Mun imported English tin, lead, and cloth, dealt in alum, and possibly acted as a factor for the Levant Company. Floated with borrowed capital, Mun's schemes came to a final crash; by 1607 he had "absconded," having been "adjudged bankrupt by a Florentine court." Was it adding insult to injury that he finally had to pawn "some of his goods with the *Mons pietatis*"?[11] Fortunately for Mun, Malynes would never find it out to cast it against him in the propaganda war of the 1620s. Of greater importance was a possible, though ultimately unverifiable, connection with the Italian economic writer Bernardo Davanzati (1529–1606). Davanzati's *Discourse upon Coins* was not published in England until 1696, but the idea (restated by Mun in chapter VIII of *Englands Treasure*) "that debasement brings a profit to the mint only once, but reduces forever the fixed incomes of the Crown" was available to Mun in any of the Italian editions published in his lifetime.[12]

In any case, his eventual failure in Italy did not detract from his prospects for success at home. By 1619 he had been elected a committee member (director) of the East India Company, remaining active in and an advocate for the Company for the rest of his life. His fellow East India merchants seem to have valued him mostly for his facility with numbers, as Mun was often called upon to check the honesty or accuracy of a member's accounts.[13] He was also something of a diplomat, being appointed to take up the off-again–on-again negotiations with the Dutch in 1632.[14] He was certainly not in favor of freedom of access to the market; he was forever urging the membership to prosecute "private traders" who shipped goods on Company vessels before the appropriate authorities.[15] But the buccaneering Mun of his youth was never entirely subsumed in the middle-aged philosopher of economic matters: his proposals for cutting out the competition in the pepper trade by poaching on the preserves of the Turkey merchants or selling supplies before they were entirely safe in hand were voted down by the Company's more cautious directors in 1633.[16]

Something, possibly personal, possibly political, caused to him to step back from company affairs to a considerable extent. Nominated in 1621 to be one of two men sent to the Indies to check into the losses posted by the Company's factors there, he begged off on the grounds of "weakness of body" and familial "tenderness," though the overall impression of his refusal is that of a man unwilling to undertake a task he viewed as impossible.[17] In March 1624 he also refused to accept election as deputy-governor of the East India Company, a position that, in the past, had led eventually to the governorship.[18]

Still, when it came to defending the East India Company against the charges of bullion exportation, Mun was their man. In 1621, he drew up a list of "Reasons to prove that the trade from England unto the East Indies doth not consume but rather increase the treasure of this kingdom," to convince the House of Commons that their attacks on the Company were unfounded.[19] In 1624, he was the one who prepared a defense to set before the Committee on Trade: "admitting the uttermost of £100,000 to be exported the returns are £400,000 at the least, whereof £100,000 of those commodities will suffice the kingdom and the rest being exported will work itself home again in money or commodities that yield money."[20]

Though he had run into financial trouble in Italy, Mun ended his days a successful and semiretired merchant, having added the estate of Otterbridge at Bearsted to other lands he had inherited in Kent. Buried in the chancel of his parish church, St. Helen's, Bishopsgate, on July 21, 1641, Thomas Mun was survived by his wife Ursula and their children John, Anne, and Mary. Mun had cautioned John against the folly by which "the memory of our richest merchants is suddenly extinguished; the Son being left rich, scorneth the profession of his Father, conceiving more honor to be a Gentleman (although but in name),"[21] but John (1615–1670) prefered to retire to his inherited estates and add to them as he could. His choice provides us with a potent reminder that even among the mercantile classes, the commercial life was not necessarily held in great esteem.

The bulk of Thomas Mun's first book, *A Discourse of Trade, from England unto the East Indies* (1621), was devoted to disproving assorted complaints against the company's activities: that the wares imported were not frivolous because spices had medicinal value and the calicoes provided a less expensive alternative to importing European cambric and linens, that the victuals for their voyages were not of a large enough quantity to endanger England's food supply and were in part derived from French grain imported for the purpose, that the company's needs did not cause such a drain on any other product (lumber, cordage, nails) as to inflate its price, and that, instead, the company actually helped the country by providing jobs for carpenters, provenders, mariners, and the like.[22] Their shipyards stood ready to serve his Majesty "with many warlike provisions."[23] Their charities aided widows, supported preachers, and sent "scholars" to school.[24] Their direct trade with the East Indies reduced the price the English paid for their calico and spices, aiding the common good at the merchants' cost: for the sacrifice of longer shipping costs, import imposts, and the like was born only by the merchant and not the state.[25] The explanations were offered in no particular order and some were contradictory: if using English resources provided employment, for example, then the purchase of French grain undid the good implied besides making a further entry on the wrong side of the trade balance ledger. If these claims show Mun was aware of the existence of links between economic sectors, they also show he had as yet constructed no system for linking them analytically.

In trying to decide how to reconcile any contradictions between Mun's two books, it would be helpful if we could determine when the second book was completed, but it is highly likely that different sections of *Englands Treasure* were written at different times. Mun's attack on the *par pro pari* and the use of a Royal Exchanger was aimed at the three works Gerard de Malynes published in 1622 and 1623.[26] Of course, Mun could have responded to them any length of time after their publication, but these sections are also the most conservative in both style and content. These paragraphs are full of causes and effects "Active" and "Passive," fine distinctions between the public purses of governments republican, aristocratic, and monarchical, and attacks on the "Quillets, Delayes and Charges" of lawyers.[27] They seem, overall, to have been written in the heat of immediate reaction, and may, in fact, be the earliest parts of the existing book.

The first few pages are entirely different, comprising an extensive memorandum on the education of a merchant: his need for arithmetic and bookkeeping, modern languages and customs, ship construction and navigation, an encyclopedic knowledge of foreign and domestic wares, and, just perhaps, a little Latin for its value as a general education tool.[28] An explanation for this seeming digression is given in Mun's dedication of the book to his son:

> My Son, In a former Discourse I have endeavoured after my manner briefly to teach thee two things: The first is Piety, how to fear God aright, according to his Works and Word: The second is Policy, how to love and serve thy Country, by instructing thee in the duties and proceedings of sundry Vocations, which either order, or else act the affairs of the Common-wealth; In which as some things doe especially tend to Preserve, and others are more apt to Enlarge the same: So am I now to speak of Money, which doth indifferently serve to both those happy ends . . . [and] the Merchant, because he must be a Principal Agent in this great business.[29]

Yet these pages read more like an advocate's summation before a jury than a book of instruction for a boy who would only have been seven years old in 1622 and thus some years away from his apprenticeship.

In fact, the treatise we have seems most likely to be the result of three separate starts. At some point in 1622–23, Thomas Mun probably began a defense of the East India Company against the attacks of Gerard de Malynes and the campaign for a new Bullion Statute. He probably intended immediate publication. The project undertaken, however, Mun found himself shifting to policies dangerous to publish. Despite the continuing exceptions that would be made for the East India Company, the *Proclamatio contra Exportationem Bullionis* issued in 1622 made it unwise to support a general lifting of the restraints on bullion movement. While James was not anxious to be dragged into the war on the Continent on behalf of the Protestant cause, he was also not anxious to antagonize the Dutch, and Mun took a stridently nationalist stance in that regard. Pym had been arrested in 1621; Chief Justice Coke was a target in 1622.[30] The years following were not a good time to assert that revenues were raised "according to the constitution of the Countreys, the government, the laws and customs of the people, which no Prince can alter but with much difficulty and danger."[31] Nor was it politic to suggest the deficit-ridden monarch lower or forgo altogether duties on items imported for reexport in the name of their long-term benefit to trade.[32] Thomas Mun's decision to refuse the deputy-governorship of the Company in 1624 may have been as much politically as personally motivated. Ironically, it may have been the realization that he was dealing with ideas that he could not publish that freed Mun's mind to advance into hitherto unexplored monetary waters. The core of the book might then belong to a draft subsequent to the earlier, more conservative, attack on Malynes and company.

In 1632, John Mun, having finished his apprenticeship, was made one of the free-brethren of the East India Company. Would this not have been an appropriate time for a presentation book? One can almost picture his father in the year or two before this event, penning that missing volume on religion and duty in his semiretirement in anticipation of his son's economic coming of age. Perhaps, at the same time, he bethought himself of that by now (in the days of the personal rule of Charles I) truly unpublishable commercial treatise and reworked it into a gift for John: a private guide for a grandson's education and personal testament of his father's philosophy. It was, finally, as a vindication that the book appeared in 1664, just after the legalization of the export of bullion the year before.

But even allowing for three separate starts and stops, the overall trend of its inconsistencies derives from Mun's efforts to erect a theoretical structure around a required end (free bullion flow) that his own premises would not support.

The first thing that strikes one about both of Thomas Mun's volumes is their lack of scholarly discourse: nary a syllable of Hebrew, Latin, or Greek, nor a single mention of Aristotle, and almost no direct citations even of roughly contemporary authors. In fact, if we tried to reconstruct a lifetime's reading from direct mentions in Mun's works, we would end up with a very short and most desultory list:

> Sir Thomas Elyot, *Castle of Health* (1534)
> Rembert Dodoens, *A New Herbal or History of Plants* (1578)
> *The French Academy* ("Second Part")
> Captain Robert Hitchcock, *A Political Plat for the honour of the Prince* (1580)
> Tobias Gentleman, *Englands Way to win Wealth* (1614)
> Hugo Grotius, *Mare Liberum* (1608)[33]

That Mun had picked up some scraps of classical education cannot be denied. Caesar, Alexander, Darius, Nero, and Galba are paraded for our edification in a discussion of how much money princes need to store up for future needs, and Philip of Macedon's penchant for bribes enters into a discussion of Dutch treachery. But the only instance of Mun's citing multiple works by any author was his devouring, for the purpose of refuting, the basic works of Gerard de Malynes.[34] If ever a man seemed to be the epitome of the countinghouse bounded merchant, that man would appear to be Thomas Mun.

But appearances can be deceiving. We are barely into *A Discourse of Trade* before we meet one of the most common economic assumptions of the age. Trade was "the verie Touchstone of a kingdomes prosperitie" as long as "some certen rules" were "diligently observed"; and chief among these:

> For as in the estates of private persons, wee may accompt that man to prosper and growe rich, who being possessed of revenues more or lesse, doth accordingly proportion his expences; whereby he may yearlie advance some maintenance for his posteritie. So doth it come to passe in those Kingdomes, which with great care and warinesse doe ever vent out more of their home commodities, then they import and use of forren wares; for so undoubtedly the remainder must return to them in treasure.[35]

If we look here for a mechanical model of a valueless market, we look in vain. To build up a positive bullion flow, no distinction need be made between one kind of import and another or one kind of export and another unless the analyst understands further the price advantage in importing raw materials and exporting manufactured items. Whether the imports or exports could be defined as necessities or luxuries would be beside the point. But Mun was equally concerned with the *moral* effects of varying goods. He harped on it in his first book:

> But where a contrarie course is taken, through wantonnesse and riot . . . there must the money of necessitie be exported, as the meanes to helpe to furnishe such excesses, and so by the corruption of mens conditions and manners, manie rich countries are made exceeding poore.[36]

And in his second:

> We may likewise diminish our importations, if we would soberly refrain from excessive consumption of forraign wares in our diet and rayment, with such often change of fashions as is used, so much the more to encrease the waste and charge; which vice at this present are more notorious amongst us than in former ages. Yet might they easily be amended by enforcing the observation of such good laws as are strictly practised in other Countries against the said excesse.[37]

The argument has been made[38] that the distinction between luxury and utilitarian imports and the argument against the former was not moral in origin but economic in the modern sense: encourage investment by discouraging importation of finished luxury goods. But Thomas Mun was as much angered over the importation of sugar, fruits, wine, and tobacco,[39] to which the employment/investment argument did not apply. The true key to understanding the grounds of this argument are the "vice[s]" being deplored: "wantonness," "excesses," "corruption," are terms from a *moral* vocabulary rather than a strictly economic one. A positive trade balance was being advocated as a way to simultaneously reform the society's values while ensuring it a *properly disciplined* prosperity. Rather than a paean to the laws of the marketplace, Mun praised the sumptuary laws[40] that attempted to restrain the most potent force in any *Market Economy:* demand. In his first book, Mun had claimed that "industry to increase, and frugalities to maintaine" were "the true watchmen of a kingdomes treasury, even when, the force and feare of Princes prohibitions cannot possibly retain the same."[41] If this was an attack on the usefulness of sumptuary laws then we have a Thomas Mun who got *less* market-law oriented as time progressed rather than the reverse.

If there was any particularly economic argument here it might be better understood as one of *political* economy: often, though again not entirely consistently, the products railed against were those of Spain or the Spanish West Indies. Monies spent on these goods went into the coffers of *Protestant* England's enemy.

Mun was well aware of the standard Aristotelian distinction between the fruits of nature and those of artifice:

> all men doe know, that the riches or sufficiencie of every kingdome, State, or Common-wealth, consisteth in the possession of those things, which are needfull for a civill life. This sufficiency is of two sorts: the one is naturall, and proceedeth of the Territorie it selfe: the other is artificiall, and dependeth on the industry of the Inhabitants.[42]

Twentieth-century distinctions go far beyond this. We recognize a number of ways in which unprocessed natural resources (whether agricultural or mineral) and the goods manufactured from them play different roles in any nation's economy. In the first place, though both provide employment, manufacturing (or processing) adds jobs to the economy that the simple transportation (or exportation) of natural resources cannot. With apologies to Malthus, one might say that without technological change in farming, jobs cannot be added to the economy through the harvesting of natural resources unless the land under use (tillage, pasturage, lumber harvesting, mining, etc.) is increased, whereas adding any level of processing (spinning, weaving, fulling, dying, finishing, etc.) adds jobs in geometric proportion. Furthermore, processing adds jobs whether applied to native or foreign resources. Second, manufactured exports earn a greater price than do raw material exports while manufactured imports cost more than raw material imports, so their impacts on the balance of trade differ, which is to say their benefits are shared out differently among the nations trading with each other according to which country does the manufacturing and which does not. Third, to the extent that processing tends to require greater capital investment even in an economy as primitive as that of the seventeenth century, it contributes proportionately more to the overall economy through the medium of the investment multiplier. Fourth, to the extent that it adds a greater number of jobs to the economy and a greater number and variety of products available for sale, manufacturing increases consumer spending, affecting velocity of circulation and the overall price level. Most important, however, is the fact that manufacturing, by adding jobs and goods to the economic pool, ends by "creating" wealth (as goods or as value): the effects of manufacturing, understood in our modern sense, make nonsense of the idea that one individual's (or nation's) gain always comes at another's loss. But not for Thomas Mun.

Like his compeers, Mun was well aware that increasing native manufacturing would not only increase the number and variety of goods available for export, but would provide employment for individuals otherwise given to occupying themselves with riot. He exhibited that common combination of Christian humanism, Calvinist discipline, and fear of riot that distinguished between the worthy and unworthy poor when he explained how the finishing of raw silks brought in by the East India Company provided for "the great relief & maintenance of so many hundreds of poore people" who were "continuallie imployed, in the winding, twisting, and waving of the same [silk]."[43] For although the "povertie of Widdowes and [the] Fatherlesse" was "a matter of great compassion," we "see how many dayly (even through their owne folly & wilfulnesse) do as it were desperately plunge themselves into adversitie."[44] Similarly, the East India Company kept the estimable "Mariners" from the "desperate courses" they attempted when left idle: "joyning, even with Turkes and Infidels, to rob and spoyle all Christian Nations."[45] So did the Company keep "the Kingdome purged of desperate and unruly people."[46] In other words, employment was a vehicle of moral regeneration for the poor as well as of "social control."[47]

Mun was well aware of the practical links between production, consumption, imports, and exports:

all kind of Bounty and Pomp is not to be avoided, for if we should become so frugal, that we would use few or no Forraign wares, how shall we then vent our own commodities? what will become of our Ships, Mariners, Munitions, our poor Artificers, and many others?[48]

He just did not think "Bounty and Pomp" could be left to have their way unrestrained, or else their disruptive tendencies would outweigh their productive ones.

In his second book, Mun appears to have at least a nascent awareness of the redistributive effects of manufacturing:

> Again, the pomp of Buildings, apparel, and the like, in the Nobility, Gentry, and other able persons, cannot impoverish the Kingdom; if it be done with curious and costly works upon our own Materials, and by our own people, it will maintain the poor with the purse of the rich, which is the best distribution of the Common-wealth.[49]

But his immediate follow-up that the poor were better set to work in the fishing trades ("if any man say, that when the people want work, then the Fishing trade would be a better employment, and far more profitable; I subscribe willingly")[50] than upon the production of those "curious and costly works" shows his intrinsically *moral* verdict that the country as a whole would be better off building its trade balance on the export of honest goods instead of indulging the vices of its upper classes, rather than an intrinsically economic verdict in favor of the greater profit in the luxury trade.

Underlying Mun's advocacy of a positive trade balance was a yardstick whose origins were not economic even if its manifestation was. When refuting Malynes's criticisms of lawyers and lawsuits in the passage just before the remarks on pomp, Mun gave us a few keys to just what yardstick he was using:

> their cases, Quillets, Delayes and Charges, are mischievous to many; these things are indeed Cankers in the Estates of particular men, but not of the Common-wealth, as some suppose, for one mans loss becomes another mans gain, it is still in the Kingdom.[51]

In this one sentence we can see operating all three of Mun's basic measures: the organic distinction between the good of the whole and any of its parts, the assumption of a finite resource pool, and the bullionism that underlay seventeenth-century balance of trade theory and caused the thinker to ignore the economic worth of domestic trade because it did not bring coin into the country but circulated the existing coin supply.

Knowing that the "natural wealth" available for export was "so much only as can be spared from our own use and necessities to be exported unto strangers," while the "artificial" was created by "our manufactures," Mun

certainly recommended increasing the natural "stock" by bringing wastelands under tillage and increasing the artificial by processing both native
and imported foreign raw materials.[52] He was clear that "Iron oar in the
Mines is of no great worth, when it is compared with the employment and
advantage it yields being digged, tried, transported, bought, sold, cast into
Ordinance . . . wrought into Anchors . . . and other instruments for
Tillage," and that cloth was more profitable than fleece.[53] Manufacturing
was favored not because it created wealth in and of itself, but because it created goods that, sent abroad, brought in wealth. Goods made and used at
home added nothing to the national wealth (though they have enriched the
manufacturer) unless they replaced foreign imports. Mun's was always a
world in which the sum total of goods to be traded was fixed: what the
English did not carry out of India the Dutch would, what the Dutch took
from English waters diminished the fishing wealth available to the English, what the English did not manufacture the Dutch or French would.
Whenever the Dutch prospered, they "encroach[ed] upon our livings."[54]

The merchant formed a point of intersection between two "cosms" (or
spheres). In the national sphere, dominated as it was by the organic model,
each "organ" was seen as contributing separately to the whole (or its center)
and receiving separately from it in a bilateral relationship, so that the
importance of each *part* (or "organ") to the other tended to be overlooked.
In the international sphere the bilateral relationship was alternately
between the country and whole fixed sum of wealth (what one country took
from the pile left less for the rest) and between any pair of nations: England
versus the United Provinces, for example. The merchant provided the
means of moving wealth from one sphere to the other.

The introduction of trade balance theory has created a tension
between the two spheres: individual states do not act as organs of the whole
(and contribute to the world's good) but in their own interest, while individuals were expected to align their private good with the public. Mun was
far from alone in not seeing that tension, but to harp on his imperfect systematization is both to diminish and distort him. He put the moral balance
ahead of the mechanical. Mun looked beyond the simple wealth of the
nation (defined as hoards of bullion) to a wealth chastely earned and
though still technically measured in bullion really measured in a disciplined
industriousness that bent the inclination of the individual to the greater
good of the whole.

To uncover the analytical gaps between Mun's basic worldview and the
policies he recommended with respect to bullion regulation, we need only
to turn to his treatment of money. For when it came to the laws of supply

and demand, money, for Thomas Mun as for Gerard de Malynes and Edward Misselden, was always a special case.

In his first book, *A Discourse of Trade*, Thomas Mun argued that there were four principal causes for the "want of money" in England. These were "breach of Entercourse," "abuse of the [international] exchanges," "neglect of dutie in some Subjects," and "dammage in our Commerce with Strangers." "Breach of Entercourse" was the tendency of countries to debase or overvalue "the price of their Coynes from that equivalence which formerly they had with the Standard and Moneys of this Realme" or tolerate exchanges at other than the official rates. "Abuse of the exchanges" was the tendency of the exchange-bankers to let the rates "rise and fall according to the plentie or scarcitie of money" to their advantage, making it "rather a Trade for some great monyed men, then a furtherance and accomodation of reall Trade to Merchants, as it ought to be in the true use thereof." Neglect of duty on the part of subjects ranged from careless coiners whose products were of unequal (and hence uncertain) weight, to goldsmiths who melted the heavier pieces for plate, state officials who did not strictly enforce the Statute of Employments, and the gullibility of "unskillful merchants."[55] All of these causes turned on the problem of the "intrinsic" value of money with the exception of the "unskillful merchants," and that touched on the question of "free" trade, or, more properly, freedom of access to trade, for it was nothing more than a prelude to a platform of restricting access to the active end of trade to the properly apprenticed merchant:

> Wherefore it were to be wished, that this mysterie of Merchandising might be left only to them, whoe have had an education thereunto; and not to be undertaken by such, who leaving their proper vocations, doe for want of skill in this, both overthrow themselves & others who are better practised.[56]

While our East India Company trader welcomed gentry investment in his company, he did not want them welcomed into the ranks of its active traders.[57]

Thomas Mun's opinions did not remain unchanged in the few years between the composition of his two major works. Certainly he spoke out directly against the bullion restrictions of the Statute of Employments in *Englands Treasure*, warning of the reciprocal action that might be taken against England by its European trading partners, as well as of the fact that forcing foreign merchants to take their profits out in English wares meant they would reap the rewards of the carrying trade that England might have otherwise kept for herself, including the employment for the mariners who were so dangerous when idle.[58] There was also a deliberate shift from the ability of humans (princes and bankers) to manipulate the exchange-rate to the stance that the abundance or scarcity of coin in any given market was the sole cause of the "under or overvaluing of moneys by Exchange," and even this was but an effect of a further cause—the trade balance.[59] At least sometimes it was the sole cause, for he spoke a few pages earlier of "forraign Coins tollerated to pass current among us, at higher rates than they are worth (being compared with our Standard)."[60] The problem seems to be that Mun had his doubts about the old idea that money was the determining and trade the determined variable but had yet to find a satisfactory theoretical foundation for either the reverse formulation or one encompassing a two-way interaction.

He knew there could be trade without money:

> Neither is it said that Mony is the life of Trade, as if it could not subsist without the same; for we know that there was great trading by way of commutation or barter when there was little mony stirring in the world.[61]

And he believed international exchange rates were the effects of trade balances rather than their cause:

> it is a certain rule in our forraign trade, in those places where our commodities exported are overballanced in value by foreign wares brought into this Realm, there our mony is undervalued in exchange; and where the contrary of this is performed, there our money is overvalued.[62]

This would seem to demote money to the position of the servant of trade rather than of its driver or goal.[63] But our merchant could not determine whether or not his trades had been successful without a reliable yardstick:

> He ought to know the Measures, Weights, and Monies of all forraign Countries, especially where we have Trade, & the Monies not onely by their several denominations, but also by their intrinsique values in weight & fineness, compared with the Standard of this Kingdome, without which he cannot well direct his affaires.[64]

Not only the merchant's affairs, but the very "common wealth" itself was affected by this uncertainty: a *just* distribution was impossible without the certainty provided by a fixed standard:

> if mony be the true measure of all our other means, and forraign Coins tollerated to pass current amongst us, at higher rates than they are worth (being compared with our Standard) it followeth that the common wealth shall not be justly distributed, when it passeth by a false measure.[65]

But if coins were not to be "tollerated" at values above those determined by their weight and fineness (or true silver content), then they would be exchanged only at *par pro pari*, the very idea of Malynes's that Mun had earlier denounced. Toleration implied a market ruled not by internal laws but human whim: the seventeenth-century meaning of "tolerate" was to allow or permit (especially with reference to that which was not approved).[66] It is most likely that Mun did not realize that his conclusion (that the trade balance regulated the exchange rate) did not rest on his argument (against toleration). In any case, Mun was only challenging Malynes on the cause of the "tolleration" but not on the effect: both men were making the case for a fixed exchange rate of some sort.

Ironically, it was in Mun's bullionist/Scholastic diatribe against governmental enhancing and debasing of coinage that he came closest to understanding the interactions between the parts of the whole (instead of between the part and the whole), and thus came closest to constructing an economic system:

> mony is not only the true measure of all our other means in the King-dom, but also of our forraign commerce with strangers, which therefore ought to be kept just and constant to avoid those confusions which ever accompany such alterations. For first at home, if the common measure be changed, our Lands, Leases, wares, both forraign and domestique must alter in proportion: and although this is not done without much trouble and damage for that is not the denomination of our pounds shillings and pence, which is respected, but the intrinsique value of our Coins. . . . Neither can these courses which so much hurt the Subjects, any way help the king as some men have imagined: for although debasing or lightning all our money should bring a present benefit (for once only) to the Mint, yet all this and more would soon be lost again in the future great In-comes of His Majesty, when by this means they must be paid yearly with mony of less intrinsique value then formerly . . . for it were vanity and against their profit to keep continually in their hands above forty or fifty pounds in a family to defray necessary charges, the rest must ever run from man to man in traffique for their benefit. . . . the gain upon the heavy, would cause our vigilant neighbours to carry over a great part thereof, and return in presently in pieces of the new stamp; nor do we doubt that some of our own Countrymen would turn Coiners and venter a hanging. . . . [And if] other Princes are vigilant in these cases to alter presently in proportion with us, and then where is our hope? . . . and shall not the price of the Merchants exchange with forraign Countries rise in proportion with our Moneys?[67]

That this re-enthroned bullion by contradicting everything he had said about money being neither the rule nor the end of trade was evidently beyond Mun's capacity to understand.

The idea of money as "the life blood" of trade takes us back to the medical analogy we saw in the work of Gerard de Malynes. In his case, it led to an adumbration of quantity theory. We are not yet at the changes in

economic thought wrought by physicians who studied William Harvey's
work on the circulation of the blood (and we certainly cannot know if
Thomas Mun ever so much as heard Harvey's name), but part and parcel of
that change concerns following money's path *throughout* the economy
(rather than merely into and out of it). We must credit Thomas Mun for at
least exploring that question. In advocating princely spending he stressed
the need for keeping the coin in circulation. Ordinary men might "lay up"
their excess revenue, but if a prince "should mass up more money than is
gained by the over-balance of his forraign trade, he shall not *Fleece,* but *Flea*
his Subjects."[68] Unlike ordinary men, princes made themselves "rich and
powerfull" by returning their revenues "to their subjects from whom it was
first taken" by "employing them to make Ships of War . . . to build and
repair Forts, to buy and store up Corn . . . [and] to erect Banks" or "Col-
lonels, Captains, Souldiers, Commanders, Mariners, and others" in their
service, "especially if care be taken that all (as neer as possible) be made out
of the Matter and Manufacture of their own subjects."[69] But this paean to
government spending equally stressed maintaining the balance of trade by
avoiding imports and protecting the merchant fleet. The domestic economy was still subordinate to the foreign,[70] and, even in its consideration of
the domestic sphere, it did not reject the redistributive function that the
organic social model traditionally assigned to the prince:

> for a Prince (in this case) is like the stomach in the body, which if it cease
> to digest and distribute to the other members, it doth no sooner corrupt
> them, but it destroys it self.[71]

What underlay the seeming confusions in Mun's attempts to explain the
economic benefits of a well-balanced trade? Perhaps it was because he
never thought of the economic effects of such a balance as unequivocably
benefits. Mun was certain that "penury and want" made "a people wise and
industrious" while "plenty and power" made them "vicious and improvi-
dent."[72] Mun would only trust a positive trade balance if it were so managed as to produce a moral balance: too much wealth was as dangerous for
a society as too much poverty. The equilibrium Mun was after was ultimately one between morality and prosperity, but that requires a formula
mere economics cannot of itself supply.

He was shifting back and forth between two incompatible worlds. He
could not permanently move from the first to the second without
sacrificing the idea of *intrinsic value,* and this he was not prepared to do.
Intrinsic (or objective) value was the cement holding the finite universe
together. It was the axis running through the center of each concentric
cosm and linking them all in the Great Chain of Being.

CHAPTER 5

Harmony and the "Balance of Trade"

In the first third of the seventeenth century, merchants routinely accepted that one nation's gain must come at another nation's loss. How could it be otherwise in a world of finite resources anchoring a closed universe? And, as usual, the personal formed the model for the political. "Covetousness," as St. Thomas Aquinas explained, was "a sin directly against one's neighbor": one person could not "overabound in external riches, without another . . . lacking them," because "temporal goods" could not "be possessed by many at the same time."[1] Here, as Jacob Viner noted, Aquinas was simply following "St. Jerome's dictum that one man's gain must be another man's loss."[2]

From that dictum would come the century's primary economic model: balance of trade theory, or the idea that a country's economic health depended upon its exporting goods valued in excess of those imported, because imports created bullion outflows while exports brought in bullion from abroad. Thomas Mun believed this rule was as important for Spain's silver-rich empire as it was for countries like England that lacked a native source of bullion, because negative trade balances eventually would drain dry even the most generous supply.[3]

St. Jerome's dictum was an economic truism long before the seventeenth century dawned,[4] though Gerard de Malynes may have been the first to link the word "balance" to it when he argued that to allow imports to exceed exports was an "overballancing of commodities" resulting in "the decrease of our wealth."[5] He accepted the theory as axiomatic,[6] but rejected any dogged devotion to annual calculations of it as both exceedingly difficult to do[7] and, even when done, as merely indicating the magnitude of the problem without solving it.[8] For Gerard de Malynes, solving it always involved fixing the exchange at *par pro pari* (the "Marchandising exchange" making English goods too expensive to sell abroad).[9]

Sir Francis Bacon is usually credited with giving the theory its actual name, in a private memorandum of "Advice to Villiers" (1616):

> Let the foundations of a profitable Trade be thus laid, that the exporta-
> tion of home commodities be more in value than the exportation of for-
> eign, so we shall be sure that the stocks of the Kingdom shall increase,
> for then the balance of trade must be returned in money or bullion.[10]

Since the third edition of Bacon's *Essays,* in which a slightly different version ("well-balancing of trade") appeared, did not see print until 1625, Misselden holds the honor of having sprung the term, if not the idea, on the
reading public, with *The Circle of Commerce or The Ballance of Trade* (1623).

Balance was a term borrowed from the Italian invention of double-
entry bookkeeping as both its advocates and enemies well knew. Misselden
explained to his readers that

> A Merchant when hee will informe himselfe how his estate standeth, is
> said to take a Ballance of Accompt . . . Which is wherefore in Merchants
> and Accomptants termes, so called a Ballance of Accompt, or a Ballance
> of Trade.[11]

Whether they argued for or against, these works were actually popularizing a new meaning of the word *balance,* because what they wished to
see was actually a permanent *imbalance* in which exports exceeded imports.
Traditionally, *balance* (derived from the image of balance scales) was conso-
nant with the Aristotelian sense of harmony and of the mean between two
extremes. Malynes used the term in this sense when he explored the issue
of the proper relationship between "natural" and "artificial" commodities:

> we ought to ballance the value of things upon this beame, laying the
> lands on the one side, and the money of things mony-worth in value on
> the other side, to find out this inequality.[12]

James I's instructions to the Commission on Trade in October 1622
conflated the older idea with the new by proposing that the commission
work on policies that would promote a greater "equality" between imports
and exports:

> That to prevent an apparent consumption and confusion, which cannot
> other wise be avoided, ye diligently observe the true balance of the trade
> of this kingdom, lest the importation of merchandize from foreign ports
> exceed the exportation of our own native commodities, and consider of
> some fitting courses to reduce the same to more equality, and to think
> upon the gain or loss that comes to our kingdom by the course of
> exchange now used by our merchants.[13]

But no one who understood bookkeeping would think that the *equality* of
debits and credits of the trial balance was the ultimate end of the system.
That equality was nothing more than a mechanical check assuring that

each item had been posted to the property category (asset, liability, capital, income, or expense) and the resulting accounts correctly added up.

The science of bookkeeping (designed to track an individual's estate) could be applied to the national sphere because of the universally accepted concept of a universe constructed of nested "cosms." Because, as we have seen, "man" was considered to be a "microcosm" or mirror of the greater cosmos, and society was held to partake of both the smaller and greater spheres, the greater could be studied through the more accessible model of the lesser (or the reverse if that proved more convenient). Where Plato thought justice more accessible of study in the social sphere than in the personal, the trade balance theorists thought the political economy better studied through the personal. Thus the model for the political was an enlargement of Aristotle's "household management" mediated by the dictum of Cato the Elder (243–149 B.C.) that the head of a household ought to be a seller rather than a buyer ("*oportet patrem-familias vendacem esse, non emacem*"). This snippet from Cato's *De Agri Cultura*, quoted by Malynes a number of times,[14] was to be found in every argument for balance of trade the century would see.

When Misselden said that "A Common-wealth is like unto a Family, the Father or Master whereof ought to sell more than he buyeth,"[15] he knew his readers would understand. To speak of a commonwealth as a "great family" was almost as much of a cliché in the seventeenth century as to speak of it as a "body politicke." Both figures of speech shared the same relation of part to whole: no organ worked for itself alone, no family member worked for himself or herself alone. In one simile, the prince made the decisions as the *head*, in the other he did so as the *father*. No wonder it found favor with James I who took great pains to remind his parliament that "Kings are also compared to Fathers of families: for a King is trewly *Parens patriae*, the politique father of his people."[16]

The soundness of the dictum Sell more than you buy was questioned in neither sphere, but to convert it from a dictum to an analytical concept, its components had to be rationally determined. Here, too, the science of bookkeeping provided a model. From a merchant's components of and charges against his income, Misselden could ascertain that a true balance of trade must include consideration of freight charges, customs duties, profits on reexports, and even money paid for smuggled goods.[17] Thomas Mun took the analysis one step farther when he realized that money transfers outside the arena of trade—such as pensions received from foreign princes or wages paid to soldiers or sent by private parties to recusants abroad— would have to be included in any balance that attempted to determine the true monetary flow to and from a nation.[18] He also stressed the need to distinguish between a nation's overall balance and that with any single trading partner.[19] The pursuit of national profit was being rationalized along with the personal.

Mun's insights into trade balance theory were likely the result of his battle as an apologist for the East India Company to convince the Crown that prohibiting the export of bullion was as bad for the nation as a whole as it was for the East India Company: having a special interest does not necessarily impede one's ability to see the overall picture; sometimes it actually fosters it.[20]

But with its emphasis on the acquisition of wealth defined as precious metal, trade balance theory was something of a two-edged sword. Popular sentiment assumed that if the East India Company would purchase Indian goods with something other than silver, much more coin would flow into England's coffers.[21] Company apologists (Misselden and Mun among them) argued against this in a number of ways: explaining that the trade was not possible without the initial silver outflow (as Indians could not be forced to purchase European goods against their will), claiming that only foreign coin was sent to India, demonstrating that income from reexporting the goods to the Continent exceeded the cost of their original purchase, and stressing the gain made by not ceding the carrying trade to third parties.[22]

As might any merchant, Mun stressed that the initial outlay had to be understood in terms of its final return. In so doing he used an analogy from an activity he thought more readily comprehensible to his readers than were some of the ways of merchants:

> For if we only behold the actions of the husbandman in the seed-time when he casteth away much good corn into the ground, we will rather accompt him a man mad than a husbandman: but when we consider his labours in the harvest which is the end of his endeavours, we find the worth and plentiful encrease of his actions.[23]

Rather than ask ourselves whether or not Mun was here making the analytic leap from "money" to "capital,"[24] we might more profitably look to this identity Mun saw between the actions of the farmer and the merchant.[25] Edward Misselden claimed that his fellow merchants were

> wont to make it their glory, to advance their fortunes, renowne their names, embellize their houses, beautifie their families with the honour of this faculty: and to perpetuate the fame unto posterities, as an hereditary title of honour unto their name and blood.[26]

In other words, merchants no more pursued profit for its own sake than did gentlemen though both would be wise to pursue it rationally. If such merchants were motivated by a different *Geist* than were their fellow countrymen, they were not aware of it. They were aware, however, that their society drew a sharp line between those *activities* (and *individuals*) it considered as belonging to the economic sphere and those it did not, and, strange as it may seem to us, the aristocrat who rented out his land for as hearty a sum as he could get did not belong, while the merchant, even after he retired to his suburban villa, did.

Misselden and Mun did not put trade balance theory forward as one of many economic indicators but as an all-encompassing economic model, and that brought it into conflict with the evolving (if as yet unnamed) quantity theory that pegged domestic prices to the "plenty" of money. The primary effect of a positive trade balance was an increase in the money supply, but such an increase was held to increase prices, and, after a century of inflation, price rises were an extremely sensitive subject. Misselden had accepted the quantity theory, but saw no insoluble problem in the resulting price rise:

> that which is equall to all, when hee that buye's deare shall sell deare, cannot bee said to be injurious unto any. And it is much better for the Kingdome, to have things deare with plenty of Money, whereby men may live in their several callings: then to have things cheape with want of Money, which now makes every man complaine. Lastly, for Landlords and Creditors, their losse is easie to be prevented by Proviso, that the Contracts made before the raising of the monies shall be paide at the value the Money went at, when the Contracts were made according to the disposition of the Civill Law in this case.[27]

But that proviso was not likely to allay the fears of the landowning classes whose tenants most commonly held long-term leases at fixed rents: one can imagine the tangled attempts to work out what money had been worth generations ago, a task made no easier by the frequent debasements of the sixteenth century.[28] One does not have to imagine the reaction of the increasing laboring classes: the tradition of price-setting riots had been both long established and acknowledged by the government in the emergency measures of 1580 through 1630 "codified" in the *Book of Orders*.[29]

So perhaps we should not be surprised that Mun tied himself into analytic knots trying to reconcile these competing "truths." On the one hand the price rise would be to the public's detriment even if to private profit:

> all men do consent that plenty of money in a Kingdom doth make the native commodities dearer, which as it is to the profit of some private men in their revenues, so is it directly against the benefit of the Publique

> in the quantity of the trade; for as plenty of mony makes wares dearer, so
> dear wares decline their use and consumption . . . although this is a very
> hard lesson for some great landed men to learn.[30]

On the other, increasing the price rise by charging higher duties on goods
for domestic consumption would increase the trade balance:

> And especially forraign wares brought in to be transported again should
> be favoured, for otherwise that manner of trading (so much importing
> the good of the Commonwealth) cannot prosper nor subsist. But the
> Consumption of such forraign wares in the Realm may be the more
> charged, which will turn to the profit of the kingdom in the Balance of
> the Trade.[31]

This would create a public benefit:

> for as the food and rayment of the poor is made dear by Excise, so doth
> the price of their labour rise in proportion; whereby the burden (if any
> be) is still upon the rich.[32]
> For when the Merchant hath a good dispatch beyond the Seas for his
> Cloth and other wares, he doth presently to return to buy up the greater
> quantity, which raiseth the price of our Woolls and other commodities,
> and consequently doth improve the Landlords Rents as the Leases
> expire daily . . . [and] it doth enable men to buy Lands, which will make
> them the dearer.[33]

But this amounted to nothing less than inflation, no matter what Mun
called it, and he had just called it an immoral encroachment on the public
good at private expense.

The problem was not one that only the apologists were having
difficulty sorting out. Theirs was still a world of "light" industry and sale on
speculation in which a quick circulation of a generous supply of coin was
the first necessity for trade.[34] A higher price level than would be found in a
stagnant economy was a side effect whose benefits they might or might not
dispute but must accept.[35]

But most important for the intellectual peace of mind of the seventeenth
century, trade balance theory posed, in a very real sense, a direct challenge
to the organic model belief that everything in this universe was designed to
work in harmony for the benefit of the whole and not that of a part.
According to Gerard de Malynes,

> God caused nature to distribute her benefits, or his blessing to severall
> climates, supplying the barrennesse of some things in our countrey, with
> the fruitfulnesse and store of other countries, to the ende that enter-
> changeably one common-weale should live with another.[36]

The idea was hardly original to him; Grotius had traced it back to Seneca:

> Seneca thinks this is Nature's greatest service, that by the wind she united the widely scattered peoples, and yet did so distribute all her products over the earth that commercial intercourse was a necessity to mankind.[37]

Edward Misselden found it in Aristotle:

> Which agreeth with that of Aristotle, *Est translatio rerum omnium coepta ab initio, ab eo quod est secundum naturam, cum homines haberent plura quam sufficerent, partim etiam pauciora negotiatione suppleri id quod naturae deest, quo commode omnibus sufficiat.*[38]

More recently, it had surfaced in a popular anonymous treatise of 1581, entitled *A Compendious or Brief Examination of Certain Ordinary Complaints of Divers of Our Countrymen in These Our Dayes . . . :*

> wherein it appeared as therefore God has ordained that no country should have all commodities but that that one lacks, another brings forth . . . to the intent men may known that they have need one of another's help and thereby love and society to grow amongst men all the more.[39]

An individual commonwealth was only one in that series of nested "cosms" within which human life was lived. All Christian commonwealths were also parts of *one* Christian Commonwealth (*Respublica Christiana*). This was why Malynes believed there should be freedom of the seas and free passage through land within Christendom for all persons (non-Christians included).[40] The harmony that was supposed to prevail within one realm was also supposed to prevail between realms. Malynes explained "equalitie & concord," the "two things required in every well governed commonwealth" as "concord within the realme amongst the several members of the same, and equality in the course of traffike between the realme and other countries."[41]

When the element of advantage was added, the argument began to change into something very different. Thomas Milles (d. 1627) believed

> albeit that Kingdome or Country be holden most wealthie and happie, that is ablest and aptest to spare and transport Commodities of their owne, wherein this Iland may compare with the best; yet since no place is extant so absolutely blist [*blessed*]; as in all points to stand and subsist of it selfe, by the benefit of *Entercourse* and *Traffique,* bounded by Lawes, *Speciall treatise, Leagues, Oathes* and *Decrees,* al wants are supplied, each Part intending the best for itself, according to Reason, Wisedome and Pollicie.[42]

The key to the change was "each Part intending the best for itself."

Malynes, like Milles, believed that it was a prince's function to enrich his commonwealth. But the only peaceable means of attaining this end was the furtherance of trade in general and the specific pursuit of a positive balance of trade. This was why the study of "Trafficke" was the "*Præheminent studie of Princes.*"[43]

But, if all nations were to seek trade surpluses as a general course, international commerce would hardly approach a harmonious balance. Some men, like Sir Francis Bacon, took a pragmatic attitude toward this economic nationalism: "the increase of any estate must be upon the foreigner (for whatsoever is somewhere gotten is somewhere lost)."[44] In fact, he advised princes to "keep do sentinel" that "none of their neighbors" did "so overgrow" them "by embracing of trade" that they became "more able to annoy them than they [previously] were."[45] Malynes was aware of a potential for tension between the two aims (international harmony and individual trade surpluses) and warned against pursuing extreme attempts to corner the market:

> And herein is to be considered, That all other nations being carefull to maintaine manufactures, cannot but take an offence, if any other nation will endeavour to doe all, and to exclude others. . . . For (as hath been noted) it is contrarie to that common entercourse and mutuall course of commodities, where of some countries are destitute, and other countries do abound, thereby supplying the barrennesse of the one, with the superfluities of the other, maintaining a friendly correspondence and familiaritie. . . . The striving of making commodities, and to undersel one another, are dangerous, and prejudiciall to both parties: for by their contention they hinder each other, and bring commodities to be lesse esteemed.[46]

But he was ultimately unable to break free of the seventeenth-century obsession with securing bullion.

Edward Misselden had similar problems. Grotius had used the idea of a geographical division of labor to put forward a doctrine not only of the right of free passage on the seas but of the freedom of all countries to tap the economic resources of the oceans, but Misselden wished to keep foreign fishermen out of "native" waters because the resources they took reduced those available to England's use.[47]

For all his support of trade balance theory, Thomas Mun also worried about the results of disturbing this harmony, warning that "the whole body of trade" would "languish if the harmony of her health be distempered by the diseases of excess at home, violence, abroad, [and] charges and restrictions at home," because "whatsoever (in this kind) we shall impose upon strangers here, will presently be made a Law for us in their Countreys."[48]

Accommodating trade balance theory into the model of a harmonious universe created a logical impasse. Trade balance theory was based, after all, on a national version of self-interest, but self-interest threatened to let loose the very Chaos the divinely ordered Cosmos had been created to conquer. Some new model might be needed altogether, but such a model would have to wait upon the emergence of a new understanding of the micro- and macrocosms.

The New Model Economics

CHAPTER 6

Mechanically Minded

The central decades of the seventeenth century were tumultuous ones for England. Rebellions in Scotland, Ireland, and England fused into a civil war that did not so much end with the execution of Charles I in January 1649 as transform into an unsuccessful eleven-year experiment in republican government. These same decades witnessed an unprecedented intellectual upheaval as the Reformation splintered into innumerable warring factions, and new mechanical and mathematical worldviews were proposed as foundations for a restored epistemological order (even though their particular goals and methods were often in "conflict with each other").[1]

The "Mechanical" (or "Corpuscular") hypothesis saw the universe as made of matter in motion. As Robert Boyle explained it:

> I agree with the generalty of philosophers, so far as to allow that there is one catholic or universal matter common to all bodies, by which I mean a substance extended, divisible, and impenetrable. . . . it will follow that, to discriminate the catholic matter into a variety of natural bodies, it must have motion. . . . matter [in motion] must be actually divided into parts . . . [and] each of the primitive fragments . . . must have two attributes—its own magnitude, or rather *size,* and its own *figure* or *shape.* And since experience shows us (especially that which is afforded us by chemical operations, in many of which matter is divided into parts too small to be singly sensible) that this division of matter is frequently made into insensible corpuscles or particles, we may conclude that the minutest fragments, as well as the biggest masses, of the universal matter are likewise endowed each with its peculiar bulk and shape.[2]

The eventual spread of the term *corpuscle* from physics to physiology in the eighteenth century[3] is an indicator of the extent to which this macrocosmic hypothesis also mechanized the microcosm. Since the human body also functioned as the seventeenth century's basic sociological model, the mechanico-mathematical worldview developed in the middle decades of the seventeenth century would reconstruct society as well.

Three of our economic writers came to maturity in this period: Sir William Petty, Sir Josiah Child, and John Locke. Petty and Locke were trained as physicians; Child was a merchant. The century's most original contribution to economic theory belongs to the physician Petty. This was no coincidence; Petty applied his new understanding of the human body to his analysis of the body politic. Locke's strictly economic work was both less original and less radically rearranging of the body politic than Petty's, but it was still built on the new model of the human body. And, merchant or no, Child could not help but be influenced by it as well.

We begin then with William Harvey (1578–1657), the Italian-trained English physician whose 1628 treatise *Exercitatio Anatomica de Motu Cordis et Sanguinis in Animalibus* (*The Movement of the Heart and Blood in Animals*) put forth the case for the circulative movement of the blood through the body via a single system composed of the heart, lungs, arteries, and veins. According to established Galenic medical thought, the veins and arteries belonged to different systems: the veins were the vessels through which "hungry" organs *drew* nutrient-rich blood created by the liver from ingested food, while the arteries carried the pneuma-rich blood created by the heart's heat to breathe life into those same organs. Harvey used observations and experiments in human and comparative anatomy to prove the direction of the flow, and a *quantitative* analysis of arterial blood flow to show the necessity of a recirculation rather than a continual manufacture of the blood.[4] The operation of this system was mechanical, but Harvey's worldview was not. His dedication of *De Motu Cordis* to Charles I reads:

> The animal's heart is the basis of its life, its chief member, the sun of its microcosm; on its heart all its activity depends, from the heart all its liveliness and strength arise. Equally is the King the basis of his kingdoms, the sun of his microcosm, the heart of the state, from him all power arises and all grace stems.[5]

In the main text, he referred to the heart as "the titular deity of the body, the basis of life, the source of all things."[6] This may have been a Copernican rather than a Ptolemaic cosmos, but it was still fundamentally an Aristotelian (or qualitative) rather than a mechanical (or quantitative) universe.[7]

Harvey's work was generally better accepted on the Continent than at home. He may have been "Physician to the King" and Professor of Anatomy of the College of Physicians in London, but his local practice suffered because his contemporaries thought him "crack-brained."[8]

René Descartes (1596–1650) first gave Harvey public credit for proving that the course of the blood was "nothing but a perpetual circulation"[9] in the same anonymously published *Discourse on Method* that proclaimed

"*Cogito ergo sum*" and launched the Cartesian revolution in 1637. The greater detail in Descartes's *Description of the Human Body* (1664) made its machinelike qualities even more apparent:

> the heat in the heart is like the great spring or principle responsible for all the movements occurring in the machine. The veins are pipes which conduct the blood from all the parts of the body towards the heart, where it serves to fuel the heat there. The stomach and the intestines are another much larger pipe perforated with many little holes through which the juices from the food ingested run into the veins; these then carry the juices straight to the heart. The arteries are yet another set of pipes through which the blood, which is heated and rarified in the heart, passes from there into all the other parts of the body, bring them heat and material to nourish them.[10]

Descartes's physiology may not have been as accurate as Harvey's—in contradistinction to Harvey, Descartes mistakenly thought the heart's diastole (dilation) initiated arterial circulation[11]—but his mechanism was more thoroughgoing (if still incomplete), because Descartes split his universe in two, separating passive matter from active spirit: the material (body) *was* moved while the spiritual (God-given soul) *did.* In *Meditations on First Philosophy* (1641), the key word in Descartes's description of his own body was *corpse:*

> I had a face, hands, arms and the whole mechanical structure of limbs which can be seen in a corpse, and which I called the body. . . . by a body I understand whatever has a determinable shape and a definable location and can occupy a space in such a way as to exclude any other body; it can be perceived by touch, sight, hearing, taste or smell, and can be moved in various ways, not by itself but by whatever else comes into contact with it.[12]

For Descartes *matter* was simply that which had *extension.*[13] *Soul* (or that which was truly "I") was "purely spiritual" and, hence, unlike extended matter, was eternal and indivisible.[14] This was a far more radical split than that implied by Edward Forset's "as in every man there is both a quickning & ruling soule, and a living and ruled bodie"[15] though Descartes's first formulation of the split appeared in print only thirteen years after Forset's *Comparative discourse of the Bodies natural and Politique.*

The "mechanical" and the physiological met and fused in the work of Thomas Hobbes (1588–1679). Hobbes had jousted with Descartes in print before finally meeting him in Paris in 1648 and befriending both Harvey and Sir William Petty (who had studied under Harvey's successors at Leiden).[16] It is the completeness of this fusion that has made possible such seemingly diametrically opposed interpretations of Hobbes's work as those that claim he had either a "mechanistic psychology of the passions"[17] or "a physiologically based psychology."[18]

Hobbes's *Leviathan* (1651) began with an extended analogy of the *body politic*:

> For by Art is created that great Leviathan called a Common-wealth, or state, (in latine Civitas) which is but an Artificall Man; though of greater stature and strength than the Naturall, for whose protection and defence it was intended; and in which, the Soveraignty is an Artificall Soul, as giving life and motion to the whole body; The magistrates, and other Officers of Judicature and Execution, artificall Joynts; Reward and Punishment (by which fastned to the seate of the Soveraity, every joynt and member is moved to performe his duty) are the Nerves that do the same in the Body naturall; The Wealth and Riches of all the particular members, are the Strength; *Salus Populi* (the peoples safety) its Businesse; Counsellors, by whom all things needfull for it to know, are suggested unto it, are the Memory; Equity and Lawes, and artificall Reason and Will; Concord, Health; Sedition, Sicknesses; and Civill war, Death. Lastly, the Pacts and Covnents, by which the parts of this Body Politique were at first made, set together, and united, resemble that *Fiat*, or the *Let us make man*, pronounced by God in the Creation.[19]

If we compare this analogy to that used by Aristotle or Malynes we will immediately see much that is new. A set of interlocking systems replaced the hierarchy of members separately linked to the head. The laws of judicial system (the "Reward and Punishment") were equated with the "nerves" because they functioned in the same way: they stimulated motion.[20] The body politic was distinguished from the natural because of its aggregate basis: its strength was an aggregation of individual prosperity, "*Salus Populi*" was its purpose, and the people were its creator (and hence purpose-givers). The new (and mechanical) focus on the physiology of the "body naturall" gave a new slant to looking at the way the parts of the "body politique" actually functioned. Here was a concept of the function of trade (albeit still taken as circulation of money rather than as constant exchange of goods for money and money for goods) directly dependent on Harvey's work:

> The Nutrition of a commonwealth consisteth, in the plenty, and distribution of materials conducing to life: in concoction, or preparation; and, when concocted, in the conveyance of it, by convenient conduits, to the public use.[21]
>
> By Concoction, I understand the reducing of all commodities, which are not presently consumed, but reserved for Nourishment in time to come, to some thing of equall value [and portable]. . . . And this is nothing else but Gold, and Silver, and Mony. For Gold and Silver, being (as it happens) almost in all Countries of the world highly valued, is a commodious measure of the value of all things else between Nations, and Mony (of what matter soever coyned by the Soveraign of a Common-wealth,)

is a sufficient measure of the value of all things else, between the Subjects of that Common-wealth . . . and the same passeth from Man to Man, within the Common-wealth; and goes round about, Nourishing (as it passeth) every part thereof; In so much as this Concoction, is as it were the Sanguinification of the Common-wealth: For naturall Bloud is in like manner made of the fruits of the Earth; and circulating, nourisheth by the way, every Member of the Body of Man.[22]

The new attitude was particularly noticeable in its treatment of the metal involved in domestic and international circulations. That the bullion content of coin was of greater importance than its legal denomination in international exchange we have seen remarked upon before, but Hobbes reversed the cause and effect. In the older argument, bullion did what it did because of what it *was* (function followed form). Hobbes has form follow the joint constraints of function (exchange measure) and environment (ability to enforce law).

This body was a natural machine.

> The cause of Sense, is the Externall Body, or Object, which presseth the organ proper to each Sense, either immediately, as in the Taste and Touch; or mediately, as in Seeing, Hearing, and Smelling: which pressure, by the mediation of the Nerves, and other strings, and membranes of the body, continued inwards to the Brain and Heart, causeth there a resistance; or counter-pressure, or endeavour of the heart, to deliver it self: which endeavour because Outward. . . . Neither in us that are pressed, are they anything else, but divers motions.[23]

Hobbes wrote one of the sets of objections to Descartes's *Meditations on First Philosophy*, in which Hobbes redefined the Ego itself (as understood in *Cogito ergo sum*) as material:

> It seems to follow from this that a thinking thing is something corporeal. . . . The knowledge of the proposition 'I exist' thus depends on the knowledge of the proposition 'I am thinking'; and knowledge of the latter proposition depends on our inability to separate thought from the matter that is thinking. So it seems that the correct inference is that the thinking thing is material rather than immaterial.[24]

In mechanizing the mind as well as the body, Hobbes stressed two characteristics that would eventually prove vital to the eventual development of "Economic Man"[25]—uniformity and predictability:

> For every man is desirous of what is good for him, and shuns what is evil, but chiefly the chiefest of natural evils, which is death; and this he doth by a certain impulsion of nature, no less than that whereby a stone moves downward.[26]
> Nature hath made men so equall, in the faculties of body, and mind; as that though there bee found one man sometimes manifestly stronger in

> body, or of quicker mind then another; yet when all is reckoned together, the difference between man, and man, is not so considerable, as that one man can thereupon claim to himselfe any benefit, to which another may not pretende, as well as he.[27]

In addition, whereas Harvey's model-making was concerned with the treatment of the body and Descartes's was constructed as a basis for his epistemology, Hobbes's model was *meant* for the work of social science. He was building

> an ideal type the application of which to reality would enable anyone to deduce actual human behaviour, provided that allowance was made for this or that set of actual conditions.[28]

It is not yet the ideal type of "Economic Man," not least because Hobbes's primary focus was on society as a politico-moral construct rather than as an economic one. To turn it into "Economic Man" one needs to keep the mechanical nature of the rationality and the analytical identity of the actors, but reduce the pleasure-pain orientation and drive for power to the narrower idea of economic rationality: the idea that human beings are rational economic actors who seek (based on their present knowledge) to maximize their future position in the marketplace so that the difference in their results is the effect of a difference in the state of their knowledge rather than any disproportion in their maximizing drive.

Sir William Petty, John Locke, and Sir Josiah Child each, in his own way, worked from a perspective of essential human uniformity and a pleasure-pain orientation operating according to knowable mechanical forces, though the extent to which they may have derived it from the work of Thomas Hobbes or simply shared with him in the developing *Zeitgeist* can never absolutely be determined. But possession of a common perspective does not mandate that the possessors reach identical conclusions. Harvey and Descartes espoused diametrically opposed views of the primary motion of the heart though both men described a thoroughly mechanical circulation of the blood. Not surprisingly, the pictures of economic circulation that Petty, Locke, and Child worked from or wished society to achieve differed almost as considerably from each other as did the physiological conclusions of Harvey and Descartes. What we have to consider is whether their personal economic interests or their general philosophical orientation had more effect on their respective ideas of the most advantageous economic circulation.

CHAPTER 7

The Number, Weight, and Measure of Sir William Petty

Sir William Petty was a pioneer in the application of the new mechanico-physiological model of the body and its emerging mathematical method to the realm of economic ideas. He explored the concepts of division of labor, national income, velocity of circulation, the multiplier, and the components of value, albeit with uneven success, a century before Adam Smith explored them in *The Nature and Causes of the Wealth of Nations*. But models and methods are intended to serve the purposes of their *makers*, and Petty's purposes were not confined to those of economics per se. He saw the economy as enclosed within, and intended to serve the purposes of, an all-encompassing political organism. So he called his new science "Political Arithmetick"—a way for governments to use numerical data to increase the efficiency of their function and the prosperity of their populace. But, beyond this, he was part of a millenarian attempt to build a New Jerusalem fusing "successful religious concord . . . social amelioration and intellectual renewal"[1] through the auspices of the state—a decidedly *seventeenth*-century venture and one of a much broader scope than found in any single social science of the twentieth century.

Sir William Petty died at his house in London on December 13, 1687, of a gangrened foot. Though there is a mid-nineteenth-century memorial erected by his descendants in Romsey Church, the exact location of his actual grave has since been lost.[2] The fate of his grave foreshadowed that of his renown. Once called by Marx one of the two founders (with Boisguilbert) of classical economics,[3] he was cast aside in the beatification of Smith, Ricardo, and Malthus, and left on a heap of seventeenth-century supporting players in spite of a recent revision upward.[4] Some of this might be said to be his own fault. He never synthesized all his economic insights into a cohesive whole, but scattered them throughout a cornucopia of essays on taxes, theology, mathematics, education, government reorganization, cloth dyes, ship design, and surveying. His restless intellect rarely stopped to spell out the steps leading to his conclusions. An estimation of national wealth in one volume was based upon a population estimate in a second and a calculation of per capita living expenses in yet a third. Petty may have complained to his friends of frequent legal interruptions, but he seems more often to have interrupted himself. But perhaps that is hardly surprising, for he lived so many different lives.

He was born on May 26, 1623, the son of a clothier rather down on his luck, in Romsey, a market-town in Hampshire.[5] He did not apprentice in his father's trade[6] but shipped away as a cabin boy on an English merchant ship only to end up on his own in France at age fourteen, stranded with a broken leg. Turning mischance into opportunity, he put his schoolboy Latin to good account by composing a successful request (in that tongue) to the Jesuit college at Caen for further instruction there.[7]

He returned to England in time to put in a short stint in the King's Navy,[8] but left the country at the outbreak of the civil war for the Netherlands where he studied medicine under Harvey's followers[9] and struck up a friendship with Dr. John Pell, the mathematician teaching at Amsterdam, while supporting himself as a jeweler's assistant.[10] In 1645, he was in Paris, reading Vesalius with Thomas Hobbes and doing the drawings for Hobbes's *Optics*.[11]

Back in England again in 1646, he began a career at Oxford that would see him successively appointed Doctor of Medicine (1648), member of the Royal College of Physicians, Fellow and Vice-Principal of Brasenose College (1650), Professor of Anatomy (1650), and Professor of Music at Gresham College (1650).[12] By 1648, his friendship with Samuel Hartlib was well enough established for Petty to dedicate a book, *The Advancement of some particular Parts of Learning*, to him.[13] Essentially a variation on the Baconian Great Instauration, it also contained an advertisement for Petty's recent invention of a duplicate-writing device, the first fruits of his lifelong fascination with the mechanical arts.[14]

His anatomy lectures gained some attention for their use of Harvey's theories,[15] and his career as a practicing physician, although brief, was not without notoriety. In 1650 he was one of two physicians to "restore to life" one Anne Green who managed not only to survive a bungled hanging but also the potions Petty and Thomas Willis (1621–1675) inflicted on her in their treatment.[16] With the aid of the renown this brought him and the efforts of his friends, Petty was appointed physician to Lieut.-General Fleetwood of the Cromwellian army in Ireland in 1652.[17]

The question of raising an army for suppressing the Rebellion that broke out in Ireland on October 24, 1641, precipitated the first of the two civil wars that marked the English Revolution of 1642–49. Before Charles I and his Parliament came to a final parting of the ways, however, two acts had been passed (16 *Car.* I., c.33 and c.34) for financing the Irish campaign by selling shares in the Irish lands to be confiscated upon the successful suppression of the rebels. With the optimistic aim of raising £1,000,000, the acts promised away 2.5 million acres of as yet unconquered land.[18] Though not nearly enough money was raised by this means, and recourse had to be made to additional taxation, Cromwell's government found itself saddled with debts to the "Adventurers" (as the investors in Irish land were known) in addition to the promises of land made to its own soldiers.[19] To cover the shortfall, an order issued July 2, 1653, banished even the "innocent" Irish to lands west of the Shannon.[20] A preliminary attempt to make sense of the hodge-podge of confiscations was already under way when Petty arrived in Ireland.[21]

Convincing the authorities that he could bring the job to completion more efficiently, Petty wangled a contract for a new survey in 1654, and, good as his word, finished the job early and under budget,[22] using most of his fee to buy up "debentures" (plots forfeited to the soldiers but put on the market by those who would not or could not relocate). His was a cutthroat rapaciousness worthy of the bad old days of Elizabethan commerce: by the end of 1657, Petty had snapped up over 70,000 acres at well under market value—so much under market value that he would spend a considerable part of his time, before and after the Restoration, defending his actions in the courts and before Parliament.[23] He also produced *The History of the Survey*, greatly devoted to vindicating his honesty and efficiency, though this remained unpublished until the nineteenth century.[24]

Though he would serve in Richard Cromwell's Parliament in 1659 and (after his knighting in 1661) as a member of the Irish Parliament for Innistioge and Enniscorthy, Petty's public career ended in disappointment. At heart the kind of constitutional monarchist who believed in government by a strong executive, and a doctrinal minimalist in religion with a pronounced belief in public conformity,[25] Petty never entirely alienated Charles II and James II with his constant political advice, but he was never given high office either. Charles II called him "one of the best Commissioners of the navy that ever was" but lamented that "the man will not be contented to be excellent, but is still Ayming at Impossible Things."[26]

Through Hartlib, Petty met and made friends with Boyle, and then through Boyle, with Hooke, Wren, Wilkins, Aubrey, and Evelyn. When the Oxford Experimental Philosophy Club called itself into being in 1649, it held its first meetings in Petty's lodgings.[27] One of the first things Petty did on arriving in Ireland in 1652 was to join Boyle in a series of experiments intended to demonstrate the accuracy of Harvey's ideas on the circulation of the blood.[28] So it was not surprising that Petty was an original and enthusiastic member of the Royal Society (1662)[29] and later became the first president of the Dublin Philosophical Society (1684) that was founded along its lines.[30] He was a member, as well, of a shorter lived group, the Rota, a club formed in 1659 by James Harrington that met for a time at Miles's Coffee-House in Old Palace Yard.[31] His mechanical bent also showed itself in the invention of a two-wheeled one-horse carriage (the "Pacing Saddle")[32] and a double-hulled boat.[33]

In 1667 he married Elizabeth, the widow of Sir Maurice Fenton. The marriage was a happy one, and his wife made a favorable impression upon his circle of scientific friends.[34] Their sons Charles (b. 1672) and Henry (b. 1675) and daughter Anne (b. 1673) all survived their father although three other siblings died in infancy.[35] The family lived alternately on Petty's estates in Ireland and England, as he divided his time between scientific and commercial pursuits and the defense of his numerous lawsuits. He supervised the farming of those of his lands so suited and ran mines, timber works, quarries, and fisheries on those that were not.[36] Most of his works were never published, and a few of the published pieces only came out posthumously. The most important of these works are the *Treatise of Taxes* (1662), *The Political Anatomy of Ireland* (published 1691, but written 1672), and the *Political Arithmetick* (published 1690, but written 1676).

An individual's work may be marred by a disorganized presentation and yet still be guided by a consistent method and purpose. Of his method Petty was quite proud; it appears as a manifesto in his *Political Arithmetick:*

> The Method I take to do this, is not yet very usual; for instead of using only comparative and superlative Words, and intellectual Arguments, I have taken the cource (as a Specimen of the Political Arithmetick I have long aimed at) to express my self in Terms of *Number, Weight,* or *Measure;* to use only Arguments of Sense, and to consider only such Causes, as have visible Foundations in Nature; leaving those that depend upon the mutable Minds, Opinions, Appetites, and Passions of particular Men, to the Consideration of others.[37]

Petty's ability as a statistician has been severely criticized: he was neither as sensitive to the varying reliability of his sources nor to the need for "some *agreed* classificatory schema" as was his contemporary John Graunt;[38] his premises and his conclusions were arithmetically inconsistent; he would make up data to suit his conclusions;[39] his data were not data at all but mere illustrations that did not even prove their respective arguments;[40] and he never used any statistical method more sophisticated than an average.[41] All of the above accusations are true, but not all of them are relevant. Petty's idea of "Political Arithmetick" was not really the same as the science we call "statistics." Petty did *use* averages to prove there were "quantifiable regularities in aggregate behaviors" that could "be empirically discovered" even where one could not "know precisely how each individual event" was "caused."[42] When he addressed the question of the "Rebuilding of London" after the fire, he insisted that "An enumeration of what things must bee knowne" had to be worked up "before any Modell can bee made."[43] But he was more interested in getting the government to act on the truths he believed were embedded in those statistical regularities than he was in creating a methodology for their compiling.

Applying his new method of "Political Arithmetick" to what he called "Political Oeconomies,"[44] he believed it produced a "Political Anatomy" of that realm. The term *political economy* was not original to Petty; Antoine de Montchrétien had used it in his *Traité d'économie politique,* published in 1616. *Political anatomy* was a coinage of James Harrington. In his *Art of Lawgiving* (1659), Harrington claimed that

> Certain it is that the delivery of a model of government (which either must be of none effect, or embrace all those muscles, nerves, arteries and bones, which are necessary unto any function of a well-ordered commonwealth) is no less than political anatomy.[45]

Harrington's source for the model (not the term) was Harvey.[46] In an anatomy lecture delivered in Dublin in 1676, Petty left no doubt his model was the body as productive engine:

> Gentlemen, the work of this day is to open the way into the practice of Anatomy and into the knowledge of Man's body. In the first place, to excite men into the admiration of God its Creator; and in the next place to cure and ease the cares and distemper that befall it; and lastly to shew proud man that his most misterious and complicated engenry is nothing to the compounded & decompounded misteryes in the fabrick of man. . . . all other their mechanicks whatsoever, are no more compared to the fabrick of an animall then putting to sticks a crost is to a loome, a clock, or a ship under sail.[47]

With its identification of money with either vital spirits or nutritive blood, the organic analogy had always contained the possibility of an alternate economic model to trade balance theory. In its narrowest sense, it led to questions about the quantity of money in circulation. William Harvey's theory was not necessary for this: Malynes had worked out a rough concept based on Galen's ideas of circulation. But Harvey's demonstration of both the existence and the mechanics of a single circulation was the basis for three important changes: (1) through its focus on the *mechanics* of circulation, it broadened the velocity question to one of how money actually moved through an economy; (2) the concept of *efficiency* opened up the question of which paths that money took through an economy would prove most advantageous to it; (3) this led to a new appraisal of what *advantageous* meant.

Cash on Hand: Volume, Velocity, and Banks

Sir William Petty's initial premise was that there was "a certain measure, and proportion of money requisite to drive the trade of a Nation, more or less than which would prejudice the same."[48] His means of illustrating that premise reveals the same medical source we have seen in the work of Malynes, Misselden, and Mun:

> Money is but the Fat of the Body-politick, whereof too much doth as often hinder its Agility, as too little makes it sick. 'Tis true, that as Fat lubricates the motion of the Muscles, feeds in want of Victuals, fills up uneven Cavitites, and beautifies the Body, so doth Money in the State quicken its Action, feeds from abroad in time of Dearth at Home; even accounts by reason of its divisibility, and beautifies the whole, altho more especially the particular persons that have it in plenty.[49]

But even this single premise—making money supply proportionate to the total trade of a nation—represents a shift from the views of Mun, Malynes, and Misselden. Petty has reversed the priority of the terms, making trade the independent and money supply the dependent variable in this equation, thus introducing the T (total transactions) of Fisher's formulation of quantity theory (money × velocity = price level × total transactions).[50]

What mediated between trade and money supply was a second innovation: the formal introduction of the concept of velocity:[51]

> the Expence [of the nation] being 40 Millions, if the revolutions were in such short Circles, *viz.* Weekly, as happens among poorer artizans and labourers, who receive and pay every *Saturday,* then 40/52 parts of 1 Million of Money would answer those ends: But if the Circles be quarterly, according to our Custom of paying rent, and gathering Taxes, then 10 Millions were requisite. Wherefore supposing payments in general to be of a mixed Circle between One week and 13. then add 10 Millions to 40/52, the half of which will be 5 1/2, so as if we have 5 ½ Millions we have enough.[52]
>
> Now as the proportion of the number of Farthings requisite in comerse is to be taken from the number of people, the frequency of their exchanges; as also, and principally from the value of the smallest silver pieces of money; so in like manner, the proportion of money requisite to our Trade, is to be likewise taken from the frequency of commutations, and from the bigness of the payments, that are by Law or Custome usually made otherwise.[53]

Petty was building his concept of Velocity not only from generalized concepts of trade, but equally from transactions whose frequencies were fixed by law or custom: how often different portions of the population received their wages and paid their rent and taxes. With his usual confidence, he estimated England's land rents at 8 million per annum (requiring 4 million to be settled semiannually), housing rents at 4 million per annum (requiring 1 million to be settled quarterly), and the mean living expenses at 7 pounds per annum for a population of 6 million (requiring 800,000 for weekly settlement): all producing the grand total of 5.8 million.[54] Accurate or not, Petty's methods reveal his grounding in and sensitivity to the externally determined rhythms of seventeenth-century economic life.

To keep the money supply in proportion to the overall volume of transactions, he advocated a kind of bank that pushed the concept of *money* well beyond that of *coin:*

> where there are Registers of Lands whereby the just value of each mans interest in them, may be well known; and where there are Depositories of the τὰ χρῆσα, as of Metals, Cloth, Linnen, Leather, and other Usefuls; and where there are Banks of money also, there less money is necessary to drive the Trade. For if all the greatest payments be made in Lands, and the other perhaps down to ten pound, or twenty pounds be made by credit in Lombards or Money-Banks: It follows, that there needs onely money to pay sums less than those aforementioned.[55]

Such land registries and public banks were much in the thoughts of those who looked to the prosperity of the United Provinces as a model for England. One can find them praised by Sir William Temple and Josiah Child.[56] Samuel Hartlib had proposed using mortgages on lands to raise "Credit in Banks" back in 1653 in response to a proposal by one William Potter to use the paper obligations created in trade to fund a national bank.[57] A land bank, however, was an idea whose time had not yet come; John Asgill and Dr. Nicholas Barbon would found the first land bank in England in 1695.[58]

Petty approved of conventional banks as well, because they would "almost double the Effect of our coined Money."[59] This was circulation as nourishment. Money in banks was *superlucration* (savings)—funds available for investment—but coin hoards or collections of plate by themselves were not:

> the most thriving Men keep little or no Money by them, but turn and wind it into various Commodities to their great Profit, so may the whole Nation also; which is but many particular Men united.[60]

Banks, of course, charged interest, which, to Petty, was simply an inducement to investment: a "Reward for forbearing the use of your own

Money for a Term of Time agreed upon, whatsoever need your self may have of it in the mean while" as bills of exchange were "Local Interest, or a Reward given for having your Money at such a Place where you most need the use of it."[61] Because merchants and manufacturers paid interest,[62] he believed lower rates were generally more beneficial to trade, but such rates were no more attainable by law than was "industry" or "parsimony"; he held the interest rate to be dependent on the total volume of trade (domestic and foreign) as well as the price of land (a competing source of investment funds) rather than the other way around because the amount of money out at loan was so much smaller than the amounts in land and trade.[63] This reversal of the earlier perspective that trade volume depended upon interest rates paralleled Petty's rejection of trade volume as dependent upon money supply, even if it was not yet a construction of a systematically interactive relationship. At the very least, it was interest considered as a mechanical rather than as a moral phenomenon.

Money into and out of investments with banks as agents of circulation was one major consideration in mapping an economy's circulatory system. Money going to and from the government in the form of taxes and government spending seemed to Petty to be the second, in the form of a public version of the private circulation managed by banks. But here his arguments seemed to be in direct opposition to his compatriot's views: everyone knew all taxes did was take money *out* of an economy.

Advantageous Paths: the Representation of Taxation

Taxation proved to be the bête noire of seventeenth-century England. It was always a political as well as an economic issue. Parliament felt it could not trust Charles I with funds for an army that might be turned on it after being used to subdue Ireland, since he had already betrayed the constitution by his extraparliamentary imposition of *ship money*. But the heart of the matter was the ever-increasing tax bill. Oliver Cromwell found himself as hard pressed as had Charles I. Addressing Parliament on April 21, 1657, Cromwell called it a decision "exceedingly past my understanding" that his Parliament would vote him an annual revenue of £1.3 million when the "present charge of the forces both by sea and land, including the government," was already up to £2,426,989.[64] The innovations introduced by the Restored Monarchy did little to close the gap. Charles II's ministers abandoned the system of farming out taxes in favor of direct collection for the customs (in 1671), the excise (in 1673), and the hearth tax (in 1674), but despite the resulting boost in revenue and the novel use of "credit Orders repayable in course," there was nothing for it but a "Stop of the Exchequer" on January 5, 1672.[65] It would seem that no matter who ran the government and no matter what the money was to be used for, the English just did not like to pay taxes.

Though the English aristocracy, unlike the French nobility, was not exempt from taxation, it did not pay its way. Contemporary analysis of the data available for the period from 1665 through 1685 shows that about 26.5 percent of the government's tax revenue came from excises and stamps on domestic production and services, 32.4 percent from customs duties on retained imports, and only 41.2 percent in direct taxes tied to wealth or income.[66] Though some of the indirect tax burden was borne by purchasers of luxury goods, poorer groups bore a decidedly disproportionate share of the burden of government. This disparity was often remarked upon in the contemporary literature. One "William Wither, Gent." went so far as to suggest a formula to remedy the problem in 1660:

> If a man having but ten pounds *per annum*, pay ten pence, another having twenty pounds *per annum*, payes twenty pence; both unjust and oppressive. . . . So after this just and golden Rule of three, If one thousand pound may pay one hundred, two thousand pound may as well, must, and ought in all justice, equity, and right pay three hundred pounds *per annum*.[67]

William Petty was certainly concerned that the burden of taxation be spread more evenly throughout the society as a whole. He claimed the current poll tax hit "rich single persons at the lowest rate" while the working poor with the largest families paid most of all.[68] Hearth taxes were no fairer. Petty well understood that it was "more easie for a Gentleman of a thousand pound *per annum* to pay for an hundred chimneys . . . then for Labourers to pay for two."[69] To remedy this, Petty conceived of a tax that was closer to being a graduated income tax than a true poll, with graduated brackets and deductions for "teeming" wives and dependant children.[70] Taxation that did not unduly burden any segment of the population would give no grounds for renewed civil discord.[71]

As to tariffs, he held that native goods should generally be exported free of duty while imports to be consumed at home (and not reexported) bore the brunt of such taxes. Similarly, bullion brought in to be coined should be free of duty (as the coins would be used in future trade), while the tax burden fell on bullion imported for plate. Also manufactured goods should only be taxed once, in their final state, rather than adding on to the final purchase price at each stage of the manufacture.[72] The general thrust of these measures would make the tax burden proportionate to income (taxing necessities less and luxuries more) while keeping it from impeding the sale of English goods abroad. Petty never abandoned the old idea of striving for a positive trade balance.

But, if efficient taxation was equitable taxation, Petty was also concerned that it be equitable not only with respect to an individual's ability to pay but also with respect to the various components of the nation's productive resources. This involved him in the problem of how much any given resource—such as land or labor—contributed to the national wealth.

Sir William Petty was quite knowledgeable about cost accounting. In an unpublished memorandum, he worked from a summary stating that the price of merchandise subsisted of "the naturall material," the "manufacture to the state of use," transportation costs, and taxes and tariffs to a list of factors under these heads sophisticated enough to include such indirect costs as shop-rent, "scot and lott" (a tax), "fraud and error in weights," losses from "Buying too much, too little, and unseasonably," and reduction of costs from by-product income.[73] He also knew interest affected the cost of goods, though his general approach to it was monetary.[74] But it was the first two factors—raw materials and labor—that he considered the key to the problem, the *value* that underlay the eventual *price*. In fact, he believed that making "a *Par* and *Equation* between Lands and Labour, so as to express the Value of any thing by either alone" was "the most important Consideration in Political Oeconomies."[75]

But making such a par entailed a problem of commensurability[76] as he well knew:

> all things ought to be valued by two natural Denominations, which is Land and Labour; that is, we ought to say, a Ship or garment is worth such a measure of Land, with such another measure of Labour; for as much as both Ships and garments were the creatures of Lands and mens Labours thereupon: This being true, we should be glad to finde out a natural Par between Land and Labour, so as we might express the value by either of them alone as well or better then by both, and reduce one into the other as easily and certainly as we reduce pence into pounds.[77]

If a common denominator could be found, it would have to be expressed in monetary terms:

> [The] common denominaction is Mony for if 40 acres of land are worth 10*l* p[er] an[num] & yt One man can Earne 10*l* p[er] an[num], Then Money is ye Commn denominator by which ye Par is made.[78]

But a true par involved an amount of money equivalent to their *intrinsic* values and not to *variable* prices set by the "fancies and opinions and errors" of particular men.[79] And Petty wanted such a par so that land and labor could be taxed according to their true contributions to the national wealth.

His attempt to find it is laid out in two paragraphs in his *Treatise of Taxes* (1662) that have become the most debated passages in all of his work, as economists and historians have tried to decide if Petty was working toward a labor theory of value (Marx and Routh), a land-labor theory (Spiegel), a land theory anticipating Physiocratic thought (Aspromourgos, Brems, and McNally), or a piece of nonsense (Schumpeter).[80] The two passages are:

> Suppose a man could with his own hands plant a certain scope of Land with Corn, that is, could Digg, or Plough, Harrow, Weed, Reap, Carry home, Thresh, and Winnow so much as the Husbandry of this Land requires; and had withal Seed wherewith to sowe the same. I say, that when his man hath subducted his seed out of the proceed of this Harvest, and also, what hath himself both eaten and given to others in exchange for Clothes, and other Natural necessaries; that the remainder of the Corn is the natural and true Rent of the Land for that year; and the *medium* of seven years, or rather of so many years as makes up the Cycle, within which Dearths and Plenties make their revolution, doth give the ordinary Rent of the Land in Corn.[81]
> But a further, though collaterall question may be, how much English money is this Corn or Rent worth? I answer, so much as the money, which another single man can save, within the same time, over and above his expence, if he imployed himself wholly to produce and make it; *viz.* Let another man go travel into a Countrey where is Silver, there Dig it, Refine it, bring it to the same place were the other man planted his Corn; Coyne it, &c. The same person, all the while of his working for Silver, gathering also food for his necessary livelihood, and procuring himself covering, &c. I say, the Silver of the one, must be esteemed of equal value with the Corn of the other; the one being perhaps twenty Ounces and the other twenty Bushels. From whence it follows, that the price of a Bushel of this Corn to be an Ounce of Silver.[82]

There are a number of logical and methodological problems in this example: what was effect on the net yield (and hence on the final equivalence) of the different prices of mining or farm land, or of the labor employed therein, or even of exchanging the goods before that par was set? Petty addressed some of these problems better than he did others. He certainly knew that skill level affected salary while location and suitability affected rent,[83] but he placed his faith in averages:

> the days food of an adult Man, at a Medium, and not the days labour, is the common measure of Value, and seems to be as regular and constant as the value of fine Silver. . . . [That] some Men will eat more than others, is not material, since by a days food we understand 1/100 part of what 100 of all Sorts and Sizes will eat, so as to Live, Labour, and Generate.[84]

The argument's logical problems resolve themselves into a question of intent, which, in Petty's case, was not primarily analytical. The ultimate purpose of the exercise was to reach an equitable taxation policy, so that if it turned out that *land* was responsible for three-eighths of an item's value and *labor* for five-eighths, they should be taxed accordingly.[85] Rather than an absolute par, he assumed different proportions between the two would arise in different countries, and hence their taxes should be differently apportioned as well.[86]

As a theory, Petty's par meant to establish relationships far beyond those of silver to corn. Petty thought he could work out similar equivalencies "between drudging Labour, and Favour, Acquaintance, Interest, Friends, Eloquence, Reputation, Power, Authority, &c."[87] He was not aiming so much at an economist's theory of value as at a scientific reorganization of society.

With his eye on an economy's circulatory system, however, Petty realized that governments taxed in order to spend, and so they did not permanently withdraw money from an economy so much as they redistributed it:

> Men repine much, if they think the money leavyed will be expended on Entertainments, magnificent Shews, triumphal Arches, &c. To which I answer, that the same is a refunding of the said moneys to the Tradesmen who work upon those things; which Trades though they seem vain and onely of ornament, yet they refund presently to the most useful; namely, to Brewers, Bakers, Taylours, Shoemakers, &c.[88]

Redistribution is something of a charged word in the twentieth century, and in the leveling sense it is only contingently used for Petty's plans. He did believe excessive inequality could lead to civil war,[89] and his words for government spending ("deliver" and "transfer") speak to a redistributive as well as a simply circulative meaning.[90] But Petty's modified poll tax (despite its progressive elements) was by no means intended to effect any radical reallocation of the social surplus. His insistence on keeping wages at a subsistence level would also have guaranteed that such a reallocation never occurred.[91] Recirculative is the better word for Petty's primary insight here: taxation acted as a circulatory system for the economy.[92]

If government spending was part of such a circulatory system, then how the government spent was as important as how they taxed. While (as seen above) almost any kind of government spending was better for an economy than no spending at all, a spending pattern that favored durable goods was better than one that favored consumables, and one that favored investment was even better:

> As for example, suppose that Money by way of *Tax*, be taken from one who spendeth the same in superfluous eating and drinking; and deliv-

ered to another who employeth the same, in improving of *Land*, in *Fishing*, in working of *Mines*, in *Manufacture, &c.* It is manifest that such Tax is an advantage to the State whereof the said different Persons are Members: Nay, if Money be taken from him, who spendeth the same as aforesaid upon *eating* and *drinking*, or any other perishing Commodity; and the same transferr'd to one that bestoweth it on *Cloaths;* I say, that even in this case, the Commonwealth hath some little advantage; because *Cloaths* do not altogether perish so soon as *Meats* and *Drinks:* But if the same be spent in *Furniture of Houses*, the advantage is yet a little more; if in *Building of Houses*, yet more; if in improving of *Lands;* working of *Mines, Fishing, &c.* yet more.[93]

But before we can declare Petty an expert on the multiplier effects of investment and government spending, we have to ask why he pressed his argument to conclude that favoring manufacture intended for export ("bringing *Gold* and *Silver* into the Country") over manufacture intended for domestic use brought the best "advantage" of all.[94] William Petty did not realize that the circulatory model he was creating did not have to be subordinated to the trade balance model he inherited.

His very definitions of wealth (for he had more than one) broadcast his belief that his new insights did not really contradict the more traditional ones. His primary (and most innovative) emphasis was on goods and the ability to create them:

> [It is a mistake to think] that the greatness and glory of a Prince lyeth rather in the extent of his Territory, then in the number, art, and industry of his people, well united and governed.[95]
> the blood and nutritive juyces of the Body Politick, namely, the prodyct of Husbandry and Manufacture.[96]
> Labour is the Father and active principle of Wealth, as Lands are the Mother.[97]

The existing concept of national wealth depended on the accumulation of bullion (coined or not). The trade balance model for accumulating it was expressed in the terminology of double-entry bookkeeping. In 1665, Petty made a calculation of the wealth of England and Wales in which his estimate of a £40 million per annum expense of feeding, clothing, and housing the presumed population of £6 million was added to the total of several items valued at current market price (land at £144 million, houses at £30million, cattle at £36 million, ships at £3 million, and plate and furniture at £31 million), and coined gold and silver at its face value of £6 million, for a grand total of £250 million.[98] He was modifying the bookkeeping model to make it serve an entirely new definition of national wealth.

In Petty's definition every thing that a nation produced (whether for its own use or for sale abroad) and every resource (whether in the form of land, labor, or raw materials and whether of domestic or foreign origin) used by a nation in producing those goods was added to a national balance sheet or net worth statement. The model for the national was still the personal, but the new way of looking at the body, the new way of seeing the positive results (health and growth) devolving from the inner working of that body, meant that new items would be included in any definition of national wealth. This new emphasis on the internal health of the body politic did not necessarily entail an absolute switch from an organic to an aggregate orientation, however. The people in Petty's national net worth statement were *assets,* that is to say, *possessions,* of the primary whole. We will see this later on in the way Petty presumed that the government of that nation would be the ultimate arbiter of resource allocation (including where people might live and for what professions they might train) for the good of the whole. But before we look into Petty's proposals for resource reallocation, we need to spend some time considering the position of gold and silver in Petty's definition of wealth.

He could consider wealth in its most abstract sense as purchasing power:

> A man is actually and truely rich according to what he eateth, drinketh, weareth, or any other way really and actually enjoyeth.[99]

And when he did so, he was apt to stress that wealth as purchasing power was a relative rather than an absolute measure:

> Let the Tax be never so great, if it be proportionable unto all, then no man suffers the loss of any Riches by it. For men (as we said but now) if the Estates of them all were either halfed or doubled, would in both cases remain equally rich. For they would each man have his former estate, dignity and degree.[100]

But he most often gave gold and silver a highly privileged position in his list of assets, because they were not only "not perishable," but were

> esteemed for Wealth at all times, and everywhere: Whereas other Commodities which are perishable, or whose value depends upon the Fashion; or which are contingently scarce and plentiful, are wealth, but *pro hinc & nunc,* as shall be elsewhere said.[101]

Although he did recognize other variables in their market price:

> silver itselfe rises and falls not onely upon difference of Time & place upon Exchange and Interest, but also in itselfe: *viz:* as workmen have more or lesse reason to bestow labour more or lesse upon it.[102]

He still valued them as less mutable in price. He was looking for the most unchangeable store of value he could find. Because he did not think of gold and silver as the sole forms of wealth, Petty never made foreign trade (and a positive trade balance) the only peaceful means of a nation's acquiring wealth, but he did favor a positive trade balance both because of the unique qualities of bullion and because a nation's relative share of the world's trade was a measure of its relative wealth in the same fashion as an individual's wealth (as purchasing power) was relative to that of other individuals within the larger society.[103] More important for understanding how he thought his "Political Anatomy" (or, National Accounting) fused with the trade balance model were his concepts of what was and was not productive economic activity.

Maximizing "Wealth"

A better-run nation would be a wealthier nation, and, if "hands and lands" were the main contributors to value (read *wealth*), then wealth was maximized through increasing the productivity of those hands and those lands. This entailed several elements: (1) making the lands and hands more productive, (2) increasing the size of the labor force, (3) educating that labor force, and (4) employing it most efficiently.

Productivity. The tide of agricultural manuals produced in the first half of the seventeenth century swelled to incredible proportions in the second. The Netherlands were looked to for their agricultural expertise as much as for their commercial skills. Treatises like Sir Richard Weston's *Discourse of Husbandrie used in Brabant and Flanders* (1650), with its advice for crop rotation, the use of turnips and clover grass to restore fertility to lands that would otherwise have to lie fallow, and calculation of profits to be reaped even unto the fifth year from such changes, were everywhere.[104] Agricultural improvement was a major concern of Samuel Hartlib, who advocated scientific exploration of "the true causes of fertility," reclamation of wastelands, and even politically charged enclosure as ways to improve yield.[105]

Far from being unaware of the millenarian purpose of such efforts, midcentury works tended to trumpet them. John Wilkins (1614–1672), not yet Bishop of Chester when he published his *Mathematical Magick* in 1648, understood "all those inventions"—agricultural and industrial—to be methods "whereby men do naturally attempt to restore themselves from the first general curse inflicted upon their labours" and gave them high praise for it.[106]

An age increasingly fixated on "works" as evidence of right theory and method in the secular sphere and of justification in the divine could hardly

avoid looking upon economic improvement as a holy task, and perhaps it
even began to impute some of God's infinite nature to the possibilities of
human science. Hartlib supposed

> that as God is infinite, and men are infinite by propagation, so the fruits
> of the Earth for their Food, and cloathing are infinite, if men will con-
> tent to put to their helping hands to this commendable Design.[107]

The finite world view that prevailed at the beginning of the century was
under siege.

Sir William Petty was not insensitive to the economic possibilities of
agricultural improvement. He especially favored it for countries such as Ireland that he considered extremely underpopulated. He knew that

> bad Land may be improved and made good; Bog may by draining be
> made Meadow; Heath-land may (as in Flanders) be made to bear Flax
> and Clover-grass, so as to advance in value from one to an Hundred . . .
> [for] one Man by Art may do as much work, as many without it.[108]

But, unlike many of his contemporaries, he looked to improvements in the
productivity of manufacturing to bring in the new golden age.

Long before Adam Smith explored the making of straight pins,
William Petty knew how division of labor creates wealth by increasing productivity:

> as Cloth must be cheaper made, when one Cards, another Spins, another
> Weaves, another Draws, another Dresses, another Presses and Packs;
> than when all the Operations above-mentioned, were clumsily per-
> formed by the same hand.[109]
> In the making of a *Watch,* If one Man shall make the *Wheels,* another the
> *Spring,* another shall Engrave the *Dial-Plate,* and another shall make the
> *Cases,* then the *Watch* will be better and cheaper, than if the whole Work
> be put upon any one Man.[110]

In fact, Petty had firsthand experience in such productive gain. He had
split the labor of his Irish survey into that which could be efficiently done
by unskilled soldiers and that which required professional attention, and he
set up workshops dividing production along modern lines to make the less
complex instruments on-site, boasting of the contribution his methods
made to his early completion of the task.[111] He was all in favor of increasing
that advantage through mechanization, as "a [wind]mill made by one man
in half a year, will do as much Labor, as four Men for Five Years together.[112]
But, as will be seen in Petty's plans for that labor force, the market was the
last agent he would trust to maximize this wealth.

Hands for lands. An increasing awareness of labor's role in producing wealth was behind the pamphlets supporting immigration that paralleled those supporting agricultural improvement. Samuel Fortrey pushed for it, in typical fashion, because "People and plenty are commonly the begetters the one of the other, if rightly ordered."[113] But Petty was the first to try to understand how this occurred.

Petty believed that labor's proportion of the value created when hands and lands met was actually increasing in relation to that of land:

> It is manifest that this accumulating of operations & Labor and art upon the first and most simple product of the Earth, doth diminish the value of the Land. That is, makes it to beare a far less proportion to the labor bestowed upon it than formerly, when raw wheate or wheate onely boyld or parched did satisfy men's appetites.[114]

On this basis alone he considered it a more efficient expenditure of effort to work on population rather than on crop rotation. The ultimate value of land, in Petty's terms, was the number of people it could feed: not to populate it with that maximum number of people was to waste it. According to Petty,

> There are in England and Wales about 30 million of acres, which being well improved, would feed 10 million of eaters; whereas there now wants about 1/3 of that number, and consequently there is already too much land. . . . Wherefore a designe of multiplying of people ought to preced all designs of multiply land [adding to its farm or grazing land through enclosure].[115]

Petty believed England's population was in a period of decline,[116] leading him to explore all sorts of schemes for reinvigorating the birthrate, such as fining married couples who did not produce at least one child every three years, and allowing for the easy dissolution of new marriages that did not produce a pregnancy within the first six months.[117] He worried, as well, over the depopulating effect of colonial emigration, though he thought incorrigible criminals might be sent to the Americas as their labor could never be harnessed to England's advantage.[118] Strictly speaking, Petty assumed a unidirectional relationship between population and wealth (population affected wealth, but there was no consideration of the reverse), making population an exogenous variable in his economic calculations.[119]

But whenever he thought of this population, it was as producers rather than as consumers. Petty favored restraint of wages. He believed the state

> should allow the Labourer but just wherewithal to live; for it you allow double; then he works but half so much as he could have done, and otherwise would; which is a loss to the Publick of the fruit of so much labour.[120]

If higher wages translated into increased spending, less would be left to export, bringing in less bullion, that most durable form of wealth. Nor would he trust the marketplace to regulate wages because he believed that an increase of population would have a positive impact on wages (unless the government stepped in to maintain the lower wage).[121]

Calculations of people as consumers were much rarer in Petty's work than his consideration of people as producers.[122] In his calculation of the population's net worth, the unseen starting point was the value of the goods they produced:

> the Expence of 6 millions of People being estimated as aforesaid at 40 million per annum, it follows that the Labour of the said People is worth 25 millions per annum. Which at twenty years Purchase (amounting to 500 millions) is the value of the People.[123]

The 25 million in question resulted from subtracting the expense of maintaining the labor force (40 million) from the value of the goods it produced (65+ million, calculated elsewhere). As 20 years' purchase (20 times its expected yearly rental income) was a common practice for land, it seemed to Petty a good rule of thumb for a worker's productivity. His abatement of poll taxes for the elderly, infants, and "teeming women" was based, after all, on their relative inability to produce. He favored fines and forced labor over corporal and even capital punishment for criminal offenders because the maimed and the dead did not produce.[124] This was Statistical Man, but Statistical Man as a producer, not as a consumer.[125] Everywhere one looks in his thought, production dominates: *supply* dominates.

Educating the labor force. Increasing the work force would accomplish little unless it was suitably trained. While Bacon had written on the importance of the *Advancement of Learning,* he had concerned himself primarily with a reform of the subject matter and method. The main institutional influence on the Hartlib Circle was probably John Amos Comenius (1592–1670),[126] a Czech Moravian minister advocating a *Pansophical* universal education of both sexes, who visited Hartlib in 1641. Hartlib and his associates produced a number of treatises urging the creation of a multitiered system to make the poor properly industrious while training the nobler classes to rule scientifically advanced states:

> the young shall have that benefit to be taught to write and reed a part of every day, besides doe some work to helpe relive them. . . . In case any should be stubborne, and will not take paines nor live orderly and peaceably, that then they be separated and sent to the house of correction, there to remaine in hard work, and hard lodging, till he or she promise amendment.[127]

[Everyone should be able] to reade distinctly and write truely and legi-
bly in his own mother tongue . . . to reckon things by number, and measure them by their weight and dimensions of breadth and length and
height and depth . . . know the summarie historie of Gods works . . .
[while those intended to] discharge some Publick Trust [should learn
such "Noble" arts as] Medicine . . . Natural Philosophy . . . Mathemat-
icks . . . Astronomie . . . Art of the Chymist, of the Apothecarie and of
the Chirurgion . . . [and] the Science of Lawes. . . .[128]

In Petty's *Advice of W.P. to Mr. Samuel Hartlib for The Advancement of
some particular parts of Learning,* we can see the basic Hartlib Circle plan for
universal primary/secondary school education and mechanical training
combined with a workhouse joined to the Baconian idea of a central scientific institution through the medium of a "Gymnasium Mechanicum"
that was to function as university, zoo, botanical gardens, natural history
museum, and experimental laboratory. All of which was to produce a
nation of healthy, industrious workers led by sympathetic leaders and free
of excessive numbers of lawyers, quacks, and unworthy preachers:

> That there be instituted *Ergastula Literaria,* Literary work-houses where
> Children may be taught as well to doe something towards their living, as
> to Read and Write. . . . That all Children of above seven yeares old may
> be presented to this kind of Education, none being to be excluded by
> reason of the poverty and unability of their Parents, for hereby it hath
> come to passe, that many are now holding the Plough, which might have
> beene made fit to steere the State. . . . That all children, though of the
> highest ranke, be taught some gentile Manufacture in their minority . . .
> [to] keep them from worse occasions of spending their time and
> estates.[129]
> In the next place for the Advancement of all Mechanical Arts and Man-
> ufactures, we wish that there were erected a Gymnasium Mechanicum
> or a College of Trades-men . . . wherein we would that one at least of
> every trade . . . might be allowed therein, a handsom dwelling Rent free.
> . . . Here would be the best and most effectual meanes, for writing a His-
> tory of Trades in perfection and exactnesse.[130]

Petty's mentors felt gentle birth was a necessary qualification for entry
into the upper levels of learning, but with his characteristic disdain for
wasted resources, Petty wanted all children taught to their individual limits. With that same concern for efficiency, he made the upper level of his
education system a factory for the finishing of the great Baconian enterprise of the Natural and Trades History of the World.

Labor reallocation. The next step was to make certain that only so
many individuals were trained for each job as were really needed:

> Knowing the fertility and Capacity of our Land, Wee can tell whether it
> hath not produced its utmost through the labours of the people. Wee can
> see whether plenty makes them lazey, and remeddy it. In briefe wee can
> find the best wayes & motives to make as many hands as possible to
> work, and that to the best Advantage. Wee can adjust the number of
> Merchants to our Manufacters, Maryners to the Merchants, Carpenters
> to the rate at which wee find Improouvement to bee made, Trades of
> Ornament to the proprietors of the said Superfluityes &c.[131]

A general survey of the country could not only form the basis of a rational
government-run economic policy, but lessen the number of public servants,
and hence rationalize if not reduce outright the revenue needed:

> It shewes what manufactures & Trades can & cannot bee maintained or
> introduced. . . . It serves to adjust the numbers of Justices of the Peace,
> constables, Sheriffs, Bayliffs and other officers; as also what number of
> Priests & Ministers are sufficient for every heterodox party.[132]

The expense of government could be kept down by replacing sine-
cured officers with salaried clerks, parishes could be restructured on the
basis of one minister and assisting curate for every thousand individuals,
physicians and nurses allocated according to the needs shown in the bills of
mortality, the number of merchants determined from data collected on the
state of trade, and the number of lawyers cut by simplifying the laws that
bred them.[133] Merchants were an especial evil, for these

> properly and originally earn nothing from the Publick, being onely a
> kinde of Gamesters, that play with one another for the labours of the
> poor; yielding of themselves no fruit at all, otherwise than as veins and
> arteries, to distribute forth and back the blood and nutritive juyces of the
> Body Politick, namely, the product of Husbandry and Manufacture.[134]

Merchants, retailers, physicians, apothecaries, nurses, surgeons, ministers,
curates, lawyers, professors, and government employees all had one thing in
common: they were providers of services rather than makers of goods.
When Petty calculated the productive power of England, he subtracted service providers as thoroughly as he did infants.[135] In Petty's construction of
an ideal circulatory system, money that changed hands without producing
concrete (and preferably exportable) goods was money diverted from the
economy.

Macpherson characterized seventeenth-century England as a "possessive market society," that is, one in which labor had become a commodity
causing "market relations" to "so shape or permeate all social relations" that
it might "properly be called a market society" and "not merely a market
economy."[136] One would expect that in such a "market society" the supply

of merchants, ministers, or miners would be regulated by the demand for them, that is, by the market. But the sole thrust of all Petty's efforts was to keep the anarchy of those "market relations" at bay. To do this, Petty bombarded the government with suggestions for the compulsory registration not just of births (or christenings), marriages, and deaths (with their causes), but of professions undertaken, changes in land ownership, nonfatal diseases (as a check on the number of positions required in the various medical professions), and religious affiliation (to take care that an adequate supply of ministers was met for each denomination tolerated). He proposed to coordinate the activities of these local offices under the umbrella of a national "Registry of Lands, Commodities, and Inhabitants" and proposed himself for the first Registrar-General.[137]

The scope of Petty's social engineering went far beyond any purely economic concerns. He often considered solving some of the sociopolitical problems of Ireland by relocating 100,000 Irish Catholic families to England and replacing them with 100,000 indigent Protestant families from England:

> This being effected, there will bee in England 11 or 12 English and Non-Papists to one Irish and Papist; and in Ireland there till bee 800m English (or 900 British, reckoning 100m Scots), 350m Irish, in all 1250m soules; vizt: 900m non-papists to 350m papists unarmed. In this care Ireland, will bee most secure against the French and against 100m Invaders of any Nation.[138]

Petty was, in fact, counting on some form of environmental acculturation to remove the causes of English-Irish friction:

> The Manners, Habits, Language, and Customs of the Irish (without Prejudice to Religion) will be transmuted into English, within less than an Age, and all Old Animosities forgotten.[139]

Well, Charles II did say Petty would attempt "impossible things"!

Before the government of England could re-form the nation, that government would itself need re-forming. For this, Petty worked out a grand combination of the executive and legislative branches whose organization chart would resemble nothing so much as a chain of councils: a monarch, a "Cabinet Councill," a "Privy Councill," a "Grand Councill," and a "Common Councill" or legislature (elected on a reformed but still property-based franchise).[140] Its ordained sphere included such hands-on tasks as "Multiplying the people," "Employing the spare Lands," "Lessening the Plague," and "Providing Stock for a forain Trade."[141]

The idea of government by a system of councils charged with expanded economic and educational functions was popular with the "Circle" of men kept in contact by Samuel Hartlib. One of the works Hartlib saw to publication was the *Description of the Famous Kingdome of Macaria* (1641) by Gabriel Plattes, an agricultural expert and mining engineer of sorts who had already published treatises on mining and husbandry. In the fictional kingdom of *Macaria* the "Great Councell" (or Parliament) met only for a brief period each year, the actual government devolving onto five "under Councels": for husbandry, fishing, trade by land, trade by sea, and for "new Plantations."[142] Plattes's "Councell of Trade by Land" was also to see "that there are not too many Tradesmen, nor too few" by manipulating the system of apprenticeship.[143]

Samuel Hartlib wanted

> all the Unlawfull and Unprofitable Ways whereby Men or Women get a livelihood, or spend their time in Idleness, in riot and vanity, are to be taken notice of; that such Employments as foment naughty Superfluities causing Pride and Sin to abound in a Nation, or such persons as live disorderly, and cannot be reduced to any certain Employment, may be banished [from] the Common-wealth, Even as weeds are to be rooted up and cast out of a fruitful garden.[144]

There were a few precedents for government by council government available to seventeenth-century theorists. Spain boasted a dual system of departmental (inquisition, military, finance, etc.) and territorial (Indies, Castile, Aragon, etc.) councils each under their supervisory boards.[145] The French *intendant* system under the control of a great minister such as Richelieu or Mazarin was also there to be copied. Clarendon conceived of a select privy council intervening between king, favorites, and Parliament that would have come perilously close to making the king a figurehead in his own government.[146] Danby and Sunderland also wished to push England down the administrative path of France.

But, for the scientists, the immediate model was not Spain or France, but the work of Sir Francis Bacon who had in his works on government, law reform, and scientific advancement conceived of a hierarchical conciliar (or committee) system applied in parallel fashion to all three arenas.[147] His final synthesis was incarnated in fictional Bensalem, the *New Atlantis*, whose all-embracing hierarchical political and scientific structures complemented each other.[148] The "College of experience" in Plattes's *Macaria* was but a variation of *Salomon's House*, that institution of big, government science found in Bacon's *New Atlantis*.[149]

Julian Martin suggested that "Bacon's insistence that 'knowledge is power'" should "best [be] understood as meaning that knowledge should be harnessed so as to augment the powers of the state."[150] The "should" had a lot to do with Bacon's awareness of the civil dangers posed by sectarian (and Paracelsian) reliers on "inward authority" and "voluntary communities."[151] But it was in the positive sense of the usefulness of knowledge in aiding the state to perform its functions that Bacon's ideas had their greatest impact on Sir William Petty—and it was a major one, affecting outlook as well as detail. Petty's "Political Arithmetick" was intended to improve the welfare of the state as much as the nation, and its chosen method to accomplish this was through the empowerment of the state.

His ultimate aim was a prosperous (because efficient and industrious) utopia with nothing left to chance or the disruptive self-interest that fueled the market, which leaves us with an unresolved paradox. Petty's insights into value, division of labor, and national accounting, stripped of their millenarian social engineering, formed part of the foundation upon which Quesnay, Smith, and Ricardo built classical economics—a narrowing of focus of which he would never have approved. To evaluate Petty as an economist, we have to make him "less" than he was in his terms, if more in ours.

CHAPTER 8

Sir Josiah Child:
What Price Money?

Sir William Petty (1623–1687) and Sir Josiah Child (1630–1699) both came from minor mercantile families. Each, measured by the wealth he left behind, proved to be an excellent businessman. But, whereas Petty pushed himself out of those limited socio-intellectual confines into the ranks of the scientific innovators and the landowning elite, Child stayed closer to home, keeping his ideas and his portfolio trained on East India Company shares. He bought land, of course; most of the merchant magnates did, but that retirement villa had little impact on his economic thought.[1] The difference in their lives tells in their thought. While Petty explored questions of taxes, land, labor, monetary velocity, value added, and the basic nature of wealth, Child remained fixed on the problem of money. He wished to have the legal interest rate lowered from 6 to 4 percent. He argued that lower interest rates created greater prosperity, but refused to consider the reciprocal effect of prosperity on the interest rate because he could not accept that there was a true market in money. He still thought of money as an exogenous variable, as something of independent value. The popularity of his works attests to that of his views.[2]

When Charles I and Parliament raised opposing armies in 1642, the established merchants of London, like the rest of the citizenry, had to choose sides. The members of the older European and East Indies companies tended to favor the cause of Charles I, while the members of the newer colonial companies favored that of Parliament,[3] though Edward Misselden's problems prove the lines could be crossed. The generation that followed Misselden and Mun had a choice to make as well: exile (in the form of service in the great company trading posts abroad) or making their way in Parliamentarian England. Not all perhaps were as assiduous as Child, the former merchant's apprentice, in making his way in that new world. From a minor navy supplier in 1650, he rose steadily to the positions of deputy to the Navy's treasurer at Portsmouth (1653), burgess (1655), mayor's assistant (1656), and mayor (1658) of Portsmouth.[4] Letters from Child or concerning his activities in the State Papers of the Commonwealth present a picture of a man who would have well understood the expression "Cover your ass." He was forever querying the Navy commissioners for explicit authorizations to victual some ship on credit or support some crew whose ship was waiting passage out.[5] He was also very careful with his own pocketbook; faced with an unexpectedly large influx of Spanish prisoners in May 1659, he doled out only 2*p.* worth of coarse bread out of an authorized 4*p.* per man per day maintenance to avoid having to dip into his own funds.[6]

The Restoration might have written *finis* to his budding career, but scorned by the Navy in 1661 and removed from the Portsmouth Corporation by the new regime in 1662, Child cultivated the friendship of Samuel Pepys and his cousin Sir Edward Montagu (afterward Earl of Sandwich) and was well on his way to restoring his fortunes by 1665.[7] He imported timber from New England to sell to the Navy and bought himself a brewery in Southwark to make it possible for him to keep more of the profits from selling the Navy its beer.

Parliamentary investigations into naval affairs after the second Dutch War ended in 1667 led to calls for the replacement of the Navy Board Commissioners. Child's appointment was enthusiastically supported by Buckingham (a "Whig"), but this, and Child's status as "a merchant" set the future James II (then Duke of York and High Admiral) "stoutly" against him.[8] James was eqully fed up with the merchant members (Child amongst them) of the Council of Trade on which the Duke also sat. Some of those merchants, like John Shorter, Thomas Papillon, and John Page, held Presbyterian or Congregationalist sentiments. Shorter and his fellow "Whiggish" Council members Thomas Papillon and John Page had, at various times, been Child's business partners.[9] Child's own religious sentiments seem to have been broadly tolerationist, and his pamphlets even supported Jewish immigration (on economic grounds). But he was as quick as any man of his century to see sectarian skeletons in every closet, going so far in his *New Discourse of Trade* as to suggest that men complained of a shortage of money because they were "uneasie in matters of their Religion."[10]

Papillon and his fellow Council member Benjamin Albin were also directors of the East India Company, and through their goodwill Child began solidifying his connections with that company. The victualing trade also brought him increased profits with the onset of the third Dutch War in 1672. A newly wealthy Child bought up £12,000 of East India Company shares before the end of 1673 and served on its directorial board from then on (with only one single interruption, in 1676, at his Majesty's instigation)[11] until his death in 1699, and as its governor from 1681 to 1690.

Though neither Charles II nor James II cared for Child, Charles, at least, understood the ways of catching flies with honey, and in 1678 Child was raised to the baronetage.[12] And as long as Sir Josiah Child controlled the East India Company, it sailed close to the Tory wind. Come the next revolution, however, Child found himself once again in trouble for his accommodating ways, and a series of attacks by former allies caused him to give up his governorship and gradually retire from the company's active management (though holding on to his directorial seat).[13] When a recoinage was on the table, however, he was still called as a financial expert by the government.[14]

The last word on Child's life should probably be John Evelyn's. His picture of Child's establishment in 1683 reminds us that not all successful seventeenth-century merchants fit Weber's ascetic model, while also revealing the continuing discomfort the traditional upper classes felt at the incursion of mercantile wealth. On March 16, 1683, Evelyn

> went to see Sir Josiah Childs prodigious Cost in planting of Walnut trees, about his seate, & making fish-ponds, for many miles in Circuite, in Epping-forest, in a Cursed & barren spot; as commonly these over growne & suddainly monied men for the most part seate themselves: He from an ordinary Merchants Apprentice, & managements of the E. India Comp: Stock, being arrived to an Estate of (tis said) 200,000 pounds: & lately married his daughter to the Eldest sonn of the Duke of Beaufort, late Marques of Worcester, with 30,000 pounds portion at present, & various expectations: This Merchant, most sordidly avaricious &c.[15]

If Josiah Child was "sordidly avaricious" he was not alone. Holdings as large as his were becoming less and less unusual. In 1675 only 31.6 percent of the shares of East India stock were in the hands of investors holding over £2,000, but by 1691 such investors held over 48.1 percent of the outstanding stock. In fact, by April 1691, over 25 percent of the outstanding stock of the East India Company was in the hands of eight men whose individual holdings were over £10,000 each, and one of these eight was Sir Josiah Child with his £51,150 (7 percent) block.[16] The rate of consolidation was not equally steep across the field of overseas trading companies,[17] but it was becoming a marked feature of the economy. The number of "major" merchants and bankers in London alone had doubled over the first three-quarters of the century, though domestic traders still outnumbered them at the rate of about 4:1.[18] This was more and more the world of "big business," and entry into it involved a far greater capital outlay than the mere £20 to £50 official entry fines: while individual members of the joint-stock companies could get by with £1,000 to start, "fully-fledged" businesses were "capitalized at £5,000."[19]

Greater capitalization requirements meant a greater role for borrowed money in business investment, and this meant greater attention was going to be paid to interest rates. So it is not surprising that Josiah Child's first work was a little treatise entitled *Brief Observations concerning Trade, and Interest of Money* (1668).

In the seventeenth century, interest was almost invariably treated as a monetary phenomenon, but within this tradition there was as yet no consensus on whether interest was properly the "price of money" or a profit *on* money. The idea of money earning money without "effort" was one with which the seventeenth century (albeit hardly uniquely) was both entranced and extremely uncomfortable.

An acceptance of profit in the sense of a wage for work done or value provided was already gaining ground at the beginning of the seventeenth century.[20] In 1612, Roger Fenton had no more trouble with the idea that "the Merchant and Tradesmen [live] upon their adventures, skill, and industrie" than he did with the idea of "the poore laborer [living] upon the sweat of his browes" or "the Husbandman and Grasier [living] upon the increase of the earth."[21] But he drew the line at the idea of borrowed money calving every six months, no matter how often interest advocates raised the claim of necessity. For Fenton,

> Necessitie is lawlesse. If Usurers therefore can put on that coate, it will bee armour of proofe against all proofe by argument; against all statute and law both of God and man. . . . I demand of those tradesmen, who cannot live in their trade without taking up at interest: Is their meaning that they cannot live in that fashion as they doe . . . [or] drive their trades to that height which they doe? . . . It may bee God would not have them carrie so great a saile as they doe.[22]

Seventeenth-century tracts on interest switched back and forth between a moral argument over usury couched in scriptural and patristic citations and a practical argument over the impact of different levels of interest. Both were equally economic debates, and both went beyond the confines of economics per se. In deciding if annuities, trustee's fees, or late charges on *free* loans were usurious, men like Roger Fenton were trying to define *socially* acceptable forms of economic behavior—and from the first, *gain* proved difficult to exclude on any consistent basis. Fenton was willing to grant that selling dearer "for time" might "be free from usurie," but only as long as selling "dearer" in such a case was not the seller's ultimate purpose.[23]

His opponents were quick to recognize the tangles of such arguments. In 1653, Robert Filmer, perhaps the most politically conservative of all the

apologists for divine-right monarchy that the century produced, delivered
the sharpest attack yet on the Aristotelian idea of money as naturally bar-
ren and therefore of gain from it as unnaturally made:

> Dr. Fenton and Dr. Dowman cannot endure to hear that usury should be
> called letting of money. . . . 'Hiring or letting (they say) is of such things
> as are not spent in the use'. . . . [But] Neither is money properly said to
> be spent in the use. . . . at the most it is but said to be spent to him that
> hath made no profitable use of it, in itself it remains unspent and useful
> to others. . . . Things let (say they) must have a fruitful use naturally in
> themselves. . . . [But] What fruitful use hath a house naturally? doth one
> house beget another or bring forth another? is it not an artificial thing,
> as tools, instruments, and furniture? all of which are lawfully let,
> although they have no more fruitful use by nature than money hath.[24]

For Filmer, renting, letting, borrowing, and selling were different
degrees of the same behavior; it was only logical that gain be as acceptable
in the one as in the other:

> letting is but a temporary kind of selling, and selling in effect a perpet-
> ual kind of letting. If such things as are bought this day for ten pound
> may be sold tomorrow for eleven pound. . . . may it not by letting
> increase in a whole year to as much? . . . [else] by this rule all gain of mer-
> chandizing is condemned, which is ordinarily far greater than that of ten
> in the hundred.[25]

Malynes had built a case for international exchange at fixed bullion
pars based on the idea of money as the rule of value. Filmer took the same
argument and made it a justification both for the charging of and government regulation of rates of interest:

> no state or commonwealth can or ever did stand without it [usury], or
> that which in contracts is equivalent to it, since the valuation of the use
> of money is the foundation and rule which govern the valuation of all
> other sorts of bargains.[26]

The state's role as the guarantor of order and the well-being of the
commonwealth made it the logical guardian of this basic foundation, or
"circulation" as even the older models of the body politic would have it, as
can be seen in this anonymous piece from 1625:

> Is not money minted by politicke Princes, out of their owne Bullion to
> bee imployed to the publike good of their publike Common-wealths,
> both in trading for the whole bodies maintenance, as also in Warres for
> the whole bodies defence. How graciously doe they disperse it in favours
> and rewards, that it may runne as charitably from member to member
> . . . throughout those politike bodies, like bloud in the naturall, in the
> veines of trading, for all and every ones maintenance, and retire to those
> royall centres againe, by many just rights for all and every ones defence.[27]

Even those like Filmer who accepted the *idea* of a price for the use of money accepted it in actuality only as regulated "as a point of state or policy."[28] A state-set interest rate was a standard interest rate, a constant that might anchor the universal measure against the shifting tides of the market.

Josiah Child's argument for lowering the statutory 6 percent maximum interest rate to 4 percent immediately (but eventually to 3 percent) does not, at first, seem to have anything to do with the problem of stabilizing value; he seems only to be concerned with the supposed ill effects of the current rate on the English economy and polity. Before attempting to prove, however, that the problem of value does lie at the heart of his argument, it would be wise to summarize that argument as presented in his *Brief Observations concerning Trade, and Interest of Money* (1668).

Child began by putting before the reader fifteen policies pursued by the Dutch that he believed led to a "prodigious increase" in their "domestick and forreign trade":

1. admission of merchants to their "Councils of State and War"
2. an equal division of inheritance instead of primogeniture
3. product quality control less easily perverted than England's "seal" laws
4. monetary rewards to inventors
5. efficient ship design and building
6. "parcimonious and thrifty Living"
7. educating both sexes in business skills to instill "thriftiness and good Husbandry" and facilitate business continuity
8. combining a low customs with a high excise tax
9. systematic welfare and workfare
10. use of public banks
11. religious toleration to increase the immigration of the industrious
12. a special law-merchant legal system
13. the allowance of transference of bills of debt
14. public registration of lands, houses, and liens against them
15. a 3 percent interest rate[29]

This list was not the result of Child's own investigations; he borrowed most of it (without attribution) from Henry Robinson's *Englands Safety in Trades Encrease* (1641) where it appeared as a general policy proposal rather than as Dutch practice.[30] Original or not, it is still indicative of the way in which this century saw the causes and effects of economic activity as deeply embedded in the society's religious, educational, moral, social, legal, sci-

entific or technological, and political fabric. It is also proof of the continuity of seventeenth-century economic thought. Items 3, 6, 7, 12, and 13 had
been of especial concern to Malynes, while 1, 3, 6, 7, 10, 12, and 13 had been
of especial concern to Misselden. It was precisely the power of market-oriented behavior to affect so much of a society's fabric that made it so dangerous.

But, having borrowed the list from Robinson, Child proceeded to
ignore it in order to claim that a low interest rate was not simply one of
many factors but the "*Causa Causans* of all the other causes of the Riches of
that people."[31] As proof he offered (1) the greater prosperity of English
merchants since the previous reductions of interest from 10 to 8 percent in
1624 and from 8 to 6 percent in 1651, (2) the increase in customs revenues
over the same period (above any changes in the rates), (3) an increase in the
price of lands over the same period from eight or ten to twenty years' purchase, and (4) a general correlation throughout Europe between low interest rates and prosperity and, in reverse, between high interest rates and a
general poverty.[32]

Child boasted of a method that consisted of nothing more than discussing the subject with the "most Ingenious men" he knew, reading "all the
Books" on the subject that he could find, and testing in his own mind the
arguments and objections raised in them.[33] He just could not believe "our
Fathers were so stupid" as to give 20 years' purchase for land at 10 percent
interest when "they might double their Money . . . at Interest upon Interest
in seven years,"[34] even though there was adequate evidence that they had
done just that. The price of land stood at 20 years' purchase from 1600 to
1646 despite the drop in the interest rate in 1625 (from 10 to 8 percent),
dropped to 15 years' purchase during the political upheavals of 1646 through
1650 despite a steady statutory rate, rose to 19 years' with the further drop to
6 percent (in 1651), but hovered at only 17 years' from 1665 through 1689
again despite a steady statutory rate.[35] A more serious problem with his
argument was his blithely taking correlation for cause, a logical error his
opponents were quick to deride. Thomas Manly reminded him that

> high interest, where money is scarce, is no more the cause of poverty,
> (though it does attend it commonly), than cheapness of provisions, and
> smallness of wages, (which are frequently found in poor Countries) the
> cause of that poverty; want of good situation, ports, money, and com-
> merce, being the cause thereof.[36]

Pushed, as well, by rebuffs of his assertions on land prices, Child found
himself forced to come up with reasons why land prices had not risen in
proportion to earlier decreases in the interest rate. He came up with some
interesting ideas—the effects of depopulation caused by the return of the

plague, the rebuilding of London after the great fire draining funds that would otherwise have been invested in land, the rise of private banking[37]— but it would have been far more interesting if he had asked himself if these demand variations might have affected the price of money as well as the price of land.

Paired with Child's support for lowering the state-regulated interest rates was his attack on the "Trade of Bankering" as one that "obstructs circulation" because the interest banks paid lured men into keeping their money on deposit with Goldsmiths (the bankers in question here).[38] The "circulation" idea was fast becoming common currency, but it was not always used as an analytical tool. Child was not actually attacking banks but making political points against the goldsmiths who supported laws against the exportation of bullion;[39] they were steadfast opponents of East India Company merchants like Josiah Child who needed bullion to trade for Indian goods.

That Child believed the price of money was a cause of economic prosperity (or its absence) rather than an effect of such prosperity (or its absence) is apparent from the objections he anticipated to his proposals, even if he picked up those from Robinson's work as well.[40] To the objection that lowering the interest rate in England would cause foreign investors (mostly the Dutch) "to call home their Estates," Child replied that the Dutch would never trade a 4 percent gain in England for a mere 3 percent at home, but should they prove so foolish, any resulting depletion of England's money supply could be offset by legalizing the transfer of bills of debt to "supply the defect."[41] To the related objection that local usurers would call in their money to the detriment of gentlemen with mortgaged estates, Child responded that they would not casually trade a "Security they know is good, for another that may be bad," but if so, the gentlemen in question could easily sell off a small portion of their lands to free the rest.[42] If that tells us anything about Child it is only that he knew very little of the lengths to which the landed aristocracy would go to hold on to their estates.[43]

Child had taken lower interest rates as a sufficient cause of an increase in land prices. To the objection that an increase in land prices would set off a chain reaction of successive increases in rents and commodities, depriving the poor of their daily bread, Child asserted that "dear" prices were themselves "an evident demonstration" of increasing prosperity,[44] again substituting correlation for cause. But he really favored higher prices because they would force the poor to greater efforts to obtain them: "in a cheap year they will not work above two days in the week" having no mind to lay away surplus funds to "provide for a hard time."[45] Besides, more work done meant more goods for export. Most seventeenth-century writers assumed that the standard legal restraints would continue to keep wages low, allowing the higher prices to function as an external inducement to work-discipline.[46] But Child immediately proceeded to sweep aside a low-wage argument as "a charitable project and well becoming a usurer,"[47] without explaining how higher prices could produce such a discipline if offset by higher wages.[48] He simply insisted that lowering interest rates would somehow incline the Nation to "Thriftiness and good Husbandry" and away from "Luxury and Prodigality."[49]

The objection that the widows and orphans who lived off the interest earned by their invested estates would suffer from a rate reduction led Child to the issue of the greater versus the lesser good: some pain was acceptable if offset by the overall benefit to the nation. The benefits proposed were considerable: the Crown's revenues would rise from the greater value of land and the greater volume of trade, and his Majesty would also be able to borrow at a cheaper rate; the nobility and gentry would find their wealth enhanced because of the increased prices of and rents for land; artisans and laborers would find more work; farmers would get better prices; and the merchants and traders would have to pay less for their venture capital and, having less ability to purchase estates due to the increased land prices, would be more likely to stay in business (and so train their sons up to it) to England's general prosperity. The only downside was the loss to those who lived off usury, and the bulk of these were not widows and orphans but such as "suck the breasts of industry."[50]

What Josiah Child was careful to avoid in his pamphlet was the issue of whether or not interest rates could be successfully controlled by law or were subject to the play of independent market forces. It is true that in England, the maximum legal rate of interest was set by statute. But there were also market rates. Child himself attested to the government's usually having to give anywhere from two to six points above the statutory rate,[51] while there is ample evidence that the great trading companies could find funds at two to three points below.[52]

The Dutch picture was far more complicated. The Dutch interest rate that Child was quoting was likely that of the return on government bonds, which had fallen to 5 percent in 1640 from a high of 8.33 percent in 1600 and was hovering between 3 and 3.75 percent at the time Child wrote.[53] But the United Provinces was a thoroughly federal government, not the unitary state with which the English were familiar. Not only did the individual provinces retain several sovereign powers, the major cities within those provinces retained a great deal of economic independence. The influence of the mercantile elite was far greater in the Dutch legislature than in the English. Even Holland's state-chartered trading monopolies were far more the result of merchant agitation for military protection than were the state creations of England. The financial climate was so much more advanced that shares in the Dutch companies traded on true exchanges, unlike the restricted and predominantly private transfers of English joint-stock shares.[54] The Exchange Bank of Amsterdam, founded in 1609, was already taking on some of the functions associated with a modern central reserve bank.[55] In fact, the Netherlands was as close to a modern financial market as the seventeenth century got until the founding of the Bank of England, but it was still a seventeenth-century market: taxes were high and regressive, and wages were regulated by municipal governments.[56]

But of much of this Child was largely ignorant at first, believing that though the Dutch had earlier legally restricted interest to 5 or 6 percent, they now "naturally" kept "down the Interest of their money . . . under the rate of what is usually paid in their Neighbouring Countries" making "the artificial Stratagem of a Law" unnecessary in their case.[57] This confused and confusing response was meant by Child to answer the objection that "the lowness of Interest of Money in Holland" was "not the effect of laws, but proceeds only from their abundance thereof."[58] But the use of "naturally" would imply the existence of the very market forces Child sought to deny existed. A more informed Child revised his argument in 1668, claiming only that the Dutch had gradually reduced their interest rates by law to keep them below England's.[59]

Child's efforts were aimed at aiding the passage of a bill before Parliament in 1668 to lower the statutory interest rate from 6 to 4 percent. Child himself gave testimony in 1669 before the Lords' committee on the bill as a representative of the Council of Trade.[60] Opposing him, Thomas Grey claimed interest was "low in Holland because they have much money and little land" and high in Scotland and Ireland because there "the reverse [was] the case."[61] In an economy where the overwhelming majority of loans were mortgages rather than for commercial ventures, this was an astute observation, but it was made in the cause of argument for holding interest rates artificially high by statute. The anonymous *Interest of Money Mistaken* (1) took Child to task for ignoring his own dictum that "nature will have its course" when he claimed that England was "prepared for an abatement of Interest," as this would mean no law was required to bring it down, (2) gave the negative argument that if the lowering of interest by law could by itself enrich a nation, all nations would have tried such a policy and succeeded, and (3) took the price of money as subject to the same law of supply and demand as governed all other goods ("the more money there is, and fewer takers, the lower is the Exchange, and when we have more lenders than borrowers Interest will be low without a law for it").[62]

Child kept up with the arguments of his opponents,[63] but he preferred not to answer them head on. He dismissed them all (and so dismissed the idea of giving serious consideration to equilibrium arguments) with a witticism: "An Egg is the cause of a Hen, and a Hen the cause of an Egg. . . . [Thus] The abatement of Interest causeth an encrease of Wealth, and the encrease of Wealth may cause a further Abatement of Interest";[64] but no sensible man would argue from the wealth to the interest rate rather than the other way round. That was as foolish as tinkering with the silver content of the coin as though merchants would be so stupid as to accept "the name it is called by" over "the intrinsick value of the Money."[65]

Sir Josiah Child may have been fond of citing "the excellent, Sir William Petty's Observation in his late Discourse, concerning Taxes" that "*Res nolunt male Administrare:* Nature must and will have its course,"[66] but the only course that he proposed was a change from one *statutory* rate to another he considered more favorable to his own interests. It was an argument based on practical considerations. A steady price for money was an important consideration in a world of speculative commerce in which merchants were routinely paid several months after deals were struck, and in which goods reached their foreign markets months after the conditions that had made them seem likely ventures had often changed for the worse. In those days, goods were more often dumped on the market below cost in a last-ditch attempt to get some return on them rather than in plots to undermine another nation's production.[67] But, as an argument, the last thing wanted was for nature to run its course.

Unlike Petty, Child was not part of the charmed circles of scientific enthusiasts that evolved into the Royal Society, but he was as shaped by the intellectual context of his day as he was by its material conditions. How it shaped him can be seen both in his efforts (1) to come up with a theoretically sound rejection of balance of trade theory, and (2) to use the work of Thomas Hobbes as a theoretical ground for profit-seeking behavior.

Balance of Trade vs. Economic "Engines"

One of the unintended consequences of the Parliamentary sovereignty that England's seventeenth-century revolutions were building was that while every statute Parliament created added a plank to their "Constitution," none of those planks was, on the face of it, more permanent than any other: any Parliament could repeal what any earlier Parliament had endorsed, thus no battle it fought was ever *necessarily* finished. The fact that, in 1663, Parliament rescinded some of its earlier restrictions on the export of coin and bullion did not mean that it could not reverse itself, and opponents of the East India Company kept up their attacks upon it.

But Josiah Child, like all of the Company's defenders, found himself in need of a new argument on its behalf. "Balance of Trade" was proving to be a two-edged sword, as handy to opponents of their need to export coin and bullion as to their propagandizing for the gains made from the reexports their free-market ways with silver eventually produced.

Rather than take on the conceptual problems of balance of trade theory, Child concentrated on the subsidiary argument of whether the nation should aim for positive balances in specific trades, with specific nations, or in its foreign trade considered as a whole, as well as on the technical problems in calculating any one of these balances. He concluded that though there was "much of truth" in the general theory, practically speaking, numerous "Accidents" and difficulties made it "too doubtful and uncertain as to our general Trade," and especially "fallible and erroneous" in reference to "particular Trades."[68] But his argument here was as evasive as his earlier attacks on market theories of interest. He used Ireland, Virginia, and Barbados as examples of "Countries" with export surpluses that remained poor because their interest rates were high or their profits were drawn off by absentee owners, even though he knew the colonies' situation was not analogous to England's because of England's power to manipulate colonial trade to its advantage.[69] And Child not only knew this was the practice, he supported such controls, claiming that New England was, of all its colonies, "the most prejudicial" to England unless strictly controlled because it traded in the same commodities as England did.[70]

He was not really arguing against the finite worldview upon which trade balance theory was built, but merely against the East India Company being held accountable for any damage it did to that balance. He firmly believed that England should look to overbalance their neighbors in their "National Profit" by their "Foreign Trade," with trade regulated to ensure "that other nations who are in competition with us for the same, may not wrest it from us, but that ours may continue and increase, to the diminution of theirs."[71]

When it came to shoring up England's trade, Child had little to add to the standard proposals of easing immigration, employing the poor, registering lands, allowing for the transfer of bills of debt, and lowering the interest rate, beyond reducing the number of holidays and easing or rescinding restrictions on the number of apprentices a merchant might accept.[72]

It was suggestions like those that gave Child, in some quarters, the reputation of being a laissez-faire pioneer, but abandoning balance of trade did not mean advocating a free market or free trade.[73] In his *Short Addition to the Observations concerning Trade and Interest of Money* (1668), Child had dismissed "the Merchants Objection" to lowering the interest rate (by encouraging trade it would increase the number of traders and hence decrease their individual profits) as valid only "if they prefer their own private Gain to the Common Good."[74] But when it came to increasing freedom of competition in the real world, Child took quite a different position, successfully opposing a 1681 bid to widen the East India Company's stock, a move that would have increased its overall strength to the detriment of the voting power of his block of shares.[75] Merchants in joint-stock companies profited from taking on apprentices, especially when those apprentices were second sons of gentry families who were using apprenticeship to gain the freedom of the trade: they increased investment in the firm but were normally not allowed into its managing ranks.[76] The eventual success of apprentices had a greater effect on the fortunes of the regulated companies with which the East India Company competed (in its reexport ventures), because entry in regulated companies was limited to "mere merchants." Child was supporting a freedom that would eat into his competitor's profits, not into his own. Child never favored letting economic behavior off the legal leash when it threatened his particular interest.

Child's support for eliminating the double taxation on reexported goods was nothing more than self-interest: it would mean a major increase in the profits the East India Company reaped on those reexports. He supported high excise taxes as being effective "sumptuary laws," which did put him in the forefront of those who wished to use economic means (taxes) instead of legal restrictions to create economic effects, but the effect he was looking for was to decrease home consumption of East Indian imports so the company would have a greater reexport stock (and that double profit). To support the repeal of laws against engrossing grain was actually to support restriction of competition, not free trade, by making it easier for large concerns to snap up whole crops before they came to market and gain monopolistic profits on their resale. Support for repeal of laws limiting the number of looms per concern[77] can also be seen as support for big/corporate business at the expense of smaller, independent concerns. While each of these points was technically a decrease in overall trade regulation, they all actually favored consolidation of trade over any real increase in competition.

Child's was a very selective attack. He certainly never supported repealing the controls on England's colonies or doing away with the restrictions of the Navigation Acts even though he felt they were economically harmful. He did not deny that profit was lost privately and publicly by the act's making it impossible for the English to ship goods in the cheapest carriers (usually the Dutch), but he held this was a less important consideration than the boost the act gave to native shipping, that necessary component of the defense of an island nation.[78] As to any inevitable market or political reaction to such English belligerence, Child was certain the king of France's hands were too soiled by the protective impositions on English cloth already in place in France to retaliate further, while the king of Denmark would find it to his economic advantage not to.[79] With almost a century of trade wars to show for such policies, and three in particular with the Dutch (1652–54, 1665–67, and 1672–74) since the passing of the Navigation Acts, there was a certain willed naïveté in this failure to carry through one's own laws of the market.

Child had an alternative theory of wealth at his fingertips that could have been an effective weapon against the balance of trade theory—the creation of wealth through labor—but he did not or could not use it. Child had read deeply enough in Petty's works to borrow the idea of the nation as a productive engine, though he did not think every occupation contributed to its productivity (and added a restriction on bringing in wealth from abroad that Petty would not have endorsed). In his very first work he distinguished the three groups he considered to be "those most profitable Engines of the Kingdom" from those who were not:

> It is (I think) agreed on by all, That Merchants, Artificers, Farmers of Land, and such as depend on them (which for brevity-sake we may here include under one of these general terms) viz. Seamen, Fishermen, Breeders of Cattel, Gardners, &c. Are the three sorts of people which by their study and labour do principally, if not onely, bring in Wealth to a Nation from abroad; other kinds of People viz. Nobility, Gentry, Lawyers, Physicians, Scholars of all sorts, and Shopkeepers, do onely hand it from one to another at home.[80]

Thus he concluded that "no Money is imployed to the advantage of any Kingdom; but that only which is Imployed in Foreign Trade, or by Artificers, and in Manufacture, or Improvement of Land."[81] And thus we are back to that distinction between those who make (goods) and those who do (services) that so confused William Petty. But whereas Petty could at least see the movement of goods through the domestic economy as a nourishing system, Child had no idea that most of what was produced by those farmers and artisans was consumed at home and thus brought no more new silver into the economy than did the efforts of shopkeepers (at least by his own theory). Child was still imprisoned by the idea that wealth was ultimately gold and silver and that these were finally increased only by exporting goods even if he fought against the public policy that this meant creating a literal export surplus.

To increase the efficiency of the economic engine Child offered his version of the by now inevitable scheme for employing the poor in workhouses. The able-bodied idle were "Unprofitable to the Kingdom" to the tune of some "Hundreds of Thousands of Pounds per Annum."[82] The laws requiring them to return to their home parishes wasted time, money, and manpower. The local authorities should have the ability to set the poor on whatever work those authorities thought fit, even to transporting them to the colonies as indentured servants. Children in the system would receive both general education and specific job-training to make them more "serviceable to their country."[83] When one remembers that included in this large class of "poor" were the seasonally underemployed workers (and all manual labor had a seasonal element in the days before electric light and indoor heating), one can see that this was far from a mind-set in which the free sale of labor was the norm.

But if wealth was, ultimately, precious metal, why all the emphasis on increasing production by increasing population and increasing productivity by disciplining that population, why all the insistence that a nation's real wealth was its productive capacity so defined? Because Child, like so many of his contemporaries, had the equation backward: money (i.e., gold and silver) was not ultimately valued because it could be turned into goods (i.e., for its purchasing power); rather, goods (land, labor, and what the two combined to produce) were valued because they could ultimately be turned into money. They were a country's "real" wealth only because they were the efficient cause of its metallic wealth. They did this, however, only when they were sent out of the country: hence the attempts to reduce domestic consumption.[84]

Domestic demand was a powerful force by Child's day. Tobacco consumption had been a favorite target of luxury-baiting economists like Mun, Malynes, and Misselden even though England consumed only 50,000 pounds of it at 20 to 40 shillings per pound in their day; however, by the 1670s the retail price had dropped below a shilling per pound, feeding a demand surge that brought England's domestic consumption up to 13 million pounds by century's end (over and above the 25 million pounds it reexported to Europe).[85] A corresponding price-drop in calicoes brought domestic consumption up to 287,000 cloths by century's end or one-third of its total imports of 861,000 (the other two-thirds being reexported), when the sum total of consumed and reexported calicoes in 1663 through 1669 had been only 240,000 units.[86] This was not the mere result of luxury consumption but of a genuine revolution in the domestic market. Mass market consumption had arrived even if the economic writers did not want to consider its consequences.[87]

Hobbes and Economic Man

We have seen the idea of a statistically calculable man emerging in the work of Thomas Hobbes and Sir William Petty. To get from there to the idea of Economic Man, two other elements were needed: one was the idea of man as motivated by a *rational* self-interest and the other was a way to comprehend his profit-seeking behavior within a eudaemonistic worldview. To the extent that our economic writers saw demand as essentially lawless, they could not accommodate it. But the ideas about human nature and the nature of knowledge and of its acquisition emerging in the century were providing, albeit unintentionally, a way to make demand law-abiding, to subjugate it to an external, universal, and hence objective order, to make it safe for economics, and thus to make economics safe for value.

The first of those elements already mentioned was the mechanical universality of human nature as taken by Child from Hobbes in the course of Child's argument for the gains England would make from admitting Jewish immigrants:

> All men by Nature are alike, as I have before demonstrated, and Mr. Hobbs hath truly asserted, how Erroneous soever he may be in other things.[88]

The next was accepting profit-seeking as the direction of that mechanical motion. Child clearly held it to be a universal trait, giving both theoretical and concrete examples. We have already seen him argue that reducing the interest rate from 6 to 4 percent would not cause a flight of Dutch funds because the Dutch would not take their money from loans earning 4 percent in England to sink it into loans earning only 3 percent at home. He believed, in fact, that "most Men by their education and Business" kept their eye so "fixed" upon their private gain that they could hardly tell the difference any longer between the public and the private.[89] It was safe to ease entry into the ranks of "mere merchants" because shopkeepers admitted to the ranks of merchants would resort to "sending out" coin or Bills of Exchange instead of merchandise for no other reason than did trained merchants: the dictates of profit.[90] While the interest rate remained at 6 percent "no Money" would be employed in those three areas that "advantage" a kingdom—foreign trade, manufacture, and improvement of land—unless it would yield the investor "above six per cent."[91] Similarly, he concluded that "if we retrench by Law the Labour of our People, we drive them from us to other Countries that give better rates."[92]

But to use Economic Man you have to accept finally that the laws that govern him apply uniformly to all his economic transactions. Put Economic Man to work in the market and he will set his own price on money. He will try to buy low and sell high. And this, Josiah Child was not prepared to let him do.

CHAPTER 9

John Locke: Nineteen Shillings do not a Pound make

John Locke's monetary works present us with a split economic personality: a man who tried to use arguments for a *market-determined* interest rate to prove the necessity of reinstating a *statutory* monetary standard that had been ignored by the marketplace for over two decades, who believed solutions derived from a stagnant economy applied to an inflationary one, and who held to a supply-driven quantity theory while building a Natural Law–based theory of demand that negated his own premises.

John Locke was born on August 29, 1632, in Somerset, the grandson of a clothier who made his fortune in the "putting-out" system, and the son of a Puritan lawyer who had briefly served as a captain in the Parliamentary Army.[1] Though his family had entered the ranks of the minor gentry thanks to his paternal grandfather's success, it never entirely lost its commercial connections: Locke's uncles were themselves tanners and brewers.

John Locke received a traditional education, going from Westminster to Christ Church, Oxford, where he received his Bachelor of Arts in 1656 and his Master's in 1658, and began teaching the same Scholasticism in which he had been schooled. Outside the classroom, however, his interests were more catholic. Locke was introduced to the new "Mechanical" philosophy through his work as an experimental assistant to Robert Boyle, and brought those insights to a new enthusiasm for the work of Descartes. The friendship with Boyle also brought Locke into that same Oxford scientific circle earlier joined by Petty and eventually into the Royal Society in 1668. Locke's study of medicine[2] partook of the same mix of old and new schools that marked his philosophical development: the courses at Oxford were still heavily tilted toward Galen and Aristotle, but his friendship with fellow medical student Richard Lower exposed Locke to Harvey's theories. This initial exposure was reinforced by Locke's connections with John Wilkins (1614–1672), then warden of Wadham College, Jonathan Goddard, M.D. (1617?–1675), Gresham professor of physic, and Ralph Bathurst, M.D. (1620–1704), president of Trinity College.

It was through Locke's interest in medicine that he first made the acquaintance of Anthony Ashley Cooper (1621–1683, created first earl of Shaftesbury in 1672), having procured some medicine for him in 1666. By the summer of 1667, Locke was in Shaftesbury's service, quickly evolving from paid physician, secretary, and political pupil to confidant and political ally. It may even have been Shaftesbury, then Chancellor of the Exchequer, who prompted Locke's response to Josiah Child's 1668 work supporting a reduction in the interest rate. Locke never published the piece ("Some of the Consequences that are like to follow upon Lessening of Interest to 4 Percent"), but the essay contained in rough form many of the conclusions found in Locke's later economic works.[3] It was at this time, also, that Locke became secretary to the Lords Proprietors of the Carolinas, of which Shaftesbury was part owner.

When the "Whiggish" Board of Trade that had so troubled the future James II was reconstituted with a much greater ministerial and much smaller merchant input,[4] it was certainly Shaftesbury who got Locke the job as secretary to the new Council on Trade and Plantations (of which Chancellor Shaftesbury was president) in 1673. When Shaftesbury's "Whiggish" ways caused him to fall from favor, it was not long before his Council was dissolved as well (on March 12, 1675), and the now unemployed Locke was off on a European tour before once again taking up his teaching duties (this time under a medical studentship) at Oxford.

By 1678, Shaftesbury was making as much political ground as he could over the charges brought by Titus Oates of a popish plot to unseat Charles II.[5] Shaftesbury and his Whigs tried unsuccessfully to push through bills to exclude the Catholic James from the succession in three Parliaments from 1679 to 1681, and in the process they gave England its first version of a modern political party with organized campaigns, member discipline, ideological content, and a partisan press.[6] But Whigs brought forth Tories, and the Tory-supported Charles II proved to be a better politician than his father. With money from the French and growing public sentiment that the Whigs had gone too far, Charles resolved to rule without Parliament. Shaftesbury was arrested July 2, 1681. Though a Whig grand jury finally threw out the bill of indictment against him in November 1681, the Whigs had lost.

Shaftesbury's fall meant Locke's as well. Locke followed Shaftesbury into exile in Holland in 1683.[7] Condemned in absentia, Locke remained a fugitive from English justice until the Glorious Revolution put William of Orange and Mary on the throne of England in place of the "abdicated" James II.

Not long after Locke's return to England in 1689, he began to publish the works for which he remains best known: the *Essay Concerning Human Understanding* (1690), the *Two Treatises of Government* (1690), and the *Letter on Toleration* (1690).[8] *Some Thoughts Concerning Education* and *The Reasonableness of Christianity* followed, in 1693 and 1695, respectively.

In October 1690, a bill was introduced in the House of Commons calling for a reduction in the interest rate from 6 to 4 percent, and the debate merged with another calling for a reform of the coinage. From 1691 to 1695, Locke published a series of pamphlets (repackaged collectively in 1696 as *Several Papers relating to Money, Interest and Trade, &c.*) opposing a reduction in the interest rate and any devaluation of the coinage. A recognized economic authority in his own right, Locke was also supported by his friend Lord Somers who had risen from being counsel to the Seven Bishops prosecuted by James II in 1688 to Lord Keeper in 1693 and Lord Chancellor in 1697. When a new council of trade was set up in 1696,[9] Locke was made one of its members, producing, in 1697, an abortive scheme for the reform of the poor laws more draconian than anything Child, Petty, Dury, or Hartlib had earlier imagined.

Ill health forced Locke to resign from the council in 1700, and he spent the years until his death (on October 28, 1704) generally at Oates, the home of Sir Francis Masham and his second wife Damaris, the daughter of Ralph Cudworth and a close friend of Locke's from his preexile days.

To prove that interest rates were a result of market forces rather than a cause of them, Locke defined money as a commodity and then applied to it the market laws that he believed governed the prices of commodities in general. Since Locke thought of the price of a commodity as the result of some "proportion" between its supply and its "vent," this involved him in two separate analytical problems: the general question of what factors affected the "vent" and the more specific question of what factors affected the "supply" of the money commodity since it could not really be discussed in terms of weather or horticultural technique. Thus we must first explore his concept of money as a commodity whose supply was affected by the balance of trade and the velocity of its internal circulation. This velocity was itself determined by the rate of turnover and the length of its circuit through the economy. Then, we must ask why a man so determined to keep his yardsticks fixed would incorporate something as seemingly subjective as demand into his economic analysis. This can be accomplished by examining his use of the elasticity of demand, his so-called labor theory of value, and his Natural Law theory of psychology.

Defining Money

Money as a Commodity

Locke believed no commodity could be used as money unless it was scarce, acceptable, durable, and divisible.[10] In this he was closely following the theory of money worked out by Jean Buridan (ca. 1300–1358) and Nicholas Oresme (ca. 1320–1382), two French Scholastic philosophers.[11] In fact, he followed their work so closely he repeated their confusion of the properties of money with those of currency.

For Locke money (as currency) served as a universal counter precisely because of its "intrinsick Value," defined as the quantity of silver it contained.[12] Its legal denomination was nothing more nor less than a public pledge of that quantity of silver (the weight of the coin less the admixture of alloy).[13] The value that "Mankind" put on gold and silver might be "imaginary" in the strict sense,[14] but once imposed it took on the weight of "immutable" law: it was no longer indifferent.[15] In another context, Locke referred to this estimation as placed on silver by "common consent,"[16] the very foundation of government in Locke's *Two Treatises*.

Though the bullion in it made the coin valuable, the stamp removed the inconvenience of having to weigh and test each lump of metal for purity.[17] The denomination was a pledge of value analogous to an oath: the "publick Authority" was "Guarantee for the performance of all legal Contracts."[18] The oath, for Locke, was still the essential cement binding the social fabric. It was, after all, the meaninglessness of oaths for atheists, the refusal of certain sectarian groups to submit to oaths, and the permission Locke believed Catholics had to lie under oath to Protestant governments that caused him to exclude these groups from his proposed umbrella of toleration in 1690.[19] Consent and public trust: the intrinsic value of money was one of the pillars supporting the continued existence of civil society.

But multiple yardsticks were in place in late-seventeenth-century England: there were standard-weight coins with milled edges and older, hammered coins whose weight had been lessened over the years by the clipping off of irregularities in their circumference. The milled coins were in short supply, and it was widely believed that they were hoarded or melted down for plate or for export as bullion (since 1663 no longer subject to the same export restrictions as was native coin).[20] But the loss of the milled coins probably contributed far less to the shortage of money depressing prices and trade than did the £2.5 million William III spent on his army in 1694.[21] The debate to which Locke was contributing was not merely one over how to reorganize the coinage to produce a uniform and more freely circulating medium, but one over how to reorganize the finances of the kingdom as a whole. Locke's support for William III was rather ironic on these grounds, given that Locke held maintaining large armies abroad was an even faster way of reducing the national money supply than was an import surplus.[22]

A number of individuals suggested accepting some average of the weight of the clipped coins as a new standard and recoining at that lower percentage of silver. To John Locke, however, that was nothing more than calling four ounces of silver five and nothing less than a public fraud. That "imaginary" valuation of silver became very real in this argument. Locke insisted that people would not accept such a coinage, that they exchanged their goods for a certain weight of silver and would not accept less: such coins would have to be weighed each time they were exchanged so that the seller was certain he received his full price. Foreign merchants would equally insist that the short weight be made up.[23]

But neither situation was exactly the case, and Locke knew it. On the domestic front clipped coin passed at full face value.[24] Locke's fellow Englishmen routinely took coins weighing one-fifth to one-half less than the standard as worth their full weight.[25] Locke himself, after arguing in one chapter that debased coin would not be accepted at face value in England ("One may as rationally hope to lengthen a foot by dividing it into Fifteen parts, instead of Twelve; and calling them inches"), went on in another to claim that the clipped coin was, in fact, routinely so accepted and would continue to be so as long as "the King receives it for his taxes."[26] The first was an argument for silver content as the efficient cause of money, the second was an argument for denomination in that role, but Locke denied the denomination argument, insisting that people really only accepted clipped coins out of ignorance, being unable to "judge right" by their "present uncertain clipped Money, of the value and price of things."[27]

The international argument was more complicated because (1) the moneys of account were bimetallic: "silver" measures were used in some instances and "gold" measures in another,[28] (2) each of these metals had a different worth in each market, (3) nations deliberately manipulated their official exchange rates to increase their bullion supply, (4) Bills of Exchange having different maturity dates were discounted at different rates, and (5) discrepancies in rates for metals, coins, and bills allowed for considerable arbitrage (the purchasing of Bills of Exchange in one market to be cashed in at a profit in another).[29] While foreign *coins* were accepted on the international market on the basis of their true metallic content rather than for their face value, the opposite was the case for calculations made in the assorted *moneys of account* and *Bills of Exchange*, so the end result was not necessarily, and perhaps not even normally, exchange at the par on the international market.

Locke dismissed each of the complicating factors as harmful deviations from some natural law of *par pro pari* exchange. For example, Locke strongly objected to the use of gold as a monetary standard. He was aware that the par between gold and silver was subject to constant fluctuation both de jure (the pars set by each government) and de facto (on the open market):[30] the Spanish government may have set their par at 16:1 but depending on what the treasure ships brought in, silver in Spain might trade for 15:1 or 14:1, and in the markets of the East India Company, routinely go for 10:1 or even 9:1.[31] One could as easily argue that this was a variation in silver's price in relation to gold as the reverse, but Locke took the position that silver's was the core value and gold's fluctuated in relation to it. He believed gold should be coined, because the stamp would give the purchaser assurance of how much fine gold was actually in the stamped piece, but he did not think it should be used for money because bimetallism introduced uncertainty into the yardstick.[32] That this yardstick had to be maintained at a constant length, he was certain, because silver, was, for Locke, "a measure of a nature quite different from all other," in that it was "the thing bargained for, as well as the measure of the bargain."[33] This was a par as strict as that desired by Malynes.

If silver was the "thing" bargained for then it was a commodity and had a price, but Locke argued that silver could have no price because a thing was always equal to itself: an ounce of fine silver was always worth an ounce of fine silver, and two ounces of that fine silver must purchase twice as much wheat as one ounce might command.[34] To the response that silver bullion could often command a higher price than coined silver of an equal purity, he argued that this was only the unfortunate result of laws that forbade the export of coin while allowing that of bullion.[35] Such laws increased the demand for bullion (or melted coin) among foreign traders (especially in cases of a negative trade balance) and gave it an artificial price edge over coined silver,[36] but this could not *naturally* be the case: the "Stamp neither does nor can take way any of the instrinsick value of the Silver."[37]

Because a thing was always equal to itself, no commodity's price could rise in relation to itself; a price increase was an increase in the proportion that a quantity of one commodity could command in exchange for another: wheat rose in price when it could be exchanged for more tobacco, or wampum, or silver, but "one Pound [of wheat] of the same goodness" would "never exchange for a Pound and a Quarter [of wheat] of the same goodness."[38] Locke locked himself into a vicious circle by confounding money's function as a medium of exchange with that as a store of value.

England's answer to the strain an expanding economy was placing on the coin supply was to turn to bills of exchange and deposit receipts: customers routinely drew on their "running cashes" at the goldsmith's by writing drafts against them, and those goldsmiths as routinely settled their interbank accounts "in Exchequer tallies and assignments" as they did in coin.[39] But for Locke, money could have no function unless it had a value of its own.[40] Credit instruments were merely stopgaps: "the Reckoning may be kept, or transferred by Writing; but on Money as a Pledge, which Writing cannot supply the place of. . . . [Credit] is nothing else but an Assurance of Money in some short time."[41]

Why were Locke's pamphlets so out of touch with the English economy in the last decade of the seventeenth century? Part of the answer lies in the fact that Locke originally set down his ideas on money in a memorandum in 1668, but only published them (with some revision) in 1691. These revisions, however, were not to his earlier conclusions but only to their supporting arguments. In fact, he boasted in the preface to the 1691 essay that

> I find not my Thoughts now to differ from those I had nearly Twenty Years since: They have to me still the Appearance of Truth.[42]

Thus some of what may seem to be nostalgia for an earlier, simpler economy, in the published works was due to the changes in the English economy from the time Locke first set down his ideas to the time they finally saw print.[43] Keeping in mind that all estimates of seventeenth-century economic conditions must be used with care, we are still looking at an economy that was in a deflationary swing when Locke first worked out his arguments in 1667 (with an estimated Consumables Index dropping from 616 in 1665 to 577 in 1670), but seriously inflationary when he published those same arguments in the 1690s (with the same index jumping from 493 in 1691 to 697 in 1696).[44] Locke's continuing satisfaction with his earlier conclusions highlights the degree to which the search for immutable market-laws still presupposed that adherence to such laws demanded equally immutable policies.

Locke was actually making an argument for maximizing the money supply by channeling its circulation through the paths most advantageous to the nation. Was there a class interest in his vision of that best path? Locke claimed his basic concern was that the "Cure" of the current "Evil" not fall "unequally on those, who have had no particular hand in it," by depriving "great Numbers of blameless Men" of some proportion "of their Estates."[45] Well, a policy of expensive money could be said to favor landowners to the extent that they were creditors. De jure or de facto, a debasement of the coinage meant landowners would receive less silver for their stated rents, just as it meant they would pay out less silver to their creditors.

A de jure debasement of the coinage (with its accompanying recoining) would increase the money supply, putting pressure on the price level. If such an upward price adjustment moved swiftly and evenly through the economy its effect on expenses would be offset by its effect on incomes, but such simultaneous price movements occur only in textbook exercises. In seventeenth-century England some prices and many wages were regulated by various authorities (guilds, municipalities, companies, or Parliament), and leases ran for decades. In a general debasement, the average landowner would find his expenses increased while his rents remained fixed, unless special provisions to deal with existing contracts were made in the law.

On the other hand, a recoining of all the clipped coins at the higher standard would drastically reduce the supply of coined money. Either way, the effect would be unevenly felt throughout the country, though when Locke wrote of the creditor "forced to receive less" or the debtor "forced to pay more than his Contract," he was thinking of the change in silver received rather than in the changed purchasing power of the altered money supply.[46] Locke admitted men would find twenty shillings "of their new Money" would buy "no more of any Commodity" than nineteen of the old would purchase,[47] but he did not see this as a price adjustment because the same weight of silver was being exchanged for the same amount of the commodity in question: "the Price of Things will always be estimated by the quantity of Silver [that] is given in exchange for them."[48]

Still, labeling this a class-based argument does not necessarily imply the perceived threat was from below. The immediate beneficiary of a debasement would be the royal treasury. The main argument against debasement in the Scholastic tradition rested on (1) the uncertainty introduced into the *publica mensura* and (2) the harm done to the common good by the private profit the monarch reaped at its expense.[49] Locke would hardly have been in a position to openly attack the motives of William III and Mary II, but he also would have hardly been unaware of the Scholastic tradition in this regard. Whether or not we think the gentry would lose money rent in a debasement, Locke believed they would, and the greatest gainer would not (in his eyes) have been the individual tenant (or debtor) who paid a few ounces less but the Crown and its mint.

Nonetheless, when Parliament finally accepted a government-sponsored coinage (as in Locke's scheme) and the deadline for using the old coins at face value had passed, it was neither the landowners nor the mer-

chants who suffered. They had prepaid their taxes and turned their money
in at face value, and had perhaps even turned in clipped money purchased
at a discount from the less fortunate. It was the poor (working or not) who
found shopkeepers refusing their coin well before the June 24, 1696, deadline.[50] The resulting riots caused the government to extend the deadline for
bringing coin into the Exchequer at prices varying from 5s. 8d. to 5s. 2d. per
ounce: if the government lost £2,700,000 on the coins it took at face value,
the general populace lost another £1,000,000 on the coins it turned in at
less than that value.[51] Ironically, the resulting shortage of coin had to be
made temporarily good by the issuing of Exchequer 'bills' (meant to be held
as an investment as they paid 3d. percent per day) passing current in
denominations as low as £1.[52]

Raw Supply, or the Balance of Trade

Locke accepted the standard argument that a positive trade balance was the
best way to increase the kingdom's supply of coin, but he turned it on its
head by valuing that coin for its purchasing power rather than its own sake:

> For we have no Mines, nor any other way of getting, or keeping of
> Riches amongst us but by Trade, so much of our Trade as is lost, so much
> of our Riches must necessarily go with it; and the over-ballancing of
> Trade between us and our Neighbours, must inevitably carry away our
> Money, and quickly leave us Poor, and exposed. Gold and Silver though
> they serve for few yet they command all the conveniences of life; and
> therefore in a plenty of them consists Riches.[53]
> Riches consist in having more in proportion, than the rest of the World,
> or than our Neighbours, whereby we are enabled to procure to our selves
> a greater Plenty of the Conveniences of Life than comes within the
> reach of Neighbouring Kingdoms and States, who, sharing the Gold and
> Silver of the World in a less proportion, want the means of Plenty and
> Power, and so are Poorer.[54]

His model was still Cato's: "A Kingdom grows Rich, or Poor just as a
Farmer doth, and no otherwise" by selling more than it/he bought.[55] Since
this was still a finite cosmos with trade incapable of enriching one nation
except at another's expense, it was best to make sure your nation was on the
gaining end. Neighboring countries that outtraded yours could keep larger
armies, lure your work force away by paying higher wages, "break" your
"Trade," and stockpile weapons to use against you.[56]

Balance of trade theory had a special attraction for Locke because it
reinforced the moral order of the universe. Since purchases eventually had
to be paid for, statutes could not prevent coin from leaving one country to
pay for goods purchased from another,[57] but statutes could encourage frugality over prodigal luxury:

Prohibited Commodities, 'tis true, should be kept out, and useless ones
Impoverish us by being brought in. But that is the fault of our Importa-
tion: And there the mischief should be cured, by Laws, and our way of
living. For the Exportation of our Treasure is not the cause of their
Importation, but the consequence. Vanity and Luxury spends them:
That gives them vent here: That vent causes their Importation.[58]

Quantity as Raw Supply Modified by Velocity

The turnover rate. Locke realized that because the same coin changed
hands several times in any one period of time, it sufficed to cover multiple
purchases, and so the "proportion" in question depended "not barely on the
quantity of Money," but also on "the quickness of its Circulation."[59]

Despite the confusions they found in his work, modern writers on
economics give Locke much credit for bringing greater clarity to the quantity theory of money.[60] His exploration of the different speeds of money in
the economy as it was paid weekly to laborers or semiannually to landlords
echoed Sir William Petty's ideas on the same subject,[61] but Locke rejected
Petty's quantitative analysis for a qualitative treatment of the question. This
led Locke to realize that a secondary level of analysis would be needed: the
problem was not merely how much pay laborers received each week or
landlords semiannually, but how much of their income went back into circulation at any given time as laborers and landlords did their marketing or
paid their bills.[62] He knew that shortening existing legal intervals of payment, such as making rents due quarterly rather than half-yearly, meant less
money would be needed "to drive the Trade of any Country."[63] But the fact
is, he meant less coin. Locke's formulation may tell us something about the
function/value of money in circulation that has nothing to do with the
material of which it is made (silver, paper, plastic cards, or electronic
impulses), but this happens to be an insight that Locke would never have
accepted.

The shorter circuit and the interest rate. For Locke, as for Petty, velocity
was also a matter of how many and whose hands those coins passed
through as they *circulated* through society. Locke was looking for the shortest circuit from producer to consumer. We can see this in the arguments he
developed for his market theory of interest.

There were two very different ways of opposing Sir Josiah Child's contention that interest should be lowered from 6 to 4 percent in order to fos-
ter the nation's economic well-being. The first was to take the position that
interest rates, being primarily an effect rather than a cause of market conditions, should be regulated by that market and not by statute. The second
was to assert that interest rates should be regulated by statute but that the
optimal rate for current conditions was the existing 6 percent. Locke's

rebuttal combined parts of both positions, maintaining that interest rates were naturally a result of market conditions and thus could not be artificially lowered by statute, but statutes could be used to set a maximum rate (pegged to the natural rate) to protect the general welfare against attempts by certain elements in the market to artificially raise rates through monopolistic practices. The argument rested on his distinguishing between two different sets of market conditions: a *natural* market of localized exchanges between small, independent units and a corrupted market dominated by large, centralized concerns seeking *monopolistic* profits.

He came down squarely on the interest-as-effect side of the argument when he maintained that since it was "the want of Money" that drove a man to the "Trouble and Charge of Borrowing," "proportionably to this Want," he would pay "whatever Price it cost him."[64] But, rather than insist on any indefeasible mechanics of supply and demand to support his position, Locke argued the inequality of letting those mechanics play out unchanneled by authority: "ingrossing" bankers would easily evade the law but widows, orphans, and "others uninstructed" in such "Arts and Management" (that is to say, gentlemen) would find they could get no more for their deposits than the law "barely" allowed.[65] "If Money were to be hired," according to Locke, "from the Owner himself," it "might then probably" be had at "the true" Rate, but "when a kind of Monopoly, by consent, has put this general Commodity into a few Hands, it may need Regulation" to make it "more equally distributed" geographically as well as more fairly lent.[66] The *natural* market produced a shorter circuit through the economy than did the *monopolistic.*

Locke claimed that when the legal and natural rates of interest roughly coincided, men would not carry their funds to London bankers but loan privately to their neighbors. But when the legal rate was below the natural rate, bankers (using their monopoly to refrain from paying more than 4 percent on deposits while using the borrower's need to get 6 percent or greater on their loans) would "be content to have more Money lye dead by them . . . [by] which means there would be less Money stirring in Trade, and a greater Scarcity [of money]."[67] But, if the bankers were loaning their deposits out to landowners and/or their tenants, the money was returning to the localities. And whether the 6 percent was being charged to farmers or merchants, the money was not lying "dead," but "stirring" about in trade simply through what the merchants and/or farmers did with it. The only way money could actually lie dead in a bank would be for the bank to refuse to loan it out again. The *deadness* under discussion here was not literal failure to circulate but the failure to take what Locke believed to be the best *circuit* through the society.

Locke was trying to maximize the social effects of money's circulation through the economy, a penchant he shared with fellow medico Sir William Petty. But the ability of a medical training to direct one's thoughts to monetary circulation did not necessarily translate into a uniform opinion of the best circuit. Though they shared a similar disregard for nonproducing middlemen (a classic *service* provider), Locke and Petty held opposing views of bankers.

John Locke asserted any number of times that bankers were brakes on circulation,[68] by which he meant they created unnecessary detours in that circulation. The source of his contention can be seen in his equation of bankers and shopkeepers in this regard:

> multiplying of Brokers hinders the Trade of any Country, by making the Circuit, which the Money goes, larger, and in that Circuit more stops, so that the Returns must necessarily be slower and scantier, to the prejudice of Trade: Besides that, they Eat up too great a share of the Gains of Trade, by that means Starving the Landholder, whose interest is chiefly to be taken care of, it being a settled unmoveable Concernment in the Commonwealth.[69]

He was thoroughly convinced that "all Encouragement" (statutory as well as market) should be given to "Artificers" and farmers to "Retail out their own Commodities" directly to "the last Buyer," thus eliminating the "Lazy and Unworking Shopkeepers" who were "worse than Gamesters."[70] As early as 1674, Locke had divided the population into two groups, those that "contributed" to trade "especially in commodities for exportation" ("men employed in husbandry, draper, mines, and navigation") and those who hindered trade either passively by being "idle" ("retainers to gentry and beggars") or actively ("as retailers in some degree, multitudes of lawyers, but above all soldiers in pay").[71]

Locke's main concern in all this was for the profits he thought would accrue to the original producer/seller/loaner if the monopolistic market gaining ground in his day were to revert to the simpler, more *natural* state of affairs of localized, direct exchanges that he believed that market was replacing. Since a nation's total supply of "Money in its Circulation" was "all shared between" the landholder, the laborer, the merchant, the shopkeeper, and the consumer, it seemed only logical that removing the middlemen would leave more money to divide among the remaining parties.[72] Hold constant the final price to the consumer and the workers' wages, and all of that freed-up money would have to revert to the landowner.

But Locke was confusing money supply and profit. And he had forgotten that even according to his own argument, the private lender got the lowest legal rate of interest (in either set of market conditions) from the private borrower: the additional 2 percent now earned by the monopolistic banker could not revert to the private lender in some *natural* market because it would not exist.

Locke's argument was shaped by his vision of a special zero-sum battle waged between agriculture and commerce:

> The usual struggle and contest, as I said before, in the decays of Wealth and Riches, is between the Landed Man and the Merchant, with whom I may join here the Monied Man. The Landed Man finds himself aggrieved, by the falling of his Rents, and the streightning of his Fortune; whilst the Monied Man gives up his Gain, and the Merchant thrives and grows rich by trade.[73]

Setting the legal interest rate below the natural (non-monopoly) market rate created a gain to the merchant directly proportional to its loss to the "Monied Man":

> For if he [the merchant] Borrow at Four per Cent. and his Returns be Twelve per Cent. he will have Eight per Cent. and the Lender Four: Whereas now they divide the profit equally at Six per Cent.[74]

The "Monied Man" here being the private lender (or gentleman), an interest rate proportionable to rack rentals would restore the balance while a lower rate would favor the borrowing merchant at the expense of the other two.

To make this claim Locke assumed the balance of trade dogma that circulation of money within a country could not increase its wealth ("it will be no matter to the Kingdom, who amongst our selves Gets or Loses"),[75] ignored the fact that according to his own ideas of demand and supply no two commodities were necessarily equal to each other ("There being no two things in Nature, whose proportion and use does not vary, 'tis impossible to set a standing regular price between them"),[76] and assumed that interest rates did have some effect on rental values even though he was about to try to prove that they did not.

For Locke, every commodity had an intrinsic value based on its ability to provide "the Necessaries or Conveniences of Life." In the case of land, this was its ability to produce income from an annual harvest of such necessities or conveniences as expressed in its "Rent"[77]—though this was its income at one remove, the tenant getting the actual productive revenue. Though Locke had been arguing that it was an *unnaturally* uneven distribution of funds in a monopolistic market that pushed interest above its natural level (a "Compact that transfers . . . the Reward of one Man's Labour into another Man's Pocket"), he accepted that a *naturally* "unequal Distribution" of Land was behind its ability to command rent.[78] Such Aristotelian prejudices aside, Locke set up the straw premise that because both inequalities were equally inevitable, equally useful, and analytically parallel, "one would expect, that the rate of Interest should be the Measure of the Value of Land in number of Years purchase for which the Fee is sold."[79] This was an easy conclusion for him to disprove: history itself revealed that interest rates and purchase prices did not move in inverse proportion.[80] Analytically, he argued that selling price being determined by the number of buyers vis-à-vis the number of sellers, land surpassed interest rates where industry produced a greater demand for land, because thrifty traders looked to land as a solid investment and were loath to invest far from their place of business.[81] The argument is faulty in that the presence of additional (and possibly countervailing) factors does not mean that interest rates have no effect on prices or rentals, but only that they are not a *sufficient* cause of those prices and rentals. As a trained Scholastic, Locke should have known better than to confuse necessary with sufficient causation, but prejudice makes for error.

Demand as a Yardstick

Elasticity

Defining scarcity as a shortage of a commodity proportionate to its "vent," Locke recognized that scarcity itself did not account for a commodity's price because it did not have an equal effect on the "vent" of every good.[82] He pointed out that while it might be "hard" to "set a [maximum or fixed] Price" on "unnecessary Commodities" such as "Wine or Silks," it was absolutely "impossible" to do the same for "Victuals in a time of Famine."[83] In modern terms, this was to recognize that the demand for some goods was more elastic than the demand for others.

Taking the demand for food as generally inelastic, and wheat as one variety of food, Locke took it that a great scarcity of wheat would cause buyers to accept a price increase for it, but only up to a point. Though preferring wheat to oats as "the healthier, pleasanter, and more convenient Food," people would "not rob themselves of all other Conveniences of Life" for scarce wheat when cheap oats were available.[84] Or, in modern terms, he held that the phenomenon of cross-elasticity of demand applied to even the most inelastic of commodities.[85] But not, of course, to the special commodity—money. For Locke, demand determined the natural interest rate in the simplest sense; interest rates rose when "the Money of a Country" was scarce "in proportion to the Debts of the Inhabitants," or, in other terms, when there were more borrowers than lenders.[86]

Actually, he was not trying to make a point about demand per se but to prove that changing the use-price of money (the interest rate) did not alter the exchange-price of money (the cost of any commodity purchased with it) because it did not alter the proportion between the supply and vent of those commodities.[87] Locke insisted that money was "in buying and selling . . . perfectly in the same Condition with other Commodities,"[88] but his attempt to erect a barrier between the actions of money used to purchase goods from those of the market in money prevented him from treating it uniformly as such.[89] He specifically denied that an inverse ratio existed between the value of money and the price of the goods it purchased:

> Money being the Counter-ballance to all other Things purchasable by it, and lying, as it were, in the opposite Scale of Commerce, it looks like a natural Consequence, that as much as you take off from the value of Money, so much you add to the price of other Things, which are exchanged for it. . . . The mistake of this plausible way of Reasoning will be easily discovered, when we consider that the measure of the value of Money, in proportion to anything purchasable by it, is the quantity of ready Money we have, in Comparison with the quantity of that thing and its Vent.[90]

The basic problem was that Locke's theory of money was not functional but physical. For Locke, money was a stamped weight of silver and nothing else.

Value and Labor

Locke was exploring the effect velocity had on circulation as a means of increasing the productive efficiency of the economy. Cutting out the middlemen—brokers, bankers, and retailers—was one way to make less coin do more work. The encouragement of manufacture was another:

> Here too we may observe, how much Manufacture deserves to be incouraged: Since that part of Trade, though the most considerable, is driven with the least Money, especially if the Workmanship be more worth than the Materials. For to the Trade that is driven by Labour, and Handicrafts Men, One two and fiftieth part of the yearly Money paid them will be sufficient: But to a Trade of Commodities of our bare Native growth, much greater proportion of Money is required.[91]

The manufacture in question has been the subject of much debate among modern scholars trying to decide whether or not Locke approved of some model of capitalism, but Locke's treatment of "Manufacture" and the "Labour" involved in it was really too generalized to fit into our pigeonholes. When Locke wrote of labor as putting *"the difference of value* on every thing" or of nine-tenths of the usefulness "of the Products of the Earth" as being the "the *effects of labour,*" he was not, in any strictly economic sense, trying to build a theory of either value or price, just as he was not trying to build a cost-basis theory when he wrote of labor constituting ninety-nine one-hundredths of the expense of any commodity.[92]

He was, according to his own remarks at the beginning of the chapter on property in the *Second Treatise,* trying to explain how individuals could have a claim to any *private* property when the Earth, in his understanding of Natural Law and Revelation, had been given to humanity *in common.*[93] Labor, both in the sense of its transforming power and that of using our faculties as God intended,[94] was Locke's bridge from communal use to private property. As God had a maker's ultimate right over our lives, we had an ultimate right over that which we made (through our labor).[95] For the most notable thing about labor for Locke was the *change* it made in anything to which it was applied: fallow land into a farm or wheat into bread, labor brought into being something that did not previously exist.[96] Thus understood, *labor* was a naturally comprehensive term, as equally applied to capital investment in a horse or the wage paid one's servant as to the act of digging: "thus the Grass my Horse has bit; the Turfs my Servant has cut; and the Ore I have digg'd . . . become my *Property.*"[97] *Labor* was, in Locke's usage, a term from a moral dictionary rather than from an economic one, since it was a fulfillment of God's purpose for humankind.[98]

Despite the usage in the chapter "Of Property," the main concern of Locke's *Second Treatise* was not exclusively about *property* as we think of it—possessions to be bought and sold in some market. The century's idea of property[99] included all sorts of things one had a "right" in; for Locke, as for his compatriots, this could (and often did) include life, estate (status), liberty of conscience, faculties, and, for those who had it, the right to vote. It was this more broadly defined *property* that accrued to us independent of government and so could not be taken arbitrarily away from us by that government we created to protect it: due process and an overriding public good were required before we could lose it.

But, even if not intended as a piece of economic analysis, was there still some endorsement of the economic system we call *capitalism* contained in it? The difficulty in answering that question is that it may depend more on our understanding of *capitalism* (and our attitude toward it) than on Locke's understanding of his own society. But do we then accept James Tully's recent contention that we abandon the "rise of capitalism" altogether as a "governing framework" for interpreting Locke's work?[100] The literature on this question is voluminous; every issue Locke took on (his proposals for the reform of the poor laws, his views on inheritance, etc.) and every point he made in his derivation of private property (spoilage limitations, origins of money, etc.) has been looked at over and over again. Rehearsing all these arguments would take us far beyond the scope of this study, but perhaps we may be able to lay out the scope of the problem by approaching it through the fairly narrow but key concept of wage labor.[101]

The passages from the *Two Treatises* forever cited in any argument over Locke and labor are:

> a Free-man makes himself a Servant to another, by selling him for a certain time, the Service he undertakes to do, in exchange for Wages he is to receive: And though this commonly puts him into the Family of his Master, and under the ordinary Discipline thereof; yet it gives the Master but a Temporary Power over him, and no greater, than what is contained in the *Contract* between 'em. But there is another sort of Servants, which by a peculiar Name we call *Slaves* . . . subjected to the Absolute dominion and Arbitrary Power of their masters.[102]

And:

> thus the Grass my Horse has bit; the Turfs my Servant has cut; and the Ore I have digg'd . . . become my *Property*.[103]

C. B. Macpherson saw a classic endorsement of the separation of labor from the profits created by the produced means of production associated with bourgeois capitalism in the second passage.[104] But Neal Wood claimed Locke's lack of appreciation for true manufacture and reliance on agricultural models proved him to be an advocate of agrarian capitalism, an earlier stage of capitalism dominated by a triad of rentier, profit-collecting tenant, and wage-worker.[105] Locke was essentially a rentier with experience on trade boards who did a little passive investing in trading companies on the side. He came from an area in England (Somerset) in which "agrarian capitalism" had made considerable headway.[106] We have already seen how his positions on interest and recoinage favored his own class.

Various "triads" were known in Locke's England. As part of his wife's estate Sir Dudley North managed lands run exactly as Neal Wood described, but he also managed her commercial leases: here also was a rent-collecting commercial landlord, a profit-reaping tenant, and wage-earning employees. The general shareholder in the East India Company had nothing to do with its active trading (although receiving its dividends), while shareholding directors such as Sir Josiah Child reaped the profits of the company-managed shipyards or from selling to the company on contract, and the sailors and clerks got their wages. All corporations embody some form of triad. The simple owner-manager has never been the only (or even the dominant) type of capitalist. But there is no triad in Locke's two examples: there we have only an owner and his servants/workers. We have to wonder why he chose the simpler model instead of a form of which he seemed to be so well aware.

James Tully looked at the first passage and claimed Locke's analysis actually left no room for the capitalist "to appear."[107] But where Locke contrasted one kind of wage earner with a slave, Tully would have it that Locke was contrasting servants with wage-slaves because servants (1) sold a complete service rather than their labor, and (2) retained the right not to serve, whereas "If a man is driven by necessity to work for another then the relationship is based on force and is, *ipso facto,* a master and vassal agreement."[108] For Tully, capitalism is just such "a master and vassal agreement" because "the precondition for the capitalist to emerge is the appropriation of all land such that a labourer is forced to work for another."[109] In which case, what alternative would the "servant" have that the "wage-slave" did not? How many footmen owned land? It would appear that Tully's own aversion to capitalism has not only colored his thinking here, but also made him conflate the term *vassal* with *serf,* forgetting that a king's vassals were earls and marquesses. There is a tremendous difference between Locke's idea of free agency as the choice of which labor to perform (or for whom to work if not for oneself) and Tully's idea of choosing not to work at all: for that, Locke's answer was the thinnest gruel possible to keep an adult alive.[110]

The key problem here is Tully's definition of wage-labor as excluding anyone who performs a "complete service or task which he directs."[111] But this imposes two very different constaints: paired, they would certainly refer to the independent craftsperson of preindustrial production. But Locke nowhere suggested in his example that the turf-cutter was working undirected. Split the two constraints apart and the first ("a complete service or task") simply means we are dealing with preindustrial production, not noncapitalist production. Tully seems to have conflated the factory system with capitalism. While the factory system certainly grew up under capitalism, it ended up as much a part of production in the Soviet Union as in the United States. And, summarized as division of labor and specialization, it is really an effect of the scale of production (rather than of any "mode" of production). One can see it among house servants as well as among factory workers: small households may have only a single maid; larger ones divide the task among upper and lower house-parlor maids, and so on. It is really only the second of Tully's two constraints that would leave no room for capitalism, and that one (control over the task performed) was not explicitly made by Locke.

If we apply a more conventional definition of wage-labor to seventeenth-century economic life we will find considerable evidence for it. Take the use of the word *servant* in the citation just given. Was the typical seventeenth-century servant a true wage-laborer? Certainly he or she was more a member of the family than is a modern factory worker, and especially so when he or she was an adolescent placed in the household for vocational training, but an adult servant was, in fact, paid a wage (in board as well as in money), did in fact, "own" the money part of the wage (or any clothing etc.), did not use his or her own tools, did not own the workplace, and neither controlled the end-product produced (good or service) nor received the profits. And factory workers were and are subject to a discipline imposed by management not entirely different from the way in which a servant was subject to a discipline imposed by the master of the house.

The guild system was not yet dead in seventeenth-century England either, but wage-laborers could be found within its ranks. A printer's journeyman, for example, could hardly be said to own the press or the workshop, did not get the profit on sales, but was paid a wage. Farming was increasingly in the hands of tenants who hired day labor, full-time as well as part-time. The carpenters in the shipyards of the East India Company did not provide the lumber or share in the profits of the voyages made by the ships they built; and whether or not they used their own saws or saws provided by the shipyard manager, all they had at week's end was their wage. Master craftsmen in the London building trades routinely employed paid laborers, keeping for themselves the profits on that labor as well as on the raw materials the masters supplied.[112] And what was the salaried underling keeping the books for the import-export merchant? England in Locke's day knew everything from the rentier to the self-employed artisan to every possible shading between that and the full-fledged factory worker, even if the factory was so small it had only eight workers. If full-fledged capitalism was far from the dominant form of economic organization, it had, in the form of "wage labor," penetrated most of England's older structures.[113] It would have been more surprising if Locke had not acknowledged its existence.

But an acknowledgment of wage labor is not necessarily an endorsement of capitalism. We have certainly seen Locke's disapproval of the monopolistic practices of financial and commercial capitalism in his attempts to cut bankers and merchants out of the profit loop. Locke was clearly unhappy with much that was emerging in the English economy at the end of the seventeenth century.[114]

A Natural Law Psychology

Locke's own model was derived from his understanding of Natural Law, and that understanding of Natural Law did contribute to something that was "new" in Locke's economic thought. Though he refused to use it consistently, John Locke took the taming of demand farther than any man before him and made what he intended to be a *restricted* self-interest at home in the economic universe. This was a considerable feat for a man who started out as mired as he did in the classic opposition of the many to the one in the finite cosmos. In the lectures he gave in 1664, Locke's focus on the destructive power of egoism given the fixed resources of the world was quite explicit. The passage is worth quoting in full if only for the way he harped on that intractable limit:

> it is impossible that the primary law of nature is such that its violation is unavoidable. Yet, if the private interest of each person is the basis of that law, the law will inevitably be broken, because it is impossible to have regard for the interests of all at one and the same time. In point of fact, the inheritance of the whole of mankind is always one and the same, and it does not grow in proportion to the number of people born. Nature has provided a certain profusion of goods for the use and convenience of men, and the things provided have been bestowed in a definite way and in a predetermined quantity; they have not been fortuitously produced nor are they increasing in proportion with what men need or covet. Clothes are not born with us, nor do men, like tortoises, possess and carry about shelters that have ordinate with them and are growing up together with them. Whenever either the desire or the need of property increases among men, there is no extension, then and there, of the world's limits. Victuals, clothes, adornments, riches, and all other good things of this life are provided for common use. And so, when any man snatches for himself as much as he can, he takes away from another man's heap the amount he adds to his own, and it is impossible for anyone to grow rich except at the expense of someone else.[115]

While it is clear that Locke's mature economic thought never completely rid itself of these limits, the only portion of that early dictum Locke never altered was his vision of utility as a result rather than as a cause. For Locke, though we act out of self-interest (or what seems to us as utility), that interest was a logical result of the obligations of our condition as creature rather than creator: made by God and not by ourselves, we had no unlimited property in our being with respect to God (that is no right to destroy his creation). We bore the same positive obligation that accompanied any such usufruct, that of preserving the property (our selves) until such time as it was lawfully reclaimed by its owner (God).[116]

Locke's exploration of the cross-elasticity of demand may have been no more than tangentially related to his treatment of interest rates as market-determined, but it does reveal a deepening acceptance of the concept of *Economic Man*. Locke was confident in his ascription of a uniform and predictable set of market behaviors to humanity in the mass, because for Locke, those behaviors were supported by what might be called his Natural Law theory of human psychology.

Locke's *Essay Concerning Human Understanding* (1690) is best known for its rejection of an epistemology based on innate ideas for one of empirically gained knowledge,[117] but the innate *faculties*—perception, reflection, composition, and abstraction—that Locke believed drew meaning from those sensory impressions functioned in his argument far more like those rejected innate *ideas* than perhaps even Locke supposed.

He certainly meant them to be as sure a guide, holding them to be "faculties fit to attain as easy and certain knowledge of them [truths in nature] as if they [those truths] were originally imprinted on the mind."[118] And though it must be admitted that the end result of all our reflection need neither be uniform nor uniformly good, both these kinds of differences seem to be reducible to nothing more than accidents of exposure to differing stimuli compounded by varying degrees of mental application ("according as they more or less reflect on them") rather than to any great innate differences in capacity.[119] Thus:

> It is not to be expected that a man who drudges on all his life in a laborious trade, should be more knowing in the variety of things done in the world than a packhorse, who is driven constantly forwards and backwards in a narrow lane, only to market, should be skilled in the geography of the country.[120]

Even though, in a less sanguine mood, he ventured that the "greatest part of mankind want leisure or capacity for demonstration. . . . The greatest part cannot *know,* and therefore they must *believe.*"[121]

In the age-old nature versus nurture debate, Locke clearly accepted nurture as the main determinant of differences in achievement, but he seems equally as clearly to have accepted nature as the main factor in keeping those differences startlingly narrow and our choices exceedingly predictable.

It was not only that human minds all worked in identical fashion, mechanically building up chains of complex ideas through reflection on simple ones, or even that there were certain propositions we could not dispute even if they were not innate—the classic one for Locke being the pre–quantum theory *impossible est idem esse, et non esse* (it is impossible for the same thing to be and not be).[122] Joined to "almost all our ideas both of sensation and reflection" were those of pleasure and pain, and these were not simply mechanical impulses but incentives attached to our ideas by "our wise Creator" to aid us in using our faculties as he intended.[123] The ultimate purpose of the "blending" of pleasure and pain in all we experienced was to lead us to seek the true "fullness of joy" in God rather than in the World,[124] but both were legitimated by their function in helping us to achieve the full lives in this world intended for us by that Creator: lives based on "convenience" as much as necessity, of "Comfort" as much as "Support," in which the world was there for us "richly to enjoy."[125] No amoral or purely egoistical hedonism was intended, and though this innate attraction for the pleasant and avoidance of the painful could be so abused,[126] for Locke it remained quintessentially a *lawful,* that is to say *purposive, meaningful, rational,* and hence *comprehensible* behavior. As creatures of our Maker we were both without the right to harm his creation and under positive obligation to ensure the survival of that creation, and thus Pleasure's and Pain's first job was to supply in the young the want of "consideration and reasoning" so that they might "take notice of what hurts or advantages the body."[127] For Locke, "God Almighty himself" was "under the necessity of being happy."[128]

Not only did Locke take pleasure and pain to be "the hinges on which our passions turn,"[129] but he believed that they affected us in a predictable fashion. It was "the *uneasiness of desire,* fixed upon some absent good" that "*immediately*" determined the will, and this preference for the present over the long-term good was so strongly ingrained in our minds that we could not be made to reach for longer term ends unless we could be made equally uneasy over them.[130] Though this tendency did appear to make it more difficult for individuals to concentrate on their ultimate good (salvation), this was not so much the fault of the focus (hunger and thirst and the like being spurs to necessary acts) as of our societies that taught us to "itch after honour, power, or riches" instead of after that salvation.[131] The "foundation of all virtue" being the ability "to resist the importunity of present pleasure or pain, for the sake of what reason" tells us "is fit to be done," even "though the appetite lean the other way," a major purpose of education was accustoming children to "cross" their own "inclinations."[132] And the most efficient way to do this, according to Locke, was to prevent as many as possible of those inclinations from being reinforced by habit. The first step on the path to luxury was too great a nicety of taste. Locke recommended that children be fed "plain" food, "very sparingly seasoned," as "our palates grow into a relish and liking of the seasoning and cookery, which by custom they are set to."[133] Locke was truly proposing a revolution in our understanding of human psychology: instead of a universe of absolute value guaranteed by a belief in *innate* ideas, he was suggesting that an ordered world could be constructed on the very malleability of our makeup. And that malleability was considerable. Locke began his *Thoughts Concerning Education* by proclaiming that "the minds of children are as easily turned, this or that way, as water itself."[134]

Locke never wrote the great treatise of morality he intended, but this was not because he did not think that morality could be any less certainly demonstrated than mathematics,[135] only that he came to feel that it was a task beyond his accomplishment.[136] So we are missing the links such a work would have forged between the incipient economic rationale in his psychology and his explanation of consumer behavior in the marketplace. We may or may not think this could be done or that his arguments as so far laid out are convincing, but we must accept that Locke thought them so. For him they formed a safety net of one weave with his idea of an immutable consent to a fixed yardstick: they were the *objective* laws of our nature as much as they were the *objective* laws of Nature. This had always been the ground of his thinking no matter how much his conclusions changed over the years:

> it is by His order that the heaven revolves in unbroken rotation, the earth stands fast, and the stars shine . . . [and] it is in obedience to His will that all living beings have their own laws of birth and life; and there is nothing so unstable, so uncertain in this whole constitution of things as not to admit of valid and fixed laws of operation appropriate to its nature.[137]

If economic behavior was acceptable because it was intended to serve one of God's purposes for man, it would also be rational (because its maker was rational and had designed a rational creature). If it was rational it was both predictable and educable: this meant polices based on its proclivities could be successfully implemented to channel it as a society needed.

Locke exposed himself to and sharpened his own ideas upon almost every strain of thought the seventeenth century had to offer or draw upon. He owed his idea of conscious existence to Descartes ("Every man being conscious to himself that he thinks");[138] his idea of the compulsively active mind was suspiciously similar to that of Hobbes (though no definite connection can be traced); and he owed his first ideas of Natural Law to the humanist drive to pursue Aristotle in the original rather than through the medieval tradition,[139] though he later refined them by modifying the positions of Hugo Grotius and Samuel Pufendorf.[140] His idea of the social contract owed much to his reading of Richard Hooker, and his "labor theory of value" derived ultimately from the Christian humanist/Protestant concern with a faith worked out through a diligently pursued calling,[141] though there are elements of neo-Stoicism in the treatment of labor as a tool for preserving national strength.[142] Locke's "State of Nature," far from being the dechristianized Nature its emphasis on self-preservation might make it appear, was really "saturated with Christian assumptions."[143] His later religious thought seems to have been shaped in part by his reactions to the most anticlerical Whigs and their heirs—Henry Stubbe (1632–1676), Charles Blount (1654–1693), and John Toland (1670–1722).[144] One could go on.

Sir William Petty was not primarily an economic writer in the sense that his economic insights were no more than tools for accomplishing a much more broadly defined societal reformation. John Locke was not primarily an economic writer in a different sense: his work on money comes out of a portion of his working life that was separate from his main interest in philosophy even if, like any other seventeenth-century thinker, he expected the philosophy of society to encompass its economic life. But as an economic writer he is a classic example of the ability of a *Weltanschauung* not only to survive a change in model and method but to turn those changes to its own ends. Perhaps we must call him an anticapitalist writer who was unaware of how much capitalism (as a system rather than as a *Geist*) had already changed his thought.

CHAPTER 10

Accounting for Economics

Sometimes supporting and sometimes in competition with the mechanical philosophy was the mathematical orientation of the century's intellectual revolution. This orientation, however, was itself subject to contradictory pulls as the century's philosophers tried to decide if the essence of mathematical thinking (and of thought itself) was deductive or inductive, rational or experiential. Numbers are everywhere in commercial activity and are central to every method designed to comprehend it, from the most mechanical tasks in bookkeeping to the most abstruse laws of economics. But, if they are everywhere, they are everywhere meaningless without some agreement on their use and significance. The debate over number was one no serious student of the market could avoid.

"Number, Weight, and Measure" was Sir William Petty's mantra as much as it was his method; the phrase, or variations upon it, appeared in his writings over and over and over again.[1] The phrase was not novel; Gerard de Malynes had used "number, weight, and measure" as a shorthand for the ranking implicit in the idea of order,[2] but Petty subscribed to a concept of reason as essentially *mathematical:*

> Ratiocination is nothing but Addition and Subtraction of *Sensata*. . . .
> Nor doe I conceave there is any sin in Ratiocination, for it is the seeking of the truth; and God is the Truth and a Rewarder of them that seek him, even allthough they should miss of finding him. Nor doe I know why God may not be as well pleased with our Considering the systeme of the World, The motion of bodyes, The Censation and Generation of Animalls, as with the manner how grace is infused, and faith inspired into the Souls of men.[3]

Petty considered himself, in many respects, a student of Thomas Hobbes,[4] but Petty had a habit of culling out pieces of *Leviathan* without paying proper attention to them. He seems to have thought his definition of reason was adapted from that of Thomas Hobbes:

> When a man *Reasoneth*, hee does nothing else but conceive a summe totall, from *Addition* of parcels; or conceive a Remainder, from *Subtrac-*

tion of one summe from another. . . . For Reason, in this sense, is nothing but *Reckoning* (that is, Adding and Subtracting) of the Consequences of general names agreed upon.[5]

But, for Hobbes, reason was a *deductive* exercise:

> The Use and End of Reason, is not the finding of the summe, and truth of one, or a few consequences, remote from the first definitions, and settled significations of names; but to begin at these; and proceed from one consequence to another. For there can be no certainty of the last Conclusion, without a certainty of all those Affirmations and negations, on which it was grounded, and inferred.[6]

However, Petty was moving it in an inductive direction in three distinct ways: (1) by counting from specifics (raw data) to reach general conclusions; (2) by counting concrete things, that is, things susceptible to sensory examination precisely because they had *weight* and *measure;*[7] and (3) by making the counting itself part of the inductive method of observation and experiment.[8] All three of these elements can be seen in the directions Petty laid out in 1684 for the Dublin Philosophical Society:

> The Society is to be called The Dublin Society for the improuving of naturall knowledge, Mathematicks and Mechanicks.[9]
> That they chiefly apply themselves to the makeing of experiments, and prefer the same, to the best Discourses, Letters and Books they can make or read, even concerning experiments.[10]
> That they provide themselves with Rules of number, weight and measure; not onely how to measure the plus & minus of the quality and Schemes of matter, but do provide themselves with Scales and Tables, whereby to measure and compute such qualitys and Schemes in their exact proportions.[11]

If anything, Petty's rules of "number, weight and measure," and his insistence that the sciences (including his new "science" of "Political Arithmetick") be limited to examining the practical cause and effect relationships between sensible things echo the thought of Marin Mersenne (1588–1648), the French Minim Father who rejected equally the opposing systems of "true physics" of Descartes and Aristotle (as grounded in ultimately unknowable final causes) for the "operational knowledge" produced by the "mathematical sciences" that "dealt with measurable appearances, not inner natures."[12] For Descartes, the "laws of mathematics" were "inborn in our minds (*mentibus nostris ingenitae*)," that is to say, implanted there by God, and hence not merely formal concepts without any connection to reality.[13] Mersenne believed numbers existed *only* in "the understanding," but were still "ontologically inseparable from" real things because "numbers existed only by virtue of the possible existence of *things to be numbered.*"[14]

Petty's "Number, weight, and measure" was part of the new philosophy's substitution of mathematics and closely defined terminology for the older rhetorical devices of simile, metaphor, and analogy in its search for a "universal language" capable of "unbiased communication."[15] The old methods (and the old model) led to a unified-field chimera as Francis Bacon well knew (though he had not the word for it):

> The ancient opinion that man was Microcosmos, an abstract or model of the world, hath been fantastically strained by Paracelsus and the alchemists, as if there were to be found in man's body certain correspondences and parallels, which should have respect to all varieties of things, as stars, planets, minerals, which are extant in the world.[16]

In the *Advice of W.P. to Mr. Samuel Hartlib for The Advancement of some particular Parts of Learning* (1648), Petty saluted "those few, that are Reall Friends to the Design of Realities" and condemned "those who are tickled only with Rhetorical Prefaces, Transitions, & Epilogues, & charmed with fine Allusions and Metaphors."[17] Men whose positions on what constituted a true physics were in total opposition to each other still recognized the need for an objective language. Hobbes believed "the Light of humane minds" was "perspicuous Words, but by exact definitions first snuffed, and purged from ambiguity."[18] Joseph Glanvill urged men to search out "the true laws of Matter and Motion" to secure "the Foundations of Religion" against what he saw as Hobbes's "Mechanical Atheism," but, in so doing, spoke out against the hunting of "Chimaera's by rules of Art" and the dressing up of "Ignorance in words of bulk and sound."[19]

This search for an objective language drew its origins from and spread to numerous strands of seventeenth-century thought. One such strand was the humanist/Renaissance-naturalist/Paracelsian assault on Scholasticism inherited by the seventeenth century from the sixteenth.[20] In Sir Francis Bacon's hand, this turned into an attack on a Scholastic "method" resting less "upon evidence of truth proved by arguments" than "upon particular confutations and solutions of every scruple, caillation, and objection."[21] A significant but supportive variation on this was the century's adoption of Senecan Stoicism with its support for Cato's "*Rem tene, verba sequentur.*" ("Hold on to the object, the words will follow.")[22] While John Locke's distaste for medieval Scholasticism predated his formal exposure to Baconian thought, it certainly took many of the same forms; the third and fourth abuses of words in his *Essay Concerning Human Understanding* were direct attacks on the "affected obscurity" of Scholasticism and its confusion of names with things.[23] Especially Baconian was Locke's reminder that notwithstanding these learned disputants, these all-knowing doctors, it was to the unscholastic statesman that the governments of the world owned their peace, defence, and liberties; and from the illiterate and comtemned mechanic (a name of disgrace) that they received the improvements of useful arts.[24]

Baconian, too, in the sense of being a Holy Grail of the *virtuosi* (Petty included), was Locke's emphasis on the correct *proportion* in a mathematical sense, though in a philosophical sense this was also an important element of the Aristotelian tradition in which Locke was steeped, argue with it as he would.[25] Locke's idea of the most advantageous circulation of money through the society sought, after all, to strike a correct proportion (or distribution of wealth) between the landowner as the source of production, the farmer, and the consumer/laborer that would exclude the strictly commercial elements of his world: bankers, wholesalers, retailers, and (import-export) merchants. Such a proportion might be said, in a practical sense, to be more Aristotelian than Baconian. It was, as well, a very different sort of proportion than that between "hands and lands" or needs and trades sought by Sir William Petty.

Another strand feeding the search for an objective language was a perceived link between rhetorical license and heretical "enthusiasm," then defined as "an inspiration, a ravishment of the spirit, divine motion, [or] Poetical fury."[26] A suspicion of poetical usage predated the civil wars: Bacon had considered an ungoverned imagination one of the "infirmities of the mind,"[27] but the tempests of the 1640s and 1650s served to harden the hearts of men as varied in their views as Meric Casaubon (1599–1671), Henry More (1586–1661), and Sir William Temple (1628–1699) against every arrow in the enthusiast's rhetorical quiver.[28] Sprat's *History of the Royal Society* praised its efforts "to separate the knowledge of *Nature,* from the colours of *Rhetorick,* the devices of *Fancy,* or the delightful deceit of *Fables.*"[29] Its members aimed at substituting a "Mathematical plainness" for the "specious *Tropes* and *Figures*" of the Scholastics and the Sectaries.[30] This was a strand fed as much by fear of the potential for politicosocial chaos in sectarianism as by concern with the logical problems caused by a multiplicity of positions supported by an equal variety of criteria for judging the validity of an argument.

More overtly political was the strand fed by the battle that raged for control of the law (and its courts), in which the language of the basic legal system—the Common Law–French—became the final victim of the attack on the King's Prerogative Courts. Both those like Henry Robinson (1605?–1664?) who attacked juries and William Walwyn (fl. 1649) who defended them had no patience for the "meanders, Quirks and subtilties" or the "Frenchified" innovations of a discourse that was, in truth, centuries old.[31] Malynes, Misselden, and Mun had nary a kind word for the problems those "Quillets" and "subtilties" created for commerce. Court law and statute law were so closely intertwined in England, and statute law was simultaneously constitutional law: this was always as much a battle over what the law said as over how it said it. Even the "how" was politically charged, because the accessibility of law's language was accessibility to the law itself.

For William Petty, finding an objective language was as much a matter of social as of epistemological necessity. Training individuals in its discipline would produce a surer (because an informed) obedience to the authority that carried out policies reached through such a method, while recognition of its objectivity would remove the discord creating claims of "self-interest" often imputed to any policy suggestions.[32] Here, Petty was less a student of Marin Mersenne than of Thomas Hobbes.[33]

Locke's numbers needed weight in a truly measurable sense. He warned his readers that "All our Names . . . are but to them [foreigners] bare sounds."[34] A clipped shilling was "in the Law and in Propriety of speech . . . no more a Shilling than a piece of Wood, which was once a sealed Yard, is still a Yard when one half of it is broke off."[35] The name for a thing was not the thing itself: the stamp was the name, the silver was the reality. Locke's formulations might be said to translate the idea of "inner nature" or "intrinsic value" from the philosophic to the economic sphere. Petty's formulations substitute "measurable appearances" for those "inner natures" but without giving up the belief in a true "ontological" link: if "number" was a true mirror of "reality," then a system built upon it would not be chaotic but would truly mirror the moral order of that reality.

Sir Josiah Child had taken much the same stand as Locke when he claimed no merchant would accept "the name it is called by" over "the intrinsick value of the money."[36] But numbers, to Child, were more overtly a matter of politics than philosophy. He advocated incarceration in workhouses or compulsory relocation for those "Unprofitable to the Kingdom," but warned against a too literal reliance on trade balance sheets whenever the numbers told against the East India Company.[37] He read Petty, he read Hobbes, and he believed each, in their own way, a guide, but he took their ideas as based in common sense rather than in particular (and divergent) analyses. And he meant that as a compliment: he valued common sense above what he would have seen as abstruse thought. To brave a pun: he valued heaping up his cents in common with each other. Of the six men whose work we have examined so far, Sir Josiah Child provides us with the closest approximation to Weber's capitalist *Geist*.

Two new economic models emerged from this period, although they were not yet as fully developed as the trade balance model with which they competed: a circulatory model and a national accounting model. The circulatory model existed in a more fragmentary form: elements such as quantity theory, interest rates, and government spending were understood to be major components in the circulation of money throughout the economy, but there was as yet no one comprehensive theory tying them together. There was still considerable disagreement, as well, as to how their mechanical and numerical elements should be combined: Petty was working toward a quantitative treatment of velocity while Locke was working toward a qualitative treatment.

Petty's national accounting theory (or, in a rougher form, Child's "productive" and "unproductive" trades) was more finished than the circulatory model in a technical sense because it could be taken from an existing business model—the balance sheet. But Petty had as yet provided no national version of the income statement to go with it, very likely because he believed the complement to his national balance sheet was still the trade balance: Petty's inclusion of individuals as producers rather than as consumers, his rejection of service providers as unproductive, and his belief that gold and silver were the most durable *forms* (not *stores*) of wealth were but a few of the ways in which his balance sheet privileged goods produced for export. He did not realize how far his ideas on value-creation went toward substituting a gross product model for a trade balance one, likely because economics was only a means for Petty and not an end in itself: he was less concerned to refine the model than to prove to the government how it could reconstruct the nation through it.

3

Balance vs. Equilibrium

CHAPTER 11

In the Balance

By midcentury the doctrine that the nation's economic health was in jeopardy whenever imports exceeded exports was so firmly accepted that a massive political overhaul of the realm from monarchy to republic and back again could not dislodge it. The "Instructions to the Council of Trade" in 1650 required its members

> to consider of some way that a most exact account be kept of all commodities imported and exported through the land, to the end that a perfect balance of trade may be taken, whereby the Commonwealth may not be impoverished, by receiving of commodities yearly from foreign parts of a greater value than what was carried out.[1]

The "Instructions to the Council for Trade" in 1668 ordered its members

> to consider how a due and exact account may be kept of all the commodities exported from or imported into any of the ports or custom houses of this nation to the end that a perfect balance of trade may be taken.[2]

The trade balance model was alive and well at the century's end. The 1697 report of the Commissioners "of Trade and Plantations" exhibits a continuing concern with merchants profiting from trade at the nation's expense, the finite my-gain-is-your-loss mentality, and the bullionist conception of wealth underlying the balance theory:

> But finding that we have imported from some countries goods to a greater original value than we have exported thither, and it being certain that some private persons may enrich themselves by trading in commodities which may at the same time diminish the wealth and treasure of the nation, to which no addition can be made by trade but what is gained from foreigners and foreign countries, and that such an overbalance has not been made good by any circulation in trade or exchange so as to make such trades advantageous for this nation as they of late been carried on, we have in our enquiries particularly distinguished the same from others that have a better foundation, conceiving that such trades have occasioned the exportation of coin or bullion or hindered the importation thereof.[3]

Perhaps the only innovation in this doctrine over the course of the century was the institution, in 1651, of the Navigation Acts. By prohibiting the importation of Asian, African, or American goods into England or any of its possessions unless carried in English vessels and of European goods unless in English vessels or those of the exporting country, Parliament could be said to have recognized the importance of the carrying trade's contribution to the trade balance. It could also have been said to have recognized the importance of taking that trade away from the Dutch.

Preventing imports from exceeding exports was hardly just an English concern. A proclamation issued by Philip IV of Spain on September 11, 1657, prohibited commerce "with the Realms of Portugal, France, and England . . . upon several penalties, even to the death of the transgressors, and loss of their Estates" because his "Realms have sustained, and do sustain very great damages, the silver and gold being carried out of them," his "Subjects and vassals estates, [were] vainly spent in useless and unnecessary things," and his enemies enjoyed "as much convenience and profit as they could have done in time of peace, by the introduction of their Merchandizes."[4] It was translated into English and published in London before the year was out.

What is different about balance of trade is that instead of being a model English economic writers merely borrowed from their general intellectual milieu, "balance" was a model to which they made important contributions. Of course, balance was both an integral part of Aristotelian moderation and the key to health according to the doctrine of the four humors, and balance scales were thousands of years older than bookkeeping balances. In fact, the use of the term *balance* probably made its way into bookkeeping from its role in weighing coins, as witness such weighty tomes as *The Scales of Commerce and Trade* (1660) by Thomas Willsford, a compendium of instruction in applied mathematics and bookkeeping with page after page of problems in exchanges worked out for the reader, whose title continues *Ballancing betwixt the Buyer & Seller, Artificer and Manufacture, Debitor and Creditor,* etc.[5] Nonetheless, we sometimes come across a borrowing so direct that it can have no other source. In his *Treatise of Vocations* (1603), William Perkins suggested that Christians take what were, in effect, trial balances of their souls:

> First, we must draw out the bill of our receipts and expenses. The bills of receipt are framed thus; we must call to remembrance what graces, blessings and gifts we have received of God, whether temporal or spiritual. . . . our bills of expenses, which are nothing else but large considerations of our sins.[6]

The borrowing was consciously made as Perkins went on to suggest that

> [as] tradesmen for their temporal estates keep in their shops books of receipts and expenses: shall we not then much more do the like for our spiritual estates.7

Of course, the doctrines of justification by faith and predestined election meant that, in this example, Christ's intercession would be needed to balance the reckoning when the time came to "appear before the great God of all the world to give up our accounting."8

Adapting a bookkeeping metaphor did not necessarily entail accepting the values of commercial society. It is easy to find much praise of merchants in midcentury pamphlets: their trade being an "honourable profession and principal fountain from whose industrious streams floweth in the riches of a Common-wealth," making merchants "necessary to the well-being, nay to the [very] being of the state."9 But this is praise for the role of these import-export dealers in bringing in the gold and silver that still consituted the century's primary understanding of wealth. Profit-seeking behavior that did not increase the amount of coin in the national coffers or came at the expense of those with a permanent (or landed) interest in the nation was still anathema. But banks, credit instruments, and profit are part and parcel of commercial life: some way was still needed to accommodate all of commercial life within the value system of the larger society.

If, by midcentury, balance of trade had become a fixed orthodoxy of political economy, balance of power had become an equally fixed orthodoxy of politics proper, though one with a much less clearly defined meaning. Balance in the political sense could refer to a diplomatic balance of powers, as in Charles Davenant's own *Essay upon the Balance of Power* (1701) stressing England's historic role of upholding "the balance of Europe," so that "neither France nor Spain might gain ground the one upon the other."10 It could also be attached to the older concept of mixed government, as Charles I had done in his *Answer to the Nineteen Propositions* (June 18, 1642):

> There being three kinds of government among men, absolute monarchy, aristocracy, and democracy, and these having their particular conveniences and inconveniences, the experience and wisdom of your ancestors hath so moulded this out of a mixture of these as to give to this kingdoms (as far as human prudence can provide) the conveniences of all three, without the inconveniences of any one, as long as the balance hangs even between the three estates.11

Or it might begin to transform into a balance of interests as James Harrington (1611–1677) intended the "Agrarian" Law of *Oceana* to do:

> But if the whole people be landlords, or hold the land so divided among them that no man or number of men within the compass of the few or aristocracy overbalance them, it is a commonwealth.[12]

According to Otto Mayr, "a self-regulating system may be pictured as a balance connected with some mechanism that, as soon as one scale drops, begins to remove weight from that scale and add it to the other until equilibrium is restored."[13] Were any of these balances self-regulating? Davenant's definition came in the middle of a complaint that William III had abandoned the policy just outlined: no functioning self-regulating mechanism there, just a dependance on state action. The whole point of mixed-government theory was to prevent the degeneration inherent in the monarchical, aristocratic, and republican principles of which it was comprised; that is to say the whole point of mixed-government theory was to set up the original constitution so that realigning was never needed.

Harrington did go to great lengths to explain how his "Agrarian" was the self-regulating mechanism for the socioeconomic balance of power even if the exact meaning of the leveling intention (or lack of it) in the £2,000 limit is still under dispute.[14] Certainly whenever an estate exceeded £2,000 worth of land, that estate was subdivided. But if this prevented a minority among the landowning classes from concentrating the ownership of all the land in Oceana within their hands, how did it *keep* the balance between the landed and the landless? Matthew Wren, in his *Considerations on Mr. Harrington's Common-wealth of Oceana* (1657), thought it could not. For Wren, it all boiled down to a simple matter of numbers. Using Harrington's own population suppositions (5,000 landowners in a population of 200,000), Wren suggested that "the whole Body of the People being intrusted with giving a Vote and keeping a Sword" would not just counterpoise the 5,000 putative landowners but so overbalance them as to change the "Agrarian" law at will.[15] It was but "the Fancie of Poets" to "say that Laws doe or can Govern," but "Wise men" knew that this figure of speech, was like any other such "only" an expression "of such Accidents and Qualifications as belong to things and Persons."[16] Government was "in the person whose Will" gave "a being to that law."[17] And the armed will of 195,000 was greater than the legislated will of 5,000.

It does not help matters that modern commentators sometimes read self-regulating factors back into these balances to make them dynamic. C. B. Macpherson believed that Harrington "based his case for a gentry-led commonwealth" on the "assumption" that "the gentry did, and always would, accept and support the bourgeois social order which then existed and which the rest of the people wanted."[18] Contemporary sources, however saw a clear opposition rather than an identity of interests between the landed and the landless. The Army Debates at Putney (October–November 1647) give us one window into contemporary thought on the issue. During a debate on how to reform the franchise, Colonel Thomas Rainsborough (d. 1648) argued that "the poorest man in England" was "not at all bound in a strict sense to that government" in which he had no voice.[19] The rebuttal of then Commissary-General Henry Ireton (1611–1651) tied the franchise to the possession of "a permanent interest" in the realm, defined as a freehold property interest, for a mere renter was free to emigrate on the morrow and take his capital with him. Ireton was certain an inclusive franchise was of itself an invitation to the abolition of property.[20] While the Putney debates centered on the question of including the lesser landless (wage earners and servants), this bias extended all the way up the ranks of landless groups. The anonymous author of *Chaos* (1659) believed the "Merchant cannot be so well confided in, who perceiving a storm arise from any foraign quarter, or in bred commotion, can easily transport himself and his into the safety of another Prince or Republiques Harbour."[21] Harrington himself admitted there might be times when a landless majority would block an opposing minority by superiority of force and numbers should a majority vote in the legislature fail of itself.[22] A resort to arms does not suggest a self-correcting balance but the failure of one.

One additional candidate for a balancer presented itself in the form of the Royal Society. As James Jacob summarized the ideology of its founders,

> where the interests of the country lie in trade, husbandry and the Reformation, they are matched by the court's interest in empire, military and naval power and a full treasury. This harmony does not come from the slavish subjection of private interests to the crown, country to court, still less of court to country. It comes instead from a due balance of forces.[23]

The mission of the Royal Society—the pursuit of experimental natural philosophy—would keep the state in balance and the various interests it represented in harmony.[24] But the Society was certainly never given the authority needed to function in such a fashion: the science it pursued would certainly serve both interests, but it could not by itself keep one interest from overpowering the other.

Balance is a centering mechanism. For royalists, the prince, even though seen as the head of the body politic, had always acted as a balancing center in his function as that body's recirculating organ, as we have already seen in the anonymous *Usurie Arraigned* (1625):

> Is not money minted by politicke Princes, out of their owne Bullion to
> bee imployed to the publicke good . . . [running] throughout those poli-
> tike bodies, like bloud in the naturall, in the veined of trading, for all and
> every ones maintenance, and retire to those royall centres again, by many
> just rights for all and every ones defence.[25]

After the advent of Harvey's work, the heart took the central role. For
a parliamentarian such as Harrington

> parlament is the heart, which, consisting of two ventricles, the one
> greater and replenished with a grosser matter, the other less and full of a
> purer, sucks in, and spouts forth the vital blood of *Oceana* by a perpetual
> circulation . . . [as] the earth remains firm for ever; that is . . . upon her
> proper center.[26]

Royalist or parliamentarian, the centering principle of the body politic
was the common good: the public interest was the center/pivot around
which countervailing interests could be balanced. It was not yet the aggregate interest of the twentieth century.[27] This was still the world of congruent "cosms": in Aristotelian ethics, virtue was the median point between
two vices. The center of a circle, after all, can be described as the intersection of the median points of all its possible diameters. Malynes wrote of
"gaine" as the "center of the circle of commerce," but strove for a national
gain, not a private one.[28] Had not Petty and Locke sought, in their respective ways, a balance between producers and consumers?

The problems of *balance* in both the political and economic spheres
were actually parallel: in both, some *balance* was an ideal to be achieved.
What was required was a *self-regulating mechanism* to maintain it. The *balance of trade* could not. But if Political Economy had provided the model of
that *balance*, could it also provide one for *equilibrium?*

In the last decades of the seventeenth century, three very different
approaches were tried. Sir Dudley North, a merchant from a gentry family,
accepted the basic premise of balance of trade (that exports should exceed
imports), but relegated it to so minor a place in his analysis of the *domestic*
economy that it is exceedingly easy for modern commentators to forget
that it was there at all. Instead, he reset the reader's focus on a number of
equilibrating mechanisms in the markets for money and land, but because
he failed to substitute an interactor analysis for the part-whole orientation
of the organic model, he was unable to tie all these mechanisms together
into an equilibrating *system.*

Nicholas Barbon, a physician turned builder, insurer, and bank speculator, openly suggested that balance of trade be scrapped as a fallacious
model and appeared to substitute for it a system of interactive economic
actors. But when his theories are closely examined, they turn out not to rest

on anything so "modern" as division of labor or economic rationality but on a much older model of the universe itself as a living organism. The substitution of *plentitude* for *scarcity* did not a system make.

Sir William Petty had begun and Charles Davenant would further develop an economic model based on a differently focused merger of bookkeeping and the body politic that competed with trade balance theory as the seventeenth century passed into the eighteenth. That model was national accounting, the production of an income statement and a balance sheet for the nation as a whole. In making up such statements, a new definition of wealth was refined in which a nation's productive power (its resources and the size of the work force it could command to transform those resources into goods) came to the fore. But when we look at the income statements and balance sheets that Charles Davenant drew up for England, we will see that all production not destined for export was subtracted from the totals calculated. In Davenant's hands these new models were used to bolster rather than replace trade balance theory. If his treatment of taxation is compared to Petty's it becomes clear that Davenant advanced Petty's methodology to bolster a worldview more conservative than Petty's own.

Sir Dudley North returned to England during the Exclusion Crisis and did not live to see the Glorious Revolution. Nicholas Barbon cut his intellectual teeth on ideas that flourished during the Interregnum but had to go underground in the ideologically conservative Restoration. Such prominence as he eventually achieved was in the heady days of the mid-1690s when the lapsing of the Licensing Acts "freed" the presses, and the demands of a war economy on England's government opened the way for such novelties as publicly funded debt and paper money. Charles Davenant died only a few months before the last of the Stuart monarchs, decidedly unhappy with the world that financial revolution was creating.

Davenant's case also makes an interesting counterpoint to Harrington's, for both men were deeply influenced by a school of thought known as civic humanism. That tradition, with its distrust of commerce and its desire to preserve a public-spirited and frugal *virtue*, also helped shape the thought of Andrew Fletcher. Davenant (1656–1714) and Fletcher (1653–1716) were almost exact contemporaries. In the introduction to the first part of this study, we met Fletcher bemoaning "the luxury of Asia and America" that sunk all "Europe into an abyss of pleasures," changing that society's "frugal and military way of living" without a thought for the "unspeakable evils" that were "altogether inseparable from an expensive" one.[29] Charles Davenant would most certainly have agreed with him.

Sir Dudley North:
Merchants and Markets

There is no doubt that Dudley North relied more on self-regulating principles in his economic arguments than had any English writer before him. He could demonstrate the effect of changes in the interest rate on the price of land and changes in the price of produce on the rent land could command. But he also insisted that falling rents were not the cause of falling prices for land, and changes in the interest rate would not affect rental prices. He could relate almost any individual economic actor to the overall economy through some market principle, but not always one group of actors to another. The same Aristotelian social division of labor permeating the century's political thought helped keep its economic thought trained on rigidly conceptualized categories. When we ask why North's was a world so prepared to use bookkeeping to describe its economy, to convert individual gain into balance of trade, to speak of the national stock as though one were making up a net worth statement, we find the same finite, bullionist, intrinsic value intellectual kit underlying Dudley North's new laissez-faire economics as we have seen in the more state-oriented thinkers preceding him.

Dudley North (1641–1691) was the fourth son of Dudley, the 4th Baron North. That he became one of the leading merchants of the Levant (or Turkey) Company is an example of the less often studied side of social mobility in seventeenth-century England, the movement of the aristocracy into the market. But the Norths were one of a number of aristocratic families that had never entirely cast off their mercantile background: the father of the 1st Baron North had been a London merchant, and Dudley's father (the 4th Baron) thought the "Church, Law, Arms or Physic . . . [and] Merchandise" all equally honorable careers for the gentry's sons.[1] The careers of Dudley and his brothers were as varied as their inclinations and abilities. Charles (1635–1691), the eldest, would succeed his father. Francis (1637–1685) pursued a career in law that led him to the Chancellorship (and a barony—Guildford—of his own) while keeping up an amateur interest in the Royal Society. Dudley was bound apprentice to a Levant Company merchant when he showed no interest in any other studies. John (1645–1683) became the Master of Trinity College, Cambridge. Montague (1649–1710) would end up as Dudley's agent in Turkey. And Roger (1651–1734) became solicitor-general to the Duke of York and attorney-general to Queen Mary of Modena. His practice falling off sharply with the change of regime following the Glorious Revolution, Roger retired to pursue his intellectual pursuits (science, history, and music), eventually becoming Dudley's executor, the guardian of Dudley's sons, and the biographer of his brothers Francis, John, and Dudley.

It is, however, Dudley North's career that concerns us here.

Leaving London in 1661, Dudley began as a factor for a member of the Levant Company in Smyrna, built up a business on his own behalf, moved to Constantinople, and was eventually elected treasurer of the Levant Company in 1670.[2] He returned to settle in England in 1680, leaving brother Montague in charge of his affairs in Constantinople, while Dudley expanded his business and political connections at home, as his marriage (in 1682 or 1683) to Sir Robert Gunning's widow Ann brought him control of a fortune even greater than his own.

The England of the 1680s was a maelstrom of party politics that threatened more than once to erupt into a repeat of the events of 1642 through 1660, and the Norths were too prominent a Tory family to avoid being drawn into the whirlwind. Paralleling the battle between Charles II and Shaftesbury for control of the three Exclusion Parliaments was the battle between Charles II and the Whiggish city financiers for control of London itself. The Whigs had taken London's seats in Parliament in the 1681 elections and won the local shrieval elections, while a Whig-packed London grand jury had quashed the 1681 indictment against Shaftesbury. Even though Charles had been quietly removing Whigs from the city militia, only a split within the Whig ranks had kept the city from being entirely lost by saving the mayoral race for the Tories.[3]

There had been a custom (although not used since 1674) of allowing the lord mayor to choose one of the two annually elected sheriffs by a special process of nomination, the Common Hall then voting for the second sheriff, but when Sir John Moore (the Tory mayor elected in 1681) tried to revive the custom by naming Dudley North sheriff in May 1682, all hell broke loose. The Whigs claimed the special nomination was invalid and tried polling the hall for both places, the Mayor ordered them to desist, each side continued to poll only its own supporters, and each side in turn seems to have barricaded itself inside the hall. The shenanigans went on for weeks, with prominent Whigs such as Josiah Child's ex-partner Thomas Papillon opposing North as Moore constantly reconfirmed North's election. When it looked as if Dudley North might refuse to serve, letters were sent off by Secretary Jenkins to his brother Roger to make sure that was not the case. Before the accusations finished flying, plans to disrupt North's installation had been turned into a supposed opening salvo in an attempt to remove James, the Duke of York, from the succession "by the sword."[4]

A by-the-book sheriff at a time when the political community refused to go by the book, all North got out of his year in office was a knighthood and the considerable enmity of the Whig portion of the merchant community. As long as Charles II or his brother remained on the throne, North prospered. He was appointed a customs commissioner in 1683, moved to the treasury in 1684 (where he would spar with Sidney, Lord Godolphin, appointed the following month), and moved back to customs on the death of Charles II. He served as Member for Banbury in James II's first Parliament and kept the city militia in line as one of its lieutenants in 1685 and 1687. But he was not uncritical of the Stuarts; Dudley joined his brother Roger in supporting the Seven Bishops against James II. He made no attempt to leave either his position or the City itself when the Glorious Revolution brought William III and Mary II to the throne, although the Whigs tried unsuccessfully to implicate him (now eight years after the fact) in the attempt to pack the juries against Algernon Sidney in 1682. The mercers struck him from their lists, and the government kept him under periodic surveillance. He spent his forced retirement supervising his business affairs until his death on December 31, 1691. His widow never remarried, and his direct line came to an end when his grandsons died without issue.

Dismissed from school at twelve as "a kind of a dunce,"[5] Dudley was eventually sent to a London boarding school (for penmanship and accounting) at the age of fifteen, to be apprenticed to a member of the Levant Company the following year. He left England in the spring of 1661 not to return (except for brief visit in 1666) for nearly twenty years, passing his most active years in a cultural climate as foreign from that of his homeland as might be found short of the antipodes.

In those twenty years, he gained hands-on experience in as broad a range of business activity as was possible in his day. In his early years as *ragione* (agent or factor) for various Levant firms he had been responsible for keeping his London principals abreast of current market conditions (prices, exchange rates, competitor's goods), getting their goods through customs, storing and finding buyers for them ("production" and shipping still being normally on speculation), keeping their accounts, and convincing those same principals that he had gotten the best deal possible under the circumstances.[6] The ability to improvise must have been vital to the success of a good agent, as this letter to one of North's fellow merchants implies:

> since which [date] is come to hand yours of the 9th past pressing the sale of your cocheneale wherein noe endeavors are omitted, but this—as all other commodities—are soe down the wind that though we court to sell we cannot. . . . Could we have had your cochineale sooner from Genoa it might long err this have binn sould but thence though there never wants conveyances, yet the bad weather in the winter tyme makes them very tedious, and we waited some time too to see whether the captain would comply with his obligation in bringing it hither, which since they doe but what they please . . . [he did not].[7]

In some respects the century's frequent outbreaks of war were the least of these men's worries.

On his own, Dudley entered into the jewel trade, procuring these goods from abroad for the bottomless market in the Seraglio and lending funds on the strength of them to temporarily strapped Beys. In all of this he was also acting as a short-term banker.

Though Dudley's interests expanded after his return to England, most of his new activities (like his exporting of British woolens to Turkey) remained connected in some fashion to the Levant trade. He dealt in Spanish bullion to purchase jewels in India for resale in Turkey. His shares in ships were an investment in his primary means of transport. He bought shares in other mercantile ventures (such as the Royal African Company) whose trades he understood and were tied to his own. His investments in the manufacture of iron goods like nails and harnesses were for an anticipated market in the Levant where English hardware was in demand.[8]

Some of his new activities after his return to London, however, were closer to those of the world he had left as an adolescent. His wife's fortune was primarily in real estate, and though most of this was in high-maintenance residential and commercial properties within the city of Bristol, he was also responsible for her estate at St. Breavil and lands in Monmouthshire and Somerset, as well as her investments in mortgages.[9]

He was also not so much of a "dunce" as he had seemed as a boy. North was an able and enthusiastic amateur experimenter in the fields of "optics, hydrostatics, and ballistics," who paid special attention to "beams, scales and balances" (here, perhaps, as befitted a merchant), "helped" his brother Francis with his "barometer," and worked on "the problem of friction in engines and pulleys."[10] A good third of these activities involve equilibrating principles.

The first problem in understanding the accomplishments and the shortcomings of Dudley North's work is determining how much of the existing corpus was actually written by Dudley North. The handwriting of the unpublished pieces has been identified as Roger's, though some have been emended in Dudley's hand, and Roger usually attributed authorship to his brother.[11] William Letwin has conclusively argued that the free-trade/free-market–praising preface to the *Discourses upon Trade* (dated 1691 but posthumously published in 1692 by Roger) was actually Roger's work.[12] And, since Roger, and not Dudley, was the dedicated follower of Descartes, he might also be responsible for the apparent methodological cohesion of the main text. This creates a considerable problem in determining which elements (Dudley's practical experience or Roger's more theoretical background) contributed more to the ideas in the work.[13]

The first section of the *Discourses* takes us back into the question of whether or not the government should lower the statutory maximum interest rate from 6 to 4 percent. North's argument appears to be a straightforward one for abandoning legal regulation altogether as detrimental to the efficiency of the market, which had its own mechanism (the supply-demand equilibrium) for setting the price of all commodities, money included, even though North's argument was based (as was Locke's) on money defined as the weight of the silver in the coin. North argued as follows:

1. Trade was defined as "a Commutation of Superfluities" produced by diligence in raising the "most fruits" or in making the "most of Manufacture," and regulated by a meeting of supply and demand: "I give of mine, what I can spare, for somewhat of yours, which I want, and you can spare."[14] Trade was not, however, really optional here, since selling its superfluities was each side's only way of obtaining that which it *wanted* (in the sense of *lacked*).

2. Money was defined through a recapitulation of its origin. All metals were intrinsically useful commodities ("necessary for many Uses"), but only silver and gold were adopted as exchange counters because of their greater scarcity and durability. Continued use over time caused them to be seen as stores of wealth, so men began to lay up their superfluous wealth in silver and gold "till occasion shall call them out to supply other Necessaries wanted." The idea that the general recognition of the value and convenience of the metals and not "any Laws" created this state of affairs was pressed to foreshadow the idea that a human law could not regulate what it did not create, and thus it could not set an interest rate nor be allowed to devalue the coinage.[15]

3. A small digression on "Publick Banks" found North claiming that "Bills of Exchange were made by Law payable in Bank, and not otherwise," because "for Dealers in Exchanges it is best that way."[16] As silver and gold

were the only natural forms of money, use of all other exchange counters (needing legal props) was to be restricted to those arenas in which some overriding concern (like the unique problems of foreign trade) made them necessary. Still later, at the very end of the section on interest, was an even more conservative handling of coin and credit in the reckoning of national wealth:

> And whereas the stock of the Nation is now reckon'd great, let it be fairly valued, and it will be found much less than it seems to be; for all the Monies that are owing upon Land Securities, must be struck off, and not estimated; or else you will have a wrong Account; for if a Gentleman of 500 *l. per Annum,* owes 8000 *l.* and you value his Land, and the Lender's stock both, you make an account of the same thing twice.[17]

This was far closer to a national net worth statement than anything else. This was not only a typical double-entry worldview but a finite one as well; in more ways than one this was still essentially a bullionist universe.

4. Differences in "Industry and Ingenuity" created differences in economic status over time. Those who acquired either more land or silver than they needed wished to "lett" it out at a profit. Those in need of land or silver "rent[ed]" it from them. Though interest was called "Rent for Stock" here, as rent was "for Land," there was no attempt to clear up the matter of whether the interest was the price of the money or of the goods which the money would be used to produce. "Stock" seems to mean the money itself, and the next sentence referred to the "hiring of money." Because the "Stock" could be physically removed from the owner while land could not, "Land ought to yield less profit than Stock, which is let out at the greater hazard."[18] This was not really any farther than Locke had gone (in 1668).

5. Interest rates, like all other prices, were caused by a meeting of supply and demand ("as plenty makes cheapness in other things, as Corn, Wool, &c. when they come to Market in greater Quantities than there are Buyers to deal for, the Price will fall"), making them results rather than causes of the general level of Trade ("it is not low Interest makes Trade, but Trade increasing, the Stock of the Nation makes Interest low").[19] So far, North seems to be building a genuine *demand* argument.

However, when the question arises of backing up this argument through illustration of the effects on the market of a high versus a low interest rate, we find ourselves back in a peculiar pattern: one-half of the supply-demand equation always gets lost in the shuffle. Josiah Child, who wanted rates lowered, argued from a demand point of view: if the merchant's profit margin was lower than the statutory interest rate, he would not seek to borrow, thus he would not produce, and a recession would occur. John Locke, who wanted rates kept high, argued from a supply point of view: no matter how many merchants wanted to borrow at a legally set lower rate, borrowers would not put their funds on the market if they could not get a return greater than they could from land (or deposit banking). North also took the strictly supply-side view.[20] Admitting that "the Usurer . . . will take half a Loaf, rather than no bread," North still contended that "high Interest will bring Money out from Hoards, Plate, &c. Into Trade, when low Interest will keep it back," because

> Many Men of great Estates, keep by them for State and honour, great Quantities of Plate, Jewels, &c. which certainly they will be more inclin'd to do, when Interest is very low, than when it is high. . . . So that it cannot be denied, but the lowering of Interest may, and probably will keep some Money from coming abroad into Trade; whereas on the contrary, high Interest certainly brings it out.[21]

As an analysis of the supply issue, this was an advance over previous arguments because of the step North took in showing the interaction between economic and noneconomic (e.g., status) factors in suppliers' behavior. Still, if we want to consider the overall analytic advance of the work, we have to ask why such an experienced merchant did not know enough to at least raise the demand side of the problem: would the merchants borrow as much at the higher rate even if the supply were more readily available? Or, in view of his use of equilibrium arguments elsewhere, why did he not consider the effect on a low rate of a great demand for it, or on a high rate of the low demand for it: would not either situation create a countervailing movement back toward the center?

The problem may be that North did know enough, but he wanted to see a policy inaugurated that such arguments might have actually defeated. After claiming that the market set interest rates, North discussed the rates in Holland so beloved of interest-rate controversialists. The commercial rate he took to be a market-set 6 percent. He admitted the existence of 3 and 4 percent mortgage rates, which the "State hath a duty" to guarantee (and good registration of titles made possible) so that "Widows and Orphans" might have a safe haven for their estates, though he considered these rates also to be set by "private consent" and not Law.[22] These low rates, however, were not the ones he was recommending. After all, when the *Discourses* were written, North had for some years been more of a lender (via his management of his wife's estate in which mortgages as investments played a large part) than an active borrower. He may have believed that freeing up interest rates from government control would not be better than regulating them; however, as the immediate aim of the pamphlet was to defeat a reduction in the statutory rate, its success would merely have meant that interest remained at the higher, still government-regulated rate, of 6 percent. Given the great complaints in all the pamphlets about the impediments to secured-loan borrowing caused by the laxer English land-titles, a deregulated rate would be expected to be higher than the 3 to 4 percent mortgages available in Holland.

It was the mortgage rate (and not the commercial rate) that really counted here:

> Then again it is to be considered, that the Moneys imployed at Interest in this Nation, are not near the Tenth part, disposed to Trading People, wherewith to manage their Trades; but are for the most part lent for the supply of Luxury, and to support the Expence of Persons, who though great Owners of Lands, yet spend faster than their Lands bring in; and being loath to sell, choose rather to mortgage their Estates.[23]

Such a position allowed North to make a pointedly class-based appeal:

> If you take away Interest, you take away Borrowing, and Lending. And in consequence the Gentry, who are behind hand, be it for what cause soever, must sell and cannot Mortgage; which will bring down the Price of Land.[24]

Since the gentry were far and away the largest block of voters in Parliament, one could hardly ignore their side of any political issue and expect one's voice to be heard. But North was actually rather unfair to the gentry as a whole. The same strict settlements that made their estates mortgageable made it more likely that they would have to turn to mortgaging those estates for extraordinary expenses (marriage portions for their daughters or start-up costs for the careers of their second sons) even if their tenants employed the most modern agricultural methods. The thrifty as well as the prodigal might find themselves in such a trap. Still, it reminds us that even the landed classes could find themselves on both sides of any economic question, even while we keep in mind that North was himself in the money-lending business.

Taking up the question of commercial lending, North used two extreme examples to bolster his case for market rates: the general trade forced to insure his ships at 36 percent and "the poor Trading Man" forced to finance his inventory at rates of twelve percent or more.[25] The second case brought in variability of creditworthiness as a price-determining factor while the first brought in variability of risk. Both were illustrations of the Scholastic tactic of setting up a straw man to knock down: both of North's examples existed, but neither was the general case. North matched supply in the normal sense with demand in the extreme sense (and failed to ask what would happen if the legal rate were 6 points higher than the market required). In fact, nowhere in his arguments do supply and demand ever go fairly head-to-head when it will damage his debating point. This is clearly a case of knowledge *selectively* applied rather than one of incomplete comprehension.

But to what extent was it theoretical and not merely practical knowledge? It is not as simple as it seems to answer this question from a methodological analysis. William Letwin based his case for Dudley North as the century's great innovator of a deductive economic system on his opening ("after a few preliminaries") with a "fundamental abstract principle" (trade as the exchange of superfluities), his subordination of "practical conclusions to a treatment of their theoretical substructure" (because his treatment of coined money looked at the general supply problem rather than clipping per se), and a mind that "led him constantly toward generalization."[26] The key feature of the deductive method, however, is the way it proceeds from general definitions to specific conclusions via a chain of reasoning in which each link is *necessarily* deduced from prior links in the chain: change one definition in a deductive system, and every conclusion that depends upon it must also change. The "Interest" chapter of the *Discourses* worked from definitions of trade, money, and the source of differences in economic status to a conclusion that interest rates were naturally regulated by the relationship of demand to supply. But there is absolutely no necessary link between North's metallist definition of money and his conclusions about interest, which would work as well or as poorly if North had defined money denominationally or functionally. Granted, North's presentation was deductive (moving from definitions to conclusions), but that was the set style of his age—we have seen it in every writer from Malynes to Locke— and we do not know how much of that arrangement was Roger's work rather than Dudley's.

Whether or not North's method amounted to anything unusually systematic, it cannot be denied that the policies he proposed were not only the most radically laissez-faire of all the major economic writers of his century, but his arguments for each of them tended to involve self-regulating mechanisms. He was, after all, really arguing for an end to statutory interest controls even if the immediate effect of defeating attempts to lower the rate by law would be to leave a high statutory rate in place.

Three examples will suffice to illustrate his positions and methods.

1. Like many of his contemporaries, North disapproved of the Poor Law as destructive of the industriousness of the population. He also believed it encouraged able-bodied men to desert their families. If the safety net provided for their wives and children were removed, men would not (he thought) abandon their families to the starvation that would surely

follow such abandonment.[27] North, however, rejected the usual prescription of workhouses as having proved impossible of rigorous enforcement because "our Natures" were too "soft and pittyful" to "hold one & another to hard labor."[28] Instead, North proposed doing away with the entire system with its restraints on freedom of movement, claiming that (1) private charity would take up the slack in the case of the truly impotent ("Mankind [is not] so Cruell to their poor neighbors to let them starve for want of a little sustenance"),[29] and (2) men allowed to move wherever they pleased would always seek the most profitable jobs for which they considered themselves suited (as it was "not possible to force a free people to work for less wages, then will produce sufficient sustenance for them & their families").[30] Such a policy would not only eliminate unemployment but also poverty itself: "By this means I doubt Not but Many of the Poor Would become Riche and wee should not hear the complaints of want of work."[31]

2. The argument for freedom of movement was expanded to cover a demand for liberalization of the naturalization laws. The idea that a "Multitude of people" was "the Greatest Riches a Nation can have," based on their productive power, was certainly made by Dudley North ("they teach us New Manufacturys"), but he also approached the argument from what was a novel demand perspective:

> It matters not what they are, whence the Come nor whither or when they goes. It is Most certein that whilst they stay here, they Eat & drink, and so help Consume the fruits of the Earth, which is all a benefit to the land owners.[32]

North believed a combination of the increases in land brought under acreage (through drainage schemes and the like) and in yields (due to growing "expertise in husbandry") had created a situation in which the food supply was growing faster than the population causing the prices of "the fruits of the ground" (and hence of rents) to fall.[33] The only way to reverse this pattern was to increase demand through (1) increased population and (2) getting more people to work in industries other than agriculture (and so reduce its yields) by "Making the poor work at reasonable rates" (i.e., by removing their social safety net).[34] While North's emphasis on increased agricultural yields could be seen as an abandonment of the finite mentality, it crept back in again when he asserted that by liberalizing its naturalization laws England's gain would be "Considerably out of other Nations."[35]

Be that as it may, the only discernible anti–laissez-faire modification of his argument concerned the question of colonies. Since they were part of England, migration to them was a reshuffling of rather a reduction in England's population, but the "Northern plantations in America" were a decidedly mixed blessing. The men employed in bringing goods to and from their shores were at least not employed in agriculture (pushing yields up and rents down), but since they yielded "little but what is or May as well be produced in England . . . If we had Never knowne them, it were better."[36]

3. North assumed an inverse relationship (an "opposite progress") existed between the interest rate and the price of land in a "proportion of 10 to 12." The rationale behind the 10 to 12 relationship was market-based (even if a result of the age's monetarist identification of interest with rent):

> Mony being the common standard of value, whereby land as well as all other things are computed, it is necessary that the profits of Mony & of land Must in some manner bear proportion with respect to the certainty of the one above the other. . . . land being more stable and secure then Mony, the profits arising from land will allwaies be less [than] what Money will yield.[37]

The fact that they moved in opposite directions was taken to be a result of the universal governance of all trades by "Advantage." The mechanism involved was that which later ages would define as opportunity cost:

> The value of land proceeds from & is Governed by the plenty of Riches or Mony. Or as that grows, it is Imploy'd in trade, put to interest, or lay'd ut upon land, for less profit then when more scarce. So years purchas[e] being the measure of land; More will be given in plentiful times.

Though it has to be granted that North forgot to finish his thought by concluding that the same plenty of money would make its price (as interest) correspondingly cheap, he did treat the purchase of land as a business no different from manufacture or money-lending ("the trade of Interest & buying of land, is like all other trades").[38]

But to what extent did he believe (or understand) the several *particular* mechanisms he described to interact with each other? The main thrust of North's argument on the value of land was to rebut the general presumption that there was any tie between the price of land and the rent it could command—two prices that he considered to be "in no sort dependeant upon each other" and thus did "not in the least affect one another."[39] The only purely economic factor affecting the price of land was the price of money. Rent he considered to be nothing more than another name for "the price of the product of it" in a literal sense, as it was simply a mirror of the prices farmers got for the "corne, hay, butter, cheese, [and] flesh" produced from it.[40] Since this was increasing faster than the demand for it (expressed as population growth), rents would inevitably fall. Wages might be another factor: North mentioned them immediately after population growth, although he did not explicitly draw the conclusion that the greater the wages a farmer must pay the less he can afford to pay in rent.[41]

It is certainly true that of any two prices, each can be more greatly affected by one variable than is the other. If Dudley North had said that the price of land was more immediately affected by the interest rate while rents were more immediately affected by the price of the goods they produced, he would have made a conventional market argument. But North said something entirely different when he severed altogether land prices from rents. Consider just two counterarguments. First, farmers are classically debtors: they borrow to sow and repay when they reap. The interest rate has a direct impact on their profit margins. If they seek to pay less rent when their revenue shrinks, will they not also seek to pay less when their expenses mount? North's own brother, Roger, understood this point, arguing (in a separate work) that "if the Value of the Product sinks, and the Price of the Labour, necessary to the raising of it, riseth, what hath the Owner? It is, in truth, a Loss of his Land."[42] Second, rent paid by the farmer was income to the landowner (and the means by which he repaid his mortgage). Would a prospective purchaser seek to pay more or less for the same piece of land if its rental income fell?

To Dudley North, the farmer and the landowner were distinct economic actors. His analysis extended only so far as to see how each was affected by the economic condition of the whole (in the form of a prevailing interest rate or price level), but not so far as to consider how one actor was affected by the other. He certainly did not consult the historical record that invalidated his elegant inverse proportion. The legacy of the organic analogy underpinning the trade balance model was difficult to escape. The emphasis even in such advanced treatments of the economy as Sir William Petty's often slipped from interactor analysis (such as how government spending circulates money) to part-whole analysis (how much does each social group contribute to or detract from the wealth of the whole). North also used such analogies. To prove his point that an "active prudent nation groweth rich, and the sluggish Drones grow poor," he suggested that the "Case" would "more plainly appear, if it be put of a single Merchant," concluding that a "Nation in the world, as to Trade, is in all respects like a City in a Kingdom, or family in a City."[43] Balance of trade analysis per se seems to have been totally extraneous to North's technique; he wrote neither for nor against it, but "his explanation of a prosperous and highly employed economy . . . depended clearly on the maintenance of a favorable balance of trade" even if maintained by the general expansion of trade rather than by bullionist restrictions.[44] Even allowing this, Dudley North seems fixated on the pre-Harvey understanding of the body in which the key relationships were those between each individual part and the whole, rather than from the new mechanical understanding of the way the actors affect each other through the flow.[45]

The best way to examine the links North did and did not make between economic actors is to follow his argument against the acceptance of clipped money. The section on interest in the *Discourses* was followed by one on "Coyned Money," in which the functional aspects of money (defined as coined gold and silver) were discussed. The argument was designed to prop up Dudley's recommendation that the government reinstate *seignorage* (the fee charged by the mint for coining silver) to discourage private citizens from melting down their coin whenever it was economically advantageous to do so only to recoin it at the government's expense when that proved more profitable. This could be seen not so much as an intervention in the market as a reminder to the government that, like any other economic actor, it should try not to operate at a loss. Removing the advantage of cost-free minting would create a more stable money supply.[46]

North's preference for a stable money supply led to his making an innovative argument concerning the opposing problems of under- or over-supply. He began by asserting that those who complained of a shortage of money were actually complaining of a want of demand: they could not find buyers because poverty was pushing down "Consumption" or war was making it impossible to sell their goods abroad.[47] According to North, "wee may want wealth, but we cannot want mony proportionable to our wealth," because it was not the quantity of money that determined the volume of trade, but the reverse:

> There will allwaies be a Convenient Quantity of Coyned Mony for the occasions of the people. . . . [though] by means of some accidents, there may be too much or too little, but it will by Cours[e] of trade, be soon Reduced to what I call a Convenient Quantity.[48]

The way this self-regulation worked was that "when Money grows up to a greater quantity than the Commerce of the Nation requires, it comes to be of no greater value, than uncoyned Silver, and will occasionally be melted down again."[49] This would certainly seem to contradict the usual maxim of the age that the money supply controlled the level of trade. Either argument can be made as each in turn affects the other, but what Dudley North (like all his contemporaries) did not do was consider that *reciprocal* effect of the one upon the other.

North thought of the *coined* money supply as something that circled round a constant center:

There is required for carrying on the Trade of the Nation, a determinate Sum of Specifick Money, which varies, and is sometimes more, sometimes less, as the Circumstances we are in requires. War time calls for more Money than time of Peace, because every one desires to keep some by him, to use upon Emergencies; not thinking it prudent to rely upon Moneys currant in dealing, as they do in times of Peace, when Payments are more certain.[50]

These "ebings and flowings" into and out of "the Hoards" did work according to a self-regulating law: "when money is scarce, Bullion is coyn'd; when Bullion is scarce, Money is melted."[51] But for all that North maintained that the domestic and foreign sectors were dependent on each other, he never attempted to explain how their differing demands affected this supply equilibrium.[52]

North also thought it made no difference to the total money supply whether or not coin was turned into plate, because turning it back into coin did not guarantee it would be spent:

A very rich Man hath much Plate, for honour and Show; whereupon a poorer Man thinks, if it were coyned into Money, the Publick, and his self among the rest, would be better for it; but he is utterly mistaken; unless at the same time you oblige the rich Man to squander his new coyn'd Money away.
For if he lays it up, I am sure the matter is not mended: if he commutes it for Diamonds, Pearl[s], &c. the Case is still the same; it is but changed from one hand to another.[53]

Or, if all the plate in England were coined,

What then? Would any one spend more in Cloaths, Equipages, Housekeeping, &c. then is [now] done?[54]

North's immediate point, of course, was that there were many things the rich man could do with his silver that would not result in its finding its way into the poor man's pockets. But it cost money to turn coin into plate; the silversmith had to be paid for his labor if not for his artistry: 100 shilling coins would be translated into a plate with 99 shillings worth of silver, which the mint would always recoin at full weight. Without an intervening devaluation or price deflation, money was actually lost in such an exercise. The case for holding the money commodity was not the same as that for holding real assets in general. And North knew it. He said:

No Man is richer for having his estate all in Money, Plate, &c. lying by him, but on the contrary, he is for that reason the poorer. That man is richest, whose Estate is in a growing condition, either in Land at Farm, Money at Interest, or Goods in Trade: If any man, out of an humour, should turn all his Estate into Money, and keep it dead, he would soon be sensible of Poverty growing upon him, whilst he is eating out of the quick stock.[55]

What seems to have bothered him was the proper proportion between hoarded funds and active funds. But trying to find his way through this led him into further contradictions. He considered "Gold and Silver, and, out of them, Money" not only to be "a proper Fund for a surplussage of Stock to be deposited in,"[56] but an inevitable one:

> Every body desires Riches or wealth, but No body desires More Mony then is Necessary for the Carrying-one [*sic* on] the designes of his trade or living. Who is there that Receives a sume of Money, but is looking about to pay it away again or to provide necessaries, etc. Now when sufficient is Coyned for this uses, What is More Must ither be carriet out againe or Melted Into Plate.[57]

Yet he simultaneously saw demand as infinite:

> The main spur to Trade, or rather to Industry and Ingenuity, is the exorbitant Appetites of Men, which they will take pains to gratifie, so be disposed to work, when nothing else will incline them to it; for did Men content themselves with bare Necessaries, we should have a poor World. The Glutton works hard to purchase Delicacies, wherwith to gorge himself; the Gamester, for Money to venture at Play, the Miser, to hoard; and so others . . . [and] the covetous man [is beneficial for] those he sets on work have benefit by their being employed. . . . The meaner sort seeing their Fellows become rich, and great, are spurr'd to imitate their Industry. . . . Countries which have sumptuary Laws, are generally poor; for when Men by those Last are confin'd to narrower Expence than otherwise they would be, they are at the same time discouraged from the Industry and Ingenuity which they would have employed in obtaining [their desires].[58]

With that kind of appetite, there would never be an excess supply of money to be turned into plate and hoarded, unless of course, the *real* engine in this economy was the finite volume of trade: then there would be no place for the demand to go but into plate. Supply reigned after all.

Further, in this argument, to the extent that demand seems to create both consumption and the production to supply it, its ability to influence price is ignored. That, as we have seen, was still, for North, a function of supply. In a sense we have an economy in which both supply and demand have identifiable but unrelated roles (as the prices of land and rents were unrelated), and one in which supply was again given the commanding role where value was concerned, even though North was capable of asserting otherwise: "How can any Law hinder me from giving another Man, what I please for his Goods? The Law may be evaded a thousand ways."[59] North accepted "appetites" as natural but was still unhappy with their lawless ways.

When Dudley North finally got around to the specific problem of the clipped coin, he proposed having the government accept the clipped coins in payment of taxes at their weight rather than at face value (to recoin them gradually at the old standard).[60] He claimed that "as long as clipt Money is taken, there will be little other," and "in a short time, all Men would refuse clipt Money in common Payment" once the government stopped accepting it.[61] Now, if the populace would trade with whatever coins the government accepted (full weight or not), the populace was accepting a denominational definition of money (though they would not think of it this way). If this was the case, then why recoin at the higher standard at all? Like Locke, North has made the wrong argument to back up a metallist position. Consider North's alternate argument that no government could successfully order its people to accept light and heavy coin at the same value: Spain did so, but Spain could not keep its coin for all its colonial mines produced.[62] This would be a laissez-faire argument for intrinsic value, though it certainly could not explain why the English had no trouble accepting light coin though new milled coins continued to be minted. Nor was a recoinage at the old standard necessary to maintain a stable standard since the de facto one was far from being a novelty. Producing milled coins at the lower standard would stabilize the currency with the least alteration in the money supply (as there were far fewer of the old coins to remint than of the new).

North believed the money supply was about 15 percent short of its correct weight because of the clipped coin.[63] Whether the recoinage was gradual or immediate, the question would still arise as to how that shortfall was to be made up. If there were not sufficient stocks of bullion in the country to melt down to make good the shortfall, the money supply itself (defined as coined bullion according to North) would shrink by 15 percent. If a sufficient store of bullion (plate) did exist to make it up, the *potential* money supply (defined by North as the sum of coin and plate) would still shrink because the portion of it that was now passing for, say, one million pounds sterling would still only pass for 850,000.

North was more concerned with who would bear the loss of recoining than the overall effect of the recoining on the money supply. He rejected having the state hand out new coins at the heavier weight while taking in the lighter coins at face value, as an unjust "general Tax" on the public. Instead, he wanted the state to accept the coins by weight only, leaving the citizenry to bear the loss. How could the first strategy harm but the second help the public? Well, according to North the loss would not hurt those with "Hoards of Money" because "those who intend to keep Money" only laid up the "good," so they would not need to turn their money in. It would not hurt the poor because they scarcely ever had "Five Shillings at a time" to call their own.[64] It would not hurt farmers who were "supposed" to hand over their rent to their landlords as fast as they had the money to pay it. The only ones hurt would be those "Trading Men" who happened to be stuck with inventories of coin in their fluctuating cycles of investment and receipts.[65] This is yet another variation on the most advantageous circulation.

North believed his solution might "be a great surprize, but no great cause of Complaint when nothing is required, but that the Publick Revenue may be paid in lawful English Money."[66] One could argue against this that like any other flat-rate tax, the 15 percent loss might mean more to the poor who lived on much tighter budgets than the rich, as Sir William Petty himself had argued, but, in North's case, the more revealing argument is the one tucked away in the *Postscript,* that a debased money favored the tenants and debtors, "For Rents and Debts will be paid less, by just so much as the intrinsick value is less, then what was to be paid before."[67] Now, North had argued that money should never be "unequall in its alloy Nor Weight," because it was a public "weight and measure."[68] Recoining at *either* weight would have sufficed to bring this about. And if money was *only* a counter, a creditor paid in lighter coin would suffer no loss since the denomination would be the same. But if money was *really* no more than some weight of silver, the creditors and the landlords would be getting less. This would seem to be Locke's commodity theory of money all over again.[69]

One final limit of Dudley North's advocacy of laissez-faire might be noted: "As an active member of the Russia, Africa, and Levant Companies, he supported their monopolies against interlopers."[70] Was it possible that he did not consider legally established monopolies to be a restraint of free trade?

Dudley North was a product of his business environment in many ways. Those who know him only from his posthumously published works do not know how long and hard that environment had to work to knock some of the seventeenth century's most precious prejudices out of him (for it seems he managed to pick some of them up even in far-off Turkey). In addition to the prejudices already discussed, he was also initially opposed to long-term deposits and private banking, an opposition eventually worn down by the exigencies of managing his wife's sizable estate, much of which was let out at interest.[71]

Dudley North's experience affords the researcher the unique opportunity to study his ideas in the context of his actual career because a considerable number of his ledgers and journals have also survived. Richard Grassby has studied them in some detail, and the picture he presents in his biography of Dudley North the businessman is far from being "modern." Though his accounts were generally arithmetically accurate (no small feat in his day), he "took no cost analysis before pricing," often posted "customs, insurance, freight, and postal charges" to the wrong venture account, mingled private and business expenditures, omitted to transfer insurance losses from his journals to his ledgers, neglected to close his accounts in a timely manner (closing some only when the page was full and others not all), kept bad debts on his books "indefinitely," neglected to revalue an inventory of perishable goods (and durable ones subject to damage in storage), took no account of depreciation (a considerable expense on his ships), rarely tried to apportion his overhead costs, and took even his gross profit calculations on whole voyages rather than on particular commodities.[72] When he died, it "took years for his executors to wind up his estate."[73] His executors' headaches aside, these are the same sorts of flaws that mark his economic thought.

This catalog of sloppy practices is not unusual. Grassby's own work on *The Business Community of Seventeenth-Century England* documents the existence of similar problems wherever business records of the day survive: "low standards of arithmetic," "retrospective" posting, irregular periodization, "infrequent and inaccurate" balancing with no record of any attempt made to find the cause of the error, no distinctions made between fixed and current assets, "doubtful debts" written off only at debtor's death, and ample evidence of a generally "casual" and "idiosyncratic" attitude toward the Italian sophistications of subsidiary ledgers and depreciation allowances.[74]

Faced with such books a modern-day accountant would be pulling out his or her hair. Nonetheless, the documented extent of these practices should make those who laud the contributions of double-entry bookkeeping to economic theory pause. Handbooks of double-entry bookkeeping have been routinely praised for their advanced rationality when they are really more in the way of examples of advanced mechanics. The mechanics of recording, posting, and keying-off have changed little, it is true, since Pacioli's pioneering 1494 opus. But, like Pacioli's, seventeenth-century manuals still did not distinguish between personal and business expenses, and gave no guidance as to how general statements of profit and loss could be turned into unit-cost/profit-margin statements. As we have seen, the practice lagged even farther behind the theory. If the rationalization of the pursuit of profit is to be considered one of the major pillars of the capitalist *Geist,* then this pillar had barely had its foundation poured before the century reached its end. What merchant could truly rationalize his pursuit of future profit when he had no real idea of how much he had actually made? Dudley North never really knew how much of the overall profit on any of his ventures was due to which of the mixed bag of goods his ships brought in. And, while common sense might suggest that taking balances at the end of each venture makes more sense than taking them from year to year, the initiated know that modern accounting allows for both to be done, simultaneously providing information on the profit of a particular venture and a particular item as well as on the ongoing health of the overall business concern. But this was a century in which balances were sometimes taken one way and sometimes the other and sometimes not at all.

Richard Grassby has proposed an interesting reason for this theoretical lag. He suggested that

> Bookkeeping developed as a system of charge and discharge for verification and audit; its primary function was to report and vindicate the responsible officer, not to depict a true financial position.[75]

Until its potential to reveal that financial position was understood, little progress could be made. In truth, it seems more likely that advances in economic thought modernized bookkeeping and accountancy rather than the other way around. For one thing, *profit* would have to be separated from the logical swamp of the *merchant's wage* before businessmen stopped deducting household linen from their business revenues and accepting the result as an accurate picture of the state of their business. And if *money* were logically separated from *coin* it might be easier for both economic thinkers and businessmen to separate it from *capital*.

Whatever was modern in Dudley North's thought, he did not get it from his bookkeeping, nor, it seems, could he see how it might be applied there.

CHAPTER 13

Nicholas Barbon and the Quality of Infinity

The century's most radical attack on balance of trade theory came not from the merchant class per se, but from a physician turned builder whose activities straddled the worlds of science and commerce. Whereas Thomas Mun and Josiah Child had stressed the difficulties in constructing an accurate balance and the need to distinguish between bilateral and overall balances, Nicholas Baron attacked the very analogy underlying balance theory: the assumed identity between the cases of an individual and a nation. In so doing he drew upon yet another strain of seventeenth-century thought: its fascination with the ancient idea of *plentitude*.

Nicholas Barbon (d. 1698)[1] was most likely the son of Praisegod Barbon (or Barebones, 1595?–1679), the leather-seller and pædobaptist preacher for whom the nominated parliament of July 1653 was, by its enemies, sarcastically named.[2] Nicholas, born in London, took his medical degree at Utrecht in 1661, and though he was made an honorary fellow of the College of Physicians in 1664, spent most of his life as an entrepreneur and speculator. He capitalized on the Great Fire of 1666 not only to make his own fortune but to start Britain's first fire insurance company (1680) and was a primary force behind the founding of what was called a "land-bank," one of a number of Tory alternatives to the Whig-dominated Bank of England. He was even, for a time, a slumlord of sorts, having converted Exeter House (the former See and Reformation plum of the Essex family) "into houses and tenements for tavernes, ale houses, cooks-shoppes, and vaulting schooles," and its riverside garden "into wharfes for brewers and wood-mongers."[3] Apart from his foreign schooling, Barbon's was essentially a London life, spent developing the land around the Gray's Inn, Lincoln's Inn, and Chancery Lane and buying up plots around St. Martin's in the Fields to sell back to the parishioners for a cemetery.[4] In the seventeenth century a successful business life was almost invariably a public life, and Nicholas Barbon's life was no exception. He took his turn at the public pulpit with *An Apology for the Builder* (1685), *A Discourse of Trade* (1690), and a

Discourse Concerning Coining the New Money Lighter (1696), as well as serving as the Member of Parliament for Bramber in 1690 and 1695. Caught up
in the rage for science and technology, as was his fellow medico, William
Petty, Barbon received a patent in 1694 for an "engine" using tidal forces to
bring drinking water from the Thames and siphon off its sediment.[5]

His business acumen was, within limits, quite noteworthy. His insurance proposal boasted cheaper rates for brick houses than for timber ones,
coverage for goods (for owners or renters) as well as for the property itself,
and fixed deductibles. Nor did it fail to point out the increased marketabil-
ity of an insured over an uninsured property.[6] It was his respect for market
forces that prompted him to seek monopoly relief for his fledgling insurance company, successfully maneuvering in 1688 for a warrant to restrain
the undertakers for the Friendly Society of London from competing with
Barbon's company for a year and limiting their competition thereafter.[7]

The "land-bank" that he and John Asgill (1659–1738) founded in 1695
might be more properly called a building society or savings and loan association, since its primary function was to "collect savings from which to
make advances on mortgages,"[8] rather than to fund them through subscriptions secured by landed property. In 1696, the Asgill-Barbon Bank and
John Briscoe's National Land Bank were subsumed under the umbrella of
a new National Land Bank approved by Parliament. It was, however, still-
born. The incredible credit crunch created by the recoinage and King
William's wars had stripped the coffers of English speculators; the subscription lists of the new bank never filled.[9] The original Asgill-Barbon
Bank survived the fiasco only to fall victim to perhaps the oldest argument
for the superiority of incorporation over partnership—the death of a partner. Nicholas Barbon died in July 1698, and the bank died with him; Asgill,
his partner and executor, advertised for a general clearing-up of debts, and
by 1699 it was all over.[10] The Bank of England was a joint-stock venture;
Barbon's business techniques were not always as cutting-edge as they
seemed, even for the seventeenth century.

Before discussing Barbon's rejection of seventeenth-century balance of
trade orthodoxy, a brief review of his positions on other economic issues of
the day (namely, money, value, interest, and wealth) may help to uncover
the range of the major influences on his thought.

Money. Barbon's understanding of money contained both innovative
and traditional elements. For Barbon, "money" rather than "silver" was "the
instrument and measure of commerce."[11] Not only was silver nothing but a
commodity without its government stamp, but periodic devaluation was a
necessary precaution for any state that did not wish to see fluctuations in

silver's value cause export of its coin.[12] Thus, he argued against John Locke
and with William Lowndes for a de jure recognition of the de facto standard of the circulating clipped coin, as

> no man will deny, but that the Broad Unclipp'd *Money* will buy as many
> Goods of the same *Value*, as the New-mill'd *Money* will do: And that all
> Bonds and Contracts are as well paid and satisfied by such old *Money*, as
> by the new.[13]

In truth, money was whatever the state said it was—"a Value made by law,"
whether it was made of gold, silver, copper, tin, shells, beads, or leather
hides: "Six Pence in [tin] farthings" bought "the same thing as Six Pence in
Silver."[14] If foreign coins went "by Weight," it was precisely because the law
that had stamped them had no force beyond its borders. Gold then had to
be exchanged for gold simply as one ten-pound sack of flour was the equivalent of another.[15]

Although this was an attempt to distinguish *money* (as an analytical
concept) from *currency* (its usual physical expression),[16] Barbon still clung
to the traditional view of *money* as the independent and *trade level* as the
dependent variable (as can be seen in his fear of "the murmer and disorder
. . . that attends a nation that wants money to drive their trade and com-
mence").[17] Nicholas Barbon was, like William Petty and John Locke, a
physician trained in William Harvey's[18] theory of the circulation of the
blood. This new way of looking at money as it moved through the economy
(rather than as it entered or left it in trade balance theories) probably reinforced the view of money as the independent variable even though this was
a line of reasoning that went (as we have seen) back through the century to
the insights of Gerard de Malynes. The more unusual view (for its day) that
trade level drove money supply we have already seen persevere in the works
of Sir Dudley North. Where Barbon put the new insights derived from
Harvey's theories to innovative use was in his candidate for the "heart"
pumping this money throughout the "Great Body of Trade":

> For the Metropolis is the heart of a Nation, through which the Trade
> and Commodities of it circulate, like the blood through the heart, which
> by its motion giveth life and growth to the rest of the Body; and if that
> declines, or be obstructed in its growth, the whole body falls into con-
> sumption.[19]

Also, like Lowndes and unlike Locke, Barbon recognized that a de
facto functional identity had arisen in his day between coin and what were
technically credit instruments. According to Barbon, "Credit is a Value
raised by Opinion, it buys Goods as Mony doe's; and in all Trading Citys,
there's more Wares sold upon Credit, then for present Mony."[20] Whatever

functioned as money essentially *was* money as far as Barbon was concerned, as money was itself nothing more than "a Change or Pawn for the Value of all other Things."[21]

Value. When Country Tories criticized "Credit" as being grounded in nothing more than "Opinion" they were attacking Whig ministries and the wars they financed through public deficit spending; when Barbon called it "A Value raised by Opinion," he was only pointing out that it was one more example of a general case; "Value" was a matter *of* "Opinion":

> The Price of Wares is the present Value; And ariseth by Computing the occasions or use for them, with the Quantity to serve that Occasion; for the Value of things depending on the use of them, the *Over-pluss* of Those Wares, which are more than can be used, become worth nothing; So that Plenty, in respect of the occasion, makes things cheap; and Scarcity, dear.[22]

He certainly believed each "Thing" had an intrinsic *virtue*, or rational usefulness. This was the result of some property of the thing itself: the natural *virtue* of the lodestone was its ability to attract iron.[23] But while *value* arose from use, it had no fixed connection to it, and *use* was itself a subjective value: "For things have no Value in themselves; It is opinion and fashion brings them in, to use, and gives them a Value."[24] While *utility* was a necessary component of *value*, it was not sufficient by itself to set value, because, no matter the use of a thing "no Man will pay for that which he have for the gathering."[25] Thus, *value* was the result of the intersection of the relative scarcity of a commodity with a subjective estimation of its utility.[26] The connection between scarcity and value was a subject for speculation throughout the century, but Barbon was one of the first to create a substantive analysis of the problem.[27]

Interest. As we have seen, most seventeenth-century treatments of interest approached it from the point of view of the investor. In this regard, interest was often identified with rent, a socially acceptable form of passive income: the claim was that a lender "rented" out his money as the gentry "rented" out their land. Discussions of their relative rates of return led to explorations of the determinants of a market-set interest rate as well as of the impact of "opportunity cost" (though not yet so named) on investment. A typical version of such an argument can be seen in Josiah Child's insistence that "no man in his wits would follow any Trade whereby he did not promise himself 14 or 12 per Cent gain at least, when Interest was at 8."[28] Barbon certainly used such an approach from time to time, claiming that interest was the

> rule by which the Trader makes up the Account of Profit and Loss; The Merchant expects by Dealing, to get more then Interest by his Goods;

because of bad Debts, and other Hazards which he runs; and therefore, reckons all he gets above Interest, is Gain; all under, Loss; but if no more than Interest, neither Profit, nor Loss.[29]

But he also turned the interest-rent analogy on its head to approach the problem from the point of view of the debt-incurring or rent-paying capitalist producer:

> Interest is the Rent of Stock and is the same as the Rent of Land: The First, is the Rent of the Wrought or Artificial Stock; the Latter, of the Unwrought, or Natural Stock. . . . Interest is commonly reckoned for Mony; because the mony Borrowed at Interest, is to be repayed in Mony; but this is a mistake; For the Interest is paid for Stock: for the Mony borrowed, is laid out to buy Goods, or pay for them before bought: No Man takes up Mony at Interest, to lay it by him, and lose the Interest of it.[30]

This approach led Barbon to a consideration of interest as a component of the market price of goods:

> The Dutch Merchant can Sell 100£ worth of Goods, for 103 £. And the English Merchant must Sell the same sort, for 106£ to make the same Account of Principal and Interest.[31]

Wealth. Sir William Petty may have been the individual who worked hardest to replace the century's bullion fixation with the proposition that a nation's productive capacity (its resources, labor supply, and level of technology) was the only true measure of its wealth, but the strength of that fixation can be seen in the frequency with which even Petty extolled gold and silver as "perpetuall and universal wealth"[32] and favored the foreign trade that brought them in over the domestic that did not:

> Now the *Wealth* of every Nation, consisting chiefly, in the share which they have in the Foreign Trade with the whole *Commercial World*, rather than in the Domestick Trade, of ordinary *Meat, Drink,* and *Cloaths,* &c. which bringing in little *Gold, Silver, Jewels,* and other *Universal Wealth.*[33]

Barbon acknowledged his debt to Sir William Petty[34] in constructing his own version of an aggregate treatment of national wealth ("That nation is accounted rich, when the greatest number of the Inhabitants are rich")[35] that also focused on the improvement of resources through the application of labor (finished cloth carrying a higher market price than raw wool or flax).[36] But, whereas Petty had sought to maintain a subsistence wage to keep unit profits up, Barbon looked at the relationship between employment and consumption ("every man that works, is paid for his time; and the more there are employ'd in a Nation, the richer the Nation grows")[37] and came to the opposite conclusion, that higher wages increased overall prosperity because "the more every man earns, the more he consumes."[38]

In distinguishing between the "unwrought" and "wrought" stock, Barbon was building on the familiar Aristotelian distinction between *natural* and *artificial* goods, with the *natural* being "the Animals, Vegitables, and Minerals of the whole Universe . . . sold as Nature produceth them," while the *artificial* were those natural wares "Changed into another Form than Nature gave them," and bearing that higher market-value that increased overall wealth but not the actual *amount* of "stock."[39]

That Barbon ultimately saw manufacturing as increasing a nation's wealth by increasing the value of its "stock" rather than by adding to its stockpile can be seen by analyzing his primary argument against his century's balance of trade theory—his claim that the stockpile was already "infinite" and thus as incapable of being absolutely increased as it was of being absolutely decreased (that which "is Infinite, can neither receive Addition by Parsimony, nor suffer Diminution, by Prodigality")[40] though it could be increased in utility and hence in market-value.

Barbon's critique of trade balance theory was something of a mixed bag. He spent a great deal of ink (as had Mun and Child before him) explaining the technical problems of reconstructing the final sale prices of all goods sold abroad from the scant information contained in the customs books and reminding his readers that international accounts were not necessarily settled in bullion[41] before moving on to the greater argument that bullion was neither the sole nor the most important form of wealth a nation should even seek in trade, because

> Gold and Silver are but Commodities; and one sort of Commodity is as good as another, so be it of the same value . . . the Trade to Denmark and Sweden . . . from whence they fetch Pitch, Tar, Hemp, and Timber, is as profitable to England, as the Trade to Spain, from whence the Merchant fetches the Bullion.[42]

But his most innovative argument was that balance of trade theory should be discarded because it was based on a false analogy (for which he blamed the popularity of Thomas Mun's work) between individual and national wealth.[43] Barbon held that

> the Stock of a Nation is vastly different from that of a private person; the one is infinite, the other finite. There is every year a Harvest, a perpetual increase of Cattel, and the mines can never be exhausted.[44]

And here is where we have to ask what Barbon understood by the word "infinite," for in his arguments against trade balance theory he claimed that both (1) demand and (2) supply were in some manner "infinite."

Infinite demand. Nicholas Barbon believed that humans were subject to "Wants of the Mind" that were as necessary to them as were the "Wants of the Body," (food, clothing, and shelter) and, in fact, were economically more useful to the state because, being "infinite," psychic wants prompted humanity to ever increasing efforts to attain them, increasing the true wealth of the nation.[45]

An infinity of wants was a logical extension of the application of the mechanical philosophy to the human body used by Thomas Hobbes. For Hobbes, "Life it selfe is but Motion, and can never be without Desire," and "Felicity is a continual progresse of the desire, from one object to another."[46] He went on to distinguish the few appetites "as of food" that were "born with men" from the infinitely variable desires "proceed[ing] from experience."[47] Barbon's divide between the few wants of the body and the infinite wants of the mind seems parallel, but whereas Hobbes sought to rein in those desires as politically disorderly, Barbon saw those forever variable desires as the "perpetual Spring" that kept "the great Body of trade in Motion." Prodigality might be a vice "prejudicial to the Man, but not to Trade."[48]

If here, Barbon parted company with Hobbes, he also parted company with Aristotle. Barbon, like Aristotle, not only distinguished between the limited *nature* of bodily wants as compared to the unlimited nature of psychic goods, but also recognized that the *utility* of the first was subject to diminishing returns while that of the second was not. But the parallel here, like that with Hobbes, was limited to the analytical emphasis, and not to the conclusions drawn or the policies recommended. Aristotle drew a further distinction between the pursuit of these psychic goods of which he approved and an unlimited pursuit of external goods that he condemned as perverse.[49] Barbon's verdict of "prejudicial to the Man, but not to Trade" moves the point of view from the individual (and Aristotle's polis was a larger image of the moderation of its "citizens") to society as a whole and rejects the concept of limitation as a social good. For Barbon, it was only "covetousness" that starved both individual and nation because it encouraged hoarding.[50] Spending and investment had a twofold impact on society: they not only enriched it in the aggregate sense but secured its orderly functioning as well, because "every man that buildeth an house" gave "Security to the Government for his good behaviour."[51]

Furthermore, he disapproved of policies designed to keep luxury goods off the market out of some concern that they corrupted the moral order. He claimed that debarring foreign commodities outright hindered "the Making and Exportation of so much of the Native, as used to be Made and Exchanged for it," causing that "Native Stock" and the rent of the land that produced it both to fall in value.[52] Since "all Trading Countries Study their Advantage of Trade," such a policy would only cause other nations to make "the same Laws" against us.[53] Tariffs might be used to encourage importation of raw materials over manufactured goods (to use more English hands in the making of them) as it was "in the Liberty of every Government, To Lay what Duty or Imposition they please."[54] But, in general, Barbon did not approve of duties so high they created a de facto prohibition: "laying too high a Duty, which amounts to a Prohibition" caused a nation to wholly lose the benefit of that trade as the merchant would not bring in a commodity on which he could make no profit.[55]

In Barbon's hands the "infinity of wants" became a necessary complement to an "infinity of supply" that he derived from another philosophy as popular among the *virtuosi* of the seventeenth century as was the mechanical worldview that was fast replacing the Aristotelian.

Infinite supply. As we have seen over and over, the standard analogy between individual and national wealth that underlay balance of trade theory was Cato's pronouncement that a man who bought more than he sold must eventually run out of wealth (money), but Barbon believed

> The Native Staple of each Country is the Riches of the Country, and is perpetual, and never to be consumed; Beasts of the Earth, Fowls of the Air, and Fishes of the Sea, Naturally Increase: There is Every Year a New Spring and Autumn, which produceth a New Stock of Plants and Fruits. And the Minerals of the Earth are Unexhaustable.[56]

This certainly looks like the most radical contradiction of the finite concept of wealth inherent in Cato's dictum that the seventeenth century would see. Barbon was not only asserting that labor could create infinite wealth from the limited but renewable resources of a finite earth; he was asserting that the resources (the *natural* stock) were themselves infinite. One can see how he came to this conclusion as far as agricultural products were concerned; they were renewable resources (which was still not the same as saying an infinite amount of them could be produced at any one time). The infinite nature of the wrought goods came both from the infinite nature of its source ("if the natural Stock be Infinite, the Artificial Stock that is made of the Natural, must be Infinite")[57] and from the art applied to it ("the earth by the arts of Husbandry produceth ten times more food than it can naturally"),[58] making labor a necessary if not a sufficient producer of wealth. But bottomless mines implied an infinity of another order entirely, and one that was intimately linked to the concept of plentitude.[59]

Plentitude was an idea that had been working its way through various strands of European thought since its first systematic presentation in the work of Plotinus, whose reason for "holding this to be the best possible world" was, as Arthur Lovejoy explained in his *Great Chain of Being*, that "the whole earth" was "replete" with "a diversity of living things . . . up to the very heavens."[60] That inexhaustible diversity revealed itself as a hierarchical Chain of Being with a fixed value/position for every animal, mineral, vegetable, or institution, but it also stood for a definition of divine goodness as "the immeasurable and inexhaustible productive energy" of the Creator and his Creation.[61]

The last decades of the seventeenth century saw the triumph of Cartesianism in French scientific circles and a vogue in England of such popularizing Cartesian works as Fontenelle's *Entretiens sur la pluralité des mondes* (1686).[62] Descartes's belief in an infinity of inhabited worlds was paralleled by Robert Boyle's belief in "an inestimable multitude of spiritual beings"— a cause taken up by Joseph Glanvill who proposed setting the Royal Society to compiling a Baconian natural history of the "Land of Spirits."[63] Antonie van Leeuwenhoek's (1632–1723) microscope revealed a hitherto hidden universe of life in miniature, lending experimental support to such ideas.[64] Henry More, the Cambridge Platonist was, for a while, "the most zealous defender" of the idea of an infinity of worlds.[65] Nor were Natural Law adherents necessarily antagonistic to such ideas. Boyle was citing Grotius in support of his claim of that "inestimable multitude."[66]

Boyle was also inclined to investigate the question of whether or not "a greater proportion of metal" could be found in ore-bearing rocks exposed to the air than they had been known to contain before the exposure. In his *Tracts containing Suspicions about some Hidden Qualities of the Air*, he spent considerable time recounting interviews he had with mine owners who had found tin, lead, or iron in previously exhausted veins, and noting the acceptance of such ideas in respected "mineralists" such as Boccatius Certardus, Gerhard, and Agricola. Boyle himself decided that no positive conclusion could be reached until true experiments replaced anecdotal evidence, but it seems clear he believed there was likely something to the theory that some minerals "grew."[67]

The neohermetic variant of this was the concept of all creation being alive: of the earth as a living being animated by a "world soul." Probably the most infamous, in his day, proponent of this view was Giordano Bruno, burned alive at the stake by the Catholic Church in 1600.[68] That same world soul appeared in *A Discovery of Infinite Treasure* (1639) by Gabriel Plattes, a member of the Hartlib circle that also included Sir William Petty. Plattes referred to it as "the universall spirit of the world."[69] The main thrust of the *Discovery* was to prove that the earth was capable of producing an infinite amount of agricultural goods if husbandry were properly improved, but this argument rested on the "infinite and inexhaustible" supply of fertilizing substances like limestone and chalk that the earth constantly produced.[70] According to Plattes, minerals (like "Trees, Plants, and Fruits") were congealed "vapours" in an eternal cycle in which, in summer, this "fatnesse" of the earth was rarefied back into vapor, only to congeal again in cooler weather.[71] The *Discovery of Infinite Treasure* and its companion treatise on mining, *A Discovery of Subterraneall Treasure* (1639), were reprinted in 1679, making them easily available in Barbon's day. So little is known of Barbon's life outside of his business activities that linking the ideas in such works to him is another matter, however.

Trained as a physician, Nicholas Barbon spent most of his life as an entrepreneur and speculator; the extent of any ongoing exact connection to the scientific community remains unclear.[72] We know he had both a slight casual and business connection to Robert Hooke, because Hooke's diary mentions meeting Barbon in 1672, and two entries from October 1677 deal with negotiations to lease (or purchase?) a house from Barbon.[73] Barbon appears not to have practiced medicine, but his honorary fellowship in the College of Physicians would seem to indicate he made some effort to keep up his medical connections.

There are hints scattered throughout Barbon's pamphlets of more heterodox sources than Petty's works or Harvey's theories. Among the short list of learned works cited by Barbon in the *Discourse of Trade*, for example, was a 1653 edition of the *Monarchia Hispania* of Thomas Campanella (1568–1639), otherwise known for his hermetically tinged theocratic utopia, the *City of the Sun*.[74] And though he knew his John Graunt,[75] Barbon's most frequently cited author on the natural and inevitable progression of population was Sir Matthew Hale (1609–1676), from whose unpublished papers a tract called *The Primitive Origination of Mankind, considered and examined according to the Light of Nature* was posthumously published.[76] Hale, chief justice of the King's Bench and one-time lord chief baron of the Exchequer, had something of a strange career himself: a "puritan" too stringent in his manner even for Baxter but who staunchly upheld the episcopacy. Barbon also maintained a long-standing friendship with John Wilkins, whose *Difficiles Nugae; or Observations touching the Torricellian Experiment* (1674) was condemned by the Royal Society as "a strange and futile attempt of one of the philosophers of the old cast to confirm Dame Nature's abhorrence of a vacuum."[77]

There are hints of heterodoxy, as well, in Nicholas Barbon's life.

When the Protectorship failed to fulfill the millenarian promise of the Commonwealth, Praisegod Barbon, his father, switched his allegiance to the Fifth Monarchy Men and was later so strident in his attacks on the Restoration that he spent considerable time in jail despite his inclusion in the general pardon of 1660. Certainly, a man may take positions opposite his father's, but Nicholas Barbon's best documented friendship was with John Asgill (1659–1738), an attorney some years his junior who became the executor of his estate as well as his partner in the Land-Bank. Asgill's literary career postdates Barbon's life, but his first noneconomic work was *An Argument proving that according to the convenant of eternal life revealed in the Scriptures, man may be translated from hence into that eternal life without passing through death. . . .* (1700). This was a distinctly heterodox position and one with marked millenarian overtones.

Whether Barbon knew of Bruno's work, or read Plattes, or picked up on these ideas through their variants in Descartes, Grotius, Boyle, or Fontenelle cannot likely be known. But their view of an essentially organic and fecund universe provides the exact ground on which Barbon built his unusual case against balance of trade theory: an infinitely renewable supply not only of trees and crops but of the very metals on which bullionism was based.

Infinite was a word with several meanings in the seventeenth century, sometimes standing in for nothing more than a number too large to conveniently count, but the implications of its true meaning of being without limit were also well understood, as in Raleigh's "There cannot be more infinities than one; For one of them would limit the other," or Cowley's "What, alas can be Added to that which hath Infinity Both in Extent and Quality," or Halley's "analogous to Eternity in time or Duration."[78]

The century actually knew, as Halley put it, "several Species of Infinite Quantity."[79] The problem was, every aspect of "infinity" disturbed the value system of the age when applied to anything besides the Deity. Alexandre Koyré's *From the Closed World to the Infinite Universe* documents the lengths to which not just Kepler but most astronomers went to avoid applying the adjective *infinite* to the universe because its connotation of "eternal" suggested a universe that was both coextensive and coexistent with its Creator.[80] Equally troubling was the idea that there were "infinite Parts in the smallest Portion of Matter."[81] Early in the eighteenth century, Bishop Berkeley countered that an "*infinitely divisible*" line had to be "*infinitely great.*"[82] Given the empirical (or sensory) epistemology coming out of the century, the infinitesimals at the heart of the new calculus were literally nonsensical (because nonsensible).[83] Mathematics had been championed during the seventeenth century as providing an objective language for the new science: how could it act as a foundation even for operational knowledge if it were only a formal exercise?

But the principle of plentitude[84] embodied just such a parallel to infinitesimals. It saw the universe as much from the perspective of the infinite number of rational and irrational numbers existing between any two whole integers as it did from that of an infinitely extended series. The infinite number of worlds it propounded was a necessary result of a *preexisting* infinite *variety* of life-forms. The necessary consequence of the infinite goodness (read as creative power) of God was that he could not have failed to create every conceivable variation on every given form of life.

Additionally, because the infinity in question was a necessary result of God's nature, it preexisted human effort and could not really be (physically) increased although it could be transformed by human effort. It was the quasi-magical life in all creation that ultimately made the supply of resources (whether animal, vegetable, or mineral) inexhaustible: human "improvement" only transformed this potential bounty into an actual harvest. Labor could be no more than the midwife here: it increased the value of the stock (by increasing its utility) but not the *size* of the stockpile.

Thus, Barbon's foundations need to be clearly distinguished from the Baconian concept of a "conquest of Nature" made possible by a correct scientific method. For Robert Boyle "a multiplicity of desires" was part of the program that God instilled in humanity to make it industrious enough to complete the conquest of nature (in the sense of knowing it as well as profiting from it) that was intended for it:

> to engage us to an industrious indagation of the creatures . . . God made man so indigent and furnished him with such a multiplicity of desires; so that whereas other creatures are content with those few obvious and easily attainable necessaries that nature has almost everywhere provided for them; in man alone, every sense has store of greedy appetite.[85]

The end result of those desires was virtue. The causal chain went from the desires to the industry required to satisfy them, to the knowledge and power gained from that industry, to the virtue resulting from the understanding that Nature presented "a model of harmony with God's purpose" that humans were meant to imitate.[86] This was, in one sense, the reason that status-elasticity of demand was accepted: it reinforced as well as reflected the harmonic limit necessary to harnessing those wants so that they served the public good. The resulting individual wealth was not so much subordinated to the public good as harmonized with it through the vehicle of industry (which saw that the wealth was correctly distributed).[87]

Barbon's harmonizing (or equilibrium) argument is more problematic. His take on commerce in general was that a "Trader takes care from time to time to provide a sufficient quantity of all sorts of Goods for mans occasions, which he finds out by the Market: That is, By the quick selling of the Commodities, that are made ready to be sold."[88] From this he drew the specific conclusion that

> there are no more Houses built every year than are occasion for; because there are Tenants for the Houses when built, and a continuancee every year to build more. For the Builders will do as other Traders, who, when the Market is overstocked with their Commodities, and no occasion for those already made, forbear to make any more, or bring them to Market, till a new occasion requireth them. And when they find they cannot lett those already built, they will desist from building, and need no Act of Parliament to hinder them. So that we may as well complain that there is too much Cloth and Stuff made, too much Corn sowed, too many Sheep or Oxen bred, as that there are too many Houses built; too many Taylors, Shoo-makers, Bakers and Brewers, as there are too many Builders.[89]

But when we turn to Barbon's arguments for the usefulness of overseas trade, we find that he valued such trade precisely for its ability to carry away surplus production:

> which surplus, if it was not carried away, would by its plenty bring down the Value of the Native Stock, and put a stop to the Labour and Industry of the People, in further improving the Wares of the Country.[90]

He valued colonization for a similar reason:

> Now there is as much Land Plowed, and all sorts of Grain sown, and reaped every year, as their is occasion for; and sometimes more: For the Crown in some years hath been at charge to Export it.[91]

When trying to come up with an alternative cause for the fall in rental values in land outside the urban belt (to offset the contention that the new buildings in London drained the countryside of its inhabitants), Barbon ascribed a negative impact to market self-regulation. He thought the drop in rental values might probably have been caused by the increase in crop yields due to the draining of fens, enclosure, and use of new seeds, "by which means the Markets are over stock'd and furnished as a cheaper rate than those Lands can afford, who have had no advantage from improvements."[92]

The infinite creative power of this world possessed a potential that needed to be carefully harnessed or it could overwhelm any national economy. Human wants might be infinitely variable and human population capable of unending growth, but not possessed of such an infinitely expandable demand that it might outpace this infinite supply. But this was to be expected: there is nothing in plentitude that supposes the potential of the created might outstrip the power of their Creator. Douglas Vickers noted that Barbon differed from his fellow economic writers in turning his "fear of goods" not into a call for "mercantilist protectionism," but a "new international liberalism."[93] If plentitude's infinity of supply made trade necessary, the confidence that plentitude gave its believers in the bounty of the universe seems to have aided Barbon in casting his "fear" upon international waters.

In attempting to incorporate Nicholas Barbon's works into an intellectual history of economic thought, careful attention must certainly be paid to his dependence on (as well as his differences from) the work of Sir William Petty, just as attention must be given to the way Barbon seemed to use his rebuttals of Locke as a teaching tool. But a wider net needs to be thrown to encompass all of Nicholas Barbon's sources: a richer understanding of the relationships between economic and philosophical thought in the seventeenth century develops when Barbon's heterodox sources are added to the mix.

CHAPTER 14

Charles Davenant and the Brave New World

Charles Davenant's work presents us with our final variation on the efforts of seventeenth-century English writers to create a science of economics in support of their inherited value system. But Davenant's chief concern was less with the values of the marketplace itself than with preventing those values from infecting society as a whole. He lived through a key turning-point in England's transition from "market economy" to "market society," and he foretold a doom as dark as any by Cassandra. Whether or not he had reason for despair, he certainly had reason for concern.

The decades straddling the transition from the seventeenth to the eighteenth centuries saw the intersection of intellectual, constitutional, and financial revolutions in England whose resolutions were still in doubt. The struggle of the Whigs and Tories to preserve their differing understandings of the constitutional settlement and to control a king determined to bring England back into the Continental arena would end by turning Britain into a modern "fiscal-military" state more powerful than and very different from its Continental cousins.[1] But no one could be certain of this during the hasty improvisations, false starts, and budget crises of the last Stuart reigns; just as no one could know which of the two emerging enlightenments—the sanctioned magisterial one led by Newton or the suspected radical one led by the likes of John Toland—would emerge victorious in the heady days at the end of the century when the lapsing of the Licensing Act in 1695 let loose a flood of heterodox treatises. Even the more conservative elements of the Enlightenment were suspect. The attacks of men like George Berkeley (1685–1753) and Stillingfleet on the ideas of Locke and Newton were neither intended nor taken as merely intellectual disagreements. Bishop Berkeley's 1710 *Treatise Concerning the Principles of Human Knowledge* saw "the Grounds of Scepticism, Atheism and Irreligion" in Locke's acceptance of "general ideas" and Newton's work on "attraction."[2] Nor was it any easier to predict the financial future when every day saw a new experiment in public and private finance—recoinages, tontines, annuities, national banks, governmental lotteries, stock exchanges, and several different kinds of paper money.[3]

During King William's War (1689–97) against France, government expenditure trebled (from under £2 million in 1688 to an average of £5–6 million per year from 1689 to 1702).[4] Customs and the Excise could yield only so much even with more efficient collection and record keeping; a land tax was added. On January 26, 1693, the government opened the subscription list for a £1 million tontine loan whose interest (10 percent through midsummer 1700 and 7 percent thereafter) was to be covered by new excise duties with provision to convert the individual subscriptions to single-life annuities at a fixed 14 percent.[5] In March 1694, a further £1 million lottery (of £10 tickets at varying interest rates) was floated, only to be joined the next month by another £300,000 in 6 percent annuities.[6] The Bank of England, established that same April by Parliament, was an attempt to bring some order into the patchwork of long- and short-term borrowing by which the government was keeping itself afloat. The subscription list for the original £1,200,000 loan (paying 8 percent) was filled within 10 days of its June 21 opening date, but the year was not even over before the government was drawing funds on the Bank far over its original limits, without eliminating any of the short-term mechanisms it had been intended to replace.[7] The recoinage, the drastic deflation caused by it, and the reaction of the foreign exchanges against it sent the whole package into a tailspin from which it almost did not recover. The Malt Lottery Loan of April 1697 was a "virtually complete failure," and only the peace of September 1697 gave the government the breather it needed to pull in its belt and settle some of the short-term debts threatening to strangle it altogether. The debt load was staggering for a preindustrial society, with the national debt standing at £12.8 million in 1702 and the debt service on it consuming as much as 24 percent of the budget.[8]

The revenue demands of the War of the Spanish Succession (1702–13) started up the whole cycle of improvisation once again. Good harvests and Marlborough's victories helped Godolphin raise funds from 1704 to 1708, but the bad winter of 1708–9, the poor harvest it engendered, and the failure of the peace talks sent Godolphin scurrying for more annuities, lotteries, and even for funds from foreign governments (borrowing £150,000 from Berne).[9] It did not help that there were party battle-lines running throughout all this. John Houblon and Michael Godfrey (the first governor and deputy-governor of the Bank) were hard-line City Whigs who had backed Shaftesbury against the court.[10] The Land Banks set up to rival it were predominantly Tory affairs, though individual subscriptions to both crossed party lines. Whig rivals of the Tory-dominated East India Company got their own nationally chartered New East India Company in 1698 when they promised to lend £2 million to the government.[11]

Even without the loans this was a government that reached farther into the pockets of its citizens than had ever been seen in England, with the average annual tax receipts of £3.64 million during King William's War themselves almost twice as large as the government's entire prewar budget.[12] The government also employed many more Englishmen than it ever had. The peacetime army increased in size to 35,000 men during this period (to say nothing of the 144,650 men under arms in 1713). Though the navy employed fewer men, there were jobs and profits galore building and victualing the ships: the 180 ships of various sizes needed periodic repair, and one single expedition of 40,000 men in 1703 required over 4 million pounds of beef and pork. And someone had to be collecting all those taxes; the fiscal bureaucracy alone jumped from 2,524 full-time employees in 1690 to 4,780 in 1708.[13]

Thanks to all those loans, an ever-increasing portion of the English population was involved in English government in an entirely new way: as its creditors. Of the 1,257 subscribers to the Tontine Loan of 1693, 88.8 percent contributed less than £100 apiece (with only 2.5 percent contributing over £1,000), while, at the other extreme, only 34.9 percent of the original 1,268 subscribers to the Bank of England contributed less than £500 apiece and 30.8 percent contributed over £1,000.[14] The financial world of England in the 1690s offered something for almost every budget. Only the poorest and the peerage proper were vastly underrepresented: the greatest blocks of shares were held by the gentry and the mercantile elite with smaller blocks by "apothecaries, carriers, clothworkers, embroiderers, farmers, mariners, [and] wharfingers."[15] Women were not excluded from this brave new world, making up 18.6 percent of the Tontine subscribers (contributing 11.9 percent of its funds) and 11.9 percent of the initial Bank subscribers (contributing 5.9 percent of its funds).[16] A similar spread can be found in the annuities and stock offering floated in 1707 and 1709: 49.2 percent of the 99-year annuities floated in 1707, 42.9 percent of the Bank lists, and 25.5 percent of the United East India Company stock of 1709 was in the hands of individuals holding less than £500 apiece with women accounting for 20.3, 16.6, and 10.6 percent of these shares (9.3, 8.3, and 3.9 percent of the funds), respectively.[17] Lending money to the Crown was fast becoming something of a national pastime.

This was also a market an investor would be wise to follow closely: shares, annuities, and lottery tickets changed hands with an ease unknown only a decade before and competed with the Navy Bills and the tallies offered by individual government departments. Stockbrokers and jobbers soon appeared on the scene; options ("refusals" and "puts") were traded as freely as the shares themselves; specialized periodicals like John Castaing's *The Course of the Exchange and other things* were soon a regular part of the scene; and for those who could not wait for the weekly quotation, at two popular coffeehouses in Exchange Alley chalkboards kept track of price fluctuations: in all but name the stock exchange had arrived.[18]

In other words, this was truly a brave new world of finance capitalism, a world in which the values of the marketplace penetrated social and political circles as never before. To this world, Charles Davenant will be our guide.

Charles Davenant (1656–1714) was the son of the royalist poet and playwright Sir William Davenant. Though he never graduated from Balliol, he managed to pick up an LL.D. by "favour and money" and practiced at Doctor's Commons.[19] At first it appeared he might follow in his father's footsteps, when his play, *Circe*, was performed at the Duke of York's theater in 1677, but he soon had his eye upon a steadier source of income. For some years the monarchy had been setting up an apparatus to collect directly those sources of revenues previously farmed out, but the path from direct collection by a government agency to a true government civil service was still far from complete. In 1678 Davenant purchased one Mr. Thynne's place as a Commissioner of the Excise with the aid of a friend, a Mr. Wintour of Gloucestershire. As a result of this purchase, Davenant got a government job and three-fifths of the annual salary of £500 that went with it (Mr. Wintour got the other £200 each year as a partial repayment).[20] Davenant remained at the excise until 1689, gathering the data he would use to underscore his points in a series of economic and political works. When James II came to the throne, Davenant was also appointed to license plays (that is to say, censor and approve them for performance and publication). Though Davenant is usually depicted as a Tory, he originally had enough of a Whig taint to have a close brush with serious trouble in the crackdowns following the dissolution of the third Exclusion Parliament, when Secretary Jenkins started receiving anonymous letters like the one that claimed that Davenant might be hiding Monmouth in his theater.[21] The temporary confusion over Davenant's loyalties was probably the result of Davenant's reliance on a "Country" rhetoric that was as often used by whatever party was out of power as by its true devotees.

The postrevolutionary regime had nothing to complain of from Davenant until his growing disenchantment with the swelling state culminated in his *True Picture of a Modern Whig* (1701 and 1702). These two dialogues attacked the postrevolutionary Whigs as cynical self-seeking liars foisting worthless credit scams upon the unsuspecting public to line their own pockets while accusing all who criticized them of being Jacobites.[22] Three other short essays, *Upon the Balance of Power*, *The Right of Making War, Peace, and Alliances*, and *Universal Monarchy*, published together in 1701, rounded out the attack with claims that the new programs for long-term debt financing were mere fiscal opiates and the New (Whig) East India Company created nothing but partisan division, while dragging out every well-known English legal authority from Bracton to Sir John Fortescue to prove that "the right of making war and peace" was never "indefinitely"vested in the kings of England "without any sort of distinction or restriction" and admonishing the public that it was a rare king who could do a better job than a Richelieu or a Mazarin.[23]

There was a genuine political rift involved, but Davenant also had personal cause to complain of the new regime, for it left him jobless. It recognized his financial expertise—he, like Locke and Child, was to be called before the Lords Justices in 1695 to determine how best to reform the coinage[24]—but it refused to employ him. Davenant remained as close as he could to the seat of affairs, however, acting as Member of Parliament for Great Bedwin in 1698 and 1700.[25]

When Queen Anne dismissed her Whig ministers as quickly as she could after ascending the throne in 1702, Davenant's fortunes began to turn. Under this reign Lord-treasurer Godolphin successfully petitioned for Davenant to be secretary to the commissioners working on the treaty of Union with Scotland, and Davenant went back to his beloved political arithmetic as inspector-general of exports and imports from 1705 until his death in 1714 (on November 6).

But Davenant created an irreparable breach between himself and his former Country Tory allies when his 1704 work, *Essays upon Peace at Home, and War Abroad*, supported the government in its advocacy of the kind of drawn-out land war he had always attacked before as fiscally unsound, and defended his own change of policy by claiming that it could not "be deemed inconstancy" to abandon a party "intirely in the wrong" for one "more moderate, honester, more disinterested" and with "righter intentions towards the publick."[26]

So, perhaps, when Charles Davenant railed about the "corruption" of the body politic brought about by the "luxury" and "faction" that were the children of mankind's boundless ambition and commercial success and bewailed its resulting loss of "military virtue," we ought to think it nothing more than the rhetoric of a Trimmer and not consider it as meaningful in regard to his economic thought.[27]

The rhetoric in question is usually labeled civic humanism. The civic humanist aimed at re-creating the spirit of a true *Respublica*—or a nation that acted as a body for the public good rather than individually for the private good of each member—rather than a literal one. As an ideology it had its roots in the organic mind-set of Aristotelian political thought: for each form of government (by the one, the few, or the many) there was a pattern of birth, growth, decay, and death that was intrinsic to it:

> For as we are said to bring with us into the world those diseases by which our decay and death is wrought; so governments, in their primitive institutions have within them the very seeds of destruction by which at last they are to be subverted.[28]

As monarchies degenerated into tyrannies through consolidation of the single rule that built them up, and aristocracies turned themselves into oligarchies by their very efforts to reproduce themselves, so republics degenerated into headless democracies through their very own success.

The republican model went something like this. Forged of the military virtue of their ever vigilant citizen-militias (as "the Romans during the second Punick War" when "the whole people were trained up to arms"), their success breeds wealth. But wealth "depraves their manners," creating discord by encouraging socio-professional specialization and breeding up men inclined to place their own private interests above those of the commonwealth. War becomes something only professional soldiers train for, while the citizenry in general decks itself out in the "effeminate" luxuries of the East and the poor indulge in "riot," leaving the dissolute state ripe for conquest. The problem was to find a way to avoid the downside of success. The program involved a reeducated citizenry ("men who have laid aside their luxury, corruption, self-ends, and private ambition") constantly maneuvering to pull the commonwealth back to its original constitution through sumptuary legislation, discouragement of expansive governments, and standing armies, or, as Davenant put it:

> All the great nations that we read of, as soon as they perceived that, either by conquest, foreign traffick, or by means of their own product, wealth flowed in among them, made early provision to restrain, by wholesome laws, the two opposite vices, avarice and luxury, wherewith might empires labour, and which, as Porcious Cato says, prove at last their ruin.[29]

First principles and original constitutions were the key here, for any "error in the first concoction" did "presently deprave the whole mass."[30] Thus, mixing in a little social contract theory and Lockean *tabula rasa* psychology, Davenant bemoaned an opportunity lost in 1689 when

> King James went away, we were reduced to what Mr. Hobbes calls the state of nature, the original contract being dissolved, and the ligaments

broken, which held us before together. The Nation was then a blank, apt to receive any impression. . . . Never had men such an opportunity of doing good, as they who had the chiefest hand in making the Revolution. . . . it was in their power for ever to have banished flattery and corruption from the court.[31]

With *The Machiavellian Moment,* J. G. A. Pocock coined "a name for the moment in conceptualized time in which the republic was seen as confronting its own temporal finitude."[32] He might just as well have said confronting the paradox of success, for the issue was not so much that a commonwealth would die but that it would die of a surfeit of its own success.

Even figuratively speaking, the republican case could not be directly applied to a monarchy, but in a constitutional monarchy such as England, it was possible to adapt the Republican argument by grafting the Aristotelian idea of a mixed government—one containing self-balancing elements of the one, the few, and the many—onto England and its Parliament. This might be done by schemes as elaborate as Harrington's radical recasting of England as the *Commonwealth of Oceana,* or by the simpler expedient of seeing the House of Commons as the embodiment of the many, the House of Lords as the few, and the Crown as the one that represents all (or acts as the balancer). This last is exactly the schema that appeared in Davenant's *Essays upon Peace at Home, and War Abroad.*[33] Thus he could conclude that a nation might "be as well called free under a limited kingship as in a commonwealth."[34]

But this still left open another issue of classification: on what sort of socioeconomic foundation was this commonwealth built? In Pocock's schema, James Harrington was the linchpin in the adaptation of the civic humanist tradition to England through his "synthesis" of "Machiavelli's theory of arms with a common-law understanding of the importance of freehold property."[35] In what we might call the neo-Harringtonian version of the evolving tradition, land was the foundation of the commonwealth, creating an agrarian-flavored discourse in which commerce was relegated to a distinctly subsidiary role. But another variation was possible, one in which commerce might have played as ambivalent a role as in the first, but one in which it and not land was seen as the true vehicle of England's greatness. This is essentially the achievement of Charles Davenant: he recast civic humanist republican rhetoric for the special situation of the commercial empire.

Which tradition was a more accurate depiction of England at the century's end? Those, like John Locke, who emphasized the contribution of land (or labor upon land) usually conflated the contribution of production (the turning of fleece into cloth or wheat into bread) with that of the actual farming, so that in their calculations, much of the value of the nation's secondary economic sector (manufacture, transportation, and construction) was merged with that of its primary sector (direct extraction). Even Sir William Petty's rough-and-ready national accounting had shown how little direct extraction contributed to what we would call England's gross domestic product, and his calculation was itself heavily biased in favor of goods over services (the tertiary sector). Modern data show an economy moving toward Petty's view. By 1700, agricultural income stood at about £18.7 million, net exports at £5 million, and income from domestic consumption of industrial goods at £14.6 million: though agriculture was still the largest sector in the economy it was already producing less than half the nation's income even in this preindustrial age.[36] On the other hand, a greater proportion of the total work force was employed by the primary than by the secondary and tertiary sectors of this economy.[37] In that sense it was truly still primarily an agricultural economy.

The question, however, is not which of the two emphases (agricultural or commercial) represented the more accurate understanding of the age, but whether or not Davenant's shift in perspective made him any more comfortable with the changes made in England by the spread of finance capitalism.

Davenant's version of the virtue-luxury paradox went like this. War being "quite changed from what it was in the time of our forefathers; when in a hasty expedition, and a pitched field, the matter was decided by courage," and become a thing "reduced to money," it was necessary that governments try to channel commerce rather than to dispense with it as Sparta had done.[38] Nations could no longer "subsist" of themselves "without helps and aids from other places."[39] Davenant was willing to accept necessary evils, because the "circumstance of time" and "the posture [of] other nations" made "things absolutely necessary" that were "not good in their own nature."[40] But he was also too much of a realist to see trade as entirely without benefit. A properly managed commerce (that is, one that maintained a positive trade balance) was England's only means of acquiring the money to defend itself and its best means of breeding up the seamen to do it.[41] And, of course, any trade abandoned by the English would only accrue to the Dutch.[42]

Credit played a multifaceted role in this new world. Davenant recognized its usefulness in greasing the wheels of commerce. During the specie shortage brought on by the war and the recoinage, "Paper-credit did not only supply the place of running cash, but greatly multiplied the kingdom's stock." It might be an "artificial wealth," but if correctly handled money and credit mutually help one another; money is the foundation of credit; where there is none, there can be no credit; and where credit obtains, money will circulate the better.[43]

Public credit (both as the flip side of government debt and as public confidence in the economy in general) was a two-edged sword. It arose from and could only be supported by two public "convictions":

> 1st, That there is a real bottom of strength, wealth, and ability in the public, to clear off, in a competent season, the great debts which have been contracted. 2dly, That there is, and shall be kept within the kingdom, a sufficient quantity of the species to turn in Trade, in the payment of rents and taxes, and in manufactures, and whereby to keep the wheels of the machine in motion.[44]

But *conviction* was only another word for *opinion*—that quintessentially subjective and hence dis-order–creating symptom of the very disease of success:

> Of all things that have existence only in the minds of men, nothing is more fantastical and nice than Credit; it is never to be forced; it hangs upon opinion; it depends upon our passions of hope and fear; it comes many times unsought for, and often goes away without reason; and when once lost, is hardly to be quite regained. It very much resembles, and, in many instances, is near a kin to that fame and reputation which men obtain by wisdom in governing state affairs, or by valour and conduct in the field. An able statesman, and a great captain, may, by some ill accident, slip, or misfortune, be in disgrace, and lose the present vogue and opinion; yet this, in time, will be regained, where there is shining worth, and a real stock of merit. In the same manner, Credit, though it may be for a while obscured, and labour under some difficulties, yet it may, in some measure, recover, where there is a safe and good foundation at the bottom.[45]

Let the public debt "swell beyond all compass," and all was lost: Spain's collapse was the best example of the effects of untrammeled borrowing.[46]

Military virtue was also not as simple a matter as some republicans would have it. It was very true that the more successful a country was, the more it needed "now and then" to be "engaged in foreign wars" in order to "awaken" its "martial temper" out of that "luxurious" and "effeminate" sleep of prosperous peace.[47] But war was by nature "a greedy monster" and had to be managed with care.[48] There were foolish wars as well as wise ones. Fighting lengthy foreign wars with great armies was a foolish policy; the money sent overseas to pay and supply these forces drained a country both of its coin and productive labor, while the debts incurred to finance them could only be paid off through ruinous taxation. Naval engagements were less of a drain. They kept men engaged in a labor that was as profitable in peacetime as in war, while the ships and the domestic goods that supplied them fed the native and not the foreign economy.[49] Long land wars also involved standing armies, and very few of Davenant's contemporaries would have had to be reminded of the battles between the Crown and Parliament over standing armies that had plagued England throughout the seventeenth century. They were still living through the most ironic result of the Glorious Revolution, the creation of a standing professional army (despite the fact that it was dependent on annual Mutiny Acts) to fight King William's Continental wars. Charles Davenant was not departing from the civic humanist tradition in condemning land wars and their concomitant standing armies, but he was modifying the rationale behind this condemnation by emphasizing the damage it did to the national economy.

There is one other significant variation in Davenant's version of civic humanist republicanism, and that concerns his general preference for a strong and intrusive executive (though not a strong monarch). One can scarcely find one of his essays or discourses that did not contain pointed praise of Richelieu, Mazarin, and Colbert for their attention to and control of trade, their "exact method," and the "entire obedience" they exacted from all "subordinate degrees," while mixed monarchies were criticized as being unduly "jealous" of powerful "master-genius[es]" in their ministries."[50] The end result of all this was Davenant's proposals for (1) the creation of a council of trade to "fit and adapt sumptuary laws," ensure enforcement of the Navigation Act, supervise standardization of the coinage, and oversee domestic manufacture and the colonial trade à la Colbert, and (2) a set of commissioners to bind the people "under great forfeiture" to accurately report their assets and incomes.[51]

One of the difficulties in sorting out seventeenth-century thought is that different schools of thought can lead to the same policy proposals. The councils of trade proposed by Gabriel Plattes or Sir William Petty had a Baconian origin, while Davenant's workhouse proposals seem to owe more to Colbert's *hôpitaux* than to Petty's in their absence of a pronounced educational component.[52] In any case, it is difficult to understand how Davenant's support for such policies can be reconciled with the twentieth-century tendency to see him as a laissez-faire pioneer for all his frequently repeated refrain that trade was "by nature free" and ran in deep "channels" from which it could not be diverted.[53] We are, after all, talking about a man who at one point advocated outright price controls.[54]

Charles Davenant considered himself a political arithmetician, a follower of William Petty and Gregory King in a field defined by Davenant as "the art of reasoning by figures, upon things relating to government."[55] As Political Arithmetic was actually used by Petty, King, and Davenant, it is better defined as Pocock put it—"a quantitative means of estimating every individual's contribution to the political stock by measuring what he put into or withdrew from the national stock."[56] It was a kind of national accounting that was still evolving in a symbiotic relationship with accounting itself. The key to it was the old analogy between the estate of the individual (or household) and that of the nation, a special case of the analogy between the human body and the body politic. But the two are far from identical, and too close an emulation of bookkeeping theory caused strange distortions in the picture drawn up of a national economy. To understand the distortions caused we need to follow two separate lines of argument, one for each of the two resulting reports, the National Income Statement and the National Balance Sheet. The first leads to questions of the balance of trade and taxation's effect on circulation. The second leads to a discussion of the nature of national wealth and the relation of demography to economics. Both finally bring us to the so-called King-Davenant Law of Demand.

The National Income Statement

Charles Davenant explained the idea of a national income statement thus:

> By annual income, we mean the whole that arises in any country, from land and its product, from foreign trade and domestic business, as arts, manufactures, &c. And by annual expence, we understand what is of necessity consumed to clothe and feed the people, or what is requisite for their defence in time of war, or for their ornament in time of peace. And where the annual income exceeds the expence, there is a superlucration arising, which may be called wealth or national stock.[57]

The parallel to standard bookkeeping can be seen in the idea that total revenue less total expense equals profit which is the net annual addition to the owner's capital account (stock), while the emerging macroeconomic tradition can be seen (1) in the idea that the portion of an individual's income which is not spent is saved (the superlucration), becoming that individual's contribution to the nation's fund of investment, and (2) in a definition of annual income that is pretty close to the modern definition of gross domestic product.

The modern definition of national income is something else, however, being the total amount earned by the owners of the resources (human as well as inanimate) used in producing the goods and services valued in the gross national product. While this sounds like it might be the same thing as Davenant's formulation, it is actually quite different. The difference between gross domestic product and gross national product (GDP includes goods and services produced by foreigners working in the country while GNP excludes such goods and services but includes those produced by nationals working abroad, a number excluded from GDP) is not the issue here. But to get from GNP to national income, an economist would subtract depreciation, sales and excise taxes, business transfers, and net subsidies to government-run businesses (because these things are not "income" to the owners of the resources used in production), while Charles Davenant is actually subtracting all consumption and government spending. There are four basic components to GNP (or GDP): consumption, government spending, investment, and net exports (exports minus imports). Do the math Charles Davenant's way and you get wealth equals investment plus net exports. Do that math and you will see the finite-bullionist worldview that underlay all of this (as well as the bias for durable goods) because investment will turn out to be the inventory of goods available for future export (and the capital goods necessary to make them). Thus we are back to the idea that the only way a nation can increase its wealth is to maintain a positive balance of trade—a position ardently supported by Charles Davenant who was fond of explaining that "by what is consumed at home, one loseth only by what another gets, and the nation in general is not at all the richer; but all foreign consumption is a clear and certain profit."[58]

Balance of trade. To hold, as Davenant did, that (1) "the wealth of a country is finite, as well as the substance of any man,"[59] so, consequently, (2) "whatever nation is at greater expence than this balance admits of, will as surely be ruined in time, as a private person must be, who every year spends more than the income of his estate,"[60] while (3) your neighbors would grab the profits from whatever trade you lost,[61] was (4) to place balance of trade theory in the broader context of balance of power, a context Charles Davenant saw as operating under parallel rules. "Machiavel," Davenant said, laid "it down for a rule seldom or never subject to exception; that in matters of empire, 'Whoever is the cause of another's advancement, is the cause of his own diminution.'" Thus it was not surprising that Davenant concluded that "One nation cannot increase in power without apparent danger to its neighbors; for Ambition was never known to set itself any bounds."[62] Davenant's own *Essay upon the Balance of Power* (1701) was a critique of William III's current alliance with France and the United Provinces, which Davenant saw as abandoning England's traditional role of holding "the balance of Europe" so that "neither France nor Spain might gain any ground the one upon the other."[63]

All commerce, domestic as well as foreign, had to be managed by the government so that a positive balance of trade was maintained while keeping competing nations from encroaching on your market share. So to find Davenant backing the Navigation Acts should be no surprise. Colonies, like commerce itself, could be as ruinous to a nation's prosperity if they began to compete with it as they could be beneficial in providing it with raw materials and markets. Colonies should not only be kept economically "as much dependant as possible upon their mother country," they should also never be taught the "art of war" by that mother country.[64] Ireland's trade had to be encouraged, but its woolens had to be kept from competing with England's.[65]

Even the English could not pick and choose which trades to enter into at will; the government had to make sure it maintained "an even hand to promote all; and chiefly to encourage such trades as encrease the publick stock" and avoid being swayed by the "distinct interest[s]" of the "distinct trade[s]."[66] In other words, the East India trade should be maintained in spite of the fact that it appeared to create a negative trade balance, because the profits from reexporting its goods actually created a positive balance.[67] This same principle applied to particular trade balances with the various colonies: they were beneficial as long as they generated a positive reexport balance.[68] Even a negative balance that generated no reexports (such as that with France) was not to be discounted outright as long as it was with the cheapest supplier of those goods.[69]

Nor could each particular branch of trade be run any way it pleased. The monopolies exercised by the great trading companies had come under considerable attack during the Exclusion Crisis, in part because the East India Company, the most influential of them all, was controlled by Tory shareholders. *Britannia Languens,* a much cited anonymous tract from 1680, mounted a concerted attack on the East India and Royal African Companies, two of the largest joint-stock enterprises. While merchants in regulated companies (such as the old Merchant Adventurers) traded on their individual accounts, joint-stock ventures acted as single buyers, and the author of *Britannia Languens* provided a well-reasoned analysis of the power this gave them of manipulating the domestic economy to their advantage via their ability to control both their buying and selling prices.[70] The arguments did not end with the Revolution, or even with the creation of the rival (Whig) East India Company, or even with their eventual merger. For Charles Davenant, however, the answer was simple. Believing in efficiency above all, he supported the East India and Royal African Companies precisely because their monopolistic power kept interlopers from disorganizing their trades and allowed them to buy cheap.[71] He particularly praised the Royal African Company for its ability to procure slaves ("the first and most necessary material for planting") cheaply for the colonies.[72]

This was a fairly limited idea of free trade, and if trade could not be left freer than this in peacetime, even more control had to be exercised in times of war:

> In times of peace, perhaps it may not be advisable to Tye up Trade or restrain it to many Rules since 'tis its Nature to prosper best in freedome. But as bodies wanting health are kept to regular diets, So in War, which is the Sickness of Trade, it cannot be Safely Left to govern itself. It may therefore in this Season be proper for the Legislative Authority to establish some Coercive power over the Merchants, to Oblige them to proceed with respect to the common good, as well as to their private profits.[73]

Since the finite mentality tended to treat all trade as a form of war, perhaps we should not be surprised if its adherents always favored considerable regulation even in those supposed seasons of peace.

Domestic trade had to be as carefully watched as its foreign sibling, because "a great part of our domestic traffick depends upon our foreign commerce, and we must sink in one, as the other decreases."[74] "The price of land, value of rents, and our commodities rise and fall, as it goes well or ill with our foreign trade."[75] The areas to watch in domestic trade were the interest rate and taxation.

For Davenant, nothing could "be more advantageous to the kingdom, than to beat down the price of money and lower interest," but this could not be done as long as the state's ever-increasing demand for funds "compelled" it to pay rates above the legal maximum. The higher the interest rate, the higher the taxes the state would need to collect to pay it off, and the combined effects of tight money and high taxation were bound to make trade "languish," chiefly because they raised the price of export goods above what the foreign market would bear.[76] Davenant's attitude toward taxation was rather complicated and, as such, will be discussed in the next section, but it is interesting to note that he had the same problem with the banking industry as did John Locke. Davenant went so far as to propose that the Bank of England be restrained by law from paying interest on deposits, as

> the ease of having from thence 3 or 4 per cent. without trouble or hard effort, must be a continual bar to industry, and has lately occasioned such a stagnation of the species in their hands, as by no manner of means can be advisable to suffer.[77]

While any twentieth-century observer might ask how Locke or Davenant expected banks to attract deposits if they could pay no interest on them, such an observer would have missed the point of the argument. Locke and Davenant knew banks could not attract savings without paying interest; what they wished to do was put an end to such banks altogether. They wished loans made directly between private individuals on the local level, assuming thereby the private lender could pocket the extra percentage points the London "banks" charged to make up for the interest they paid on deposits. The shorter circuit through the economy provided the greatest velocity (as well as a possible class advantage). This was the logic behind the idea that money in a bank was not circulating.

By the time Charles Davenant began to write, the circulation analogy was so well established that one would hardly see a tract without it. In Davenant's case it turns up numerous times, though one example may suffice:

> Trade and Money are like Blood and Serum, which tho Different Juices, yet run through the veins mingled together. And this present Corruption of our Coyn is like a dangerous Ulcer in the Body Politick which is never to be throughly Cured by applying Remedies to the Part, but by mending the whole Mass of Blood which is corrupted.[78]

It was this identification of the shortest circuit as the swiftest that made the problem of taxation conceptually so vexatious: did it contribute to circulation or detract from it? William Petty considered it an aid to circulation, because the government's spending of its receipts moved money through the economy. But here Petty and his pupil parted company. Charles Davenant thought it "a strange notion" to hold "that taxes make money circulate" and set out to prove otherwise.[79]

Taxation, sumptuary laws, and circulation. Taxation's effect on circulation had become something of a political football. From the Exclusion Crisis to the Glorious Revolution, Country Whigs had taken the position that taxation was a drain on the economy, while Tories like John Houghton defended government spending (the other side of taxation) as providing employment for the poor and profits for the luxury trades.[80] But, after the Revolution, Whig ministries began to hold the economic reins. Now Country Tories argued that taxation drained the economy, while Court Whigs claimed it was a circulating pump. Taxation can actually be either, depending on both its sources and its uses. Typically, a pump analysis would focus on its uses and a drain analysis on its sources. The two-pronged analysis offered by Sir William Petty would not be seen again in his century.

Charles Davenant basically saw the economy as divided into two sectors represented by the people and the government, but in which the government sector was itself a subsector of the first. Thus after calculating the balance of trade or the net national income, he concluded:

The revenue of the government is a part of this annual income, as likewise, a part of its expence; and where it bears too large a proportion with
the whole, as in France, the common people must be miserable and bur-
thened with heavy taxes. . . . But, in countries where the revenue of the
government bears but a small proportion with the annual income, as in
England, there the people are in plenty, and at their ease.[81]

The government's share was rapidly mounting. With National Income
running at from £45.73 to £55.70 million per annum for the period from
1690 through 1710, the share of that income appropriated for taxes was running anywhere from 6.7 to 9.2 percent. Back in 1680, the government had
taken only 3.6 percent of a £41.76 million National Income.[82] It was important that the government be provided with the revenue it needed to do its
job with the least damage to the greater sector. Since Davenant rejected
deficit financing as far too injurious to trade, he was left with direct taxes
(on land or by poll or hearth), indirect taxes (on imports or consumption),
or increasing the overall revenue (and hence the government's net at the
same percentage) by reducing consumption through import prohibitions or
sumptuary laws.

His basic position on such matters was first laid out in his *Essay upon
Ways and Means of supplying the War* (1695). This also represents his most
measured treatment of the problem, the one least affected by his political
disagreements with one administration or another. Actually, aside from
some minor flip-flops on sumptuary laws, his later positions modified
rather than reversed his first argument. What follows, then, is from *Ways
and Means*.

Here, Davenant rejected land taxes because raising funds to pay them
put the gentry into the power of their creditors (who thus became the "true
owners" of the land), and there could be no "circumstance more dangerous
to the liberty of a nation, than to have the real right, interest, and property
of land in one hand, and the power of being chosen into parliament in
another."[83] Could any other civic humanist have said it better? The poll tax
was rejected because its popularity was so low the amounts collected never
exceeded "more than half what in reason might be expected from it."[84] The
hearth tax was not discussed, presumably because it was too small a source
of revenue as it stood, and to increase it would create the same problems as
occurred with the poll tax.

Davenant treated excise taxes as a preferred alternative to customs
duties, because they had less of an impact on foreign trade. Customs duties
on imports could create a ripple effect on prices (and eventually on exports)
as imported raw materials were processed for reexport, or bring on retaliatory measures from England's trading partners: neither effect was desir-

able.[85] Excises, on the other hand, especially when correctly placed on the final point of sale, affected only the end consumer, so they could be used to reduce consumption of foreign or domestic goods. They could be set so high as to amount to an import "prohibition" on commodities that hindered "setting our own poor to work," or, like brandy, were "prejudicial to the health of the nation"; or to "depress several luxuries, of which our laws could never get the better."[86] Thus they were generally preferable to sumptuary laws.

An excise is a flat tax, and as such, consumes a greater percentage of one's income the poorer one is. But Davenant, like many of his contemporaries (and again, unlike William Petty) did not see a flat consumption tax as inequitable because "the disproportion between what the rich and the poor consume[d]" made excises "fall easily upon the poor." He was not entirely insensitive to the problems of the working poor; he did suggest excises should fall mainly upon luxury goods so "the poor would be least affected," but he also felt beer, ale, and brandy should be taxed for the very good of those same poor.[87]

In *Discourses on the Public Revenues* (1698), Davenant suggested reviving the policy of farming out the excises. Tax-farmers who stood to lose money from their own pockets if their collections did not meet the amounts contracted for would be more efficient collectors than salaried government officials, and the smaller the government payroll, the less the taxes needed to support it: "Multiplicity of officers is chargeable to the king, vexatious to the common people, and ministers occasion of jealousy to the country gentlemen."[88] Civic humanism and fiscal frugality went hand in hand. It was in this work as well that Davenant clarified his stand on charging excises only on the last point of sale:

> All excises should be laid as remotely from land as possible; it is true they yield less when so put, because the first maker is best come at; but when the last manufacturer or vendor is charged, they list with most equality upon the whole body of the people, and come not upon land in so direct a manner.[89]

Land continued to play an important role even in Davenant's commercial version of civic humanism.

When Davenant reconsidered his position on excises in *The Probable Methods of making a People Gainers in the Balance of Trade* (1699), it was not to reject them, but to urge greater care in setting them because of the injurious effect on foreign trade of making them too high or taxing too many of the basic goods used by the common people. If their market-basket became too expensive, their wages would have to rise to cover it, and then the price of the goods they produced would be higher than overseas markets would bear. Here Davenant followed the ripple effects throughout each group in the economy, explaining how the rich would have to retrench, which meant the manufacturers and retailers who supplied them would have to, which would lead only to further poverty for those farthest down on the scale. But Davenant's final conclusion was that all this "would signify little, if nothing but our own dealings among one another were thereby affected."[90] The systemwide view that arose from following the circulation analogy was not lost, but it was still subordinated to balance of trade theory.

Davenant's position on sumptuary laws did not so much change as shift, depending on the use to which they were to be put. He had suggested without elaboration that a council of trade consider imposing them in his 1695 memo, "Concerning the Coyn of England."[91] In his *Essay on the East-India Trade* (1697), he rejected sumptuary laws as ineffective, not so much because they were routinely ignored, but because they had no positive effect on foreign trade. Prohibiting the wearing of silk would not help the producers of domestic woolens:

> The natural way of promoting woollen manufacture, is not to force its consumption at home, but by wholesome laws to contrive, that it may be wrought cheaply in England, which consequently will enable us to command the markets abroad.[92]

But in his report to the commissioners charged with executing the act for *Taking, examining, and stating the publick Accounts of the Kingdom* (1712), he decided that they were better than high import duties or import prohibitions in "putting a stop to losing trades."[93] In other words, laws against the wearing of French silks would have no effect on the wearing of English woolens but could be used if all you wanted to do was decrease the use of French silks.

Davenant also favored a policy that could either supplement or replace sumptuary laws, a combination of government example and cultivation of religion (with appropriate sermons from the pulpit). Many different schools of seventeenth-century thought took such a position. Davenant's happens to have come from Hobbes as much as from his civic humanism. Believing that "the welfare of all countries in the world depends upon the morals of their people," he reminded his readers that "to preserve societies of men from that perpetual war with which the state of nature must be attended," the "founders of cities" had "set afoot forms of religion."[94] He used Hobbes as well to remind the nation that its leaders needed as great a training in statecraft as the general populace did in religion.[95] Actually his whole outlook on human psychology seems to have come from Hobbes, or at least Hobbes would have agreed with Davenant that humanity's "good inclinations" were "few and short," while their "irregular and bad appetites" knew "no end."[96]

This Hobbist psychology also worked its way into a passage in Davenant's unpublished "Memorial Concerning the Coyn of England" (1695) that modern commentators seize on as showing a particular sophistication on Davenant's part because of its use of interchangeable economic actors (if A will not do something, B will).[97] This was a trend begun, as we have seen, by Thomas Hobbes,[98] and to a certain extent picked up by our other Political Arithmetician, Sir William Petty, himself a friend of Hobbes. The passage in Davenant's "Memorial" actually concerned why the population would not accept clipped coins at their face value but only as worth their lesser weight. It also used a demand argument based on the Hobbist law of self-preservation (in which the market reproduces the war of all against all) to bolster an argument explaining the difference between intrinsic value and price as a result of supply (scarcity): in other words, why foreign trade affected domestic prices. The argument, considerably condensed, went like this:

> The Originall value of every thing is according as it is necessary to the Common uses of Life. . . . time, practice and consent have in a manner weighed in a Ballance what each of those Commodities shall be worth respectively. . . . 'Tis true indeed that the particular price of Goods is ambulatory, sometimes high, sometimes Low, but this arises from an Externall cause of their being at that time either Scarce or plentifull. . . . Which no Law can hinder. But Why must so much corn be worth such a Weight in silver? Because if B. will not give it, the same may be had from C. & D. or if from neither of them, it will yeild such a price in foreigne Countries; and from hence arises what wee commonly call Intrinsick Value. Nor can any law hinder B. C. & D. from supplying their Wants, Nor will any Law (in discretion) prevent such Transportation when the plenty admitts it. . . . The supream power can do many things, but it cannot alter the Laws of Nature, of which the most originall is, That every man should preserve himself. This thought of self preservation drives him to supply his necessities from others, which he cannot do but upon equal foot and Value for Value, which must be determin'd by common usage, and Consent, and this in a matter of Trade, must be the common Consent and usage of Trading People.[99]

Charles Davenant's connection to Thomas Hobbes was, in a sense, biological. His father, Sir William Davenant, had become close friends with Hobbes in Paris during the second half of the 1640s when many Royalists found it prudent to absent themselves from England. Hobbes did some in-progress editing of William Davenant's *Gondibert* and had considerable influence on his *Proposition for Advancement of Moralitie* with its scheme of using the dramatic arts to educate the populace in the civic religion Hobbes thought necessary to the health of any commonwealth.[100]

National Balance Sheet

When Charles Davenant got down to actual numbers it was usually data on population, tax revenues, or the nation's annual spending, though at one point he did produce something along the lines of a national balance sheet (or at least the asset portion of it) when he reproduced Gregory King's valuations of the land and livestock, houses, commercial buildings and commercial stock in, and ships belonging to England and its inhabitants. He assumed the data proved that England could well (as Petty had insisted) support twice its estimated population of 5.5 million.[101] He came to such a conclusion because he treated these numbers as indicative of productive power: that is, he was treating the land, the buildings, and even the streams as part of the national "stock"—the capital with which and from which it would produce the goods that its population needed. This was why his data usually concerned itself with annual spending, because it was a guide to how much different kinds of national stock might be expected to yield.

Equating spending with production was a major step toward the development of gross domestic/national product, but as we have seen, Davenant did not equate this with any incremental change in true national wealth. His main interest in such production data was in how it might be most efficiently harvested by the state in the form of taxation (that is, yield the state the greatest revenue with the least harm done to wealth-producing trade). In both instances when he reproduced Petty's data, it was to introduce a discussion of what was currently or should be taxed. His conclusions reveal the usual bias against middlemen and services. Taking taxation as falling "chiefly upon land, and foreign trade," Davenant concluded that "usurers, lawyers, tradesmen, and retailers, with all that troop that maintain themselves by our vice and luxury" were getting off virtually scot-free.[102]

Defining national wealth. The basic conceptual problem in devising a national balance sheet concerns the definition of national assets. Malynes, Misselden, and Mun had taken gold and silver as equally personal and national assets whether coined or in plate, drawing a distinction between them along the essentially modern lines of varying liquidity. Sir William Petty broadened the concept of national assets to include all the resources, animate and inanimate, that could be turned into (or did the turning into) commodities for exchange. Petty's idea of including the population in his national net worth statement was not as much of a radical departure as it seems, if we step out of accounting proper and think of the way we might refer to good health as one of our "assets." Petty did, after all, try to calculate the productivity of the population.

Davenant's definitions of "the riches of a nation" ran along the same lines and into the same problems as Sir William Petty's. Included in Davenant's vision of a nation's wealth were "numbers of men," "numerous merchant fleets and powerful navies," with stores and munitions to supply them, buildings for whose adornment a "great stock" of "iron, lead, brass copper" could "lie dead," large inventories of export commodities, large stores of gold and silver plate in private hands, homes adorned with "costly furniture, statues and pictures," a population able to afford "rich apparel and jewels," a "good annual income from the earth," livestock, mines, coin, and "even perishable goods" if they were "convertible" though not yet "converted into gold and silver," and, above all, the "Industry, and skill" to produce commodities for export.[103]

Two items from this list, however, proved in need of considerable qualification to be considered true assets: money and men. For Davenant, as for Locke, money had both a real and a functional identity, and like Locke, Davenant considered the real more important than the functional.[104] Where in the one instance Davenant would call money the "measure of trade," in another he would refer to gold and silver in the same words. He recognized that gold and silver were "themselves but a Commodity," but insisted (as did Locke) that "Time, Common Consent and Practice Seeme to have fixed a Constant value upon them." This "true Naturall and Intrinsick value" did not alter, so that to speak of them as being "dear or cheap abroad" meant only that they were "Dear or Cheap in Comparison with other Commodities," or one varied in price with respect to the other. The stamped denomination was "no more than a Declaration" of a coin's weight and fineness, a means of preventing fraud, that "in no other Sence can be said to put a value on it."[105] Davenant considered "Purity of Coin" a "true sign of Wealth in a Nation" and "its Corruption" a "marke of Poverty and Want of strength in the Laws and Government," because he was certain that international exchange was based on intrinsic value: no "valuation the Government here can put upon our money can alter its course abroad." Since England was a "Trading Nation," the prices of both the products it sold abroad and the raw materials it imported to make them would be adversely affected by devaluation.[106]

Money (coined gold or silver) was a national asset, but one that had to be managed. Too little in circulation, and trade stagnated: Davenant recommended Petty's calculation of keeping enough coin on hand to pay one installment of the semiannual and quarterly rents, the weekly wages, and one-quarter of the commercial turnover.[107] But go beyond this and trade was damaged as well: excess coin needed to be turned into other assets, such as "foreign materials for building" or even plate to keep the "surfeiting diet" of circulating coin from inflating prices. Davenant considered the situation exactly parallel to that of the individual merchant who started a business with considerable cash on hand, but quickly turned it into inventory if he wished to prosper.[108] And what of credit? It was a functional equivalent of money and one the nation could not do without:

> If men in England spend, one with another, but seaven pounds per annum, The Expence of the nation in the Common Turning and winding of mony must be fifty Millions per annum; To which our quantity of Cash could at no time in any Measure answer. It must follow then That the remained is all Transacted by Creditt.[109]

Nonetheless, it was not "wealth":

> Tis not from hence to be argued that the Nation is by So much [credit] Richer now than it was before, but, as a Landed Merchant who engages his Estate to raise Money to carry on his Trade, may be said to have a greater stock, but cannot be esteemed the Wealthier for it.[110]

The bookkeeping parallel remained unbroken: credit created an asset but was not wealth because it also created an offsetting liability (in this case, the mortgage on the land).

Population being the active part of the national stock, more was generally better than less.[111] Davenant was in favor of increasing the population through liberalization of the naturalization laws (with the caveat that only the rich, the skilled, and the industrious should be included under this head) and even of using monetary rewards and fines to encourage the English to have more children (that is, for those groups who contributed to the national wealth).[112] But, as was the case with money, mere numbers of people could not simply be added to the national balance sheet; a country could be "populous and yet poor." According to Davenant, it was "a wrong opinion" to think that

> all mouths profit a country that consume its product: and it may be more truly affirmed, that he who does not some way serve the commonwealth, either by being employed, or by employing others, is not only a useless, but hurtful member to it.[113]

One of the features of Davenant's national accounting was the fairly rigorous conceptual consistency he maintained in going from his income statement to his balance sheet. In his balance sheet, he included only the producing part of the population by subtracting nonproducers (or mere consumers) from the whole; in his income statement, he included only that portion of their production that was used to create true wealth (bullion or the assets it could purchase) by subtracting all production domestically consumed.

The economics of Davenant's demographics. Like any good political arithmetician, Davenant would use statistical data to illustrate his contention that only certain members of a commonwealth were profitable to it. In this instance, however, the data he used were not his. He reproduced them (with permission), as he explained, from the unpublished work of Gregory King. But who was Gregory King?

The *Dictionary of National Biography* sums up Gregory King (1648–1712) as a "herald, genealogist, engraver, and statistician,"[114] but this son of a Staffordshire mathematician and surveyor was also a mapmaker (for London and Westminster), surveyor (laying out the streets around Soho Square, originally King Square), superintendent of municipal and private lotteries (for Bristol and for John Ogilvy the printer), diplomat (sent as herald to present the order of the Garter to the Electors of Brandenburg and Saxony), and secretary to the commissioners of the public accounts and to the controllers of the army's accounts. He might more properly be called a Political Arithmetician (à la William Petty) or a Political Economist rather than simply a statistician, though he was a pioneer in that field, because when he compiled his *Natural and Political Observations and Conclusions upon the State and Condition of England* (1696),[115] he was not merely interested in estimating England's population but in determining how that population was (and was not) contributing to its politicoeconomic strength.

King's "Scheme of the Income and Expence of the several Families of England, calculated for the Year 1688"[116] divided the population of England into two groups. In the first were listed lords temporal and spiritual, baronets, knights, esquires, gentlemen, officeholders, import-export merchants, lawyers, clergymen, freeholders, farmers, professionals in the arts and sciences, artisans, and naval and military (army) officers. King calculated the total annual income of the 2,675,520 persons in these 500,586 households at £34,488,800, and their annual expenses at £31,465,100, giving them a combined annual increase in estate of £3,023,700.

In the second group were listed common seamen and soldiers, wage-laborers, out-servants, cottagers, paupers, and vagrants (gypsies, thieves, and beggars). King calculated the total annual income of the 2,825,000 persons in these 849,000 families at £9,010,000, but their total annual expenses at £9,572,000, creating an annual deficit of £622,500. Thus he came to the simple conclusion that the first group were "Encreasing the wealth of the kingdom" to the tune of £3,023,700 while the second group were "Decreasing" it to the tune of £622,500, giving England a net annual increase in wealth of £2,401,200. By this he meant, according to Davenant, the first group not only "add every year something to the nation's general stock" but "out of their superfluity, contribute every year so much to the maintenance of others"; while the second group (and especially their non-working "wives and children" or "sick and impotent") were "a yearly burthen to the public, consuming annually so much as would be otherwise added to the nation's general stock."[117] This kind of characterization is both the logical result of the blanket application of bookkeeping theory to a national arena and a logical corollary of the finite-bullionist mentality that saw all domestic trade as adding nothing to the wealth of a nation.

Since, for Davenant, the only way a nation could actually increase its wealth was to maintain a positive balance of trade (which required producing goods for export), it was necessary to increase the percentage of the population that worked for a living. To this end Davenant proposed a reform of the poor laws, replacing outdoor relief with "workhouses" administered by officers with the authority to compel the able poor to enter them, and in which the wages were to be no more than three-fourths of the usual wage "because board is also included." The impotent poor were not to be cared for at home either; a series of hospices was to be erected as a more cost-efficient means of providing for them.[118]

Even among the productive portion of the population, not all professions were equally useful. The "strength of a government" did not lie in the "brewers, malters, victualers," or "traders and retailers" who "get by the public," but in "the body of the people who subsist by labour," "the middle rank of men who subsist from arts and manufactures," and "the gentry of the nation."[119] Again those who produced commodities were favored over those who performed services, because eliminating middlemen created a more direct circulation. As for the brewers and malters, well, they were producing product rather than performing a service, but it was a product Davenant thought the poor would be better off without.

The Law of Demand

If for no other reason, Charles Davenant has earned a permanent place in the history of economic thought with a small chart concerning the price of grain that appeared in his *Essay upon the Probable Methods of making a Peo-*

ple Gainers in the Balance of Trade (1699). According to Davenant, "a defect in the harvest" would "raise the price of corn in the following proportions":[120]

Defect		Above the common rate
1 tenth		3 tenths
2 tenths		8 tenths
3 tenths	raises the price	1.6 tenths (actually 1 and 6 tenths)
4 tenths		2.8 tenths (actually 2 and 8 tenths)
5 tenths		4.5 tenths (actually 4 and 5 tenths)

In the economic literature, this much-debated table is generally referred to as the King-Davenant Law of Demand and marks a true milestone: the first mathematical formulation of a law of supply and demand. At numerous points in the essay in which the table appeared Davenant not only acknowledged his access to Gregory King's unpublished data but reproduced chunks of it for his readers. No such table appears in what remains of King's work, but economists remain undecided as to the law's ultimate authorship.[121] A second problem with the law concerns its basis. Although originally assumed to be derived inductively, most economists now take it to be "hypothetically based on a mathematical formula,"[122] an idea first proposed by William Whewell (1794–1866) back in 1850. Since the time Jevons first reduced the table to a function (price of corn equals .824 over the square of harvest size minus .12), economists have been arguing over the derivation of the constants, and the more sophisticated the mathematics proposed for their derivation, the more the question of authorship has tended to swing back toward Gregory King because of his demonstrated greater mathematical skill.[123]

In building his national accounting system, Davenant used both King's data and King's underlying assumptions. There is no reason the two men thought differently about the demand table, no matter who refined whose idea. But what kind of demand table was it?

The context of the table is actually production for export. The whole essay was taken up with ways to mend the balance of trade: what portion of a population did not contribute to the economy because by living off public assistance it drained resources that might otherwise be invested in export-directed production, how much more could be produced if naturalization laws were liberalized and larger families encouraged by law, and which taxes would hurt foreign trade by raising the prices of goods consumed by the working poor, forcing up both their wages and the selling prices of the export goods they produced. Domestic demand was the stumbling block in the way of achieving a positive balance of trade; demand was what had to be controlled.

Like just about every economic writer of the century, Davenant reminded his reader over and over again that the "Want or Plenty of any Commodity" gave "the Rule to its Price,"[124] but when it came down to explaining how this worked, supply was almost always the operative mover and demand the thing moved:

> And Considering the various Necessitys of mankind, at different Seasons of time in Different Countreys, Occasioned by Warr, Plague, Drowth [Drought] and other Accidents which by altering the Experience or Need, many Change the Price of Severall Commodities.[125]

This was meant to explain a variation in the price of a particular commodity. To explain a variation in the general price level, the supply argument shifted to the question of the money supply itself:

> gold and silver being the measure of trade, all things are dear or cheap as that sort of wealth is wanted or abounding, and in all countries of the world where money is rare and scarce, the product of the earth is cheap.[126]

Variations in supply were the result of objective forces (such as the weather) or factors that could be objectified (the amount of acreage under the plow, the percentage of the population actively employed in some form of production, or even the amount of money in circulation). Demand was that dangerous, egotistical, and thus subjective vehicle of the passions. For Charles Davenant, demand was the true source of the "corruption" commerce brought and the one he tried hardest to see controlled—through his strong advocacy of sumptuary laws, tariffs, excises, and monopolistic trade.

How then should we fit Davenant's Demand Law into its context? We might begin by asking what is different about the demand curve for wheat than for that of any other product in England in the seventeenth century. Davenant had hinted at it before, when he said that so much "corn" must be worth so much silver because if B will not give that price for it, C or D would.[127] But John Locke actually came much closer to laying bare its secret when he claimed that though it was "impossible" to set a maximum or fixed price on "Victuals in a time of famine," people would not "rob themselves of all other Conveniences of Life" for scarce wheat when cheap oats were available.[128] The demand for the basic dietary staple of any people is the most inelastic, most intransigent, and hence most predictable form of demand there is because of the strength of the cultural preference involved. If anything, Locke still understated its power: individuals will come far closer to robbing themselves of those "Conveniences" than he thought despite the availability of cheaper substitutes. In the case of a dietary staple, what really causes the drop-off in units sold as the price rises is the increasing numbers of people who cannot afford to continue buying the wheat and *must* switch to the substitute. Nothing as ephemeral as fashion complicates the picture.

The economic writers of the seventeenth century were well aware of the need to explain the essential nature of both supply and demand if they wished to produce a *cosmology* of the marketplace, but, over the course of that century, they also became aware that the creation of a *cosmography* of the marketplace would only require an explanation of the mechanical workings of those same two forces. Fitting demand into a cosmology of the market always brought up the issue of those mutable, individual, subjective, and *ultimately* (in the Aristotelian sense) unknowable "fancies." Fitting demand into a cosmography only required the demonstration of the existence of a predictability in preferences (or *practically* knowable tastes). Both courses were attempted. In attempting to create a *true* science of humankind, Hobbes was following the cosmological path, though incidently laying down guidelines for the cosmographical. Taking Hobbes's work as a given, Petty moved directly to the cosmographical road. Locke seems to have tried to travel down both paths at once. Davenant believed there was a *real* foundation involved (hence his remarks that, however fanciful credit seemed, it also, like fame, had some real center around which it fluctuated),[129] but with his Demand Law, he demonstrated that the behavior of demand in the marketplace could be shown to follow rational laws (and hence be *practically* known) whether or not its *true* essence was ever completely understood.[130]

There was nothing in this of a confidence trick: wheat was not deliberately chosen by Davenant, Locke, or Petty because of the special nature of the demand for it. Wheat dominated the discussion of the domestic economy as wool had long done that of its foreign trade because each was the dominant product in its sphere. Wheat (or rice or corn or potatoes) looms as large in the worldview of an agricultural society as cattle in a pastoral. And even if English society was no longer as overwhelmingly agricultural as it had once been, agriculture was still the largest single sector in its economy.[131] Nonetheless, the unique behavior in the marketplace of a dietary staple made wheat an extremely comforting commodity to work with for a world still largely unwilling to trust the concept of flux as a manifestation of stability.

Davenant's explorations of demand in the marketplace were not as bold as they seem: he certainly attempted no "Law of Demand" founded on the prices of French silks, wig-powder, or petticoats. Outside of the mar-

ketplace proper he drew an even sharper distinction. Not everything in life
was intended to be a commodity.

It was not merely a self-seeking politics that motivated Davenant's
attacks on "corruption." It was a true fear of what the proliferation of credit
was doing to England's political life that kept Davenant harping on the
links between "luxury," public debt, and disaster. It was a profound discomfort with the values of the *market* itself that drove this man to create an analytical framework restricting its action to commercial life proper and advocate policies (such as excises and monopolistic organization) to keep its
potential for disorder contained even in that limited sphere.

He was far from alone in this discomfort with the changing economic
universe. The very continuation of civic humanist republican arguments
demonstrated by J. G. A. Pocock probably hinged on its ability to justify
that discomfort in the face of the rising power and prosperity commerce
was creating. Pocock put the "neo-Machiavellism" first, giving us the situation of an "Englishman" who "had begun to envisage himself as a civic individual through the use of Aristotelian and civic humanist categories, which
required among other things that there be a material foundation" for virtue
as well as for value, who found the post-1675 advent of "parliamentary
patronage, a professional army, and a rentier class maintaining the two for
its own profit, posed a threat of corruption to the whole edifice."[132] It seems
likely that in the case of this one Englishman the story needs to be
reversed: it was the discomfort with the spread of capitalism throughout
the sociopolitical structure that made this political school so convenient a
rhetorical vehicle for Charles Davenant. It was but one more variant in the
long tale of economic thought in seventeenth-century England and the
struggle of its molders to create a new science to support an old value system.

Conclusion

One of the longest-running disagreements in the interpretative literature concerns who among these nine authors deserves to be considered a forerunner of laissez-faire liberalism and who was simply some variety of mercantilist. E. A. J. Johnson saw Mun and Misselden as liberals, but Sir Eric Roll moved them (along with Malynes and Petty) into the mercantilist column. Pierre Vilar put Child, Locke, North, and Davenant among the mercantilists and Barbon among the liberals, but Richard Wiles's Barbon was a mercantilist while Vickers thought North a liberal. H. T. Dickinson's Locke was a semiliberal and his Davenant a full-fledged one, while Beer cast Locke as a proto-Physiocrat.[1]

This disparity is more the result of an ongoing debate over the meaning and validity of the label *mercantilism* than of disagreements over how close a theorist has to be to a particular pole of this bipolar arrangement to be labeled one or the other. Was there ever anything we might call mercantilism?

Of all the analytic models applied to seventeenth-century economic literature, mercantilism is the least anachronistic in a strict sense. Defining "political oeconomy" as the "branch" of "the science of a statesman" concerned with providing "a plentiful revenue" for the people and the state, Adam Smith believed the "progress of opulence in different ages and nations" had created two different systems of political economy, the agricultural and the commercial (or mercantile)."[2] The salient characteristics of the mercantile system were its definition of wealth as gold and silver, its concentration on a positive balance of trade to the exclusion of the domestic economy (because it saw that domestic economy as not bringing gold/silver into the economy), its reliance on monopoly to accomplish that positive balance, and its sacrifice of the desires and needs of the domestic consumer to the requirements of the export-producer.[3] Thus it was a set of government policies supported by the commercial exporter devolving from a false definition of wealth.

Having dismissed mercantilism as a set of deficient policies based on incorrect assumptions, classical economists ignored it. Historians of economic thought, however, could not. Their interpretations branch off into two main schools—the statist and the wealth—each subject to considerable internal variation. Gustav Schmoller saw mercantilism as part of the historical process of political centralization, the transfer of power from local to national organs,[4] while James Bonar saw it as growing out of (rather than along with) "the conditions of absolute monarchy,"[5] and Eli Heckscher saw it as a form of raison d'état common to all European governments (finding its epitome in Colbert) from the beginning of the sixteenth to the end of the eighteenth centuries evolving out of a policy of provision.[6] The works of these pioneers form what we might call the statist school; it sees mercantilism as the end product of economic policies pursued by governments for political ends. National variants become minor themes, the result of accidental differences in national political situation. Two recent examples might suffice. In 1995, Murray Rothbard called mercantilism "the economic aspect of absolutism," or "a comprehensive system of state building, state privilege, and what might be called 'state monopoly' capitalism."[7] The so-called theories (fallacious special interest pleading) follow rather than lead the ill-advised government policies.[8] In 1998, Mark Perlman and Charles R. McCann Jr. defined mercantilism as "an economic theory dedicated to the advancement of national power through the encouragement of collective antagonisms, or countervailing power centers" and promoting "autarky," which grew out of a change in emphasis from the fifteenth to the sixteenth centuries "from a concern with the role of the state as political unifier to the role of the state as a coordinator, as an entity providing a sort of organizational framework for economic activity."[9] Its roots lie not in the "continuing theme" of "power relations" running through the literature but in the craft guilds and their function as "order-preserving collectives."[10] Mercantilism is the state as the ultimate guild.

The alternative argument grows out of a challenge posed by Jacob Viner to Heckscher's thesis. Viner believed the governments in question did not seek power to the exclusion of wealth or even wealth merely as a means to power, but, instead, saw power and plenty as interrelated and harmonious ultimate ends.[11] The wealth argument (even though still about state policy) opened up the question of which of the policies proposed by mercantilist authors was their ultimate aim and which merely the means to that goal. In such arguments the economic writers are treated less as minions than as independent advisers of the state. William Dyer Grampp believed English mercantilism was "one phase in the development of liberal doctrine" and English mercantilists seekers after national (not state) prosperity, who, if they "had wanted a favorable balance of trade for its own sake

... surely would not have given as much attention as they did to the money supply, employment, spending, and domestic trade."[12] More specifically, he took the ultimate goal to be full employment.[13] Richard C. Wiles suggested a mercantilist "ideal type" could be constructed around the view "that the all encompassing aim and goal was economic development or 'progress.'"[14] Recently Robert Burton Ekelund Jr. and Robert D. Tollison saw it as nothing more than a special-interest grab for monopolistic rents.[15] National variation was due to institutional developments that affected the efficacy of various rent-seeking measures, "intellectual developments" having little "impact on public policy."[16]

A study of seventeenth-century English economic thought cannot, obviously, come to any final conclusion about the nature or origins of a phenomenon spanning half a continent and three centuries. What it can do is see if there was anything we might call *English mercantilism* in the seventeenth century.

There were certainly marked similarities of goals and methods among seventeenth-century economic writers if not any absolute uniformity. The key areas of agreement may be summarized as follows.

1. The ultimate goal of these writers was a politicoeconomic growth that their finite view of the world's resources led them to assume would be at the expense of their neighbors' power and prosperity.

2. This growth was expressed in terms of an analytical identity between state wealth and national power. There was no similar identity between individual wealth and national power, because the drive for gain assumed to motivate merchants was understood to be capable of being (if not necessarily) in conflict with the common good.

3. Gold and silver were almost universally considered the most desirable form of wealth, and by a considerable majority (at least in the earlier half of the century) to be the only form of wealth. As a consequence, money was generally thought of as some quantity of coined gold or silver (with the stamped denomination acting as no more than a guarantee of weight and purity), although in the second half of the century a rudimentary *functional* definition of money began to compete with this metallist or *physical* definition.

4. Another consequence of the metallist concept of wealth was the development of balance of trade theory: the ultimate purpose of trade being to increase the nation's wealth/power, its immediate purpose was to secure a positive flow of bullion by exporting more goods than were imported. The tension between this us–versus–the world theory and the "harmonious" or mutual-support justification of commerce was never resolved but subsumed beneath the concern with maintaining a "harmo-

nious" (i.e., advantageous) circulation of the resulting wealth through the society.

5. This led to general support for a considerable governmental role in the organization of commerce. Since the state already played such a role, these writers could be characterized as proposing variations in the status quo rather than true innovations. Nonetheless, conscious state policy (especially with respect to trade balances) follows rather than leads economic thought in this century. The governmental role proposed is not absolute. None of these writers accepted an unlimited role for the state: they were as afraid of regulations they believed impeded production as they were in favor of those they felt encouraged it. As the century progressed, however, the general trend of economic thought was toward a shrinking rather than a growing role for the state, but true examples of laissez-faire advocacy (with reference to both the domestic market and international trade) were extremely rare.

6. The preferred form of international-trade organization was monopolistic, though there was considerable disagreement as to whether regulated or joint-stock companies best accomplished this aim. This was the result both of the age's inherited mind-set equating order with hierarchy and chaos with leveling (free access) and the greater effectiveness of monopolies in cutting out *foreign* competition. It was also a logical development of the guild system that once dominated and still heavily influenced domestic trade.

7. Because of the technological limitations of the age that dictated production for export could only be increased by increasing the number of hands at work, as well as concerns with the political havoc wreaked by the unemployed, and the importance of the idea of "the calling," to say nothing of dismay over the increasing expense of the Poor Rates, these works were full of schemes for workhouses, vocational schools, and other measures to increase the work force. Since a great majority of these works were also full of suggestions for curbing demand for imported goods and consumption of domestically produced goods that might otherwise be exported, the idea of separating the goal of full employment from that of increasing production for export seems unwise.

8. Though subordinate to the question of work-force size, there was a continuing concern over the overall size of the population. In the first half of the century, a fear that population growth was outracing society's ability to supply it led to the recommending of colonies as ways to siphon off the excess (as much as for any new products or markets they could provide). In the second half of the century, buoyed by confidence in science's ability to

boost agricultural and industrial yield, writers called for liberalization of naturalization laws and encouragement of larger families to provide the workers necessary to make the most of the new knowledge. This led to a closer assessment of whether or not a colony's goods competed with those of its motherland in the international market. No one suggested leaving colonies free to trade as they wished.

Many of the policies and their underpinning assumptions pre-date the beginning of "mercantilism" whether one picks the beginning or the end of the seventeenth century as the time of "mercantilism's" inception in England.[17] But where basic ideas were borrowed from the previous century, they evolved into markedly different policies throughout the seventeenth: if the idea of state intervention was a constant of both centuries, there was a qualitative difference between the Tudor laws against "forestalling, regrating, and engrossing," and the Navigation Act of 1651.[18] The Tudor laws were an attempt to prevent restraint of competition in the domestic marketplace in order to maintain "just prices," while the Navigation Acts were designed to prevent foreign competitors from bringing goods into England and upsetting monopolistic prices. Alternately, a number of the seventeenth century's preoccupations and biases survived the demise of its main theories. Adam Smith and his successors were as nationalistically oriented as their predecessors, would never assume power did not depend on plenty, and were equally driven to see the national economy grow. But Adam Smith assumed that the freer trade was from state intervention the faster the economy would grow. That was not a common assumption in the seventeenth century.

It may prove impossible to determine authoritatively whether we are dealing with an ideology or a less self-consciously held *Weltanschauung*. While the word *mercantilism* might best be avoided, the adjective *mercantile* should still be used to describe this body of thought because the specific problems addressed in these works—interest rates, exchange rates, the reliability of a coin's stamp as an indicator of its true metallic content, the impact of domestic consumption on exports and the varying impacts of sumptuary laws/export prohibitions/tariffs in this regard, whether or not the bullion earned by reexports of East Indian goods offset the bullion lost originally procuring those goods, how to increase the work force, and calls for the codification of a Law Merchant, facilitating the transfer of credit instruments, and easing the bankruptcy laws—are overwhelmingly those of the import-export merchant though not entirely exclusive to him. There is also no getting away from the fact that when the literature is read en masse, most of it turns out to have been written by merchants, mercers, and the goldsmiths who financed them. For these reasons, if for no other, the body of economic literature created in seventeenth-century England should be called *mercantile*.

The type of economic thought codified by the nine writers under discussion is, in effect, a school of "Political Economy." In the seventeenth century, *oeconomics* was still a word denoting household management. For Adam Smith, as we have seen, *political economy* was a branch of statecraft. The term had been coined in 1616 by Antoine de Montchrétien (ca. 1575–1621) in his *Traité d'économie politique*. Sir William Petty called his "new" science "Political Arithmetick" while reserving "political economy" for the thing described: Political Arithmetic described the political economies of England and Ireland the way bookkeeping described the economy of a business or household. In this sense, seventeenth-century economics was political economics because it described the economy of the *polis,* the commonwealth, the political community. But the political community was simultaneously the *body* politic. The seventeenth century inherited a view of the universe as a series of concentric spheres each understood by its congruence both with the sphere in which it sat and that which sat within it. Thus political economy was consciously modeled on household economy and evolved in tandem with the changes in the way in which the seventeenth century understood the human body to work.

The century's economic thought was political in a different sense: since most of the economy was still heavily regulated by the state, all the policies desired by these writers had to be put to the state in a manner emphasizing the advantages the government would reap from such policies rather than necessarily emphasizing the advantages the nation (or any group within it) might reap. This would apply even if the policy being put forward involved the partial retreat of the state from the regulation of the market. Money was also understood as a prerequisite for power, so the state could not afford to ignore the economic activity of the nation.

This political emphasis was not merely a result of practical reality. The state and the nation were not identical in the seventeenth century. Following the anatomical analogy, the body represented the nation as a whole, but the head represented the state, and, at least at the beginning of the century, the head was considered to be the only independently active member of that body: all production flowed from the members to it before being redistributed to those members as the head decided was best.

Being a political economics in every possible sense of the word meant that it was also a *moral* economics. In the *studia humanitatis* of the Renaissance, politics, ethics, and "oeconomics" were the three branches of "moral philosophy." The key classical sources for moral philosophy were the political tracts of Cicero, Seneca, and Tacitus, and, of course, Aristotle's *Politics*, *Ethics*, and the pseudonymous *Oeconomics*, which last three were treated as though they were three parts of the same work. Even where distinguished from them, the purely economic effects of any policy were always subordinate to the greater matrix of the political, social, theological, and moral concerns of the society.

England's economic structure changed considerably over the course of the seventeenth century. It was still certainly more agricultural than commercial at the century's end, and more commercial than industrial, but it was also much more sophisticated: paper currencies, publically funded government debts, public banks, transferable credit instruments, and stock exchanges were foreign novelties to Gerard de Malynes but everyday realities to Charles Davenant. Just as important, this level of sophistication penetrated much farther into the populace at large and the politicosocial structure than it ever had. Shoemakers held shares in international trading concerns and stock in the public debt—not so very many shoemakers, of course—but the gentry were deeply involved, as were the mercantile and professional men. Capitalist practices were, at varying speeds, transforming all the sectors—agricultural, commercial, financial, and manufacturing—of the economy. But practice was far in advance of theory, even in a technical sense: profit was still conflated with estate growth, and money with capital, at the century's end.

The changes in England's economic life played themselves out against a century of civil wars and revolutions: two constitutional upheavals in England, the assassination of Henri IV and the Fronde in France, the Catalonian revolt and the loss of Portugal in Spain, the evolution of the revolt of the Netherlands into a Thirty Years' War in central Europe, three trade wars between the English and the Dutch, and three others between the French and the Dutch (the last being simultaneously the War of the Spanish Succession).

This was equally a century of intellectual upheaval. The intellectual inheritance passed on from the sixteenth century to the seventeenth was both rich and richly contradictory: magic and science, the closed Aristotelian-Ptolemaic universe and the boundless one of hermetic plentitude, geo- and heliocentric perspectives, mechanical and vitalist universes, right reason and illumination, Christian humanism and civic humanism, divine right and social contract, civil and common law, Catholic and Protestant, and, within Protestantism, Arminian inclusiveness and Calvinist exclusion. The best minds of the seventeenth century would devote themselves to repairing these rifts.

Thus the century would prove in many ways to be the high-water mark of the *esprit de système:* the great constructions of Descartes, Hobbes, Grotius, Pufendorf, and Spinoza were designed to restore a moral and philosophical cohesion they felt the world had lost. Sisters in spirit were the century's utopian systems of social engineering drawn up in a millenarian zeal to establish the New Jerusalem: *Macaria, Oceana,* all those hundreds of pamphlets for improving husbandry, and Sir William Petty's ambitious plans for a total socio-political reorganization of England. But it was equally the age of the *esprit systématique:* of the refining of empirical, deductive, and mathematical methods for establishing a body of objective, practical knowledge intended to serve the same improving ends. The ideological clashes between the advocates of system and those of method were mirrored by clashes between the different schools of each: there would be no true synthesis until the seventeenth century had turned into the eighteenth.

Although that ultimate synthesis lies beyond the chronological bounds of this study, almost every strand in it helped shape the thought of the nine men covered within these pages. From the cross-pollination of the basic analogy of the body, the concept of congruences, the idealization of Aristotelian harmony (balance), and the new science of bookkeeping came the balance of trade theory that so dominated the century's thought. Malynes, Misselden, and Mun laid down the basic pattern, though it did not remain unaltered as the century progressed. But the model they inherited was of a finite universe ranged in a hierarchical order. Their economics judged each individual's worth by his or her contribution to the welfare of the whole (seen as his or her ability to bring in bullion). Their policies were intended to create an ever increasing amount of goods for export but they only understood this as guaranteeing for England a greater share of the world's fixed supply of wealth and never as adding to the world's wealth overall.

As the century progressed, that basic analogy of the body was itself transformed by a tide of mechanization that spread from physics to physiology. Locke and Petty used the perspective they gained from the new medicine to follow the circulation of money through the economy and found a new understanding of the relationship between the members of the body politic (rather than merely the relationship of each member to the whole). In Petty's work, the millenarian conquest of nature and the idea of nature as a machine (and hence of society as a machine) blended to produce a new concept of wealth as resources and the productive power to harness them. But William Petty still could not use this as a way to break through the last crystalline sphere: he only thought that sphere was much farther away than usually supposed. In his hands the hunt for a universally applicable objective language turned into the search for a universal standard of value. Locke had undergone the standard training in Scholasticism before he turned to medicine; that may be why there was so much more of the traditional in his economic thought that there was in the less traditionally schooled Petty. Locke took the new insights into the circulation of money and tried to restore the harmony of an older order with them: to roll back the advance of commercial and financial capitalism until only a natural society of producers and users remained—no oligopolies, no bankers, no middlemen. For Locke, wealth remained little pieces of coined silver.

When this new perspective on the body economic sought expression, the idea of congruences between natural and politic bodies drew it back to bookkeeping, and in the new National Accounting the older and newer perspectives did not quite mesh.

One of the ideas inherited by early modern Europe from both its Christian and classical roots was that of change as essentially degenerative: whether the progression was from Eden to the expulsion, the purity of the primitive church to what Protestants saw as the corruption of the papacy, from the Golden to Iron Ages in Greek thought, or even of the corruption, in the Hermetic tradition, of knowledge from the days of the *prisci philosophi*. The political version of this was Aristotle's three types of government (monarchy, aristocracy, republic) and the three forms into which they degenerated over time (despotism, oligarchy, and democracy). The solutions centered on mixed government and constant restoration to original principles through the ideology of civic humanism. In Charles Davenant's hands this restoration of original principles involved a statistical analysis of which segments of a population did and did not contribute to its well-being as a basis for constructing a socioeconomic policy to favor the propagation and protection of contributing groups over those of noncontributing groups. Economic thought was drawn back into a variation of the part-whole analysis of the original Aristotelian social division of labor with merchants, bankers, and the government alternately seen as parasitic growths draining the whole.

A powerful tie between bookkeeping, economic thought, and science was the idea of number whether pushed in an empirical direction by Petty or in a deductive one by Hobbes. But there was also an alternate idea of number celebrated in a Pythagorean and a hermetic-Paracelsian stream that we first saw in the thought of Gerard de Malynes and that came to the fore in the plentitude argument of Nicholas Barbon. Advocates of plentitude took the logical position that creation had to be as infinite as its creator. But supposing value to be infinite did not solve the problem of relating it to price, nor did it produce a coherent theory upon which to ground the resulting optimistic faith in a world of endless wealth.

Aristotle's natural-unnatural dichotomy helped provide the foundation for the constructing of the edifice that was Natural Law and that, in Locke's hands, began to turn the analytically identical man created by Hobbes from the statistical man developed by Petty into *Homo Economicus.* Petty took that same natural-unnatural dichotomy and pushed it deliberately into division of labor and unintentionally into value added, but seeing what he had done, he tried as best he could to bridge the natural-unnatural chasm with a land-labor par theory of value.

The sacralization of the secular and the culture of discipline that had been the hallmarks of Christian humanism merged with the millenarian thrust of Protestantism and was tempered by a Baconian discipline into a debate on schools, workhouses, poor laws, and productivity that no century will ever finally solve but all of whose basic components were laid before the public in the seventeenth.

But the seventeenth century saw economic activity through the lens of a greater matrix of political, social, religious, moral, and metaphysical order. Thus economic activity could not be justified unless its results benefited that greater whole, and it could not be comprehended unless its rules proved to be of the same genus as those of the whole (as the rules of all the other particular subsystems were held to be). If we think for a minute of that elaborate taxonomy of laws expounded by Richard Hooker—of local laws embedded within the Law of Reason, which was the Law of Nature for humans (as there was a matching but involuntary Law of Nature for unthinking beasts), embedded itself (as Revelation) within the law of God's own Nature—we have a model for our matrix. Was the Cosmos itself not enclosed within a crystalline sphere embedded with stars held within the infinite mind of God? Was not its essence, value?

Running through the works of Gerard de Malynes, Edward Misselden, Thomas Mun, Sir William Petty, Sir Josiah Child, John Locke, Sir Dudley North, Nicholas Barbon, and Charles Davenant is a dialogue about value (in a social and moral sense) disguised as a debate over money under the subheads of international exchange, debasement, interest rates, circulation, and Petty's land-labor par.

International exchange. Let us suppose for a moment that the seventeenth century had found a way to fix the international exchange at Malynes's *par pro pari.* A Dutch coin containing twice as much silver as an English coin would command two of those English coins in every international transaction, and, allowing for "usance" (or interest for the delayed payments involving Bills of Exchange), Bills of Exchange would be turned into coin under the same standards. But if the general price level in the two domestic markets were not the same, the coins would not actually have been exchanged at their equivalent purchasing powers. Malynes, however, thought they would be (despite all his examples of commodities actually selling for different weights of silver in different markets), because he thought of the purchasing power of money as something dependent on its silver content. Misselden claimed to accept many of the reasons for monies not being exchanged at the silver par (and the profit motives involved), but he still railed about English coin being undervalued abroad (i.e., treated as though it contained less silver than it did). This may have helped him turn attention away from the East India Company's bullion exports, but it also reveals him to be as concerned as was Malynes to keep his yardstick fixed. Exchanging English coin at its proper silver weight was exchanging it at *par pro pari*. Thomas Mun blamed the undervaluation of English coin abroad on its negative trade balance, but he was equally adamant that the crown not allow foreign coins "to pass current amongst us, at higher rates than they are worth (being compared with our Standard)." The purpose of the office of Royal Exchanger proposed by Malynes was to prevent such unequal exchanges within England. Though they would not admit it, Misselden and Mun were both implicitly calling for such regulation, since the market mechanisms they proposed as the true regulators (the profit-motivated arbitrage in Misselden's case, or the balance of trade in Mun's) seemed to cause the very problem they wished to undo.

Recoinage. The recoinage debate of the second half of the seventeenth century transposed the *par pro pari* mentality from the international to the domestic sphere, though advocates for and against restoring the de jure standard did pay some attention to the effect of bullion variations in international exchange. The efficient cause of the crisis was England's adoption of the technological advance of producing coins with milled edges. While the irregular edges of the older hammered coins could be clipped without producing any obvious visual change in the coins, the milled edge of the new coins instantly revealed any tampering with their size. So the milled coins tended to be melted down for plate or export as bullion while the lighter hammered coins remained in domestic circulation. By 1690, the coin in domestic circulation seems to have weighed somewhere between 50 and 75 percent of what it should according to the last legally set standard. The government accepted it at face value in payment of taxes, and so it was accepted by buyers, sellers, lenders, and borrowers.

All the arguments for recoining at the old standard rest openly on the need to keep the yardstick stable and uniform. But a simple recoinage at the lighter de facto standard would have accomplished the same purpose: once turned into milled coins the currency's weight would remain stable. Locke argued that lenders and landowners were being cheated because they were receiving less silver than originally contracted for. Petty argued in an identical fashion: if the denomination and the metal did not agree, the coin was not true money and not "fit to pay ancient Debts"—and this even though he had argued that coin could always be made of something other than metal. Child insisted merchants would never accept "the name it is called by" over "the intrinsick value of the Money." North's arguments concentrated on making sure (certain sections of) the public and not the government bore the loss of recoining at the higher standard, but he was just as insistent as Petty, Child, and Locke that "Rents and Debts" would be "paid less" by just so much as the "intrinsick value" was less if the old standard was abandoned. Over and over again we get the refrain that a public measure must not be allowed to change. The body of Charles Davenant's work postdated the recoinage, but he, too, railed against the "Corruption of our Coyn" that he considered "a dangerous Ulcer in the Body Politick," on identical grounds.

You or I might have countered that the lender was not receiving proportionately less purchasing power because the coin received today bought the same amount of wheat whether it was milled or clipped. Since, for Locke, money had no purchasing power apart from its bullion content (and what the bullion had was actually fixed value rather than purchasing power), that counterargument was false. In any case, it was not explicitly made. Nicholas Barbon argued for a denominational definition of money ("a Value made by Law"), stressing the alternative materials historically used for currency and the historical tendency of governments to debase their metallic coinage. But while he argued that no commodity could ever have a fixed price, he never pushed the point to establish an inverse relationship between commodity prices and money's purchasing power. Most of Locke's opponents just argued that recoining at a higher standard would result in a reduction in the overall money supply, which would depress prices (that is, depress trade) and take purchasing power from the poor who would take sixpence to the mint only to receive back five. But this was still to peg the purchasing power of money to some fixed quantity of money (however defined).

No one was arguing for a floating coining standard: one side wanted the standard fixed at the de facto weight, the other at the de jure. The question was whether to accept the standard wrought by the market over the past two decades. The answer of Locke, Child, North, and Petty was to roll back time: they could not separate the concept of the purchasing power of money from its metallic content.

Interest rates. The debate over whether or not England should lower its statutory interest rate seems to show the modern and premodern perspectives at war with each other. Malynes, Mun, and Misselden accepted the charging of interest on commercial loans, though they wanted it regulated by the government because they saw it more as a necessary evil than a positive good. Market-set pawnbroking they damned outright. By the final third of the century the ground of the debate had changed, in part because of the new prominence of estate mortgaging: the competing interests of lenders (a group now including a considerable block of the gentry as well as the goldsmiths) and borrowers (merchants, landowners, and tenant farmers). Locke and North argued for a market-set rate while Child argued for a lower legal maximum. Of course, in arguing that the legal rate should not be reduced, Locke and North were opting for the continuation of a higher legal maximum in a practical sense even if arguing that the market set rates in a theoretical sense. After all, neither one of these men suggested a simple repeal of all the laws involved, and both North and Locke were arguing from a supply perspective (lower rates would cause the gentry to sit on their money) while Child was arguing from a demand perspective (lower rates would cause more borrowing). But precisely because Child worked from demand he wanted the rate legally set, avoiding altogether the case where demand might push the rate above the desired level.

Petty seems to have been the only one to both think that lower rates were better and that they could not be kept so by law. He assumed the interest rate was dependent not just on the total volume of commerce but on the relative proportion of that volume commanded by land and trade as these were competitive uses for funds. This was still an analysis of the supply of lendable funds rather than of the demand for loans, but it was a more sophisticated treatment of the relationship between returns on land and interest rates than his successors developed. North, Locke, and Davenant thought that if a true (read *natural* rather than *monopolistic*) market in money was allowed, a 12–10 relationship would occur between the interest rate and return on land (as a function of selling price). Locke claimed that as money measured the price of everything and as land historically earned 5 percent (that is, went at twenty years' purchase) and money carried a slightly greater risk (one could always repossess land) it ought to go at six. Every argument we have seen about what land should be purchased for accepts a 20/21 year base as that center around which prices should circle in England (though they easily accepted 30 years as the center for Holland) just as 11:1 or 12:1 was taken as the natural center of silver-gold price ratios.

The question is, why, if money measured everything, should its price be
pegged to this one thing? Why not say that if profits on woolen cloth were
normally 6 percent, money should go at 7 percent? Land was as much the
center of every agricultural society as cows/sheep/llamas were of pastoral
societies: all acted as value anchors. One did not really have to be a member of the landed classes to think this way.

Only Nicholas Barbon pushed the land-interest analogy to the conclusion that interest was part of the price of goods (produced by the money
borrowed) rather than a cost of the money itself. He suggested the interest
rate was then the rule of profit (or, in our terms, the gauge of opportunity
cost). He was not interested in how the rate came about but in its effects on
economic choices. Since he took the price of wares to fluctuate he might
have assumed interest rates would as well, but too free-floating an interest
rate would detract from its value as such a "Rule" for adding up "Profit and
Loss" as Barbon proposed.

Consider the reluctance shown by Locke, North, and Davenant to
accept any tie between the interest rate and the rental of land itself, because
they held that rental value to be dependent on the profitability of the crop.
This was to wall off the purchasing power of money from affecting its own
price (as well as affecting land's price). To keep the fluctuating purchasing
power of money from affecting land's price was to keep the net worth of the
gentry stable. To keep the fluctuating purchasing power of money from
affecting the interest rate might be the same at one remove, but it also
probably had a lot to do with the difficulty these thinkers had in seeing
interest as the price of goods rather than of money itself. The question here
is not whether one or the other is the correct understanding of interest but
of understanding that a monetary definition made it easier to avoid the vex-
ing question of purchase power fluctuation. Malynes had argued that the
practice of allowing interest to be paid on money was itself a factor in creating a "general" uncertainty in the value of money. To argue for pegging
that rate to land was to move the line of defense rather than to abandon it
altogether.

Circulation: Quantity, velocity, and credit. Though the mechanical philosophy's effect on physiology aided in the substitution of a horizontal for
a vertical perspective on the economy, the simple following of the functional circulation of money through that economy did not change the
value/price stalemate as much as one might think. Malynes had thought of
money as an Aristotelian harmonizer keeping the natural and artificial
products of a country in balance (perhaps making him the first of the nine
to think along the lines of pegging interest rates to rents). When we follow
Locke and Davenant (and even Petty and North) as they traced money's

path through their society, we can see them trying to create a balance that would reward what they saw as the production of concrete value (whether read as use or esteem). In their estimation, the preponderance of profit belonged to those who produced (always including those who provided capital as land or stock) and not to those who performed services. They did not agree on which services were necessary to an economy (they especially disagreed on the role of banks), but they treated services as contributing far less to a society's wealth than did its goods. Of course, services were also far harder to export than were commodities, so to the extent that these writers supported a favorable trade balance for its ability to import the most durable (if not the sole) form of wealth, services would be shortchanged anyway.

Locke's argument against banking (duplicated by North) happens to make the problem clearest: he presumed that as the banker paid the gentry 4 percent on his deposits while loaning the money out at 6 percent, if the gentry did its own lending it would reap the extra 2 percent. Removing what Locke took to be an unnecessary detour in the circuit of money would better equalize the profit/cost ratio between the two parties really involved: the first lender and the final borrower. Gerard de Malynes had been just as suspicious of the spread between the interest paid by banks on deposits and collected by them on loans. Josiah Child paid less attention to the circulation/velocity argument than to defending the East India Company, but when he divided the population into those who were "profitable Engines of the Kingdom" and those who were not, a clear line between goods and services emerged.

Locke gave us two contradictory examples of what happened when the raw quantity of coin in circulation was cut in half: in one, trade contracted by 50 percent (and/or prices drop by 50 percent or some combination of the two); in the other, credit and barter replaced the coin, and the volume of trade was not affected. Then he insisted that credit instruments were not part of the money supply because they were not money (after all, they had no silver content). Locke understood that increasing the turnover rate of coin (paying rents and the like more frequently) allowed a society to support a greater volume of trade. Credit happens to be a classic way of increasing velocity: Sir William Petty supposed the establishment of banks would "almost double the Effect of our coined Money." He believed money in a bank was *superlucration* (savings), that is, available for investment, while coin hoards and plate collections were not, but he did not consider Locke's alternative of direct lending. On the other hand, while Locke would allow moving silver coins more quickly through the economy to increase the functional power of money, he would not make the parallel case: no piece of paper was ever going to have the same purchasing power as a little disc of silver because it was not the same thing. Now two things equal to the same thing are equal to each other: Locke says this over and over again in his *Essay upon Human Understanding*. But not, it would seem, two stores of purchasing power.

Davenant understood that credit could at least temporarily substitute for money, but when he added up a nation's wealth he wanted mortgages on land to be deducted from the market value of that land (where one individual's asset is another's liability nothing is added overall). He was even more concerned that credit not become a permanent source of budget funding or transfer the true ownership of land from the gentry's hands to those of their creditors. He moved the argument from a more narrowly economic realm to a broader social one, concentrating on credit's ability to undermine the social/political/moral fiber of a nation.

Nicholas Barbon provides us more with a variation upon than an exception to this line of argument: he had no complaint against bankers, retailers, or any form of service provider per se, but for all his claim that bullionist balance of trade policy could be abandoned because of nature's infinite resources, he pushed for government policies to favor labor-intensive manufactures over their opposite, knowing this would increase the amount of goods available for export. He also favored the use of high import tariffs on goods that competed with native manufactures.

Land and/or labor. Sir William Petty stands apart from his compeers in trying to find an alternate measure of value, but his land-labor par not only rested on the same principle of intrinsic value in a general sense, it also required the acceptance of there being a special intrinsic value in the money commodity (being, at that time, silver). In Petty's formulation the intrinsic value of land was its ability to produce the necessary commodities (wool, wood, and wheat)—taken as wheat, the most necessary of all. The intrinsic value of any individual was his or her ability to transform raw materials into useful goods—taken as labor-power (remember women, children, and the elderly paid less tax based on their lesser productive power measured by their reduced incomes). To find the true (rather than the market) equivalence between these two, Petty introduced money as a common denominator. He did not rely on the mere prices of these goods as expressed in money. What he tried to do was use labor to calculate an equivalence between the land's value (measured as its net product in wheat) and money's value (measured as a mine's net product of silver): as much silver as could be produced and minted by the same labor-time as could produce and process (or at least thresh) some amount of wheat was the correct monetary equivalent of the intrinsic value of that wheat. Then, in its turn, wheat became the common denominator between money and labor as a day's wage was taken to be a day's subsistence (a day's consumption mostly of wheat with an allowance for clothing, etc.). Petty was, in effect, applying the same principle of two things equal to a third thing must be equal to each other, but all he created was a series of circular arguments because some equality was always assumed before it was proved. He single-handedly discovered the concept of net product (or surplus) upon which the classical theory of value would be built and diverted it into a caucus race à la Lewis Carroll because of his obsession with a universal standard of *value*.

Money may be borrowed or exchanged as though it were a commodity, but money is neither a commodity nor *the* commodity that is actually being borrowed or exchanged: the commodity changing hands is purchasing power, and like any other commodity, it has no set value. As Barbon said over and over (and even Locke admitted as long as money was not the commodity in question), no one commodity has any set relationship to the price of any other commodity.

The problem of money's fluctuating purchasing power is not exactly parallel to the problem of the size and location of the stars revealed by the telescope: the question there was simply whether they were smaller or farther away. Put in terms of the starry paradox, money's threat to the concept of the closed universe of eternal order was that it was never in the same place in the heavens from moment to moment. While Sir Isaac Newton may be said to have set the stars themselves sailing across the universe, he also insisted that there was such a thing as absolute space (as well as absolute time) in that universe. In the economic universe constructed by these seventeenth-century economic thinkers, commodities orbited around the fixed sun of money.

The seventeenth century began as the century before it had ended, thinking by analogy: by similitude and congruence. But it also thought by differentiation. Order was the product of hierarchical differentiation: trees were different from grass, they held a different unique place in the universe, and animals were equally different from and differentially placed than trees, and humans to animals and angels to humans. The international exchange "overruled" national monies as money "overruled" commodities.

When the hierarchical body was replaced by the mechanical one, the problem of differentiation did not entirely disappear. Locke divided his economic universe into three separate species: producers (including suppliers of capital), consumers (limited to those who, like children, consumed without producing), and the gamblers or brokers who fattened off the efforts of producers. He never really understood these as roles alternately played by the same individuals, just as he was loath to consider the gentry as debtors (because as owners of capital in the form of land they would be producers of profit and hence lenders). When Dudley North tried to sever the relationship between rental values and the interest rate (making the first solely dependent on commodity prices and the second the sole cause of land's sales value) he was falling into the same trap: the tenant farmer who was simultaneously a capital borrower and produce seller was not within his scope. Of course, Locke and North had a practical knowledge that individuals did both: it was the fact that labor insisted on consuming that caused all those problems for the balance of trade. What Locke and North lacked was the theoretical comfort level with the idea of economic actors as multiply faceted personalities that would allow them to build the analytical framework to express that fact. For Locke and North, an individual who played every role had no *particular* role (read *status*) at all, and how then could one individual be differentiated from another so that order (*logos*) was preserved? Petty came somewhat closer, but always ended up paying more attention to *homo productus* than to *homo consumptis*. In Barbon's universe people seem essentially to consume while the earth endlessly produces (and if they don't consume fast enough, there is always foreign trade to dump the excess on another nation's shores).

The century's reliance on congruent analogical reasoning paved the way for double-entry bookkeeping to shape the economics of the polis as it was coming to dominate business and estate management. In double-entry bookkeeping, each action in the running of a business or estate is simultaneously registered as a debit and a credit. But the century saw each action as two opposing and thus canceling perspectives on the same event (think of Davenant's netting out of mortgaged lands in his national balance sheet). This was far from realizing that each individual was simultaneously (in potentiality if not always in reality) lender, borrower, spender, earner, and investor.

At a deeper level still we are down to the basic paradox of seventeenth-century economic thought: their tendency to treat supply as objective and only demand as subjective. That table drawn up by Charles Davenant (with or without the aid of Gregory King) shows what happens to price when a harvest fails. Variation in supply tended throughout the century to be treated as the result of factors beyond individual human control whether those factors were drought or war or even the machinations of foreign bankers. Demand was the product of irregular human desires, the better to be controlled with everything from sumptuary laws to export duties to workhouses (in the case of the desire for leisure paid for by the public purse). With the identically mechanical man worked out by Hobbes, converted into statistical man by Petty and Davenant, and taken a considerable distance toward economic man by Locke, demand was made increasingly subject to objectification, to some economic parallel to Kepler's laws. No demand-based economic theory would be possible until this objectification of demand was complete. If all our subjects had wanted to do was tame demand analytically, their desire would actually be of little interest for this study. What is of major interest is the way they consistently pushed policies to tame it in the real world as well. Taming it analytically was only the side effect of trying to curb it in the flesh: the high import duties proposed for luxury goods and time-wasters like tobacco and the sumptuary laws were one side of a two-edged disciplinary effort whose other side was work discipline. This was a fight for social values as well as for "value."

There is another side to this coin, and that is the subjective element in supply, though that is difficult to discuss with respect to seventeenth-century thinkers because they themselves rarely discussed it. Price-elasticity applies as much to supply as it does to demand: given a particular market price for some commodity (and its margin of profitability), how much of that commodity will actually be produced? We have seen what we call *opportunity cost* (although the seventeenth century had no special name for it) enter into their calculations when they asked whether or not money would be invested in land or trade, or let out at interest at various ratios of interest rate to profit margin. But though they acknowledged that producers were to some extent motivated by profit, they never extended the argument to true price-elasticity of supply. There are two possible reasons. The lesser revolves around their general inability to calculate true profit: their confusion of personal with business expenses, their erratic balance taking, their failure to account for depreciation, and the rest of their sloppy (to us) accounting practices mean they had only the roughest of cost calculations to set against their revenues. These are symptoms of their confusion of profit with a merchant's wage and of a business with a personal estate; they are signs that the rationalization of the capitalist *Geist* was still far from complete.

The greater reason involved their overall discomfort with unbridled economic behavior. After all, to speak of price-elasticity of supply was to say that a producer was making the same kind of selfish (self-oriented) decision about producing for the market (for the whole society) as a consumer was in favoring French silk over English woolens. Self-centered profit was the main complaint against merchants in general and the East India Company in particular: they imported (supplied) based on their own private gain and not with an eye to how their actions affected the nation's overall economic health. Nicholas Barbon stood alone against this tide. He not only suggested a major refinement of the concept of profit (by equating it with the interest rate), he was supremely confident that self-centered economic behavior could do no harm. His answer to the problem of how then to assure a just (or harmonious) distribution was the inherent abundance of the universe (though he certainly believed it had to be worked for). This was not the way a laissez-faire system would be built. More importantly, however, to rely on plentitude was still to rely on a preexistent value.

Notes

Introduction

1. John Maynard Keynes, "Notes on Mercantilism, the Usury Laws, Stamped Money and Theories of Underconsumption," in *The General Theory of Employment, Interest and Money* (1936), in *Collected Writings* (London: Macmillan Press Ltd., 1973), 7:343.

2. Sir Eric Roll, *A History of Economic Thought*, 3d ed. (Englewood Cliffs, NJ: Prentice-Hall, 1956), 115.

3. Douglas Vickers, *Studies in the Theory of Money, 1690–1776* (Philadelphia: Chilton Company, 1959), 52, 72.

4. Sir Thomas Elyot, *The Book Named the Governor* (London, 1531), 2d ed., ed. S. E. Lehmberg (London: J. M. Dent and Sons Ltd., 1962), 1–5 (I.1), 9 (I.2).

5. Ibid., 2 (I.1), 7 (I.2).

6. Thomas Milles, *The Customers replie. or Second Apologie....* (London, 1604), preface (B2).

7. Alexandre Koyré, *From the Closed World to the Infinite Universe* (Baltimore: Johns Hopkins University Press, 1957), 58, 61–62.

8. See, for example, Richard H. Popkin, *The History of Scepticism from Erasmus to Descartes* (Assen: Koninklijke Van Gorcum and Comp. N.V., 1960), 112–30 (on the "counter-attack" to Pyrrhonism); Theodore K. Rabb, *The Struggle for Stability in Early Modern Europe* (New York: Oxford University Press, 1975), 49–59 (on the initial response to the "crisis"), 39–40 (on his agreement with Popkin); Stephen L. Collins, *From Divine Cosmos to Sovereign State: An Intellectual History of Consciousness and the Idea of Order in Renaissance England* (New York: Oxford University Press, 1989), 109–48 (on Jacobean England); Barbara J. Shapiro, *Probability and Certainty in Seventeenth-Century England: A Study of the Relationship between Natural Science, Religion, History, Law, and Literature* (Princeton, NJ: Princeton University Press, 1983), 30, 75, 90–91 (on the problems of "moral certainty," of producing "an unambiguous mode of scriptural interpretation," and of reconciling "innate ideas" with newer empirical models of human knowledge); A. J. Krailsheimer, *Studies in Self-Interest, From Descartes to La Bruyère* (Oxford: Clarendon, 1962), 16 (the responsibility of liberty in Rabelais), 24 (Montaigne's fideism), 35–38 (Descartes's "radical" ego-centrism), etc.; Nannerl O. Keohane, *Philosophy and the State in France: The Renaissance to the Enlightenment* (Princeton: Princeton University Press, 1980), 183–87 (the opposition of *amour-propre* to *charité* and the "consonance" between the *libertins* and the Augustinians); and Stephen Toulmin, *Cosmopolis: The Hidden Agenda of Modernity* (Chicago: University of Chicago Press, 1992), 65–82 (on Donne and "cosmopolis").

9. Thomas S. Kuhn, *The Structure of Scientific Revolutions*, 2d ed. (Chicago: University of Chicago Press, 1970), 4–7.

10. Terence Wilmot Hutchison, *On Revolutions and Progress in Economic Knowledge* (Cambridge: Cambridge University Press, 1978), 11, 86, 121 (accepted candidates), 289–91 (rejected candidates).

11. Guy Routh, *The Origin of Economic Ideas* (London: Macmillan Press Ltd., 1975), 13, 27.

12. Kuhn, *Scientific Revolutions*, 18–20, 23–24, 137–38, 164–65. Note also ibid., 209, Kuhn's own concern with the wholesale application of his thesis without reference to the existence of analogous "communities."

13. Ibid., 11.

14. Robert V. Eagly, *The Structure of Classical Economic Theory* (New York: Oxford University Press, 1974), 13.

15. Hans Brems, *Pioneering Economic Theory, 1639–1980: A Mathematical Restatement* (Baltimore: Johns Hopkins University Press, 1986), 19–22.

16. Routh, *Origin*, 15.

17. C. B. Macpherson, "Scholars and Spectres: A Rejoinder to Viner," *Canadian Journal of Economics and Political Science* 29, no. 4 (Nov. 1963): 562.

18. Ronald L. Meek, *Studies in the Labour Theory of Value* (London: Lawrence and Wishart, 1956), 7.

19. Ibid., 18.

20. Murray N. Rothbard, *Economic Thought before Adam Smith: An Austrian Perspective on the History of Economic Thought*, vol. 1 (Aldershot: Edward Elgar Publishing Ltd., 1995), vii.

21. Ibid., 325.

22. Ibid., 324, 302, 323. Nor does it seem especially useful to fulminate against the "quantophrenic and metromanic folly of modern historians of economic thought" (309) or modern economists (303).

23. Joseph A. Schumpeter, *History of Economic Analysis*, ed. Elizabeth Boody Schumpeter (New York: Oxford University Press, 1954), 369.

24. Ibid., 211.

25. Rothbard, *Before Adam Smith*, 277.

26. B. E. Supple, *Commercial Crisis and Change in England, 1600–1642: A Study in the Instability of a Mercantile Economy* (Cambridge: Cambridge University Press, 1959), 197–98.

27. E. A. J. Johnson, *Predecessors of Adam Smith: The Growth of British Economic Thought* (New York: Prentice-Hall, 1937), 97.

28. Roll, *Economic Thought*, 68.

29. Keynes, "Notes on Mercantilism," 335–36. See also ibid., 340; he is quite clear, however, that these "truths" were only practically and not scientifically reached.

30. D. C. Coleman, ed. *Revisions in Mercantilism* (London: Methuen and Co., Ltd., 1969), 14–15. For a quick and witty tour of the "complaints, explanations, and excuses often thrown together" to explain the theoretical failures of seventeenth-century economic writing, see William R. Allen, "The Position of Mercantilism and the Early Development of International Trade Theory," in *Events, Ideology and Economic Theory: The Determinants of Progress in the Development of Economic Analysis*, ed. Robert V. Eagly (Detroit: Wayne State University Press, 1968), 78–80.

31. Wilson was certain Keynes's interest in the relationship between state policy

and employment colored his views of mercantilism, causing him to put the horse (employment) before the cart (bullion balance). For which, see Charles Henry Wilson, *Economic History and the Historian: Collected Essays* (London: Weidenfeld and Nicolson, 1969), 48. The greater fault may be Keynes's failure to *read* the works on which he passed judgment. He preferred to rely on the quotations used by Heckscher: "They are the more suitable for my purpose because Prof. Heckscher is himself an adherent, on the whole, of the classical theory and much less sympathetic to the mercantilist theories than I am. Thus there is no risk that his choice of quotations has been biased in any way by a desire to illustrate their wisdom." For which, see Keynes, "Notes on Mercantilism," 7:341 (note 1).

32. Schumpeter, *Economic Analysis*, 52.

33. Schumpeter, *Economic Doctrine and Method: An Historical Sketch*, trans. R. Aris (New York: Oxford University Press, 1954), 9–10.

34. William Letwin, *The Origins of Scientific Economics* (London: Methuen and Company Ltd., 1963), 197.

35. Karl Pribham, *A History of Economic Reasoning* (Baltimore: Johns Hopkins University Press, 1983), 37. His three forms/stages of mercantilism are bullionism, Baconian mercantilism, and refined mercantilism, but only the first two apply to the seventeenth century (so he has divided it in half where I have further divided it into thirds).

36. Ibid., 50.

37. Ibid., 62. Aside from reading Hobbes, Pribham seems to have relied on only one source for Hobbes's thought, a work by Talcott Parsons (*The Structure of Social Action*) from 1937.

38. Ibid., 65.

39. Schumpeter, *Economic Analysis*, 1–2.

40. Ibid., 79, 78.

41. See Richard Henry Tawney, *Religion and the Rise of Capitalism: A Historical Study* (New York: Harcourt, Brace and World, 1926; reprint, Glouchester, MA: Peter Smith, 1962), 104–5, 177 (page references are to the reprint edition).

42. Joyce Oldham Appleby, *Economic Thought and Ideology in Seventeenth-Century England* (Princeton, NJ: Princeton University Press, 1978), 7–10, 16. Appleby's recent collection of essays, *Liberalism and Republicanism in the Historical Imagination* (Cambridge, MA: Harvard University Press, 1992), made no modification to this part of her thesis.

43. See Appleby, *Economic Thought*, ix, 4, 248, 257–58.

44. See Coleman's contention that Appleby "castrated" her chosen subjects "of their political essence" by ignoring the contexts in which they wrote, Winch's claim that she "offers a teleological or Whig history of liberalism in modern guise," and Pocock's claim that "there is reason to suspect that Appleby's concern with words like 'liberal' and 'liberalism' is inhibiting her capacity to locate the phenomena she treats in the historical context capable of giving them the greatest meaning." For these, see, respectively, D. C. Coleman, "Review of *Economic Thought and Ideology*," *Journal of Modern History* 53, no. 1 (Mar. 1981): 106; Donald Winch, "Economic Liberalism as Ideology: The Appleby Version," *Economic History Review*, 2d ser., 38 (May 1985): 288; and J. G. A. Pocock, "To Market, to Market: Economic Thought in Early Modern England," *Journal of Interdisciplinary History* 10, no. 2 (autumn 1979): 306–7.

Chapter 1

1. The original meaning of *agora* was "assembly," usually political, and by extension, the place where such an assembly was held. Merchants, not being citizens, were denied access. Agora as marketplace in a commercial sense was a later development. There is an excellent summary of the ambivalent treatment of commerce and the commercial classes by Greek thinkers (despite an unwillingness to see Xenophon as an economic analyst) in M. I. Finley, "Aristotle and Economic Analysis," *Past and Present* 47 (May 1970): 17–24. The attitudes range from Aristotle's contention that the *kapelos* was unnecessary to Xenophon's ideas for increasing the number of *metics* because of the community's dependence on their services, but the essential wall between merchant and citizen was never breached.

2. Cato the Elder, *De Agri Cultura*, II.7

3. Plutarch's "Life of Cato" (5.1) in *Plutarch's Lives*, Dryden's translation revised by A. H. Clough (New York: Hearst's International Library, 1914), 2:354.

4. Gratian, *Decretum*, pt. I, dist. lxxxviii, cap. xi.

5. Thomas Aquinas, *Summa Theologiæ*, 2a2æ.77,4.

6. "Howe to reforme the Realme in settying them to werke and to restore Tillage," ca. 1535–36 (possibly by Clement Armstrong) in R. H. Tawney and Eileen Power, eds., *Tudor Economic Documents: Being Select Documents Illustrating the Economic and Social History of Tudor England* (London: Longmans, Green and Co. Ltd., 1924), 3:126.

7. Thomas Lever, *Sermons* (1550), *English Reprints*, ed. Edward Amber (New York: AMS, 1966), 6:130 (the assorted works bound into each volume of *English Reprints* are individually paginated).

8. Sir Thomas More, *Utopia* (1516), trans. Paul Turner (London: Penguin Books Ltd., 1965), 73. On the specific linking of the communal property systems of *Utopia* and Plato's *Republic*, see ibid., 64; though, in More's schema, there was no communal sharing of wives. On the Utopians' contempt for the "lust for gain," see ibid., 86–89. They did, however, keep stocks of gold and silver earned in foreign trade to provide for mercenaries in times of war; for which, see ibid., 85.

9. Thomas Wilson, *A Discourse uppon Usurye. By waye of Dialogue and oracions, for the better varietye and more delite of all those that shall reade thus treatise* (1572), ed. R. H. Tawney (London: G. Bell and Sons Ltd., 1925), 379.

10. James I, *Basilikon Doron. Or His Majesties Instructions to his dearest Sonne, Henry the Prince* (Edinburgh, 1599), in *The Political Works of James I* (reprinted from the edition of 1616), ed. Charles Howard McIlwain (Cambridge, MA: Harvard University Press, 1918), 26.

11. William Laud, *The Works of William Laud, D.D.*, ed. William Scott (London, 1847), 1:6.

12. James Harrington, *The Commonwealth of Oceana* (1656), in *The Political Works of James Harrington*, ed. J. G. A. Pocock (Cambridge: Cambridge University Press, 1977), 296–97.

13. Andrew Fletcher, *A Discourse of Government with Relation to Militias* (Edinburgh, 1698), in *Andrew Fletcher of Saltoun: Selected Political Writings and Speeches*, ed. David Daiches (Edinburgh: Scottish Academic Press, 1979), 5.

14. Adam Ferguson, *An Essay on the History of Civil Society* (Edinburgh, 1767),

ed. Duncan Forbes (Edinburgh: University of Edinburgh Press, 1966), 19. Had he been reading Plutarch on Cato?

15. Especially when it took the form of monopolistic restraint of competition. See, for example, Adam Smith, *An Inquiry into the Nature and Causes of the Wealth of Nations* (1776), two volumes bound as one, ed. Edwin Cannan (Chicago: University of Chicago Press, 1976) 2:147 [IV.vii.iii].

16. William Godwin, *Poetical Justice*, 3d ed., ed. F. E. L. Priestley (Toronto: University of Toronto Press, 1969), 2:513, 2:514.

17. Thomas Carlyle, *Chartism*, in *Selected Writings*, ed. Alan Shelston (London: Penguin Books Ltd., 1971), 193.

18. Karl Marx, *Capital: A Critique of Political Economy*, vol. 1, *The Process of Capitalist Production*, trans. Samuel Moore and Edward Aveling, ed. Friedrich Engels (New York: International Publishers, 1967) 166.

19. Ibid., 165n.

20. Émile Durkheim, *The Division of Labor in Society* (1893), trans. George Simpson (New York: Macmillan/Free Press, 1933), 41.

21. Ibid., 137–38.

22. Ibid., 133.

23. Ibid., 1. On morality as "the daily bread without which societies cannot exist," see ibid., 51.

24. Ibid., 3.

25. Ibid., 25–31.

26. Max Weber, *The Protestant Ethic and the Spirit of Capitalism*, trans. Talcott Parsons, ed. Anthony Gibbons (New York: Charles Scribner's Sons, 1976), 17–18.

27. Ibid., 24, 27, 51–53. Weber located the font in the more radical forms of Protestantism as opposed to the centrality of Lutheran or Calvinist thought proper, but this has been a subject of much controversy. See, for example, Michael Walzer's contention that Puritan Calvinism was the main instrument of sociopolitical as well as socioeconomic change, in *The Revolution of the Saints: A Study in the Origins of Radical Politics* (New York: Athenaeum, 1969), passim, and Margo Todd's counterclaim that the Puritans learned it from the Christian Humanists in *Christian Humanism and the Puritan Social Order* (Cambridge: Cambridge University Press, 1987), passim but especially 16–17. In all three versions, however, the resulting *Geist* is an unintended rather than an intentional result of behaviors designed to promote a social as well as a personal reformation.

28. See, for example, Weber, *Protestant Ethic*, 48, 50, 64, 71, 82, 124, 151, 158, 180, 192, 195, 263, for Benjamin Franklin as an ideal type.

29. C. B. Macpherson, "Harrington's 'Opportunity State,'" *Past and Present* 17 (Apr. 1960): 46.

30. Thomas Hobbes, *Leviathan, or The Matter, Forme, and Power of a Commonwealth Ecclesiastical and Civill* (London, 1651), ed. C. B. Macpherson (London: Penguin Books Ltd., 1985), 151–52 [chap. 10].

31. Macpherson, *Possessive Individualism*, 37–38. For Hobbes's state of nature as "a logical abstraction drawn from the behaviour of men in civilized society," upon which ground Macpherson believed he was warranted in drawing such conclusions about Hobbes's world, see ibid., 26.

32. Keith Thomas, "The Social Origins of Hobbes's Political Thought," in *Hobbes Studies*, ed. Keith C. Brown (Oxford: Basil Blackwell, 1965), 193, 202, 230. On

fame, a related aristocratic (and equally disruptive) social currency, see David M. Levy, *The Economic Ideas of Ordinary People: From Preferences to Trade* (London: Routledge, 1992), 156–59.

33. *O.E.D.* (1933), 12:28, 29.

34. Which is not to say he was an enemy of commerce per se. See Jacob Viner, "'Possessive Individualism' as Original Sin," *Canadian Journal of Economics and Political Science* 29, no. 4 (Nov. 1963): 550–52. Rejecting Macpherson's models as the distortions of Marxian analysis (550–52), but generally accepting his characterization of Hobbes, Viner still concluded (552) by conceding "that much of Hobbes's argument follows the pattern, as Hobbes sees it, of a competitive economic market . . . and treats honour and power as in a high degree dependent upon the possession of riches and as important means of attaining riches. It does not at all follow from all of this, however, . . . that Hobbes thought that the elimination of economic competition would eliminate, or even substantially moderate, the need for strong and coercive government."

35. Maurice Herbert Dobb, *Studies in the Development of Capitalism,* rev. ed. (New York: International, 1963), 8.

36. R. H. Hilton, "Capitalism—What's in a Name?" *Past and Present* 1 (Feb. 1952): 32–43.

37. Alan Macfarlane, *The Origins of English Individualism: The Family, Property, and Social Transition* (London: Basil Blackwell, 1978), 95, 104, 107, 151–52, 154, 163.

38. A good example of this vein of criticism can be found in Govind Sreenivasan, "The Land-Family Bond at Earls Colne (Essex), 1550–1650," *Past and Present* 131 (May 1991): 3–37.

39. Weber, *Protestant Ethic,* 19–22.

40. Alvin R. Johnston, "Introduction" to *Paciolo on Accounting,* trans. R. Gene Brown and Kenneth S. Johnston (New York: McGraw-Hill, 1963), 9. Note, however, that Pacioli is the preferred spelling of the name.

41. Pacioli, *Paciolo on Accounting,* 71–73, 83, 97.

42. Aristotle, *Politics* VII.viii (1328b2, 1328b15); a slightly different version appears in IV.iv (1290b38, 1291a22).

43. Ibid., I.i (1253a19–25): "Thus also the city-state is prior in nature to the household and to each of us individually. For the whole must necessarily be prior to the part"—although Aristotle had just proven that the household was historically prior to the state (1252b10–35).

44. Richard Hooker, *Of the Laws of Ecclesiastical Polity,* in *The Works of that Learned and Judicious Divine, Mr. Richard Hooker: with an account of his life and death by Isaac Walton* (Oxford: Clarendon, 1890), 1:196 [Book I, Chapter X, Section 13].

45. William Perkins, *Christian Oeconomy, or A short Survey of the right Manner of erecting and ordering a Family, According to the Scriptures,* in *The Work of William Perkins,* ed. Ian Breward (Appleford, United Kingdom: Sutton Courtenay, 1970), 418.

46. Perkins, *A treatise of the Vocations or Callings of Men,* in *Work,* 449.

47. Thomas Starkey, *A Dialogue between Reginald Pole and Thomas Lupset* (probably written 1533–35), ed. Kathleen M. Burton (London: Chatto and Windus, 1948), 22.

48. Perkins, *A Treatise of Vocations,* in *Work,* 467–68.

49. Robert Burton, *The Anatomy of Melancholy* (1621), ed. Holbrook Jackson (London: J. M. Dent and Sons Ltd., 1932), I:65.

50. Edward Forset, *A Comparative discourse of the Bodies natural and Politique. . . .* (London, 1606), 3.

51. Perkins, *An Exposition of the Symbol or Creed of the Apostles,* in *Work,* 265.

52. Richard Baxter, *A Holy Commonwealth, or Political Aphorisms, Opening The true Principles of Government: For The Healing of the Mistakes, and Resolving the Doubts, that most endanger and trouble England at this time. . . .* (London, 1659), 55, 62.

53. *Chaos: Or, a Discourse, wherein Is presented to the view of the Magistrate, and all others who shall peruse the same, a Frame of Government by way of a Republique. . . .* (London, 1659), 1.

54. Forset, *Comparative Discourse,* 45–46.

55. Perkins, *A Treatise of the Vocations,* in *Work,* 466.

56. Hooker, *Sermon VI,* in *Works,* 2:787.

57. Forset, *Comparative Discourse,* 50.

58. Hooker, *Ecclesiastical Polity* (preface iii §4), in *Works,* 1:102.

59. Sir Francis Bacon, *The Twoo Bookes of Francis Bacon of the Proficience and Advancement of Learning Divine and Human* (1608), in *Selected Writings of Francis Bacon,* ed. Hugh G. Dick (New York: Random House, 1955), 328.

60. Ibid., 374.

61. Ibid., 163.

62. Hooker, *Sermon VI,* in *Works,* 2:780.

63. There is a good summary of the problems of the hierarchical challenge posed by merchants, lawyers, and clergy in Lawrence Stone, "Social Mobility in England, 1500–1700," *Past and Present* 33 (Apr. 1966): 18–20. Each group re-created the age's hierarchical model by creating their own parallel hierarchy. But the merchants remained the most difficult group for the order to accommodate, unless, as individuals, they chose to purchase land and move into the traditional social structure.

64. Schumpeter, *Economic Analysis,* 79.

Chapter 2

1. Gerard de Malynes, *Consuetudo, Vel Lex Mercatoria, or The Ancient Law-Merchant. Divided into three Parts: According to the Essentiall Parts of Trafficke. Necessarie for all Statesmen, Judges, Magistrates, Temporall and Civile Lawyers, Mint-men, Merchants, Marriners, and all others negotiating in all places of the World* (London, 1622), 263.

2. Ibid., 281.

3. R. E. G. Kirk and Ernest F. Kirk, eds., *Returns of Aliens dwelling in the City and Suburbs of London: from the Reign of Henry VIII to that of James I, Part II: 1571–1597* (Aberdeen: Huguenot Society of London, 1902), 383. See also ibid., 314–15, 412, 466, for other mentions of Gerard de, Gerard A., and Jarrat de Malines. The date of the 1583 reference (314–15) is only tentative.

4. This is given greater credence by a possible mention of his father's being in England in 1562. For which, see William Page, ed., *Letters of Denization and Acts of Naturalization for Aliens in England, 1509–1603* (Lymington: Huguenot Society of London, 1893) 84, for "John Du Moleyn: from the dominion of the king of Spain. 20 Feb. 1562 (*Pat.* 4 Eliz. P.II, m.12)." Nor was it unusual for members of "foreign" churches in England to be the children of denizated aliens. For which, see Ole Peter Grell, *Dutch Calvinists in Early Stuart London: The Dutch Church in Austin Friars, 1603–1642* (Leiden: E. J. Brill, 1989), 8. For an oppposing view, see Raymond de Roover, *Business, Banking, and Economic Thought in Late Medieval and Early Modern Europe,* ed. Julius Kirshner

(Chicago: University of Chicago Press, 1974) 346–48, stressing possible links to a Belgian aldermanic family, von Melechen. De Roover wished to make Malynes as much of a compatriot as possible despite what he admitted was a lack of evidence in Belgium.

5. See Malynes, *Lex Mercatoria*, 281, and *The Center of the Circle of Commerce. Or, A Refutation of a Treatise, Intituled The Circle of Commerce, or The Ballance of Trade, lately published by E. M.* (London, 1623), 26. In *The British Librarian: Exhibiting a Compendious Review or Abstract of our most Scarce, Useful, and Valuable Books in all Sciences, as well in Manuscript as in Print*. . . . (London, 1738), 97, Sir William Oldys suggested Malynes "was appointed one of the *Commissioners of Trade* in the *Low Countries*, for setting the Value of Monies about the year 1586." Malynes was there at the right time; for which, see *Calendar of the Salisbury Manuscripts, Part IV* (London: HMSO, 1892), 53. But when Malynes discussed the commission, he claimed no part in it, though as a merchant on the scene he might very well have been called before it. For which discussion, see *Lex Mercatoria*, 185, and *Center of the Circle*, 25. The same stricture applies to a 1576 commission he discussed in *The Maintenance of Free trade, according to the three essential Parts of traffique: Namely, Commodities, Monies and Exchange of Monies, by Bills of Exchanges for other Countries*. . . . (London, 1622), 16.

6. Max Beer, *Early British Economics from the XIIIth to the Middle of the XVIIIth Century* (London: George Allen and Unwin Ltd., 1938), 108.

7. Malynes, *Center of the Circle*, 26.

8. Malynes, *Lex Mercatoria*, 211–12.

9. This account is taken from Lawrence Stone, *An Elizabethan: Sir Horatio Palavicino* (Oxford: Clarendon, 1956), 81–82, 220–30. One "Daniell Vermaiden" is referred to as the brother-in-law of Malynes in the June 10, 1600, proceedings of the Privy Council. For which, see *Acts of the Privy Council, N. S. 30, 1599–1600* (London: HMSO, 1905), 365. Guillam Veruyden may have been Daniel's father.

10. *Calendar of the Salisbury Manuscripts, Part VI* (London: HMSO, 1895), 455–56 [174/7].

11. *Calendar of the Salisbury Manuscripts, Part IX* (London: HMSO, 1902), 11 [58/87]. Malynes and company were sailing under the Venetian flag.

12. *Historical Manuscripts Commission, 8th Report, Part I* (London: HMSO, 1881), 435, records two letters from Gerard de Malynes to the mayor of Leicester concerning the king's "white farthing tokens" dating from December 15, 1615, and January 18, 1615/16.

13. Malynes, *Center of the Circle*, 75–76.

14. Lynn Muchmore, "Gerrard de Malynes and Mercantile Economics," *History of Political Economy* 1, no. 3 (fall 1969): 356–57.

15. See Milles, *Customer's Replie*, unpaged "Epistle"; Lewes Roberts, *The Merchants Mappe of Commerce. Wherein the universall Manner and matter of Trade is compendiously handled* (London, 1638), unpaged "Epistle"; and [William Lowndes], *A Further Essay for the Amendment of the Gold and Silver Coins*. . . . (London, 1695), 2.

16. Thomas Mun, *Englands Treasure by Forraign Trade. Or, The Ballance of our Forraign Trade is The Rule of our Treasure* (London, 1664), reprint (Fairfield, NJ: Augustus M. Kelley, 1986), 42.

17. *An Essay on the Fishing Trade* (Edinburgh: Privately printed for William Adams, Jr., 1720) from *Lex Mercatoria*, 241–49. The "editor" replaced seventeenth-century spellings with eighteenth-century versions and capitalized the few nouns not so honored in the original, but otherwise did not amend the text.

18. Oldys, *British Librarian*, 96–105 (no. 2, Feb. 1737).

19. Tawney, *Religion*, 177.

20. E. A. J. Johnson, "Gerard de Malynes and the Theory of the Foreign Exchanges," *American Economic Review* 13 (1933): 442; see also 446n, 454.

21. Dobb, *Development of Capitalism*, 204.

22. William Dyer Grampp, "The Liberal Elements in English Mercantilism," in *Essays in Economic Thought: Aristotle to Marshall*, ed. Joseph J. Spengler and William R. Allen (Chicago: Rand McNally, 1960), 79.

23. Raymond de Roover, "Scholasticism and Mercantilism: A Contrast," in Spengler and Allen, *Economic Thought*, 96. The harshness of the verdict makes one wonder why de Roover was so anxious to claim Malynes as a compatriot, but has less to do with de Roover's opinion of Malynes than with his general advocacy of Scholastic economic thought. For de Roover's tendency to disparage the mercantilists in order to celebrate the Scholastics, see Julius Kirshner, "Raymond de Roover on Scholastic Economic Thought," in de Roover, *Business*, 35.

24. Appleby, *Economic Thought*, 43.

25. Beer, *Early British Economics*, 126.

26. Schumpeter, *Economic Analysis*, 344.

27. Letwin, *Scientific Economics*, 197.

28. Henry William Spiegel, *The Growth of Economic Thought*, 3d ed. (Durham: Duke University Press, 1991), 102–3.

29. Malynes, *Lex Mercatoria*, 19–58 (weights and measures); 259–323, 360–62 (coins and mining); 70–82 (commodities); 17, 61, 362–71 (mathematics and bookkeeping); 120, 167, 175 (maritime laws); 229, 272, (foreign proverbs). Other foreign proverbs appear in *Free Trade*, 26, and *Center of the Circle*, 124, 129.

30. Malynes, *Lex Mercatoria*, 54–59 (color theory), 17–18 (on number, possibly loosely borrowed from Bodin's *Republic* IV.2), 10–16 (on calendars). Malynes could be politically obtuse in the extreme. That he had sent his calendar recommendations to James in 1604 was one thing (16), but to boast in 1622 of having done so after he had quoted from a 1609 speech by James I revealing the king's hatred of the reform was quite another. For the king's speech, see James I, *Political Works*, 311.

31. Thus his preemptive strike at Edward Misselden (whose books are replete with Greek, Latin, and Hebrew texts) as that "Babylon of learning." For which, see Malynes, *Center of the Circle*, 1 and 116. Except for the odd and inaccurately spelled derivation (e.g., monopoly: from μονος and πωλιο [*sic*]) so common it could have come from any of his Scholastic sources, Greek was nowhere used in his works. For monopoly, see Malynes, *Lex Mercatoria*, 214.

32. Malynes, *Free Trade*, 38, 85; *Lex Mercatoria*, 71, 486; *Center of the Circle*, 43; and *A Treatise on the Canker of Englands Common Wealth. Divided into three parts: Wherein the Author imitating the rule of good Phistians, First, declareth the disease. Secondarily, seweth the efficient cause thereof. Lastly, a remedy for the same* (London, 1601), 1–2.

33. See Malynes, *Englands view, in the Unmasking of Two Paradoxes: With a replication unto the answer of Maister John Bodine* (London, 1603), 1; *Free Trade*, 5, 105; *Lex Mercatoria*, unpaged "Epistle," 3, 60; and *Center of the Circle*, 137, among many other citations.

34. Malynes, *Lex Mercatoria*, 120, 146; *Free Trade* 48, 59; and *Saint George for England, Allegorically described* (London, 1601), 39.

35. See Malynes, *Lex Mercatoria*, 258.

36. See Malynes, *Free Trade*, 26; *St. George*, 25, 28, 35, 37, 38, 43, 50; *Center of the*

Circle, 7, 17, 19, 80, 112; and *Lex Mercatoria,* 499. Less ancient tales, such as those of Canute and the tides (Malynes failing to see Canute's irony) or the tribulations of Patient Griselda also found their place in his works. For assorted folktales and lore, see *St. George,* 29, 30, 35, 36, 54; or *Center of the Circle,* 42, 78.

37. Malynes, *St. George,* 21–22. See Peter Burke, *Popular Culture in Early Modern Europe* (New York: Harper and Row, 1978), 208, 212, 270–81 (on the attack on popular culture and license).

38. Malynes, *Canker,* 17; also *St. George,* 16, 34.

39. Malynes, *Lex Mercatoria,* 229, 234.

40. Malynes, *St. George,* 40; see also ibid., 26, 43, 44. This may look like a touch of Machiavellian republicanism, but given his limited exposure to Machiavelli, and his multiple citations of Cato and Pliny, Malynes was more likely to have picked up this idea from the *De Re Rustica* (I.4) or Pliny's *Natural History* (XVIII.26). Machiavelli's name only appears twice in Malynes's works. In *Englands View,* 79, Malynes disagreed with what he believed to be an estimate of England's population done by Machiavelli, while *Lex Mercatoria,* 437, quoted what Malynes believed to be Machiavelli's saying that "It is miserable that we cannot do all things; More miserable to do that which we would do; and most miserable to do that which we can do."

41. Malynes, *Lex Mercatoria,* 10–11, 17.

42. See Malynes, *Lex Mercatoria,* 5, 375, 452, 461–73.

43. Malynes, *Lex Mercatoria,* 187–89, 308–9; and *Free Trade,* 86–87.

44. Malynes, *St. George,* 1. A comprehensive analysis of his borrowings in this work from Chaucer and More can be found in Helen E. Sandison, "An Elizabethan Economist's Method of Literary Composition," *Huntington Library Quarterly* 6, no. 2 (Feb. 1943): 205–11. Malynes did not read More simply for his literary devices; there was also an extensive analysis of the incident of the Flatulentine ambassadors in *Englands View,* 98–103.

45. Hugh Trevor-Roper, *Renaissance Essays* (Chicago: University of Chicago Press, 1985), 153, 161–62, 178–79.

46. Malynes, *Lex Mercatoria,* 189, 255–59 (with an extended quotation from Paracelsus's *De Transmutione Rerum*). Malynes first referred to Paracelsus in *Englands View,* 104.

47. Malynes, *Lex Mercatoria,* 205.

48. Malynes, *Canker,* 14, 56.

49. Carlo Ginzburg, "High and Low: The Theme of Forbidden Knowledge in the Sixteenth and Seventeenth Centuries," *Past and Present* 73 (Nov. 1976), 33.

50. Malynes, *Center of the Circle,* 137. This is his translation of Horace, *Odes* IV.ii (lines 1–4).

51. Malynes, *Lex Mercatoria,* 182–83, 185, 236–37.

52. Malynes, *Lex Mercatoria,* 66, 235; and *Englands View,* 135–37. Including Wales, England actually measures some 37,340,160 acres, and a more accurate estimate of her population at the time would be 4.1 million.

53. Malynes, *Free Trade,* 72; *Lex Mercatoria,* 214–16, 233, 242; and *Center of the Circle,* 85, 127 (in which he particularly recommended "Master Hill his booke of husbandrie" for its information on beekeeping, and the work of Tobias Gentleman on fishing).

54. Malynes, *Lex Mercatoria,* 62.

55. Malynes, *Center of the Circle,* 123–24. Malynes never mentions Bodin's

Démonomanie des Sorciers with its rejection of Pyrrhonism, nor is there any evidence he had read Montaigne, the seminal figure in Richard Popkin's account of the dispersion of the *crise pyrrhonienne*. For which, see Popkin, *Scepticism*, 43.

56. Malynes, *Lex Mercatoria*, unpaged "Epistle"; similarly, ibid., 3, 60, 491.

57. The most accessible discussion of the macro-microcosmic correspondence is probably that in Eustace Tillyard's *The Elizabethan World Picture: A Study of the Idea of Order in the Age of Shakespeare, Donne and Milton*, paperback edition (New York: Vintage Books/Random House, n.d.), 68–69, 83–85.

58. Malynes, *Free Trade*, 5–6.

59. See, for example, Aristotle, *Politics*, I.i [1252a1], I.ii [1252b15, 1252b27] and Plato, *Republic*, II.xi.

60. Plato, *Republic*,II.x.

61. See, for example, Plato, *Republic*, V.xx.

62. *Hermetica: the Ancient Greek and Latin Writings which contain Religious or Philosophic Teachings Ascribed to Hermes Trismegistus*, trans. Walter Scott (Boston: Shambhala Publications, 1985), 179 [*Lib. VIII.5*]

63. Ibid., 289 [*Asclepius I.2a*]

64. Ibid., 293 [*Asclepius I.4*]

65. Ibid., 305 [*Asclepius I.10*]

66. Nicholas of Cusa, *Nicholas of Cusa on Learned Ignorance: A Translation and an Appraisal of De Docta Ignorantia*, ed. and trans. Jasper Hopkins, 2d ed. (Minneapolis: Arthur J. Banning, 1985), 131 [3.3].

67. Tillyard, *Elizabethan*, 28.

68. Paracelsus, *Selected Writings*, trans. Norbert Guterman (Princeton, NJ: Princeton University Press, 1979), 25, 63.

69. Malynes, *Canker*, 3.

70. Malynes, *Lex Mercatoria*, 377–78.

71. Malynes, *Free Trade*, 38, repeated word for word in *Lex Mercatoria*, 486. The longest and most detailed of his physiological analogies can be found in *Center of the Circle*, 128–32; that in *Lex Mercatoria*, 11, displays another cosmic correspondence: the body had a total of 365 veins, making "residences" for the Spirit "agreeable to so many dayes of the yeare."

72. See Galen, *De usu respirationis* 2.1, 5.7, *An in arteriis natura sanguis contineatur* 4.3, 6.1, and *De causis respirationis* 3 in *Galen on Respiration and the Arteries*, ed. and trans. David J. Furley and J. S. Wilkie (Princeton, NJ: Princeton University Press, 1984), 83–85, 129–31, 157–59, 165–67, 241–43. Malynes was, however, guilty of conflating Erasistratus's arguments with Galen's refutations of them.

73. Malynes, *Lex Mercatoria*, 257.

74. Malynes, *St. George*, 16.

75. Malynes, *Lex Mercatoria*, 62. Lewes Roberts, an active member of the East India and Levant Companies, not only acknowledged a general debt to Malynes in the preface of his *Merchants Mappe of Commerce* (1638), he borrowed Malynes's social classification virtually intact. For which, see Roberts, *Merchants Mappe*, unpaged "Epistle" and 20.

76. Aristotle, *Politics* VII.viii (1328b2, 1328b15), already cited.

77. See Malynes, *Free Trade*, 37–38; also *Lex Mercatoria*, 62, 416 (mispaginated as 316), 486.

78. Malynes, *St. George*, 40.

79. Malynes, *Lex Mercatoria*, 216, referring to the Statute of Artificers (1563).
80. Ibid.
81. Ibid., 1.
82. Aristotle, *Politics* I.v (1254b2–1254b15).
83. Malynes was aware of that preference; for which, see *Lex Mercatoria*, 63.
84. Ibid., unpaged dedication to James I.
85. Elyot, *Governor*, 7, 9 [1.2]
86. Milles, *Customers Replie*, unpaged "Epistle."
87. Jean Bodin, *The Six Books of a Commonweale. Written by J. Bodin a famous Lawyer, and a man of great Experience in matters of State. Out of the French and Latine Copies, done into English, by Richard Knolles* (London, 1606), 84 [I:8].
88. James I, *Political Works*, 307.
89. Ibid., 55.
90. Ibid., 64.
91. Ibid., 438.
92. Malynes, *St. George*, unpaged "Epistle." Similarly, *Englands View*, 5; and *Lex Mercatoria*, 327. "All extreames being vicious" was a fundamental Aristotelian concept accepted by Malynes; for which, see *Lex Mercatoria*, 205.
93. Malynes, *Lex Mercatoria*, 205.
94. Malynes, *Canker*, 1–2.
95. Malynes, *Englands View*, 118–19.
96. Malynes, *Free Trade*, 67. Malynes tended to view all change as "corruption" requiring a return to first principles for reformation. For which, see *Lex Mercatoria*, 413, or *Free Trade*, 2.
97. See, for example, Malynes, *Canker*, 6, or *Lex Mercatoria*, 58.
98. Malynes, *Lex Mercatoria*, 463.
99. Malynes, *Canker*, 5–6. Similarly, *St. George*, 28, 43; *Englands View*, 9, 119, 120 (but labeled 104; there is irregular pagination between 107–22), 124; *Lex Mercatoria*, 60, 71; and *Free Trade*, 57. The tradition Malynes inherited was actually a corruption of the rough analogy in Aristotle's *Politics* between the method of producing goods (growing versus manufacturing) and the use of the terms *natural* (household management) and *artificial* (commerce for gain) ascribed to their means of acquisition. For which, see the *Politics*, I.ix (1256b40–1257a27), I.x (1258a38–1258b8), I.xi (1258b9–1258b33).
100. Malynes, *St. George*, 15, 18–22, 40.
101. Malynes, *Canker*, 66–67; *Englands View*, 94; *Lex Mercatoria*, 6, 84, 213; and *Free Trade*, 58, 104.
102. Malynes, *St. George*, 18.
103. A good parallel to Malynes's analysis, suggested by James Jacob, can be found in Robert Burton's *The Anatomy of Melancholy* (1621), ed. Holbrook Jackson (London: J. M. Dent and Sons Ltd., 1932), 1:64–65, 87–88, and especially 108–9.
104. Mark Blaug, *Economic Theory in Retrospect*, revised edition (Homewood, IL: Richard D. Irwin, 1968), 11–12. Blaug considered this a technical deficiency rather than an analytic confusion as supposed by Jacob Viner, *Studies in the Theory of International Trade and Economic Theory* (Glencoe, IL: Free Press, 1952), 31. The analytic confusion seems rather to be between currency, money, and capital than between the functions of money per se.
105. Malynes, *Lex Mercatoria*, 360–62, 386–91.
106. Malynes, *Canker*, 60–61.

107. The stamp did not necessarily overrule the weight domestically either: if there was a sufficient discrepancy between the stamped denomination and the market price of the bullion therein coins might be melted down for plate or export. Malynes, however, was concerned with the international problem rather than the domestic one.

108. Malynes, *Lex Mercatoria*, 383. Although the Troy ounce is heavier than the avoirdupois ounce, the greater number of ounces in the avoirdupois pound make it equal to 1.21528 Troy pounds. See C. E. Challis, *The Tudor Coinage* (Manchester, UK: Manchester University Press, 1978), appendix 1 (table 9) for a conversion table on the Troy, Tower, and avoirdupois standards. Table 10, immediately following, converts conversions between the assorted gold and silver standards.

109. Gold was divisible into 24 carats of 4 grains each. Standards existed for two gold coins: the "Angel" containing 23 carats 3.5 grains of gold and .5 grains of alloy, and the "Crown" containing 22 carats gold to 2 carats alloy.

110. This had actually been the case in England from 1551 through 1560; for which see D. M. Palliser, *The Age of Elizabeth: England under the Later Tudors, 1547–1603* (London: Longman Group UK Ltd., 1983), 135, on "coins containing 6 oz and 3 oz of silver . . . freely circulating at the same face value."

111. Beer, *Early British Economics*, 95.

112. Challis, *Tudor Coinage*, 235. But compare B. E. Supple, "Currency and Commerce in the Early Seventeenth Century," *Economic History Review*, 2d ser.,10, no. 2 (Dec. 1957): 241–42. Supple notes an enhancement in 1601 and a par change in 1604 (because the 1601 change produced an effect opposite to that desired). A further increase of the par to over 13:1 in 1611 brought a "chronic efflux of silver" (ibid., 242).

113. Muchmore, "Malynes," 350.

114. Before a 1604 adjustment sent it up over 12:1.

115. Malynes, *Canker*, 8–9. The par was between Crown gold (rather than Angel) and sterling silver because these shared the same ratio of fine metal to dross.

116. Malynes, *Englands View*, 175, citing Bodin's *Response*, 64.

117. Malynes, *Lex Mercatoria*, 313.

118. Ibid., 291.

119. Ibid., 430; emphasis added.

120. Hooker, *Ecclesiastical Polity*, in *Works*, 148 (I.2.2), 153–54 (I.3.1).

121. Ibid., 310 (III.8.14).

122. Ibid., 67 (I.7.3).

123. Ibid., 169 (I.7.7).

124. Malynes, *Lex Mercatoria*, 461. Thus he approved of Cato's dictum that usurers repay their victims fourfold but thieves only double and disapproved of bankruptcy laws that punished improvidence as strictly as fraud. For which, see ibid., 222–23, 330 (Cato's *De re rustica*); compare Aristotle, *Nicomachean Ethics* V.iii (1131a21–23).

125. Malynes, *Englands View*, 4; similarly *Lex Mercatoria*, 461.

126. Malynes, *Canker*, 64.

127. Malynes, *Free Trade*, 62.

128. Malynes, *Canker*, 5, 7, 11; also *Free Trade*, 3; and *Lex Mercatoria*, 61, 251, 307, 383, 386, among other citations.

129. Malynes, *Englands View*, 103–4; similarly *Lex Mercatoria*, 275.

130. Lynn Muchmore took the stand that "the 'doctrine' outlined by Malynes" was "firmly rooted in the economic conditions and institutional peculiarities of early seventeenth-century England," rejecting all interpretations based "upon some precon-

ceived school of thought" (namely, Heckscher's interpretation). For which, see Muchmore, "Malynes," 336–37.

131. Malynes, *Englands View*, 190.

132. Malynes, *Lex Mercatoria*, 382; similarly, *Free Trade*, 3.

133. Malynes, *Lex Mercatoria*, 382. Similarly, *Canker*, 15–16; and *Center of the Circle*, 14. On bankers as "commaunders or rulers of this exchange," see *Canker*, 20, 28; on
merchants, see ibid., 19, and *Free Trade*, 4.

134. Malynes, *Lex Mercatoria*, 378.

135. Malynes, *St. George*, 42.

136. Malynes, *Canker*, 14; in *Lex Mercatoria*, 490, Malynes called setting "a price
on his owne incoyne" "one of the greatest prerogatives the King" had. While it is tempt-
ing to propose that Malynes saw in the "Merchandising Exchange" a form of taxation
without representation, the phrase was not used either by Malynes or by any of his contemporaries; the argument is always over the royal prerogative, which did not, of course,
include taxation.

137. Malynes, *Englands View*, 161.

138. Malynes, *Canker*, 56.

139. Ibid., 31.

140. Ibid., 32–33, 36, 48.

141. Ibid., 27–28, 35.

142. Malynes, *Canker*, 38. Note, *Lex Mercatoria*, 416 (mispaginated as 316), that
though plenty of money increased the price level, the "exchange hath a contrairie meane
of working, for plentie of money maketh a low exchange, and scarcitie of money maketh
a high exchange." He just refused to allow supply and demand this authority over the
exchange.

143. Malynes, *Canker*, 39.

144. Ibid., 43.

145. Malynes, *Free Trade*, 2.

146. Malynes, *St. George*, 60.

147. Milles, *Customers Replie*, 4–5, 12–13.

148. Ibid., 6–7.

149. Malynes, *Englands View*, 9.

150. Charles Henry Wilson, *England's Apprenticeship, 1603–1763* (London: Longmans, 1965), 53. Wilson gives it at about 90 percent of England's foreign trade, citing
Supple, *Commercial Crisis*, 266.

151. Wilson, *England's Apprenticeship*, 52–54.

152. Malynes, *Free Trade*, 46. Malynes seems never to have lost his high opinion
of Cockayne. The contention that it was a problem of quality rather than price was
repeated in *Center of the Circle*, 79. As Lynn Muchmore pointed out, Malynes's refusal
"to concede that price was a crucial determinant of quantity sold" was "central to his
model." For which, see Muchmore, "Malynes," 352; similarly, ibid., 355. Lawrence H.
Officer credited Malynes with having "all the ingredients for the PPP [Purchasing
Power Parity] theory" and coming "ever so close to exhibiting the theory for both fixed
and floating exchange rates," but failing "to draw the conclusions indicated by his analysis" to "complete" the theory. Officer was trying to see if sixteenth-century Spanish (the
Salamancan school) scholars were the only ones to develop the theory at the time. For
which, see Officer, "The purchasing-power-parity theory of Gerrard de Malynes," *History of Political Economy* 14, no. 2 (summer 1982): 258. Absolute purchasing-power-parity

occurs when the exchange rate equals the ratio between relative purchasing power of the two currencies being exchanged. Relative purchasing-power-parity measures percent changes in these values. While Officer's verdict on Malynes was accurate, it missed the point that Malynes would never have found such a theory acceptable, which may very well be why he did not draw the conclusions Officer thought so logical.

153. Malynes, *Free Trade*, 56.

154. See Marian Bowley, "Some Seventeenth-Century Contributions to the Theory of Value," *Economica*, n.s. 30, no. 118 (May 1963): 124–26. Bowley maintained that the "case for freedom of the foreign exchange market had focused on the argument that there was no absolute or objective basis for value in exchange, either with or without ethical implications, for it was simply the consequence of a relation between scarity and wants" (126). Based on the implications of this freedom for the concept of absolute value, Malynes argued against freeing the exchange (124) even though he allowed supply and demand to determine other commodity prices (125).

155. Malynes, *Canker*, 101; See also *Englands View*, 194, in which it is clear that he rejected this approach.

156. Malynes, *Canker*, 102–3. The office was originally established by 9 Edw. III, c.7 (1335) but had been allowed to lapse in the sixteenth century. By the time of the publication of *The Maintenance of Free Trade* in 1622, Malynes seems to have given up hope that the office of Royal Exchanger would ever be revived and wrote only of the first solution. For which, see *Free Trade*, 84. A remark in *Lex Mercatoria*, 490, makes Malynes appear back to the Royal Exchanger solution, but this may simply have been written earlier than the passage in *Free Trade* though *Lex Mercatoria* appeared later in the same year.

157. De Roover, "Scholasticism," in Spengler and Allen, *Economic Thought*, 93.

158. Muchmore, "Malynes," 347.

159. Malynes, *Lex Mercatoria*, 5.

160. Ibid., unpaged Dedication to James I.

161. Ibid., 59. The merchants who dealt in commodities were not actually engaged in barter but those who having sold English wool in France would then purchase French silk with their proceeds to resell in England, or brought raw materials in from the East Indies to process in England and resell abroad.

162. Ibid.

163. Malynes, *Free Trade*, 4; similarly, *Center of the Circle*, 14, 45; and *Lex Mercatoria*, 60 (the keel of the ship was "Equitie").

164. Malynes, *Free Trade*, 85. On the other hand, Malynes was willing to accept regrating, forestalling, and engrossing (three monopolistic practices of the day) when they were necessary to ensure a regular supply of some needful commodity in spite of the increased prices they caused. For which, see Malynes, *Englands View*, 82, 87–88, and *Lex Mercatoria*, 213. To regrate was to go to a particular market and buy up some commodity (especially foodstuffs) in order to resell it at a profit in the same (or a nearby) market. To engross was to buy all or as much as possible of some commodity (on the wholesale level), for the purpose of regrating it or retailing it at a monopoly price. To forestall was to buy up goods before they reached the market (as in to buy up a crop before it was harvested).

165. Malynes, *Free Trade*, 5. Also, *Center of the Circle*, 45, "which caused the wise man to say: *Consult not with a Merchant concerning Exchanges*." There is a marginal note to *Ecclesiasticus* 37:11 ("Never consult . . . a merchant about a bargain").

166. Malynes, *Center of the Circle*, 53.
167. Malynes, *Free Trade*, 18 (marginal note cites Bodin's *Republic*).
168. Malynes, *Canker*, 22–24.
169. Ibid., 25.
170. Ibid., 21–27; also *Lex Mercatoria*, 132–33.
171. Malynes, *Englands View*, 172–73; also *Center of the Circle*, 42.
172. Similarly *Leviticus* 25:36–37; *Psalms* 15:5; *Ezekiel* 18:8; and *Luke* 6:34. See Malynes, *St. George*, 65. Expulsions of non-Christians in the late medieval and early modern period along with the rise of Christian banking houses seems to have made the brotherhood v. otherhood argument a thing of the past by the seventeenth century as it had the dependence on non-Christian lenders to avoid the "my people" restriction in the biblical texts.
173. Malynes, *Englands View*, 2.
174. Malynes, *Lex Mercatoria*, 335.
175. Ibid., 339.
176. Malynes, *Center of the Circle*, 66; the opponent was Edward Misselden.
177. Aristotle, *Politics*, I.3.23 (1258b).
178. As for example, Malynes, *Canker*, 104; and *Center of the Circle*, 10.
179. Wilson, *Discourse*, 313; compare Malynes, *Canker*, 56. Compare also Wilson, *Discourse*, 301, with Malynes, *Free Trade*, 2, on the merchandising exchange condemned for violating money's role as an equalizer. Or compare Wilson, *Discourse*, 241, 285, with Malynes, *Canker*, 113, on usury as the stinging of the "Serpent *Aspis*" and its derivation from *Neschech*.
180. Wilson, *Discourse*, 236, 253.
181. Compare Malynes, *Lex Mercatoria*, 336, to Wilson, *Discourse*, 236.
182. Wilson, *Discourse*, 288.
183. Malynes, *Lex Mercatoria*, 329–30.
184. Malynes, *Englands View*, 161.
185. Malynes, *Free Trade*, 39–40.
186. Ibid., 40.
187. Malynes, *Lex Mercatoria*, 253. Similarly, *Canker*, 10; *Englands View*, 7, 66; *Free Trade*, 36; and *Center of the Circle*, 14. There are also "occasional" factors: "when armies are dearer in time of warre, then in time of peace: victuals in time of famine: wood in winter, and water in desert places," for which, see *Englands View*, 67. Hamilton's first statement of his thesis can be found in E. J. Hamilton, "Imports of American Gold and Silver into Spain, 1503–1660," *Quarterly Journal of Economics* 43, no. 3 (May 1929): 436–72. Briefly, Hamilton suggested that the price revolution of the sixteenth century was caused by the influx of American treasure. For Malynes's linking of the influx of bullion from the Americas to the price rise, see also *Canker*, 10, and *Englands View*, 7.
188. Jean Bodin, *The Response of Jean Bodin to the Paradoxes of Malestroit, and the Paradoxes*, trans. George Albert Moore (Washington, DC: Country Dollar, 1947), 48.
189. Ibid., 23, 29, 33–36.
190. Malynes, *Englands View*, 64, 118.
191. Malynes, *Center of the Circle*, 83.
192. E. A. Wrigley and R. S. Schofield, *The Population History of England, 1541–1871: A Reconstruction* (Cambridge, MA: Harvard University Press, 1981), 528 (table A3.1).
193. N. J. Mayhew, "Population, Money Supply, and the Velocity of Circulation in

England, 1300–1700," *Economic History Review* 48, no. 2 (May 1995): 244. Mayhew uses Wrigley and Schofield's population estimates.

194. E. H. Phelps Brown and Shiela V. Hopkins, "Seven Centuries of the Prices of Consumables, Compared with Builders' Wage-Rates," *Economica, n.s.*23, no. 92 (Nov. 1956): 296–314. As to their continued use, see Mayhew, "Population," 244. The market basket used by Phelps Brown and Hopkins excluded the durable goods outlays that make modern CPIs less volatile.

195. See Challis, *Tudor Coinage,* 237–47. Challis was still the main source for Mayhew, "Population," 244.

196. Malynes, *Canker,* 60; *St. George,* unpaged "Epistle"; *Englands View,* 67; *Free Trade,* 97; and *Center of the Circle,* unpaged dedication.

197. Niccolò Machiavelli, *Discourses on the First Ten Books of Titus Livius,* trans. Christian E. Detmold, in *The Prince and the Discourses,* ed. Max Lerner (New York: Random House, 1950), 308–12.

198. Francis Bacon, "Of the True Greatness of Kingdoms and Estates" and "Of Sedition and Troubles," in *Essays and New Atlantis* (New York: Walter J. Black, 1942), 124, 59. Compare Malynes, *Canker,* 124.

199. James I, *Political Works,* 324, 29.

200. Malynes, *Englands View,* 2; similarly, *Free Trade,* unpaged "Epistle"; borrowed from Fortescue's reference to Justinian; for which, see Sir John Fortescue, *De Laudibus Legum Anglie,* ed. and trans. S. B. Chrimes (Cambridge: Cambridge University Press, 1942), 5 (Cap. I).

201. Palliser, *Age of Elizabeth,* 109.

202. Wilson, *England's Apprenticeship,* 91.

203. James I, *Political Works,* 319–21.

204. Ibid., 317.

205. *Chaos,* 1.

Chapter 3

1. See, for example, Beer, *Early British Economics,* 182; Appleby, *Economic Thought,* 44–45, 47, and J. A. W. Gunn, *Politics and the Public Interest in the Seventeenth Century* (London: Routledge and Kegan Paul, 1969), 231–33.

2. There has been considerable debate among economic historians as to which factor was *actually* the more decisive. Astrid Friis put the emphasis on the Cockayne scheme in *Alderman Cockayne's Project and the Cloth Trade* (Copenhagen: Levin and Munksgaard, 1927), passim; while B. E. Supple put the emphasis on eastern European currency manipulations in *Commercial Crisis,* passim. Supple had already laid out this position in "Currency," 249–50. Supple had himself been anticipated by J. D. Gould, who opted for the currency manipulations in "The Trade Depression of the Early 1620s," *Economic History Review,* 2d ser., 7, no. 1 (Aug. 1954): 89–90.

3. Wilson, *England's Apprenticeship,* 54–55. Supple documented the 43-plus percent drop in the silver content of Polish coins in "Currency," 248, and the corresponding drop in shortcloth exports (250).

4. Ibid., 245.

5. Ibid., 252. As to the feasibility of maintaining such a balance, Supple has also picked up on the "necessary assumption" of an inelastic demand for English goods; see

ibid., 253, in which he cited Malynes, *Canker,* 3–4, 53–55. Gould used citations such as this to discount the idea that the Thirty Years' War was the true cause of the trade depression, in "Trade Depression," 88–89.

6. The inability of any of these committees to come up with decisive policies appears to have left the Crown fuming. Note, for example, *Calendar of State Papers, Domestic: James I (vol. 10), 1619–1623,* 384 (Order in Council dated 3 May 1622, "desiring the Merchants' Committee for inquiring into the decay of merchandise and inequality of trade, to make their report with diligence, as extreme injury will arise from any delay therein"). See also *Acts of the Privy Council (vol. 5), 1619–1621,* 393; and *(vol. 6), 1621–1623,* 40, 71, 79, 201, 208.

7. *Court Minutes* (17–21 Oct. 16) in *Calendar of State Papers, Colonial (vol. 4), 1622–1624,* 165; also ibid., 168–69, 171, 174, 218, 230, 242, 244, 265–67.

8. *Calendar of State Papers, Domestic: Charles I (vol. 4), 1629–1631,* 112 (3 Dec. 1629); and *Calendar of State Papers, Colonial (vol. 8), 1630–1634,* 2, 34, 41, 101, 115, showing the negotiations still under way in 1631.

9. *Calendar of State Papers, Colonial (vol. 7), 1628–1630,* 136 (18 Oct. 1628).

10. *Calendar of State Papers, Colonial (vol. 4), 1622–1624,* 292, 321, 334, 336, 415.

11. For a defense of James's efforts to resolve the Amboyna crisis (against both contemporary and modern critics), see Karen Chancey, "The Amboyna Massacre in English Politics, 1624–32," *Albion* 30, no. 4 (winter 1998): 583–98.

12. Misselden seems to have run into personal problems with Forbes, the minister to the Merchant Adventurers' Congregation, and complained to Windebank of Forbes's nonconforming practices as much to assure himself of the Crown's help in overcoming his own administrative problems as to resolve any religious dispute. Pressure was put on William Boswell, the ambassador at the Hague by Windebank and Laud, but Forbes had an ally in Samuel Avery, the chief elder of the congregation who had connections to Sir John Coke, secretary of state (1625–1640). This is not to say that the practices described—ordaining ministers at will, lack of sacramental "solemnities" and regularized prayers, omission of the Prayer Book and approved catechisms—were not nonconforming. For which, see *Calendar of State Papers, Domestic: Charles I (vol. 5), 1631–1633,* 432, 575; *Charles I (vol. 6), 1633–1634,* 30–31,152–53, 225, 297, 364; and *Charles I (vol. 8), 1635,* 151.

13. Charles's efforts ranged from advising the Merchant Adventurers to give Misselden "all encouragement in the present and future elections" to threatening them with recalling their charter to London. See, for example, *Calendar of State Papers, Domestic: Charles I (vol. 6), 1633–1634,* 74–75; *Charles I (vol. 8), 1635,* 77; and *Charles I (vol. 9), 1635–1636,* 36.

14. *Calendar of State Papers, Domestic: Charles I (vol.15), 1639–1640,* 117, 485.

15. See John Thurloe, *A Collection of the State Papers of John Thurloe* (London, 1742), 3:13, for a letter from Misselden to Cromwell in which he complains that he "never received an answere, nor soe much as his charges for lawyers' fees, and length of time, study, and labour" during the Amboyna negotiations.

16. Edward Misselden, *The Circle of Commerce, or The Ballance of Trade, in defence of free Trade: Opposed to Malynes Little Fish and his Great Whale, and poized against them in the Scale. . . .* (London, 1623), unpaged dedication to Middlesex, 21, 66, 103; and *Free Trade. Or, The Meanes To Make Trade Florish. Wherein, The Causes of the Decay of Trade in this Kingdome, are discovered: And the Remedies also to remoove the same, are represented. The second Edition with some Addition* (London, 1622), 69.

17. Misselden, *Circle of Commerce*, 18–19.

18. Ibid., 15–16.

19. Ibid., unpaged dedication to Middlesex, 11, 42, 118; and *Free Trade*, 37, 61–62, among other citations.

20. Misselden, *Free Trade*, unpaged dedication to the reader.

21. See John Venn and J. A. Venn, *Alumni Cantabrigienses: a biographical list of all known students, graduates and holders of office at the University of Cambridge from the earliest times to 1900; Part One: From the Earliest Times to 1751* (Cambridge: Cambridge University Press, 1924), 3.195.

22. Kenneth Charlton, *Education in Renaissance England* (London: Routledge and Kegan Paul, 1965), 258–71.

23. Charlton, *Education,*118.

24. Misselden, *Circle of Commerce*, 9, 11–13.

25. See ibid., 29–30. An Elizabethan manuscript attributed to Sir Thomas Gresham listed twenty-four ways in which bankers could manipulate the exchange. It appeared in Malynes's *Lex Mercatoria* and in his *Maintenance of Free Trade*. Misselden also accused Malynes of having taken his analogy of the Body, Soul, and Spirit of trade from the *Customers Alphabet and Primer* of Thomas Milles (ca. 1550–1627), even going so far as to cite the page (15) from this work in which it appeared.

For Gresham's list, see Raymond de Roover, *Gresham on Foreign Exchange: An Essay on Early English Mercantilism with the Text of Sir Thomas Gresham's Memorandum for the Understanding of the Exchange* (Cambridge, MA: Harvard University Press, 1949), 300–302. Misselden had himself borrowed a trade balance calculation from Gresham without attribution. For which, see *Circle of Commerce*, 119–20 (noted by Spiegel, *Growth*, 106). The balance, dated *Anno 28 Regis Edward III* (1354) was appended by Gresham to his memo on the exchange. For the date of the original document used by Gresham and the links in the chain from Gresham to Misselden, see de Roover, *Gresham*, 252–55. A passage Misselden "borrowed" from Grotius will be cited later.

26. While unattributed borrowing had long been a crime in established literary genres such as poetry (where writers were expected not simply to *use* standard sources but to *improve* them), it was not yet the case in the newer and less legitimate genre of the "muck-raking pamphlet." For the accepted difference between literary adaptation and literary theft during the period, see Harold Ogden White, *Plagiarism and Imitation during the English Renaissance: A Study in Critical Distinctions* (Cambridge, MA: Harvard University Press, 1935), 112, 122–24, 146–47; the classical position is laid out in ibid., 5–6.

27. Misselden, *Free Trade*, unpaged dedication and 2.

28. Ibid., 3.

29. Misselden, *Circle of Commerce*, 97.

30. Misselden, *Free Trade*, 35.

31. Ibid., 4.

32. Ibid., 2–3, 53.

33. Misselden, *Circle of Commerce*, 37.

34. Bacon, "Of Seditions and Troubles," in *Essays*, 57.

35. Misselden, *Free Trade*, 12. On the difference between "distributive" and "commutative" justice (following Aristotle), see *Circle of Commerce*, 112–13.

36. Misselden, *Free Trade*, 109.

37. Ibid., 132, 137.

38. Ibid., 118–19.
39. Misselden, *Circle of Commerce*, 137.
40. Misselden, *Free Trade*, 12.
41. Ibid., 108.
42. Ibid., 28; or 109, for the hand, eye, mouth, and "languishing body" of the Commonwealth.
43. Ibid., 9–10.
44. Ibid., 79, 93, 97, 111, 125, 133.
45. Ibid., 103.
46. Ibid., 104.
47. Ibid.
48. Ibid., 9–10.
49. Ibid., 4. Similar defenses can be found in *Circle of Commerce*, 18; but the most fulsome was his repeating, word for word, Scaliger's *Carmen de Mirandis Batavie* on the miraculous bounty of cloth, wheat, and wine that trade had procured for a land in which flocks of sheep, fields of wheat, and vineyards were scarce if at all to be found. For which, see Misselden, *Free Trade*, unpaged dedication to the reader. The poem appeared in the 1615 edition of Scaliger's *Poemata*. For a modern text and translation, see *The Autobiography of Joseph Scaliger with Autobiographical Selections from his Letters, his Testament, and the Funeral Orations by Daniel Heinsius and Dominicus Baudius*, trans. George W. Robinson (Cambridge, MA: Harvard University Press, 1927), 24–25.
50. Misselden, *Free Trade*, 91–92; similarly, ibid., 93 (here "subsidies" for "supplies").
51. Ibid., 99. One of the main thrusts of R. W. K. Hinton's work has been to elevate navigation to the position of a *summum bonum* of "Mercantilism." See, for example, R. W. K. Hinton, "The Mercantile System in the Time of Thomas Mun," *Economic History Review*, 2d ser., 7, no. 3 (April 1955): 282. But such explanations fail to take into account differences in aims between the various constituencies. The general health of England's navigation was important to the import-exporters, but we might expect it to rank higher on the Crown's list, while a larger pool of money for investment (and cheaper interest rates) might rank somewhat higher on the merchants' list.
52. Misselden, *Circle of Commerce*, 17.
53. Ibid., 17.
54. Ibid., 19.
55. Ibid., 132.
56. Misselden, *Free Trade*, 96–97.
57. Misselden, *Circle of Commerce*, 135.
58. Misselden, *Free Trade*, 60.
59. Misselden, *Circle of Commerce*, 112.
60. Most of the great trading companies had, at various times in their existence, a feature or two more commonly associated with the opposite type, so that the expressions "regulated" company and "joint-stock" company should not be understood to mean that a given firm was a perfect model of its type but only that it partook of more of the features of one than of the other.
61. K. N. Chaudhuri, *The English East India Company: The Study of an Early Joint-Stock Company, 1600–1640* (London: Frank Cass and Co., 1965), 3, 22, 97.
62. Chaudhuri, *East India*, 26 (although the Muscovy Company was technically an intra-European concern).

63. Hinton discussed the plight of the Eastland Company, which unsuccessfully requested the confirmation of its privileges by Act of Parliament in 1624 and 1660; for which, see R.W.K. Hinton, *The Eastland Trade and the Common Weal in the Seventeenth Century* (Cambridge: Cambridge University Press, 1959; reprint, Hamden, CT: Archon Books, 1975), 72 (page references are to reprint edition). One cannot, however, posit a consistently followed policy pre-1649 in this regard as Acts of Parliament were, on occasion, employed.

64. Brenner has massed some impressive statistics on the doubling and trebling of these commodity imports in the first four decades of the seventeenth century. For which, see Robert Brenner, *Merchants and Revolution: Commercial Change, Political Conflict, and London's Overseas Traders, 1550–1653* (Princeton, NJ: Princeton University Press, 1993), 25–27, 42–43. Even allowing for a generous reexport factor, this is impressive growth.

65. W. G. Hoskins, *The Age of Plunder: King Henry's England, 1500–1547* (London: Longman, 1976), 10.

66. See Gregory King, *Natural and Political Observations and Conclusions upon the State and Condition of England* (1696) in *The Earliest Classics,* ed. Peter Laslett (London: Gregg International Publishers Ltd., 1973), 226.

67. Chaudhuri, *East India,* 29, 97.

68. Chaudhuri, *East India,* 29.

69. And, as Robert Ashton pointed out, while shortfalls under Elizabeth I had been due to "the extraordinary charges of the Spanish War and the Irish Revolt," James I was racking up deficits of "*ordinary* expenditure." For which, see Robert Ashton, "Deficit Finance in the Reign of James I," *Economic History Review,* 2d ser., 10, no. 1 (Aug. 1957): 18.

70. Theodore K. Rabb, "Investment in English Overseas Enterprise, 1575–1630," *Economic History Review,* 2d ser., 19, no. 1 (Apr. 1966): 70, 73.

71. Rabb, "Overseas Enterprise," 72, 74. Compare, however, Brenner, *Merchants and Revolution,* 107. Robert Brenner takes the predominance of smaller investors in the Virginia Company (an average of £35 per gentry investor) to mean that gentry involvement was widespread but merely casual. Whether one company's records should be used as the basis of such a characterization is highly arguable. But even Brenner agrees with Rabb on the preponderance of even an unwilling Parliamentary investment in keeping foreign trade on the table.

72. Chaudhuri, *East India,* 36.

73. Rabb, "Overseas Enterprise," 75.

74. See, for example, J. E. Neale, *Elizabeth I and her Parliaments, 1584–1604* (New York: St. Martin's, 1958), 370, 384–88.

75. Robert Ashton, "The Parliamentary Agitation for Free Trade in the Opening Years of the Reign of James I," *Past and Present* 38 (Dec. 1967): 41, 43. The controversy over whether this was mainly a center-provincial or a stock-regulated conflict can be followed if one begins with Theodore K. Rabb, "Sir Edwin Sandys and the Parliament of 1604," *American Historical Review* 69, no. 3 (Apr. 1964): 646–70, and then continues with the Ashton article cited above, Rabb's rejoinder, "Free Trade and the Gentry in the Parliament of 1604," *Past and Present* 40 (Jul. 1968): 165–73, and Ashton's response, "Jacobean Free Trade Again," *Past and Present* 43 (May 1969): 151–57.

76. See, for example, references in *The Case of the Army* and *The [first] Agreement*

of the People cited in Maurice Ashley, *Financial and Commercial Policy under the Cromwellian Protectorate*, 2d ed. (London: Frank Cass and Company Ltd., 1962), 34–35.

77. For which, see Robert Burton Ekelund Jr. and Robert D. Tollison, *Mercantilism as a Rent-Seeking Society: Economic Regulation in Historical Perspective* (College Station: Texas A&M University Press, 1981) 5, 18–21, 155–56. Although, in making the balance of trade "nothing more than the by-product" of the "supply and demand for monopoly rights" (5), the authors push their case further than the evidence will support.

78. Misselden, *Circle of Commerce*, 69–70.

79. Misselden, *Free Trade*, 84–86.

80. Ibid., 79, 111, 133. See also *Calendar of State Papers, Domestic: James I (Vol. 10), 1619–1623*, 247 (no. 95, 17 Apr. 1621). There had been a regulated Spanish Company chartered in 1577. Its charter lapsed in 1585, was renewed in 1605 after peace was restored, but Parliament disallowed the charter in 1606, and competition from the Dutch after their truce with Spain in 1609 further complicated matters. See Friis, *Alderman Cockayne*, 156–58, 161–62, 169–71, on the various attempts to reconstitute a Spanish Company. See also Misselden, *Free Trade*, 74, 76–80. His argument was far from consistent. He also put the diminution of the Hanse's trade to their own loss of privilege and had to allow that Holland prospered with unregulated trade but only because of the civic-mindedness of its citizens. He also included the East India Company among those companies helping to improve England's economy, though a major thrust of his book was against the exportation of *European* coin out of Christendom, and he specifically cited joint-stock companies as most likely to be true monopolies (ibid., 70).

81. See Misselden, *Circle of Commerce*, unpaged dedication to Middlesex, and 66. The accusation was raised (66) that the office of Royal Exchanger would itself be a monopoly; this was technically true, given Misselden's characterization of the same, but what it would really do was interfere with the East India Company's ability to export specie.

82. Misselden, *Free Trade*, 57–58. Misselden based (and acknowledged) his definition of monopoly on the discussion of the same in Johannes Althusius, *Politica methodice digesta, atque exemplis sacris et profanis illustrata* (1603), cap. 31–32.

83. For Aristotle, there could be no true reciprocity between (social) unequals, though there could be a proportional reciprocity between the value of products exchanged. For which, see *Ethics* V.v.1–14 and the discussion of friendship between unequals in ibid., VIII.vii.1–6.

84. Misselden, *Free Trade*, 63.

85. Ibid., 65–68.

86. Ibid., 58, 60–61.

87. Ibid., 134, with marginal citation to Cicero's *De legibus*. But the passage does not appear to be in that work, nor in Cicero's *De Re Publica*. The closest parallel would seem to be Mark 3:24–25 ("And if a kingdom be divided against itself, that kingdom cannot stand. And if a house be divided against itself, that house cannot stand").

88. Spiegel suggested that the term had to wait for Chamberlin's 1933 reintroduction of it in his *Theory of Monopolistic Competition* because the word only appeared in the original Latin edition of *Utopia* and not in its seventeenth-century English translations. For which, see Spiegel, *Growth*, 105. Marginal notations in Misselden's works, however, make it clear that he had read his More in the original Latin. Misselden did not have much of a sense of humor and likely missed the playful irony as well as increased exactitude More meant the term to convey.

89. Compare Richard Olson, *The Emergence of the Social Sciences, 1642–1792* (New York: Twayne, 1993), 68. While we agree on the importance of medical theory in the development of economics, I take the physician's manipulative role as both an earlier influence (Olson sees it as coming in with Petty) and, in a sense, a more obstructive one in the development of the idea of economic laws (where Olson sees it as a force in the development both of cameralism and economic liberalism).

90. Misselden, *Free Trade*, 7.

91. This is the "maker's right" on which John Locke would later build his justification of private property. For this century, a right always implied a power to execute that right.

92. Misselden, *Free Trade*, 107–8. Similarly, ibid., 10–11.

93. Chaudhuri, *East India*, 29, 116–17, 119.

94. Misselden, *Circle of Commerce*, 97.

95. Ibid.

96. Ibid., 95, 97.

97. Ibid., 97. Misselden's placing these remarks just after some paragraphs on More's *Utopia* and the nature of barter would seem to indicate he was relegating this kind of equal exchange to an earlier stage of civil development if not to that fictional state of nature itself. For Misselden on *Utopia*, see *Circle of Commerce*, 95.

98. Ibid., 98.

99. Misselden, *Free Trade*, 21.

100. Misselden, *Circle of Commerce*, 20.

101. Misselden, *Circle of Commerce*, 100, 113.

102. Ibid., 112 (marginal note to Bodin's *Republic*, Book I).

103. Eric Roll suggested that it might "also be claimed that when he [Misselden] came to write *The Circle of Commerce* he had appreciated better the general class interests for which he stood and ceased to represent a narrow self-interest." For this, see Roll, *Economic Thought*, 76. He had certainly reached a better understanding of the need of the import-export trade to rid itself of bullion and credit restrictions but this did not require a deep understanding of prices and values.

104. Misselden, *Circle of Commerce*, 131. In 1621, Thomas Mun, a director of the East India Company, had published a defense of its practices under the title of *A Discourse of Trade*. Edward Misselden praised the work in passing in his *Free Trade*, without, it would seem, noticing that Mun was advocating bullion policies Misselden's own work attacked. In truth, Misselden's praise for the work likely had as much to do with its ancillary critiques of the state of affairs in England—the idle poor, coin-culling, plate-hoarding, and the like—as with its support for an export surplus (and rejection of *par pro pari*). For which, see Misselden, *Free Trade*, 78.

105. Misselden, *Free Trade*, 13, 35, 70, 103, 111, 115–16.

106. Misselden, *Circle of Commerce*, 139.

107. Misselden, *Free Trade*, 19–20.

108. Ibid., 23: "the more the stocke of Christendome is thereby encreased in Wares, the more it decreaseth in Treasure."

109. Ibid., 20. Within the context of this argument, the "true nature" was not a definition of commerce but an opinion as to which was the proper form of commerce for a nation to engage in. Like Malynes, Misselden covered trade as wares for wares (not as barter but as trade within the limits of the Statute of Employments), money for wares

(trade from Christendom to the Indies), or money for money (the "Merchandizing Exchange" for Malynes or the "Politique Exchange" for Misselden).

Chapter 4

1. Mun's *Discourse of Trade* went through a second "corrected and amended" edition in 1621 before being reprinted in Purchas's "Pilgrimes" in 1625 and then disappeared from print until the Political Economy Club brought it back in a collection of rare tracts in 1856.

2. Smith, *Wealth of Nations,* 1:453 (the seed-time analogy quoted), 1:453n (the name of the book) [IV.1].

3. See Roger Coke, *Discourse of Trade* (1670), 37; and his *Treatise wherein is demonstrated that the Church and State of England are in equal danger with the Trade of it* (1671), 72, 75; Nicholas Barbon, *Discourse of Trade* (1680), preface, but check 3–6 where Barbon argues against Mun; *Britannia Languens, or A Discourse of Trade: shewing The grounds and Reasons of the Increase and Decay of Land-Rents, National Wealth and Strength.* . . . (London, 1680), 91; *England's Great Happiness; or a Dialogue between Content and Complaint.* . . . (London, 1677), 10.

4. See, for example, Appleby, *Economic Thought,* 38 (on Mun's "Grand design that linked country to country and knit together the interest of merchants, landlords, and servants"); Spiegel, *Growth,* 112 (on the "germ" of "monetary theory" in Mun's works); and Blaug, *Economic Theory,* 13 (that Mun was the first to realize that market forces made favorable trade balances impossible of being sustained in the long run).

5. James R. Jacob, "The Political Economy of Science in Seventeenth-Century England," *Social Research* 59, no. 3 (fall 1992): 527.

6. See Mayling Stubbs, "John Beale, Philosophical Gardener of Herefordshire. Part II: The Improvement of Agriculture and Trade in the Royal Society (1663–1683)," *Annals of Science* 46, no. 4 (Jul. 1989): 325, 348, 350–51.

7. See ibid., 354–55. Stubbs also draws on an earlier article by James R. Jacob, "Restoration Ideologies and the Royal Society," *History of Science* 18 (1980): 33.

8. This is not to say that one cannot construct a coherent economic theory based on value; in the eighteenth century classical economics would do just that. But the classical economists not only developed sharper analytical tools (in their concepts of the surplus, factors of production, and the rate of profit), they did so within the confines of a radically different intellectual context (especially with respect to the Enlightenment's ideas of growth and progress).

9. Challis, *Tudor Coinage,* 318–21 (appendix III).

10. Mun, *Englands Treasure,* 44–47; he made an additional mention of his long sojourn there on page 126. See also Raymond de Roover, "Thomas Mun in Italy," *Bulletin of the Institute of Historical Research* 30 (1957): 81–83; de Roover placed Mun's arrival in Italy between 1596 and 1598.

11. De Roover, "Thomas Mun in Italy," 82–83.

12. Bernardo Davanzati, *Discourse upon Coins* (1696 edition), 20; quoted in de Roover, "Thomas Mun in Italy," 84.

13. See, for example, *Calendar of State Papers, Colonial Series (vol. 4), 1622–1624,* 179, 182, 238, 382.

14. For Mun's appointment to the group of commissioners to reopen negotiations with the Dutch, see *Calendar of State Papers, Colonial (vol. 8), 1630–1634*, 300, although nothing seems to have come of it.

15. See ibid., 148, 404–5, 408, 453–55.

16. See ibid., 310, 319–20, 448–49.

17. See *Calendar of State Papers, Colonial (vol. 3), 1617–1621*, 484, 485, 488.

18. *Calendar of State Papers, Colonial (vol. 4), 1622–1624*, 262, 299–300. Mun having begged off, one Clitherow was elected deputy, but Mun remained on the Director's Committee.

19. *Calendar of State Papers, Colonial (vol. 3), 1617–1621*, 431 (1621?); not the list itself, but see the citation to *Commons Journals* I:510–01 (6 Feb. 1621).

20. *Calendar of State Papers, Colonial (vol. 4), 1622–1624*, 267; also 256, for Mun's being charged with proving to Parliament that the Company would not export £80,000 in bullion as charged by the House of Commons.

21. Mun, *Englands Treasure*, 3–4.

22. Ibid., 6–8, 25, 31, 34, 56.

23. Ibid., 31.

24. Ibid., 42–43.

25. Ibid., 12, 45.

26. Mun, *Englands Treasure*, 42. De Roover ("Thomas Mun in Italy," 80) used the revival of the Office of Royal Exchanger in 1627 and a cutoff of trade with Spain and France lasting from 1625 to 1628 to suggest a composition date of 1626–1628. But it is impossible to tell from Mun's reference to the Office of Royal Exchanger whether he is attacking a newly resurrected office or the suggestion that such an office be resurrected. The trade with Spain and France was not officially reopened until 1630. Blaug (*Economic Theory*, 13) put the work only "as early as 1630," perhaps having decided that Mun was aware of this restarted trade. Supple ("Commercial Crisis," 91–94) came up with 1622/1623 based on marked similarities between certain sections of *Englands Treasure* and four (unpublished) memoranda submitted by Mun to the Commission for Trade during that period.

27. Mun, *Englands Treasure*, 49, 53, 60.

28. Ibid., 1–3.

29. Ibid., viii.

30. Max Beer (*Early British Economics*, 177, 182–83) suggested there was a direct correlation between Mun's increasing political distance from the Crown and his decision not to publish *Englands Treasure*.

31. Mun, *Englands Treasure*, 61.

32. Ibid., 12.

33. Mun, *Discourse*, 6; *Englands Treasure*, 186, 188.

34. On classical cites, see, for example, ibid., 65, 80, 186, 188; on Malynes, see ibid., 42ff, with marginal notes to Malynes's *Canker, Free Trade, Lex Mercatoria*, and *Center of the Circle*.

35. Mun, *Discourse*, 1–2.

36. Ibid., 2–3.

37. Mun, *Englands Treasure*, 7; similarly, ibid., 72–73.

38. As, for example, by Dobb, *Development of Capitalism*, 204n.

39. Mun, *Englands Treasure*, 72.

40. These are the "good laws" referred to in *Englands Treasure*, 7.

41. Mun, *Discourse*, 3.

42. Mun, *Discourse*, 49–50. See, similarly, *Englands Treasure*, 12.

43. Mun, *Discourse*, 7.

44. Ibid., 42.

45. Ibid., 35–36.

46. Ibid., 36.

47. See Stubbs, "John Beal," 357–58, and Jacob, "Restoration Ideologies," 28.

48. Mun, *Englands Treasure*, 60.

49. Ibid.

50. Ibid.

51. Ibid.

52. Ibid., 7.

53. Ibid., 13.

54. Mun, *Englands Treasure*, 9, 11, 12, 48–49.

55. Mun, *Discourse*, 51–54.

56. Ibid., 55.

57. This might also have been the result of Mun's connection with the Levant Company. Though originally a joint-stock company, it had drifted into regulation before its dissolution in 1603 and was so reconstituted as a regulated company in 1605. For which, see Ashton, "Parliamentary Agitation," 50. Regulated companies, as discussed in a previous chapter, were extremely anxious to keep nonmerchants out of their markets. Mun's own continued activity against interlopers into the East India trade has already been discussed.

58. Mun, *Englands Treasure*, 32, 34–36.

59. Ibid., 39–40.

60. Ibid., 32.

61. Ibid., 16–17.

62. Ibid., 87.

63. Appleby (*Economic Thought*, 39, 41) took the position that Mun was successful in this effort and that it represented a consciously chosen theoretical promarket and antibullionist position.

64. Mun, *Englands Treasure*, 1.

65. Ibid, 32.

66. *O.E.D.* XI:112–13. In *Englands Treasure*, 54, Mun claimed that no prince could "make the staple of Money run where he pleaseth," but this does not explain how a prince who could not directly control the flow of money could prevent its "tolleration" at nonstandard values.

67. Mun, *Englands Treasure*, 28–30.

68. Ibid., 69.

69. Ibid., 69–70.

70. Compare Marian Bowley, *Studies in the History of Economic Theory before 1870* (London: Macmillan Press Ltd., 1973), 19, on Mun's not appearing "to have considered that similar activities by individuals [to those discussed of princes] had any implications for economic activity in general terms."

71. Mun, *Englands Treasure*, 70.

72. Ibid., 73; similarly, ibid., 82.

Chapter 5

1. Aquinas, *Summa Theologiae* II-II (a.1)

2. Jacob Viner, "Religious Thought and Economic Society: Four Chapters from an Unfinished Work by Jacob Viner," ed. Jacques Melitz and Donald Winch, *History of Political Economy* 10, no. 1 (spring 1978): 62.

3. Mun, *Englands Treasure*, 22–23.

4. For citations going back to 1381 and spanning the sixteenth century in particular, see Viner, *International Trade*, 6–7.

5. See Malynes, *Canker*, 3, 16, and *Englands View*, 6, among other cites. Without the use of the term *overballancing* but with the same sense, see his *Free Trade*, 77, and *Center of the Circle*, 44. For the equation of a trade deficit with "inequalitie in a commonwealth," see *St. George*, unpaged epistle to the reader. See Viner, *International Trade*, 8, for terms such as *overplus* and *countervail* used in the same sense in late-sixteenth- and early-seventeenth-century pamphlets.

6. See Malynes, *Englands View*, 6, 70, 148; *Canker*, 12, 17; *Free Trade*, 22; and *Lex Mercatoria*, 59.

7. Malynes, *Center of the Circle*, 55–56, 58. Suviranta appears to have been the first to notice that Malynes had himself (in *Englands View*, 148) pointed to the customs' records as a source for a possible balance: "this overballancing is knowne by the increase of the custome of the goods inwarde, and the decrease of the custome of the goods outwards." For which (and the same idea in Misselden and Mun), see Bruno Suviranta, *The Theory of the Balance of Trade in England: A Study in Mercantilism* (Helsingors: privately printed, 1923; facsimile reprint, New York: A. M. Kelley, 1967), 35.

8. Malynes, *Center of the Circle*, 55, 66.

9. Ibid., 57.

10. Sir Francis Bacon, "A Letter of Advice, written by Sir Francis Bacon to the Duke of Buckingham, when he became Favorite to King James I," First Version, in *The Works of Francis Bacon*, ed. James Spedding, Robert Leslie Ellis, and Douglas Denon Heath (London: Longman and Company, Ltd., 1857–1874; facsimile reprint, New York: Garrett, 1968), 13:22 [full text runs 13–26]. The "Letter" itself first appeared in print in Blackbourne's 1730 edition of Bacon's *Opera omnia*. See also Bacon, "Of Seditions and Troubles," in *Essays*, 61. Beer (*Early British Economics*, 139) gave Bacon credit for popularizing the term and the idea "among the public at large," though it was probably in general use in the trading community beforehand. But as to actual coinage, see Viner, *International Trade*, 8 (and his citation of W. H. Price's "The origin of the phrase 'balance of trade,'" *Quarterly Journal of Economics* 20 (1955): 157ff), on the use of the term in a balance drawn up by two customs officials in 1615.

11. Misselden, *Circle of Commerce*, 130. See the balance drawn up in ibid., 127–29, for the terms *debitor* and *creditor* used in this regard; also, Beer, *Early British Economics*, 136–37. See Malynes, *Center of the Circle*, 55, for the use of *trial* with this balance. For the trade balance equated with the Commonwealth's "income and expenses," see Malynes, *Englands View*, 106.

12. Malynes, *Canker*, 5.

13. "Instructions to the Commission on Trade, October 1622" in *Seventeenth-Century Economic Documents*, ed. Joan Thirsk and J. P. Cooper (Oxford: Clarendon, 1972), 20. Beer (*Early British Economics*, 150–52) took the words "the true ballance of the trade" in the instructions to the 1622 Commission in this light. Compare, however, Otto

Mayr's contention that balance as equilibrium was essentially a liberal-leaning idea while "the older aspect" of balance as "an illustration of comparison or difference" was (as the "centerpiece of the doctrine of mercantilism") "congenial to absolutist governments and helped to confirm them in their authoritarian centralism." For which see Otto Mayr, *Authority, Liberty, and Automatic Machinery in Early Modern Europe* (Baltimore: Johns Hopkins University Press, 1986), 146–47.

14. With and without identifying it as from Cato. See, for example, Malynes, *Englands View*, 1, 148; *Free Trade*, 5; and *Lex Mercatoria*, 60. The line is from *De Agri Cultura* II.7 (also known as *De Re Rustica* from the various sixteenth-century combined editions of Cato and Varro).

15. Misselden, *Free Trade*, 12. For this image in Malynes, see, for example, *Canker*, 2; *Englands View*, 1, 148; and *Center of the Circle*, 56.

16. James I, "Speech to Parliament of 3/21/1609 (o.s.)" in *Political Works*, 307.

17. Misselden, *Circle of Commerce*, 124–25.

18. Mun, *Englands Treasure*, 83–85 (also discussing allowances for freight, insurance, and resale profits). In ibid., 43, he also discussed the problem of transactions handled solely through bills of exchange. In our terms, Mun was moving from "balance of trade" to the more comprehensive "balance of payments," but without recognizing these as two distinct concepts. Suviranta (*Balance of Trade*, 34) believed Mun's categorization of nontrade transfers as "things uncertain" might be an attempt at such a distinction.

19. Mun, *Englands Treasure*, 40.

20. Among those who stressed the importance of the East India Company's needs in pushing Mun into the analytical distinction between general and particular balances was Dobb; for which, see Dobb, *Development of Capitalism*, 216. Similarly, Chaudhuri, *East India*, 9.

21. As we have seen, Misselden himself supported such a case in his first book when he supported trade balance theory while backing export restrictions on bullion.

22. For such arguments in Misselden, see *Circle of Commerce*, 32–36. In Mun, see *Englands Treasure*, 18–19, and *Discourse of Trade*, 9, 20–21. Mun's claim that only foreign money was used to buy Indian goods was rather disingenuous. In 1632, while trying to decide whether to apply for a license to export £100,000 in coin or bullion as per the prior year or to ask for an increase, the company decided to keep the request to the lower number, but ask for permission to export up to £40,000 of that amount in Spanish *or* English coin! For which, see *Calendar of State Papers, Colonial (vol. 8), 1630–1634*, 285.

23. Mun, *Englands Treasure*, 19.

24. Roll (*Economic Thought*, 79–80) believed that in the seed-time analogy, Mun not only developed the concept of "stock" (meaning "capital") but turned the "special pleading of the East India Company" into "a pleading for commercial capitalism as such." Grampp ("Liberal Elements," 69) believed it was Mun "who made clear the importance of demand conditions in the export market."

25. With, of course, the analytic caveat that Mun thought the merchant's profits added to the national wealth while the farmer's did not.

26. Misselden, *Circle of Commerce*, 18.

27. Misselden, *Free Trade*, 106–8. In *Circle of Commerce* (21), Misselden rejected Malynes's argument that changes in exchange rates could increase prices across the board, but this was a rejection of the claim for exchange rates as the determining variable and not of the emerging quantity theory itself.

28. Ironically, there is considerable evidence that the movement of rents out-

paced that of prices during the period. For which, see Eric Kerridge, "The Movement of Rent, 1540–1640," *Economic History Review*, 2d ser., 6, no. 1 (Aug. 1953): 17, 19, 21–22, 28. A table (28) using 1510–19 as an index (@ 100) gives rent:wheat prices for Wiltshire in 1600–1609 as 672:435, and for 1620–1629 as 699:513. General price movements, even if any particular landlord had been aware of them, would have been small comfort to the individual whose tenants' leases still had thirty years to run.

29. See E. P. Thompson, "The Moral Economy of the English Crowd in the Eighteenth Century," *Past and Present* 50 (Feb. 1971): 108.

30. Mun, *Englands Treasure*, 17. On "plenty of money" and the price level, see also ibid., 20.

31. Ibid., 12.

32. Ibid., 62.

33. Ibid., 21. See also ibid., 37, 87, on the difference between treasure forced into the kingdom and that brought in by a positive trade balance.

34. See Hinton, "Mercantile System," 282. His is an excellent encapsulation of the problem of the disproportionately high (by modern standards) proportion of working to fixed capital even in the heaviest of their industries, mining.

35. Hinton, "Mercantile System," 285.

36. Malynes, *Canker*, 6; see also *Englands View*, 107; *Lex Mercatoria*, 60, 182.

37. Hugo Grotius, *Mare Liberum sive de ivre quod batavis competit ad indicana commercia, dissertatio* (1608); trans. Ralph van Deman Magoffin, ed. James Brown Scott (New York: Oxford University Press, 1916; reprint, New York: Arno, 1972), 9 (page references are to reprint edition). Grotius's note was to Seneca's *Natural Questions*, III.IV. Misselden copied both the passage from Grotius and the citation error. For which, see Misselden, *Free Trade*, 26 (mispaginated as 24). Book Three of Seneca's *Natural Questions* being about rivers and not about winds, the citation is more likely from V.18.4: *"Quid quod omnibus inter se populis commercium dedit et gentes disspatis locus miscuit? In gens natureae beneficium, si illud in iniuriam suam non vertat hominum furor!"* or "And, too, wind has made communication possible between all peoples and has joined nations which are separated geographically. A great benefit of nature, if the madness of men did not turn it to his own destruction." For which, see Seneca, *Naturales Questiones*, trans. Thomas H. Corcoran (Cambridge, MA: Harvard University Press/Loeb Classical Library, 1971), V.18.4. This adds a very different color to the remark.

38. Misselden, *Free Trade*, 26 [but labeled 24]. This is a translation into Latin of a Greek passage in the margin labeled *"De Repub.* lib.I.cap.9," or, by its more common title, Aristotle's *Politics* I.9 (1257a28). Beer (*Early British Economics*, 56–57) suggested the thirteenth-century Schoolman Ricardus [Richard of Middleton] as a prime source for the transmission of the theory from the ancient to the early modern world; there was "no direct evidence that the writers knew their source." Jacob Viner treated these harmony theories as an alternate tradition coming down through Christian thought from classical sources (tracking it back to Euripides) designed "to serve as evidence of the providential design of the universe, and of the universal brotherhood of man as part of that design." For which, see Jacob Viner, *Essays on the Intellectual History of Economics*, ed. Douglas A. Irwin (Princeton, NJ: Princeton University Press, 1991), 41, 42 ("Each country provides for itself what its climate refuses to it by maritime expeditions of its vessels," from the *Suppliants* of Euripides). Irwin himself gives a number of Christian variants going back to Origen in *Against the Tide: An Intellectual History of Free Trade* (Princeton, NJ: Princeton University Press, 1996), 16.

39. [Smith, Sir Thomas?], *A Discourse of the Commonweal of This Realm of England* (London, 1581), ed. Mary Dewar (Charlottesville: University Press of Virginia, for the Folger Shakespeare Library, 1969), 63. The edition has modern spelling and punctuation. The work was earlier ascribed to Sir John Hales by Elizabeth Hammond. Smith and Hales were both subjects of speculation from the first manuscript circulation of the work in the 1560s. Smith will be used in this paper, more out of convenience than conviction, though Dewar makes a strong case.

40. Malynes, *Lex Mercatoria*, 182.

41. Malynes, *St. George*, unpaged dedication.

42. [Thomas Milles], *The Customers Apology. That is to say, A generall Answere to Informers of all sortes, and their injurious complaints, against the honest reputation of the Collectors of her Maiesties Custome specially in the Out-Portes of this Realme. . . .* (London, 1599), D2.

43. Malynes, *Free Trade*, unpaged dedication; also *Lex Mercatoria*, unpaged dedication; *Center of the Circle*, unpaged dedication; and *Canker*, 125.

44. Bacon, "Of Seditions and Troubles," in *Essays*, 62.

45. Bacon, "Of Empire," in ibid., 79; they were also to avoid letting their neighbors increase their territory or their "approaches".

46. Malynes, *Lex Mercatoria*, 229–30. He was referring to the disastrous outcome of the experiment of the King's Merchant Adventurers. Ultimately, however, he did believe "we should live by the gaines of our home commodities being sold unto other nations." For which, see *Canker*, 44.

47. Misselden, *Free Trade*, 36–39.

48. Mun, *Englands Treasure*, 34–35, already cited.

Chapter 6

1. Richard S. Westfall, *The Construction of Modern Science: Mechanisms and Mechanics* (New York: John Wiley and Sons, 1971), 1. On the function of the new science in reconstructing an epistemological order nearly shattered by Pyrrhonism, see, for example, Popkin, *Scepticism*, 132–33 (Mersenne on "requisite knowledge" as an alternative to Pyrrhonism) or 143–47 (on Gassendi's "atomism"); also Richard Tuck, *Hobbes* (Oxford: Oxford University Press, 1989), 20 ("Hobbes's general purpose of transcending scepticism").

2. Robert Boyle, *The Origins of Forms and Qualities According to the Corpuscular Philosophy* (1666), in *Selected Philosophical Papers of Robert Boyle*, ed. M. A. Stewart (Manchester: Manchester University Press, 1979), 18, 20.

3. The earliest citation of corpuscle in a physiological sense in the *O.E.D.* is from 1741.

4. William Harvey, *The Circulation of the Blood and Other Writings*, trans. Kenneth J. Franklin, with an introduction by Andrew Wear (London: J. M. Dent and Sons Ltd., 1990), 19, 34–37 (comparative anatomical observations), 54–57 (ligature experiments), 49 (output calculations). The mechanical nature of the operation of the circulatory system as described by Harvey is not of itself lessened by his failure to understand the function of the pulmonary transit or by his belief that the heart itself was "enriching" the blood by heating it.

5. Harvey, *Circulation*, 3.

6. Ibid., 46–47.

7. That Harvey, in his *Generatione Animalium* (1651), may have dethroned the heart in favor of the blood itself makes no difference; to change one qualitative sovereign for another does not dethrone the qualitative principle itself. What others read into Harvey's work was a machine; what Harvey saw in it was more the (albeit machinelike) workings-out of the "pulsative faculty or power of the soul." See Wear's "Introduction" to Harvey's *Circulation*, xii. A basic summary of Harvey's "thorough-going Aristotelian[ism]" can be found in Westfall, *Construction*, 90–92. An opposing view of Harvey as a (closet?) republican hermetic neo-Platonist can be found in Christopher Hill, "William Harvey and the Idea of Monarchy," *Past and Present* 27 (Apr. 1964): 60, 63, and Hill's rebuttal in ibid. 31 (Jul. 1965): 97–103, to Gweneth Whitteridge's "William Harvey: A Royalist and no Parliamentarian," in ibid. 30 (Apr. 1965): 104–9. On the link's between Harvey's Aristotelianism and his monarchism, see also I. Bernard Cohen, "Harrington and Harvey: A Theory of the State based on the New Physiology," *Journal of the History of Ideas* 55, no. 2 (Apr. 1994): 192.

8. John Aubrey (fl. 1626–1697), *Brief Lives*, ed. Oliver Lawson Dick (Ann Arbor: University of Michigan Press, 1957), 131.

9. René Descartes, *Discourse of the Method of rightly conducting one's reason and seeking the truth in the sciences, and in addition the Optics, the meteorology and the Geometry, which are essays in this Method* (Leiden, 1637), in *The Philosophical Writings of Descartes*, trans. John Cottingham, Robert Stonehoff, Dugald Murdoch, and Anthony Kenny (Cambridge: Cambridge University Press, 1985–1991), 1:136.

10. Descartes, *Description of the Human Body* (Paris, 1664), in ibid., 1:316.

11. Ibid., 1:316–17. See Westfall (*Construction*, 94) on Cartesian physiology as "basically Galenic physiology reattired in the robes of mechanical philosophy."

12. Descartes, *Meditations on First Philosophy* (Paris, 1641), in *Philosophical Writings*, 2:17. On Descartes's more thorough mechanization of the body as a deliberate elimination of "Harvey's vitalism," see Westfall, *Construction*, 93.

13. Descartes, *Meditations*, in *Philosophical Writings*, 2:20.

14. Ibid., 2:17, 20–21, 59; and *Rules for the Direction of the Mind* (Holland, 1684), in ibid., 1:42.

15. Forset, *Comparative Discourse*, 3.

16. For Hobbes's friendships with Descartes, Harvey, and Petty, see Aubrey, *Brief Lives*, 154, 157–58.

17. For a good summary of this view, see Laurence Berns, "Thomas Hobbes," in *History of Political Philosophy*, 3d ed., ed. Leo Strauss and Joseph Cropsey (Chicago: University of Chicago Press, 1987), 398.

18. See Christensen, "Hobbes and the Physiological Origins of Economic Science," *History of Political Economy* 21, no. 4 (winter 1989): 690. For a view that both influence Hobbes, but giving primacy to the mechanical, see I. Bernard Cohen, "Harrington and Harvey," 195–97.

19. Hobbes, *Leviathan*, 81–82 (Hobbes's introduction).

20. Compare Malynes, *Free Trade*, 38; and *Lex Mercatoria*, 377–78 (already cited), especially for the clearer emphasis on *functional* similarity in Hobbes's choice of nerves than in Malynes's use of the same.

21. Hobbes, *Leviathan*, 294–95 (Chapter 24).

22. Ibid., 300 (Chapter 24).

23. Ibid., 85–86 (Chapter 1). Note also Tuck (*Hobbes*, 48) on an earlier adaptation

by Hobbes of Harvey's concept of the heart as a pump in Hobbes's idea of the sun as alternately contracting and expanding and so pumping light toward the earth (although this view was abandoned by Hobbes after 1645).

24. Hobbes, "Third Set of Objections [Second Objection]," in Descartes, *Philosophical Writings*, 2:122–23. For the contrasting view, linking Hobbes's use of *endeavor* as a synonym for the Latin *conatus* with a concomitant "intensification of the subject," see William Sacksteder, "Speaking about Mind: Endeavor in Hobbes," *Philosophical Forum* 11, no. 1 (fall 1979): 72. See, however, Tuck (*Hobbes*, 43–45) for Hobbes's argument (as part of this "Second Objection") that (1) the sense of a "self" existing apart "from its own perceptions" was "simply a construct arising from our inability to conceive of thinking without a thinker to *do* it," and (2) Hobbes's belief that self-movement was "literally impossible."

25. Although not so intended by Hobbes himself. See Bonar, *Philosophy*, 82.

26. Thomas Hobbes, *Man and Citizen* (*De Homine and De Cive*), ed. Bernard Gert (Indianapolis: Hackett Publishing Company, 1991), 115 (*De Cive* I§7).

27. Hobbes, *Leviathan*, 183 (Chapter 13).

28. Sir Isaiah Berlin, "Hobbes, Locke and Professor Macpherson," *Political Quarterly* 35, no. 4 (Oct. 1964): 448. As Schumpeter noted (*Economic Analysis*, 122), "We need only replace [it] by the opposite [assumption] to realize that this would change the whole picture of the economic process."

Chapter 7

1. Charles Webster, *The Great Instauration: Science, Medicine and Reform, 1626–1660* (New York: Holmes and Meier Publishers, 1976), 8; similarly, ibid., 500–501.

2. Marquis of Lansdowne, ed., *The Petty-Southwell Correspondence, 1676–1687* (London: Constable and Company Ltd., 1928; reprint, New York: Augustus M. Kelley, 1967), 333–34 (page references are to the reprint edition).

3. Karl Marx, *A Contribution to the Critique of Political Economy*, trans. W. Ryazanskaya, ed. Maurice Dobb (New York: International Publishers, 1970), 56.

4. Hutchison (*Before Adam Smith*, 30, 40), for example, thought him "the outstanding economist of the seventeenth century," introducing "a general theoretical and scientific foundation for sounder policy-making, together with the endeavour to estimate quantitatively the elements involved."

5. Aubrey, *Brief Lives*, 237.

6. Though he may have worked as a clothier for a brief period upon his return to England in 1646; for which, see Charles Henry Hull, "Introduction," *The Economic Writings of Sir William Petty. Together with the Observations upon the Bills of Mortality more probably by Captain John Graunt* (Cambridge: Cambridge University Press, 1899; reprint, Fairfield, NJ: Augustus M. Kelley, 1986), xiv (page references are to the reprint edition).

7. Lansdowne, *Correspondence*, 216–17 [Petty to Southwell, 14 July 1686]. Also Aubrey, *Brief Lives*, 237.

8. Petty's silence on his navy service likely had, as Strauss noted, a political cause, since it would have coincided with "the defection of the fleet from Charles I." For which, see Erich Strauss, *Sir William Petty, Portrait of a Genius* (Glencoe, IL: Free Press, 1954), 25.

9. Hull, *Economic Writings*, xiv, gives the date of his matriculation at the University of Leiden as May 26, 1644. Petty also studied at Amsterdam and Utrecht.

10. Strauss, *Petty*, 26, 29.

11. Aubrey, *Brief Lives*, 237.

12. See Hull, *Economic Writings*, xv. According to Aubrey (*Brief Lives*, 238), John Graunt played a major role in Petty's getting the Gresham appointment. See also Strauss (*Petty*, 39–41) on the role of the general reshuffling of academic appointments by the Commonwealth in forwarding Petty's career and on the precedent of a professor of medicine being given the music appointment.

13. Sir William Petty, *The Advice of W. P. to Mr. Samuel Hartlib, For The Advancement of some particular Parts of Learning* (London, 1648). A possible companion piece would have been a *History of Trades* planned but never completed in 1647; for which, see Strauss, *Petty*, 21. The compilation of such a history was a favorite project of the Baconians and the ancestor of the *Encyclopédie*.

14. See Strauss, *Petty*, 30.

15. Olson, *Emergence*, 60. See also Marquis of Lansdowne, ed., *The Petty Papers: Some Unpublished Papers of Sir William Petty* (London: Constable and Company Ltd., 1927; reprint, New York: Augustus M. Kelley, 1967), 2:168–78, for portions of an essay on the art of medicine and an anatomy lecture given in Dublin in 1676 that document his continued advocacy of Harvey's methods and conclusions.

16. Petty's own account of this "resurrection" (giving a decidedly secondary role to Willis) can be found in Lansdowne, *Petty Papers*, 2:157–67. There is a briefer but no less laudatory relation in Aubrey, *Brief Lives*, 238.

17. See *Calendar of State Papers, Domestic: Commonwealth (vol. 4), 1651–1652,* 236, 613; also *Calendar of State Papers, Ireland (vol. 3): 1647–1660 (and Addenda, 1625–1660),* 643.

18. Karl S. Bottigheimer, *English Money and Irish Land: The "Adventurers" in the Cromwellian Settlement of Ireland* (Oxford: Clarendon, 1971), 41, 51, 53.

19. Ibid., 54, 56.

20. Ibid., 133.

21. This is the survey usually known as the "grosse survey" as it was so referred to in the Act of 26 September 1653. Petty's survey became known as the "Down Survey" because its details were set "down" on maps.

22. The Down Survey, technically begun December 11, 1654, with the acceptance of Petty's proposals, was actually completed within the stretch from February 1655 to March 1, 1656. See Hull, *Economic Writings*, xvi–xvii; and Aubrey, *Brief Lives*, 238.

23. See, for example, *Calendar of State Papers, Ireland (vol. 4): Adventurers : 1660–1662 for Land, 1642–1649,* 357, 360–65; *(vol. 5),* 306; and *(vol. 8): 1669–1670 (and Addenda, 1625–1670),* 456–57. Also Hull, *Economic Writings*, xvii–xxi; and Lansdowne, *Correspondence,* 219 [Petty to Southwell, 17 Jul. 1686].

24. William Petty, *The History of the Survey of Ireland commonly called the Down Survey by Doctor William Petty, A. D. 1655–1656,* ed. Thomas Aiskew Larcom (Dublin: Irish Archaeological Society, 1851; reprint, New York: Augustus M. Kelley, 1967). Webster (*Great Instauration,* 453) suggested the problem of sorting out profitable from unprofitable land set Petty on the value-theory road.

25. Petty considered fines the best way to deal with people stubborn enough to insist on a public display of their private liberty of conscience. See, for example, "Liberty of Conscience and Worship," and "Political Observations (1671)," in Lansdowne, *Petty*

Papers, 1:140, 2:235. As examples of his doctrinal minimalism and insistence on public conformity, see ibid., "Religio Catholice Catholica (1685)" and his own Will (written 1685) in ibid., 1:130–31, 2:115.

26. Lansdowne, *Correspondence*, 281.

27. Olson, *Social Sciences*, 60; and Hull, *Economic Writings*, xxii.

28. See Toby Christopher Barnard, *Cromwellian Ireland: English Government and Reform in Ireland, 1649–1660* (New York: Oxford University Press, 1975), 238.

29. In a single Royal Society meeting, Petty submitted papers on the manufacture of woolen cloth, "divers" recommendations for the improvement of shipping and plans for a new type of keel. For which, see John Evelyn, *The Diary of John Evelyn*, ed. E. S. de Beer (Oxford: Clarendon, 1955), 3:304. Petty's paper on cloth dyes was included by Thomas Sprat in his *History;* for which see Thomas Sprat, *The History of the Royal Society of London, For the Improving of Natural Knowledge* (London, 1667), ed. Jackson I. Cope and Harold Whitmore Jones (St. Louis: Washington University Press, 1958), 284–306.

30. Petty's drafts for the Dublin Society's Rules can be found in Lansdowne, *Petty Papers*, 2:88–92.

31. See Samuel Pepys, *The Diary of Samuel Pepys*, ed. Henry B. Wheatley (London: Macmillan and Co. Ltd., 1918), 1:14 (10 Jan. 1660).

32. It was an adaptation of the Calash meant for longer-distance uses. See Lansdowne, *Petty Papers*, 149–50, and Evelyn, *Diary*, 3:416.

33. There were at least three versions of this boat (two hulls joined by transverse connections not unlike the modern catamaran although much, much larger); Strauss makes it four counting a prototype (*Invention I*); for which, see Strauss, *Petty*, 116. The first boat had a successful launch but the two later versions sank. For their various fortunes, see Evelyn, *Diary*, 3:369, 4:57–58; Pepys, *Diary*, 3:217, 223, 283, 369, 4:20, 23–24, 26–27, 293, 330, 333, 354; and *Calendar of State Papers, Ireland (vol. 6): 1663–1665*, 185–87 (25 Jul. 1663), 191–92 (1 Aug. 1663).

34. Aubrey, *Brief Lives*, 240, and Evelyn, *Diary*, 57 ("she was an extraordinary witt, as well as beauty, & a prudent woman"), 60.

35. Aubrey also records the existence of an unnamed natural daughter (mother also not named) acting at "the Duke's Playhouse." For which, see *Brief Lives*, 240.

36. See Alessandro Roncaglia, *Petty: The Origins of Political Economy*, trans. Isabella Cherubini (Armonk, NY: M. E. Sharpe, 1985), 9–10, on Petty's innovative use of vertical integration (copper works taken "from the mine to the blast furnace" and fishing from "the sewing of the fishing nets to the building and operation of the boats") in these ventures.

37. Petty, *Political Arithmetick*, preface, in Hull, *Economic Writings*, 1:244.

38. On Graunt's methodological superiority, see A. M. Endres, "The Functions of Numerical Data in the Writings of Graunt, Petty, and Davenant," *History of Political Economy* 17, no. 2 (summer 1985): 248, 253; and Hull, *Economic Writings*, 1:lxxv–lxxix. John Graunt was the author of *Natural and Political Observations upon the Bills of Mortality* (1662). Petty supplied some rhetorical flourishes and may even have convinced Graunt to publish it, but Petty did not write the treatise. Graunt was a haberdasher who served in the Cromwellian forces (as captain and later as major), was earlier more successful than Petty (and hence able to recommend Petty for the Gresham post), and was recommended to the Royal Society by Charles II on the strength of the *Observations*. Graunt lost any chance of future advancement under the dual blows of financial losses due to

the Great Fire of London (1666) and his conversion to Catholicism. Money and religious matters seem to have initiated the break with Petty. On Graunt's life, see Aubrey, *Brief Lives*, 14–115; and Hull, *Economic Writings*, 1:xxxiv–xxxviii. On the respective contributions of Graunt and Petty to the *Observations*, see Hull, *Economic Writings*, 1:xlix, lii. For the older view favoring Petty, see Lansdowne, *Petty Papers*, 2:273–84.

    39. Hull, *Economic Writings*, 2:533–36.

    40. Letwin, *Scientific Economics*, 145–47.

    41. Ibid., 148.

    42. Olson, *Emergence*, 62.

    43. Lansdowne, *Petty Papers*, 1:27.

    44. Petty, *Political Anatomy of Ireland*, in Hull, *Economic Writings*, 1:181.

    45. James Harrington, *The Art of Lawgiving in Three Books.* . . . (London, 1659), in *Political Works*, 656.

    46. A good analysis of Harrington's use of a specifically Harveyan anatomy can be found in Cohen, "Harrington and Harvey," 199–204.

    47. Lansdowne, *Petty Papers*, 2:171–72. Compare Petty's unpublished essay "Concerning the Study of the Art of Medicine" in ibid., 2:177, in which he compared the "fabrick & the use of the muscells" to the rigging of a ship, the "veines, nerves, arteryes," etc., to the victualing of a ship and so forth. Structural modeling could be applied to the body as well as be drawn from it.

    48. Petty, *Treatise of Taxes*, in ibid., 1:35.

    49. Petty, *Verbum Sapienti* (published 1691 as a supplement to the *Political Anatomy of Ireland*, but probably written 1665), in ibid., 2:113.

    50. Now *Y* as used in GDP calculations.

    51. Roll, *Economic Thought*, 113; also Suviranta, *Balance of Trade*, 66.

    52. Petty, *Verbum Sapienti*, in Hull, *Economic Writings*, 1:112–13.

    53. Petty, *Treatise of Taxes*, in ibid., 1:35–36.

    54. Petty, *Political Arithmetick*, in ibid., 1:310.

    55. Petty, *Treatise of Taxes*, in ibid., 1:36 (τά χρήσα here in the sense of "acceptable alternatives"). On land banks providing "money" to run trade, see also Petty, *Political Anatomy of Ireland*, in Hull, *Economic Writings*, 1:219; and "Registry of Lands, Commodities, and Inhabitants (1660–1661)," and "A Colloquium between A. B. C. concerning a New Instrument of Government (1682)" in Lansdowne, *Petty Papers*, 1:78, 1:87, 1:109. Petty was especially concerned to see such a bank established for Ireland which he believed to be suffering from a shortage of coin sufficient to drive its potential trade.

    56. Sir William Temple, *Observations upon the United Provinces of the Netherlands* (1673), ed. Sir George N. Clark (Oxford: Clarendon, 1972), 56–57, 112, 115; and Sir Josiah Child, *Brief Observations concerning Trade, and Interest of Money* (London, 1668), in William Letwin, *Sir Josiah Child, Merchant Economist* (Boston: Harvard Graduate School of Business Administration, 1959), 43–44. In Petty's version, the banks would take plate, jewels, cloth, and "other durable Commodities" in deposit as well as coin. For which, see *Treatise of Taxes*, in Hull, *Economic Writings*, 1:26. Petty can be found praising Dutch banks and land registries in *Political Arithmetick*, in ibid., 1:264–65.

    57. Hartlib's *An Essay upon Mr. William Potter's Design concerning a bank of lands* appearing in *A Discoverie for Division or Setting out of Land.* . . . (1653), 25–33, and Potter's *The Key of Wealth* (1650), 38, 45, 66, are discussed in J. Keith Horsefield, *British Monetary Experiments, 1650–1710* (London: G. Bell and Sons Ltd., 1960), 94–95. For a discussion of Petty's proposals, see ibid., 98.

58. On the priority of the Asgill-Barbon bank over those of Chamberlen and Briscoe, see ibid., 197.

59. Petty, *Quantulumcunque*, in Hull, *Economic Writings*, 2:446.

60. Ibid.

61. Ibid., 2:446, 2:447.

62. Interest rates were also a particular concern of landowners for they consistently exceeded the expected gross return on investment in land, though they did generally respond to declines in the number of years purchase (to the extent that statute allowed). For a discussion of which, see Robert C. Allen, "The Price of Freehold Land and the Interest Rate in the Seventeenth and Eighteenth Centuries," *Economic History Review*, 2d ser., 41, no. 1 (Feb. 1988): 34 (table I). The expected gross return on 20 years' purchase is 5 percent but the mortgage interest rate from 1600 to 1646 when land regularly sold at 20 years' purchase was set by statute first at 10 and then later at 8 percent. For the period (ca. 1651–1689) when Petty alternately gives 20 or 21 years as the usual purchase rate, Allen documents a rate varying from 17 to 19 years' purchase or an expected gross return of from 5.26 to 5.88 percent as against a mortgage interest rate of 6 percent, although there would have undoubtedly been cases of lenders who demanded and got more from particular borrowers.

63. Petty, "Of Interest" and "Interest," in Lansdowne, *Petty Papers*, 1:246–48. Note also "the natural fall of Interest, is the effect of the increase of Mony." For which, see *Political Arithmetick*, in Hull, *Economic Writings*, 1:304.

64. Oliver Cromwell, *Speeches of Oliver Cromwell*, ed. Ivan Roots (London: J. M. Dent and Sons Ltd., 1989), 162. For the ongoing budget problems of the Protectorate, see Ashley, *Financial and Commercial Policy*, 96.

65. See Howard Tomlinson, "Financial and Administrative Developments in England, 1660–1688," in *The Restored Monarchy, 1660–1688*, ed. J. R. Jones (Totowa, NJ: Rowman and Littlefield, 1979), 100–104.

66. Patrick K. O'Brien, "The Political Economy of British Taxation, 1660–1815," *Economic History Review*, 2d ser., 41, no. 1 (Feb. 1988): 9 [taking the totals of the five-year averages from the table].

67. [William Wither], *Proposals to the Officers of the Army, And to the City of London for The taking of all Excise, Taxes, and Custom with A Perfect Unity of the Army, City, and Commons of England, for a Free Parliament, And a firm Peace, throughout the Three Nations* (London, 1660), 4.

68. Petty, *Treatise of Taxes*, in Hull, *Economic Writings* 1:62 (referring to *12 Car. II, c.9* of September 1660).

69. Ibid., 1:94.

70. Petty, "Heads of Irish Revenue, (c. 1682)" in Lansdowne, *Petty Papers*, 1:96–97. The professions and titles used in the proposals were meant as shorthand for income levels, not as titles qua titles; Petty believed that "Titles of Faculties and callings ought to be no Qualification in a Poll-money, because they do not necessarily nore probably inferr ability to pay." For which, see *Treatise of Taxes*, in Hull, *Economic Writings*, 1:64. An alternative schedule of taxation levels along the same principles appears in "Of a Poll Bill (1685)" in Lansdowne, *Petty Papers*, 1:182–87.

71. See Peter Buck, "Seventeenth-Century Political Arithmetic: Civil Strife and Vital Statistics," *Isis* 68, no. 241 (Mar. 1977): 75.

72. See Petty, *Treatise of Taxes*, in Hull, *Economic Writings*, 1:55–56, 91–92.

73. Petty, "In Merchandize (n.d.)," in Lansdowne, *Petty Papers*, 1:190–92.

74. Petty, *Political Anatomy of Ireland*, in Hull, *Economic Writings*, 1:187: "Interest must enflame the price of Irish Commodities, and consequently give to other Nations the means of underselling."

75. Ibid., 1:181.

76. It is Hadden's thesis (building on the work of Franz Borkenau) that the mathematicians learned how to do this from the merchants, making the "mathematical-mechanistic world-picture" a "reification of the social relations of commodity exchange." For which, see Richard W. Hadden, *On the Shoulders of Merchants: Exchange and the Mathematical Conception of Nature in Early Modern Europe* (Albany: State University of New York Press, 1994), xv. Certainly the two use parallel solutions.

77. Petty, *Treatise of Taxes*, in Hull, *Economic Writings*, 1:45.

78. "Sir William Petty: An Unpublished Manuscript," ed. Shichiro Matsukawa, *Hitotsubashi Journal of Economics* 17, no. 2 (Feb. 1977): 47.

79. Petty, "In Merchandize," in Lansdowne, *Petty Papers*, 1:192.

80. Characterized as an attempt at a labor theory, Routh (*Origin*, 37–38). As a land-labor theory, Spiegel (*Growth*, 128). As a land theory anticipating Physiocratic thought: Tony Aspromourgos, *On the Origins of Classical Economics: Distribution and Value from William Petty to Adam Smith* (London: Routledge, 1996), 22; Hans Brems, "Cantillon versus Marx: The Land Theory and the Labor Theory of Value," *History of Political Economy* 10 (winter 1978): 669; and David McNally, *Political Economy and the Rise of Capitalism: A Reinterpretation* (Berkeley: University of California Press, 1988), 52. As a land theory if anything at all (meaning as primarily nonsensical), Schumpeter (*Economic Analaysis*, 214). As "brilliant" but merely *obiter dicta*, Meek (*Studies*, 96). Karl Marx, *Theories of Surplus Value*, trans. Emile Burns, ed. S. Ryazanskaya (Moscow: Progress Publishers, 1963), 1:346, 352, treated it as a labor theory but noted its similarities to Physiocratic thought in taking rent of land as the "*true form* of surplus-value" and use of the day's food rather than the day's labor as a measure in one instance.

81. Petty, *Treatise of Taxes*, in Hull, *Economic Writings*, 1:43.

82. Ibid.

83. Ibid., 1:43, 49–50.

84. Petty, *Political Anatomy of Ireland*, in ibid., 1:181. Sir Eric Roll held that this "anticipates Ricardo's natural price of labour." For which, see Roll, *Economic Thought*, 108.

85. Petty, *Verbum Sapienti*, in Hull, *Economic Writings*, 1:110.

86. Ibid., 1:117.

87. Petty, *Political Anatomy of Ireland*, in ibid., 1:182.

88. Petty, *Treatise of Taxes*, in ibid., 1:33. It was in remarks like these that Petty began to separate himself from his fellow Baconians. For the more orthodox Baconian line, see Jacob, "Political Economy of Science," 508, 516–17 (Wren on "moderate riches"), 519 (Wilkins of "occasions" and "status"), 526 ("just desserts" and industriousness).

89. Petty, *Treatise of Taxes*, in Hull, *Economic Writings*, 1:23.

90. Petty, *Political Arithmetick*, in ibid., 1:269. According to Hutchison (*Before Adam Smith*, 32) Petty was a veritable proto-Keynesian, believing that "If the money supply was excessive, a budget surplus, or government hoarding, would be in order; but if, on the other hand, the money supply were insufficient, then, excess taxation, or a budget surplus, would 'leave less money than is necessary to drive the nation's trade.'" But (1) Petty's idea of "excessive" taxation was higher taxes than an economy could bear, not taxes unspent, and (2) he never under any circumstances advocated government

hoarding. Compare Roncaglia (*Petty,* 47), who presents a Petty who rejects policies designed to create a deliberate surplus as well as those which would rely on deficit spending.

91. See Roncaglia (*Petty,* 44, 68) on avoiding overequalization of incomes and on wage limits. According to Aspromourgos (*Classical Economics,* 24) for Petty "taxation and public expenditure constitute[d] extraction and redistribution of surplus product, in the service of political purposes." The question then becomes, to what political purpose.

92. Compare Olson (*Emergence,* 68). Olson wished to extend the idea of a medical influence on the development of economic theory to allow for differing medical traditions creating differing theories. To wit, a cameralist approach (in Becher) resulting from a Paracelsian emphasis "on the use of proper diet and medication to assist natural processes," as contrasted to a "liberal" approach (in Petty, Locke, and Quesnay) resulting from a "Cartesian" anatomical emphasis "on removing pathological conditions." Considering the tremendous role Petty allocated to the state in force-feeding the population that "proper diet," I cannot imagine what Olson meant here.

93. Petty, *Political Arithmetick,* in Hull, *Economic Writings* 1:269. Or, as Roncaglia put it, "a sector is more productive the more durable the output that it produces." For which, see Roncaglia, *Petty,* 56.

94. Petty, *Political Arithmetick,* in Hull, *Economic Writings,* 1:269.

95. Petty, *Treatise of Taxes,* in ibid., 1:22.

96. Ibid., 1:28.

97. Ibid., 1:68.

98. Petty, *Verbum Sapienti,* in ibid., 1:105–7. Brewer stressed the pervasiveness of an "accounting framework" in Petty's economic constructions. For which, see Anthony Brewer, "Petty and Cantillon," *History of Political Economy,* 24, no. 3 (fall 1992): 713. Spiegel, *Growth,* 126, considers Petty's "conceptual derivation of the national income" to be his "outstanding achievement."

99. Petty, *Treatise of Taxes,* in Hull, *Economic Writings,* 1:91. See also ibid., 1:51, for a definition of wealth as hiring power.

100. Ibid., 1:32.

101. Petty, *Political Arithmetick,* in ibid., 1:269.

102. Petty, "Political Observations (1671)," in Lansdowne, *Petty Papers,* 2:231–32.

103. Petty, *Political Arithmetick,* in Hull, *Economic Writings,* 1:295.

104. Sir Richard Weston, *A Discourse of Husbandrie used in Brabant and Flanders; shewing The wonderful improvement of Land there; and serving as a pattern for our practice in this Commonwealth* (London, 1650), 4, 18–19.

105. Samuel Hartlib, *Samuel Hartlib his Legacy of Husbandry. . . .* (3d ed., London, 1655), 37–38, 41, 55.

106. John Wilkins, *Mathematical Magick: or, the Wonders that may be performed by Mechanical Geometry. . . .* (London, 1649), in *The Mechanical and Philosophical Works of the Right Rev. John Wilkins, Late Lord Bishop of Chester. To which is prefixed the Author's Life, and an account of his Works* (London, 1708); facsimile reprint (London: Frank Cass and Company Ltd., 1970), 92.

107. Hartlib, *Legacy,* 175. There is at least one extra "to" in this sentence, and probably a missing "be" (be content?).

108. Petty, *Political Arithmetick,* in Hull, *Economic Writings,* 1:249.

109. Ibid., 1:260. For Smith, see *Wealth of Nations,* 7–11. Marx believed the credit for this concept belonged to Petty rather than to Smith; see Marx, *Contribution,* 57n.

But the earliest mention is probably Xenophon's (*Cyropaedia*, 8.2.5.) example of the division of labor in the palace complex of the Persian monarch. Finley ("Aristotle," 3–4) rejected this as economic analysis because it focused on the difference in quality rather than on quantity produced by the division of labor. Compare, however, S. Todd Lowry, *The Archaeology of Economic Ideas: The Classical Greek Tradition* (Durham: Duke University Press, 1987), 69–70. Lowry saw that Finley's rejection was really based on the ahistoric nature of Finley's definition of an economy as a "market system" and a "separate entity" within the social order. As such a market system did not exist in Xenophon's day, it was not then unreasonable to view economic functions as "embedded" within a social fabric and treat them analytically as such. The difference, then, is not one of analytical depth but of underlying assumptions.

110. Petty, *Another Essay*, in Hull, *Economic Writings*, 2:473.

111. This practical application of the division of labor and its links to Petty's later writings was discussed by Strauss, *Petty*, 62–63; Petty, *Down Survey*, 53, 111 (also Larcom's "notes," 322–23); and Webster, *Great Instauration*, 436–41. Webster also noted that Petty's methods "made the survey a model demonstration of the potentialities of Baconian collaborative enterprise" (437).

112. Petty, *Political Arithmetick*, in Hull, *Economic Writings*, 1:256.

113. Fortrey, *Englands Interest*, 219. The most detailed treatment of the push for greater population is still that of Furniss; for which, see Edgar Stephenson Furniss, *The Position of the Laborer in a System of Nationalism: A Study in the Labor Theories of the Later English Mercantilists* (Boston: Houghton Mifflin Co., 1920), Chapter 2, passim.

114. Petty, "An Explication of Trade and its Increase (n.d.)," in Lansdowne, *Petty Papers*, 1:213–14.

115. Petty, "Inclosing Commons," in Lansdowne, *Petty Papers*, 2:129–30.

116. Petty, *Another Essay in Political Arithmetick* (1683), in Hull, *Economic Writings*, 2:468.

117. "Of Marriages," in Lansdowne, *Petty Papers*, 2:50.

118. Petty, "Crimes and Punishments," in ibid., 2:212.

119. Brewer, "Petty and Cantillon," 714.

120. Petty, *Treatise of Taxes*, in Hull, *Economic Writings*, 1:87. On the need to regulate wages in general to keep them "certain," see ibid., 1:52.

121. There is a fascinating series of exchanges between Petty and Southwell on this, Southwell insisting that "if Diamonds grew as common as pebbles, they would be but of the same account," while Petty insisted that the greater the harvest of pilchards the higher their price. For this, see Lansdowne, *Correspondence*, 144–47, 153–59, 160–65.

122. For one of those rare examples, see Lansdowne, *Petty Papers*, 1:247, to the effect that "Encrease of Trade depends chiefly and naturally upon encrease of People and luxury in their consumption."

123. Petty, "A Gross Estimat," in ibid., 1:182.

124. Petty, *Treatise of Taxes*, in Hull, *Economic Writings*, 1:68–69.

125. The best discussion of this is in Glenn Hueckel, "Sir William Petty on Value; a Reconsideration," *Research in the History of Economic Thought and Methodology*, vol. 4 (1986): 37–66; especially his linking of Petty's ideas on "pecuniary mulcts," a magistrate determined "distribution" of the labor force, and a reluctance to depend on market factors (41–44).

126. Né Jan Amos Komenský. See Webster, *Great Instauration*, 42–43, 210. An

earlier account of the mixed influence of Bacon and Comenius can be found in Richard L. Greaves, *The Puritan Revolution and Educational Thought: Background for Reform* (New Brunswick, NJ: Rutgers University Press, 1969), 27–37, but Greaves was more interested in the redirection of this influence into Puritanism rather than into the Hartlib circle proper. Kearney treats Comenius as a Ramist and thus makes Ramus the ultimate source for the utilitarian aspects of this educational movement. For which, see H. F. Kearney, "Puritanism, Capitalism and the Scientific Revolution," *Past and Present* 28 (July 1964): 96.

127. [Samuel Hartlib], *The Parliaments Reformation Or a Worke for Presbyters, Elders, and Deacons, to Engage themselves, for the Education of all poore Children.* . . . (London, 1646), in Charles Webster, *Samuel Hartlib (1600–1662) and the Advancement of Learning* (Cambridge: Cambridge University Press, 1970), 112–13. Reformed adolescents were not released into the parish but returned to the workhouse (113).

128. [John Dury], *Some Proposalls Towards the Advancement of Learning*, an unpublished, unsigned manuscript from 1653, in Webster, *Samuel Hartlib*, 178–81.

129. Petty, *Advice of W. P.*, 3–6.

130. Ibid., 7; see also pages 8–10 on the botanical garden, zoological garden, museum of engines, astronomical observatory, map-room, library, and hospital attached to the college for the compiling of this history as well as for training purposes.

131. Petty, "The Registry of Lands, Commodities, and Inhabitants (1660–1661)," in Lansdowne, *Petty Papers*, 1:90.

132. Petty, "The Uses of the Booke Mention'd by W.P. (1679)," in Lansdowne, *Petty Papers*, 1:173–74. Various versions of Petty's census schemes can be found in "Register Generall of People, Plantations, & Trade of England (1671)," "To Bee the Kings Accomptant (n.d.)," "Of Lands & Hands (n.d.)," "Ten Tooles for making the Crowne and State of England more powerful than any other now in Europe (1686)," and "Advantages humbly offered to the King (1686)," all in ibid., 1: 171–72, 178–79, 193–98, 256, 257.

133. Petty, *Treatise of Taxes*, in Hull, *Economic Writings*, 1:24–30.

134. Ibid., 1:28. Petty's condemnation of "Merchants" was actually broader than most, for his definition was broader. He included anyone "who buys and sells": "grain merchants, grossers [wholesalers], retaylers, speeders [facilitators or go-betweens]," along with the usual importers and exporters. For which, see Petty, "In Merchandize," in Lansdowne, *Petty Papers*, 1:189. For a bullionist like Misselden, merchants brought in wealth so only retailers would be gamesters.

135. Petty, "Political Observations (1671), in Lansdowne, *Petty Papers*, 2:238–39.

136. Macpherson, *Possessive Individualism*, 48.

137. See "Employment for W.P. (1686)," in Lansdowne, *Petty Papers*, 1:258. It is intriguing to think of what Petty would have made of our birth, marriage, and death certificates, social security and national health numbers, professional licenses, and title registry for cars and houses as well as real property. He might think it a statistician's heaven, but one wonders if this man so determined to streamline government payroll ever really considered the size of the bureaucracy needed to gather and sort all that information.

138. Petty, "Of Reconciling the English and Irish and Reforming both Nations (1686)," in Lansdowne, *Petty Papers*, 1:62; the data on the number of families to be moved is on pages 60–61. The project of transplanting is taken up several times. For example, "The State of the Case between England and Ireland (1686?)," in ibid., 1:59.

139. Petty, *Treatise of Ireland*, in Hull, *Economic Writings*, 2:573.

140. See, for example, "Of the House of Commons" in ibid., 1:7–8; Petty was incensed that "The 160m freeholders who chuse but 91 members [are worth] about 160 millions. . . . Whereas the 40m chuse 422 [members] and are not worth 20 millions." Petty did once produce a republican variation on this scheme in a little Latin paper written before the Restoration. Aside from his use of a universal male franchise tempered by increasing indirect elections and the substitution of a civil religion for the Anglican Church, this chain of *centumvirale, chiliarchy, comitatus,* and *province* functioned in much the same way as its monarchical variant. For which, see Frank Amati and Tony Aspromourgos, "Petty *contra* Hobbes: A Previously Untranslated Manuscript," *Journal of the History of Ideas* 46, no. 1 (Jan. 1985): 127–32.

141. This description of the components and functions of the government and of the councils is taken from "The King and His Four Councills (Chiefe, Privy, Cabinet & Comon) and the 3 armyes, (1679?)," in Hull, *Economic Writings*, 1:5–7. For variant versions, see "Of a Grand House of Peeres," "Of a Grand Councill for Plantation and Trade," "Of a Generall Councill for Plantation, Manufacture, Trade, Religion, and Applotment," "Of Uniting England and Ireland by a Common Parliament," and "An Expedient in Order to an Union of England, Ireland and Scotland," in ibid., 1:8–16.

142. [Gabriel Plattes], *A description of the Famous Kingdome of Macaria. . . .* in Webster, *Samuel Hartlib,* 81–82. *Macaria* was published anonymously and earlier thought to be by Hartlib himself. For the attribution of *Macaria* to Plattes, see Charles Webster, "The Authorship and Significance of *Macaria,*" in *Past and Present* 56 (Aug. 1972): 34–48.

143. Plattes, *Macaria,* in Webster, *Samuel Hartlib,* 82–83.

144. [Samuel Hartlib and John Dury], *Considerations Tending to the Happy Accomplishment of Englands Reformation in Church and State. . . .* (1647), in ibid., 124.

145. An excellent organizational chart of the Spanish conciliar system can be found in J. H. Elliott, *Imperial Spain, 1469–1716* (London: Penguin Books Ltd.,1990), 172.

146. Tomlinson, "Financial and Administrative Developments," 105.

147. Julian Martin, *Francis Bacon, the State, and the Reform of Natural Philosophy* (Cambridge: Cambridge University Press, 1992), 2, 43, 45, 93–94, 169–70.

148. Ibid., 135–37.

149. Plattes, *Macaria,* in Webster, *Samuel Hartlib,* 83.

150. Martin, *Bacon,* 5.

151. Ibid., 42–43, 57, 59.

Chapter 8

1. On the land-buying habits (mostly of suburban houses and tracts rather than of true country estates) of the mercantile magnates, see Richard Grassby, *The Business Community of Seventeenth-Century England* (Cambridge: Cambridge University Press, 1995), 335.

2. As for example, as a possible influence on Turgot through the translation of Child's work by Gournay, a personal friend of Turgot's. For which, see Schumpeter, *Economic Analysis,* 245. On the frequent reprinting of Child's works (the *Brief Discourse,* for

example, reappearing as a chapter in the *Discourse* of 1690 as well as in the *New Discourse* of 1693), see Letwin, *Child*, 26.

3. Robert Brenner, "The Civil War Politics of London's Merchant Community," *Past and Present* 58 (Feb. 1973): 73–77, 85, but 83–84 on the greater fragmentation within the Merchant Adventurers. The divisions are explored at greater length, though to the same conclusion in his *Merchants and Revolution*, 316–89.

4. Unless otherwise noted, this account of Child's life is taken from Letwin, *Child*, 12–24; see especially ibid., 12n. for the "considerable confusion" over Child's origins. The chapter on Josiah Child (3–51) in Letwin's *Scientific Economics* was more of a reprint than a reworking of the earlier study, and so citations have been taken from the former work.

5. *Calendar of State Papers, Domestic: Commonwealth (vol. 9), 1655–1656*, 522, 540, 563; *Vol. 8, 1655*, 424, 431, 489, 498, 564; *Vol. 10, 1656–1657*, 456, 458–59, 509, 516; *Vol. 11, 1657–1658*, 359; *Vol. 12, 1658–1659*, 325, 326, 368, 461, 466, 563, 567, 572, 575; *Vol. 13, 1659–1660*, 380, 453, 479, 483, 495–96, 501, 540–41, 548–49.

6. *Calendar of State Papers, Domestic: Commonwealth (vol. 12), 1658–1659*, 567 (from Child to the Navy Commissioners of 14 May 1659).

7. On the "Mr. Child" who bid unsuccessfully on Navy contracts in 1661, see *Calendar of State Papers, Domestic: Charles II (vol. 2), 1661–1662*, 9, 18. For his successful bid to supply masts to the navy, see *Vol. 4, 1664–1665*, 540, 564, 568. From then on he appears in the State Papers fairly regularly. See, for example, *Vol. 5, 1665–1666*, 4, 30, 62, 129–30, 135, 301, 371, 381; *Vol. 6, 1666–1667*, 390, 572. See also Pepys's *Diary*, 1:215, 250, 254, 257, 304; 2:30; 5:100.

8. The behind-the-scenes maneuvers of James and Buckingham for control of the Board and the lucrative contracts it oversaw can be followed in Pepys, *Diary*, 8:83, 106, 112, 265, 267, 295, 300.

9. For Papillon's political and religious connections, see Margaret Priestley, "London Merchants and Opposition Politics in Charles II's Reign," *Bulletin of the Institute of Historical Research* 29 (1956): 209, 218. For Shorter and Child or Papillon and Child as partners, *Calendar of State Papers, Domestic: Reign of Charles II (vol. 8), 1667–1668*, 260; *Vol. 12: 1671–1672*, 41, 66, 85, 98–99, 156; *Vol. 28: Addenda, 1660–1685*, 428.

10. Josiah Child, *A New Discourse of Trade. . . .* (London, 1693), facsimile reprint in *Sir Josiah Child: Selected Works, 1668–1697* (Farnborough, UK: Gregg, 1968), preface.

11. See *Calendar of State Papers, Domestic: Reign of Charles II (vol. 18), 1676–1677*, 75. Charles had two reasons for being displeased with Child and Papillon. First, because they had the audacity to resign the victualling contract in December 1673 over late government payments (*Vol. 16: 1673–1675*, 41), and, second, because they had been accused by Thomas Salter of suborning his testimony against Danby in the 1675 impeachment hearings (Letwin, *Child*, 18).

12. James II could only overcome his distaste for Child enough to make him one of the Deputy Lieutenants for Essex; for which see *Calendar of State Papers, Domestic: Reign of James II (vol. 3), June 1687–Feb.1689*, no. 1018 (page 187, order of 16 Apr. 1688). Items in the *Calendars* for the reign of James II are indexed by item number rather than by page.

13. See, for example, the charges referred to a Committee of the House of Commons that Child had ordered one Captain John Tyrell to plunder and sink the *Bristol*, in *Calendar of State Papers, Domestic: Reign of William and Mary (vol. 1), 1689–1690*, 129 (May 1689). For other "Whig" attacks on Child after the Glorious Revolution (the for-

mer exclusionist Papillon prominent among the attackers), see Henry Horowitz, "The East India Trade, the Politicians, and the Constitution: 1689–1702," *Journal of British Studies* 17, no. 2 (spring 1978): 1–2.

14. For the determination to include him among the expert witnesses, see *Calendar of State Papers, Domestic: Reign of William and Mary (vol. 6), 1 July 1695–31 Dec, 1695 and Addenda, 1689–1695,* 71, 74.

15. Evelyn, *Diary,* 4:305–6. According to Letwin's calculation of Child's estate, Evelyn's estimate of £200,000 might have been just a bit of an understatement; for which, see Letwin, *Child,* 23n. The level of display seems to have been a bit unusual even for a wealthy merchant (although not altogether unique), according to the picture presented in Grassby, *Business Community,* 340–41.

16. K. G. Davies, "Joint-Stock Investment in the Later Seventeenth Century," *Economic History Review,* 2d ser., 4, no. 3 (1952): 295–97. The total value of the shares outstanding April 1691 was £739,782.

17. See, for example, the contrasting figures for the Royal African Company where the percentage of shares held by large investors (defined as holding over £2,000) increased only from 7.7 percent to 14 percent from 1675 to 1691, in Davies, "Joint-Stock," 295.

18. Grassby, *Business Community,* 56–57. See also ibid., 247–49, on the respective worth of the London business community ca. 1694–1714, for which period, Grassby calculates there were at least 15 businessmen worth over £100,000, another 25 in the £30,000–100,000 range, perhaps another 60 in the £20,000–30,000 group, and 300 in the £10,000–20,000 range.

19. Grassby, *Business Community,* 83. Even factors required as much as £1,000 by 1689.

20. In other words, not in the modern sense of a return on a factor of production. See Smith, *Wealth of Nations,* 59–60 (I.vi) for the first clear critique of this confounding of wages with profit.

21. Roger Fenton, *A Treatise of Usurie, Divided into three Bookes: The first defineth what is Usurie. The second determineth that to be unlawfull. The third removeth such motives as persuade men in this age that it may be lawfull* (London, 1612), facsimile reprint in *The Usury Debate in the Seventeenth Century: Three Arguments* (New York: Arno, 1972), 5.

22. Ibid., 121.

23. Ibid., 21.

24. [Robert Filmer], *Quaestio Quodlibetica: Or a Discourse, whether it may be lawfull to take use for Money* (London, 1653); reprinted from *The Harleian Miscellany* X, 2d supplement (London, 1813) in *Usury Debate,* 127–28.

25. Ibid., 135–36.

26. Ibid., 112.

27. [Anonymous] *Usurie Arraigned and Condemned. Or A Discoverie of the infinite Injuries this Kingdome endureth by the unlawfull trade of Usurie* (London, 1625), facsimile reprint in *Usury Debate,* 1–2.

28. Filmer, *Quodlibetica,* in *Usury Debate,* 112.

29. Sir Josiah Child, *Brief Observations concerning Trade, and Interest of Money* (London, 1668), in *Works,* 3–6.

30. See Henry Robinson, *England's Safety in Trades Encrease. Most humbly Presented to the High Court of Parliament* (London, 1641), 4–5, 43, for the items that form nos. 3, 4, 8, 9, 10, 12, 13, 15 on Child's list. Also Letwin, *Child,* 8–9; and appendix II, for

an index of Child's borrowings from Worsley and Lambe as well as from Robinson in this regard. Child's omission here is quite curious given his insistence later in the same work on crediting Samuel Fortrey's similar remarks on the benefits of lowering interest "to give the Author his due Honour of being the first Observer." For which, see Child, *Brief Observations,* in *Works,* 38. Actually, Child seems to have adopted Robinson's ideas so strongly as to forget they were not originally his own, for in his *New Discourse* he accused the author of *Interest of Money Mistaken* of having stolen "nineteen Observations of mine, as means whereby the Dutch have encreased their Trade and Riches." For which, see *New Discourse,* in *Works,* 2. The *fifteen* points and four subsidiary observations are, in fact, correctly cited in *Interest of Money Mistaken* as being taken from Child's work in order to be refuted. For which see [Anonymous], *Interest of Money Mistaken. Or A Treatise, Proving, that the Abatement of Interest is the Effect And not the Cause Of the Riches of a Nation, and that Six Per Cent. Is a Proportionable Interest to the present condition of this Kingdom* (London, 1668), 3–8.

31. Child, *Brief Observations,* in *Works,* 7.

32. Ibid., 7–9.

33. Ibid., 10.

34. Child, *New Discourse,* in *Works,* preface.

35. Allen, "Price of Freehold Land," 34.

36. Thomas Manley, *Usury at Six per Cent examined, and Found unjustly charged by Sir Thomas Culpepper, and J.C. with many Crimes and Oppressions, whereof 'tis altogether innocent. . . .* (London, 1669), preface.

37. Child, *New Discourse,* in *Works,* 16–18.

38. Ibid., preface.

39. See, for example, Thomas Violet, *An Appeal to Caesar: wherein Gold and Silver is Proved to be the Kings Majesties Royal Commodity. . . .* (London, 1660), passim.

40. Letwin, *Child,* 8–9.

41. Child, *Brief Observations,* in *Works,* 10–11, 15. In support of his arguments, Child reprinted Thomas Culpepper's *A Tract against Usurie, Presented to the high Court of Parliament* (London, 1621) in his *Brief Observations.* Culpepper's observations, however, were often more astute than Child's. Culpepper observed that it was better the Dutch took out one hundred pounds now than one hundred and ten pounds later. For which, see Child, *Brief Observations,* in *Works,* 35.

42. Ibid., 11–12. Again, Culpepper was sharper: it was not so much a case of exchanging a known (good) security for an unknown (bad) but of calling in an old loan at a higher rate only to have to make the new loans at lower rates (the proposed laws allowing for the continuance of existing loans at their original rates). For which, see ibid., 33.

43. For the assorted strategies from entails to adoption of surrogate heirs used by the gentry to preserve land holdings intact from generation to generation, see Lawrence Stone and Jeanne C. Fawtier Stone, *An Open Elite? England, 1540–1880,* abridged ed. (Oxford and New York: Oxford University Press, 1986), 66–91.

44. Child, *Brief Observations,* in *Works,* 11.

45. Ibid. Seventeenth-century economic writers seem to have held the notion that the work force was simultaneously lazy and consumption-prone. Manley (*Usury at Six per Cent,* 19) believed high wages were not caused by a shortage of laborers but by an "evil disposition" among the people to "live the better above their station."

46. Dobb, *Development of Capitalism,* 203.

47. Child, *Brief Observations,* in *Works,* 11.

48. Nor did he consider whether or not lower interest rates would combine with higher wages to raise commodity prices to the point they would "frustrate the drive for exports." For which, see Spiegel, *Growth,* 147.

49. Child, *New Discourse,* in *Works,* 161.

50. Child, *Brief Observations,* in *Works,* 13–14.

51. Ibid., 12.

52. Davies, "Joint-Stock," 287. Other examples can be found in Grassby, *Business Community,* 88.

53. Jan de Vries, *The Economy of Europe in an Age of Crisis, 1600–1750* (Cambridge: Cambridge University Press, 1976), 212.

54. Jonathan Israel, *The Dutch Republic: Its Rise, Greatness, and Fall, 1477–1806* (Oxford: Clarendon, 1995), 276–77, 285–86, 321–22, 326, 341, 344–45, 533, 769. On the more primitive nature of English share sales, see Davies, "Joint-Stock," 294.

55. Through its monopoly of the exchange. The original idea behind the Dutch banks seems to have been one of specialization. With the exception of small loans to the Indies Company and the municipality of Amsterdam itself, direct customer loans were not handled by the Bank of Amsterdam but through the municipal Loan Bank set up in 1614. Deposit receipts from the Exchange Bank began to circulate as "money" as early as 1658 according to Ralph Davis, *The Rise of the Atlantic Economies* (Ithaca, NY: Cornell University Press, 1973), 185–86, 246–47. Vilar put the formal recognition of these banknotes as occurring in 1683, the same time the Bank of Amsterdam began to pay interest to its depositors. For which, see Pierre Vilar, *A History of Gold and Money, 1450–1920,* trans. Judith White (London: N.L.B., 1976) 207, and on its direct loans, ibid., 206.

56. Israel, *Dutch Republic,* 630.

57. Child, *Brief Observations,* in *Works,* 19.

58. Ibid., 18.

59. Child, *A Short Addition to the Observations concerning Trade and Interest of Money* (London, 1668), in ibid., 5. By the time of the *New Discourse,* Child had finally gotten the dates of changes in the Amsterdam interest rates up to the 1655 change to 4 percent correct; for which, see *New Discourse,* in *Works,* 31. Child referred to rates set by "Placard," a term that normally referred to a municipal regulation.

60. Testifying on October 28, 1669, Child claimed that interest was low in Holland without a law, though in his *Short Addition* he had already claimed statutory limits were in place there. For his testimony before the Committee of the House of Lords, see the *Eighth Report of the Royal Commission on Historical Manuscripts: Report and Appendix (Part I)* (London: HMSO, 1881), 133–34 (no. 215, 28 Oct. 1669). Letwin deals with the rebuttals to Child's testimony in *Child,* 3–4. A transcript of the testimony, including a repeat of the laundry list of Dutch virtues, can be found in Thirsk and Cooper, *Economic Documents,* 69–70.

61. *Eighth Report, H. M. S.,* 134.

62. *Interest of Money Mistaken,* 10, 13, 14, 18. Manley brought up the interesting question of weighing variables, wondering why a 2 percent drop in interest rates would be expected to have a bigger economic impact than bringing wages down 15 to 30 percent (to Continental levels). For which, see Manley, *Usury at Six per Cent,* preface and 7.

63. In the preface to his *New Discourse* (1693) Child referred to having read *Interest of Money mistaken* in 1669 and Manley's tract at some time later; for which see *Works* (A).

64. Child, *New Discourse*, in *Works*, 35–36.

65. Ibid., preface.

66. Child, *Brief Observations*, in *Works*, 17.

67. There is a very poignant complaint from a frustrated client of one Jacob David who was trying to get his iron sold at "the market price" when the English, having bought it at an inflated price, were dumping it below cost rather than hold it against a further rise in the market—a behavior the writer found inexplicable even though he was urging his goods be sold before the expected arrival of large quantities from Sweden. For which, see Henry Roseveare, ed., *Markets and Merchants of the Late Seventeenth Century: The Marescoe-David Letters, 1668–1680* (Oxford: Oxford University Press for the British Academy), 473 [no. 360; L. Tripp to Jacob David, 6 Aug. 1677].

68. Child, *New Discourse*, in *Works*, 136–37; also 143–45 on the fallacy of judging by only one particular trade.

69. Ibid., 137–41. He also did not see that the fact that there was a profit for the absentee owners to draw out worked against his own argument.

70. Ibid., 204–5; similarly, ibid., 206.

71. Ibid., 153, 160. The persistence of the idea of a fixed volume of trade in Graunt, Child, and even in Petty has been astutely noted by Irwin (*Against the Tide*, 31) who rejects the use of a zero-sum analogy because of the seventeenth-century belief that trade was, in essence, "mutually beneficial," although its volume (and the resulting profit) being fixed, each writer wished his country to have the greatest share of that volume (and profit).

72. Child, *New Discourse*, in *Works*, 153–56.

73. Beer (*Early British Economics*, 203) called Child a free-trader. Grampp ("Liberal Elements," 71–72), took him for a liberal but seems to have confused him with someone else entirely, putting Child among those who favored an indirect means of reducing the interest rate over a statutory one. Dobb (*Development of Capitalism*, 216) was much better at smelling the difference between special pleading and real free trade advocacy. Hutchison (*Before Adam Smith*, 59–60) saw the special pleading as the cause of Child's doctrinal inconsistency.

74. Child, *Short Addition*, in *Works*, 12–13.

75. Letwin, *Child*, 21(n). For the king's decision in favor of Child's position, see *Calendar of State Papers, Domestic: Reign of Charles II (vol. 23), 1682*, 194–95 (2 May 1682).

76. On the control maintained by the East India Company over its shareholders, see Davies, "Joint-Stock," 294. Grassby documents the consistent level of gentry recruitment; for which, see Grassby, *Business Community*, 168 (fig. 5.5).

77. Child, *New Discourse*, in *Works*, 27, 47, 131, 157.

78. Ibid., 93. He even wanted the act extended to exclude shipping in vessels of country of origin so the Norway trade would be carried on in English ships instead of in Danish ones; for which, see ibid., 99–100.

79. Ibid., 102, 104–5.

80. Child, *Brief Observations*, in *Works*, 16.

81. Child, *Short Addition*, in *Works*, 11.

82. Child, *New Discourse*, in *Works*, 56.

83. Ibid., 61–63, 67, 70, 74.

84. Even though Child did not notice that his acceptance of higher wages tended in the opposite direction.

85. Ralph Davis, "English Foreign Trade, 1660–1700," *Economic History Review,* 2d ser., 7, no. 2 (Dec. 1954): 151–52.

86. Davis, "Foreign Trade," 153.

87. Joan Thirsk considered this revolution essentially accomplished by 1630 but saw a time lapse in the theoretical awareness of it, suggesting that Misselden and Mun, for example, were unaware of the change or they would not, unlike writers from the second half of the century, have fixated on foreign trade. She did not, however, really test her thesis of the impact of the consumer revolution on those later writers: Petty would have worked in favor of her case up to a point, but Child would not. For which, see Joan Thirsk, *Economic Policy and Projects: The Development of a Consumer Society in Early Modern England* (Oxford: Clarendon, 1978), 18, 134–38. Certainly neither Petty, Child, Locke, nor Davenant really underwent the "radical change" for better in "their attitude toward middlemen" she spoke of (18).

88. Child, *New Discourse,* in *Works,* 125.

89. Ibid., preface. The monarch, presumably, was fixing his eye on the welfare of the whole and not merely on his own coffers.

90. Child, *New Discourse,* in *Works,* 86.

91. Child, *Short Addition,* in *Works,* 11; similarly, *New Discourse,* in ibid., 22: "no man in his wits would follow any Trade whereby he did not promise himself 14 or 12 per Cent gain at least, when Interest was at 8." Robinson had anticipated him in this, however. See *England's Safety,* 6–7, for Robinson's opportunity-cost take on interest.

92. Ibid., preface.

Chapter 9

1. Unless otherwise noted the biographical material in this chapter was taken from Maurice Cranston, *John Locke: A Biography* (London: Longmans, Green and Co. Ltd., 1957).

2. He did take his M.B. in 1675.

3. The best treatment of the problems in the argument of the essay, along with the text of the essay itself, can be found in Letwin, *Scientific Economics,* 169–74, 295–323 [appendix 5].

4. On the deliberate diminution of the merchant influence, see Hinton, *Eastland Trade,* 154.

5. As to Oates, Shaftesbury was later to admit "I will not say who started the Game, but I am sure I had the full hunting of it." For which, see L. Echard, *History of England* (London, 1718), 3:460, quoted in J. R. Jones, *The First Whigs: The Politics of the Exclusion Crisis, 1678–1683* (London: Oxford University Press, 1961), 23.

6. See Jones, *First Whigs,* 92, 133–35, 159–61, 168–69, 174, 178.

7. Locke had good reason to think he was next; his rooms at Oxford had been searched more than once that year; for which see *Calendar of State Papers, Domestic Series: Reign of Charles II (vol. 25), 1 July–30 Sep. 1683,* 109. Shaftesbury died in Amsterdam on January 21, 1683, after having arrived there in early December 1682.

8. The original Latin *Epistola de Tolerantia* was published in Holland in 1689.

9. For a detailed account of Locke's involvement with this and the earlier trade councils and boards, see Peter Laslett, "John Locke, the Great Recoinage, and the Ori-

gins of the Board of Trade: 1695–1698," in *John Locke: Problems and Perspectives*, ed. John W. Yolton (Cambridge: Cambridge University Press, 1969), 137–64.

10. John Locke, *Some Considerations of the Consequences of the Lowering of Interest, and Raising the Value of Money. In a Letter sent to a Member of Parliament, 1691* (2d ed., London, 1691), 31–32. See also Karen Iverson Vaughn, *John Locke, Economist and Social Scientist* (Chicago: University of Chicago Press, 1980), 33–35, on the requisite qualities.

11. For Buridan and Oresme, see the chapter on the "Properties of Money" in Odd Langholm, *Wealth and Money in the Aristotelian Tradition: A Study in Scholastic Economic Sources* (Bergen: Universitetsforlaget, 1983), 79–88. The parallels between their work and Locke's in this regard are too striking to be coincidental (especially given Locke's university training).

12. Locke, *Some Considerations*, 31. He also called the amount of pure silver in the coin its "real value." For which, see ibid., 135, 141, 145. See also the repeated stress on "intrinsic value" in "Propositions sent to the Lords Justices (1695)" in *Locke on Money*, ed. Patrick Hyde Kelly (Oxford: Clarendon, 1991), 2:374–75. But note Kelly's introduction in ibid., 86, on the three "confusingly" different senses in which Locke used the term "intrinsick value" with respect to money: its origin, as "the source of its exchange value, and the ratio at which money exchanges for other commodities."

13. Locke, *Some Considerations*, 32, 146. Also *Further Considerations concerning Raising the Value of Money. Wherein Mr. Lowndes's Arguments for it in his late Report concerning An Essay for the Amendment of the Silver Coins, are particularly Examined* (2d ed., London, 1696), 5.

14. Locke, *Some Considerations*, 31.

15. Ibid., 171.

16. Locke, *Further Considerations*, 1.

17. Locke, *Some Considerations*, 146. Also *Further Considerations*, 8–9, 22.

18. Locke, *Further Considerations*, 9.

19. John Locke, *A Letter Concerning Toleration* (London, 1690), reprint (Buffalo: Prometheus Books, 1990), 62–64. See also Raymond Polin, "John Locke's Conception of Freedom," in Yolton, *Locke*, 17, on the exclusion of atheists because of the essential links between "moral and political obligations" and "moral and political virtues" in Locke's thought.

20. 15 Charles II, c.7, s.12 (1663) allowed "the re-export of foreign coin or bullion if entry were made of it at the customs house by which it was hoped the better to guard against the export of English coin." For which, see Sir Albert Feavearyear, *The Pound Sterling: A History of English Money*, 2d ed., revised by E. Victor Morgan (Oxford: Clarendon, 1963), 4. It was still illegal to melt the coins to export them, but there was a brisk trade in stamping the melted coins to make them look like foreign bullion; for which, see Haynes, *Brief memoires* (B. L. Lansdowne MS-801), cited in Stephen Quinn, "Gold, Silver, and the Glorious Revolution: Arbitrage between Bills of Exchange and Bullion," *Economic History Review* 49, no. 3 (Aug. 1996): 480.

21. Feavearyear, *Pound Sterling*, 124.

22. Locke, *Some Considerations*, 30.

23. Ibid., 157, 160; and *Further Considerations*, 16.

24. This was the argument advanced by William Lowndes (1652–1724), newly appointed (24 Apr. 1695) Secretary to the Treasury, in *Further Essay*, 6–8.

25. See Quinn, "Gold," 476, 481, on the decline in the average silver content of the circulating coin from 81 to 88 percent (1685–1690) to 79 percent (1691) to 51 percent

(1695) and 45 percent (1696), ascribed by Quinn to the arbitrage fed by England's need to pay the troops stationed abroad during the Nine Years' War (1689–1698) as it "increased the supply of pounds in London seeking bills of exchange payable in the Low Countries." See also Kelly, *Locke on Money,* 1:59, to the effect that the lowest percentages finally did set off a "widespread refusal" of the coin by late 1694 due to the inflationary pressures of the war. There is no evidence that the 80+ percent weight coin had been any problem over the two preceding decades.

26. Compare Locke, *Further Considerations,* 11–12 (the weight argument) with ibid., 94, 97 (the denominational argument). Similarly, *Some Considerations,* 161 (a weight argument) and 50 (a denominational argument).

27. Locke, *Some Considerations,* 33.

28. Locke seemed to think moneys of account were universally in silver. For which, see *Further Considerations,* 20.

29. See Quinn, "Gold," 475–76. Quinn maintained that because of the costs of transporting bullion (about 3 percent of their value round trip), the small bullion price differentials in European markets discouraged arbitrage in metals alone; bills, of course, cost nothing to transport. His example of a typical metal-to-metal price differential was "the exchange rate using gold guineas at 21s. 6d. was 38.87 S/£ (Dutch *schellingen*/English *pounds*) and the exchange rate using the mint price of English silver was 38.46 S/£."

30. Locke, *Some Considerations,* 162.

31. Feavearyear, *Pound Sterling,* 151. Lowndes wished the gold-silver par kept as it was, so that his plans for recoinage at the lower weight entailed an adjustment in the gold coinage as well. For which, see Lowndes, *Further Essay,* 11.

32. Locke, *Some Considerations,* 167–69, and *Further Considerations,* 20–21, 23.

33. Locke, *Further Considerations,* 4.

34. Ibid., 2.

35. Newton noted a discrepancy of two to three pence per pound between the market and Mint price for silver when the East India Company fleets were preparing to leave. For which, see Sir Isaac Newton, *Memorial concerning the proportion of gold and silver in value* (London, 1701), cited in Feavearyear, *Pound Sterling,* 151. See Kelly, *Locke on Money,* 1:82–83, on Locke's use of the Scholastic idea of intrinsic value ("the inherent capacity of an object to perform certain functions, e.g. the 'intrinsic value' of bread is to assuage hunger") as a necessary but "by no means a sufficient" cause of exchange value. For Locke, silver was a singular exception to this necessary but not sufficient rule.

36. John Locke, *Short Observations on a Printed Paper, Intituled, For encouraging the Coining Silver Money in England, and after for keeping it here* (London, 1695), 4–6. Similarly, *Further Considerations,* 59.

37. Locke, *Short Observations,* 2.

38. Locke, *Further Considerations,* 27.

39. Feavearyear, *Pound Sterling,* 109–10.

40. Locke, *Further Considerations,* 1.

41. Locke, *Some Considerations,* 32–33. Locke was not always consistent on this point. In this pamphlet (78) he argued that if the coin supply dropped to half of what was needed to drive the current level of trade, "'tis certain, that either half our Rents should not be paid, half our Commodities not vented, and half our Labourers not imployed, and so half the Trade be clearly lost; or else, that every one of these must receive but half the Money." But in *Further Considerations* (67), he asserted that if the total goods for sale in England at one point were equal in value to "a Million Ounces of

Silver," but the coined money was only equal to half that amount, "Credit or barter" would supply the rest.

42. Locke, *Some Considerations*, 4.

43. Compare Joyce Oldham Appleby, "Locke, Liberalism and the Natural Law of Money," *Past and Present* 71 (May 1976): 55, 63, 65. Appleby considered Locke's idea of money's intrinsic value putting it outside of government manipulation and his idea of property rights devolving from natural law to be part of an end-of-century oligarchic reaction to the egalitarian market advocacy she saw as building up throughout the century. For which, see her *Economic Thought*, 221–23, 229–30, 254. Appleby's footnotes contain several references to Letwin's *Scientific Economics*, which both discusses the points of agreement between the 1668 essay and the published works and reproduces the 1668 essay itself (in appendix V), but she appears not to have considered whether Locke might more properly belong in a Restoration reaction or if the path of that egalitarian movement was not as straight as she imagined.

44. See Phelps and Brown, "Seven Centuries," 313.

45. Locke, *Further Considerations*, Dedication.

46. Ibid., 10–11.

47. Locke, *Some Considerations*, 143.

48. Ibid., 186.

49. See Langholm, *Wealth and Money*, 90 (Oresme), 95–96 (Buridan).

50. Set by 7 William III, c.1, and 7 William III, c.2, with allowances for prepayment of certain taxes due after that date.

51. Feavearyear, *Pound Sterling*, 138–42. The effect on the poor had been predicted by Lowndes, in his *Further Essay*, 11–12.

52. Feavearyear, *Pound Sterling*, 145.

53. Locke, *Some Considerations*, 14.

54. Ibid., 15.

55. Ibid., 26, 30.

56. Locke, *Further Considerations*, 15–16.

57. Ibid., 36–37.

58. Ibid., 41–42.

59. Ibid., 33.

60. See, for example, Letwin, *Scientific Economics*, 173 (based on Locke's use of the phrase "quickness of its circulation" in the 1668 essay). However, Blaug (*Economic Theory*, 20) wondered why Locke could not see his quantity theory was "obviously destructive of mercantilist principles." A possible solution might be found in Vaughn's contention (*Locke*, 37) that Locke thought of velocity as basically constant (being legally and culturally determined) so that quantity remained the determining variable (and hence the need for an export surplus).

61. How much Locke borrowed from Petty is an open question. Neal Wood has noted "Petty's definition of the function of money 'to drive the Nations Trade,' his stress on labor as the primary source of value, and his sense of the vital role of land and agriculture," as well as his work on rents, his "labeling retail merchants 'gamesters'," his use of the bushel of wheat "as the standard unit of value," and his assumption of the subsistence labor wage as reappearing in Locke's 1668 essay. For which, see Neal Wood, *John Locke and Agrarian Capitalism* (Berkeley: University of California Press, 1984), 37. Blaug (*Economic Theory*, 23–24) believed Locke's idea that the interest rate varied inversely with the money supply had also been anticipated by Petty. In terms of general influence,

Kelly (*Locke on Money*, 98) considered Mun and Petty as equally important sources for Locke.

62. Locke, *Some Considerations*, 34–41. Schumpeter (*Economic Analysis*, 291n, 298n, 317) dismissed Locke as a metallist in whose work on money there was "little that was not said as well or better by other writers at the same time," but believed Locke, like Cantillon, pushed velocity "in the strict sense" into velocity as "rate of spending."

63. Ibid., 40–41.

64. Ibid., 2.

65. Ibid., 2–3, 9.

66. Ibid., 103. See also G. S. L. Tucker, *Progress and Profits in British Economic Thought, 1650–1850* (Cambridge: Cambridge University Press, 1960), 26, on Locke's acceptance of a state-regulated rate as long as it was high enough to prevent "the concentration of money in the hands of a growing class of middlemen that stood between the ultimate lender and the borrower."

67. Locke, *Some Considerations*, 7–9.

68. For example, see ibid., 84: "making a Law to reduce Interest, will not raise the Price of Lands: It will only, by driving it more into the Bankers Hands, leave the Country barer of Money."

69. Ibid., 42.

70. Ibid., 42–43.

71. Locke, "Notes on Trade," in Thirsk and Cooper, *Economic Documents*, 96.

72. Locke, *Some Considerations*, 30–31.

73. Ibid., 116.

74. Ibid., 13. This is one of the rare instances in which Locke changed a tenet instead of just the shape of his argument in the years separating the 1668 memo from the published works. In the earlier piece the 8–4/6–6 divide is between the merchant and the "usurer" to the loss of the "monied man" as a third party. Evidently by the later date, Locke had a clearer idea of what "monied" gentlemen did with their money. On the earlier argument, see Letwin, *Scientific Economics*, 295 [appendix V].

75. Locke, *Some Considerations*, 13.

76. Ibid., 169–70.

77. Locke, *Some Considerations*, 51.

78. Ibid., 55. Marx proposed that Locke was not identifying interest with rent in order to legitimate interest but to condemn aristocratic rent as usury! For which, see Marx, *Surplus-Value*, 1:356.

79. Locke, *Some Considerations*, 56–57.

80. Ibid., 58–59.

81. Ibid., 60–61.

82. Vaughn (*Locke*, 25–26) took Locke's use of *vent* to mean the "rate of sales to final consumers per time period" and thus "a point on a demand curve" rather than a stand-in for the demand curve itself. Perhaps, but not consistently so.

83. This is one example of a conclusion taken over virtually word-for-word from his 1668 manuscript; for which, see Letwin, *Scientific Economics*, 299 [appendix V].

84. Locke, *Some Considerations*, 48.

85. See Bowley, "Seventeenth-Century Contributions," 130–31: Locke's argument "also outlines in general terms the process of distribution of expenditure between different uses to maximize satisfactions, and shows that this distribution will be affected by changes in prices of commodities."

86. Locke, *Some Considerations*, 10.

87. Ibid., 48–49.

88. Ibid., 55.

89. Compare Keynes ("Notes on Mercantilism," 343): "Locke explains that money has two values: (1) its value in use which is given by the rate of interest . . . and (2) its value in exchange . . . 'depending only on the Plenty or Scarcity of Money in proportion to the Plenty or Scarcity of those things [to be exchanged for it] and not on what Interest shall be'. Thus Locke was the parent of twin quantity theories. . . . But—standing with one foot in the mercantilist world and with one foot in the classical world—he was confused concerning the relationship between these two proportions, and he overlooked altogether the possibility of *fluctuations* in liquidity preference." Vickers (*Theory of Money*, 57) claimed that though Locke's "interest analysis, or financial sector analysis" was "kept separate from and distinct from the money-price, or goods sector analysis," Locke did explicitly recognize "the possibility of an interdependence between them" and just decided not to develop it (it "is not in this place to be considered"). I am arguing that he was determined that no such argument be developed.

90. Locke, *Some Considerations*, 45. Similarly, ibid., 69–70, 76, 77, 135.

91. Ibid., 43.

92. John Locke, *Two Treatises of Government: In the Former, The False Principles and Foundation of Sir Robert Filmer, And His Followers, are Detected and Overthrown. The Latter is an Essay concerning The True Original, Extent, and End of Civil-Government* (London, 1698; originally 1690), ed. Peter Laslett (Cambridge: Cambridge University Press, 1988), 296 (II.5.40). I agree with Schumpeter's conclusion (*Economic Analysis*, 120, 214) that Locke was building a political/juridical argument here and not, like Petty, an economic one. Aspromourgos (*Classical Economics*, 149) characterized Locke's ideas on labor as the "elaborate expressions of a single-minded practical intention deeply embedded in his political theory—the preservation of individual property rights (more against threats from monarchy than from 'below')." For the view that Locke's *principal* aim in all this was to defend English colonialism in the Americas, see Barbara Arneil, "Trade, Plantations, and Property: John Locke and the Defense of Colonialism," *Journal of the History of Ideas* 55, no. 4 (Oct. 1994), 602–3, 606. Arneil seems unaware that others had already noticed that Locke's ideas in this regard could be used to justify colonialism (though they might have had as much to do with justifying enclosure in England). For example, see Wood, *Locke*, 66. Arneil elaborated her thesis in her *John Locke and America: The Defence of English Colonialism* (Oxford: Clarendon, 1996), passim, but see especially 2 (on Locke's state of nature as a "historical reality" existing "in the Americas of his day"), 7, 90 (on Locke's links to the mercantile tradition favoring colonies).

93. Locke, *Two Treatises*, 285–86 (II.5.25).

94. Ibid., 286 (II.5.26), 291 (II.5.34).

95. Ibid., 287–88 (II.5.27), 284 (II.4.23).

96. Ibid., 298 (II.5.43). James Tully pointed out that (1) "the workmanship model" was "a fundamental feature of all Locke's writing" and (2) its use in Locke's epistemology forms a strong link between Locke, Bacon, and Descartes as well as Aristotle (especially as interpreted by Boyle), but also to Presbyterians such as Richard Baxter. For which, see James Tully, *A Discourse on Property: John Locke and His Adversaries* (Cambridge: Cambridge University Press, 1980), 4, 22, 42. Tully also stressed that for Locke "there is not a thing which persists through making and altering and from which one would have to subtract the value added by the labourer" and that this is essentially

a "Baconian picture of man's creative and transformative powers." For which, see ibid., 117.

97. Locke, *Two Treatises,* 289 (II.5.30).

98. See Thomas A. Horne, *Property Rights and Poverty: Political Argument in Britain, 1605–1834* (Chapel Hill and London: University of North Carolina Press, 1990), 49: "Locke used labor to help demonstrate the moral component of possession or occupation against Pufendorf's criticism that such acts were mere seizures."

99. For what follows in this paragraph, see Jacob Viner, "Possessive Individualism," 554–58, and Viner, "The Perils of Reviewing: A Counter-Rejoinder," *Canadian Journal of Economics and Political Science* 29, no. 4 (Nov. 1963): 562–66. There is a sweet irony here in having an economist point out a historian's failure to pay attention to a word's history.

100. James Tully, *An Approach to Political Philosophy: Locke in Contexts* (Cambridge: Cambridge University Press, 1993), 127.

101. Compare Keith Tribe, *Genealogies of Capitalism* (Atlantic Highlands, NJ: Humanities, 1981), 38. For Tribe, "Capitalism can be briefly summarized as a form of economy in which consumption is separated from production, enterprises are separated and in a state of competition, and the national economy is co-ordinated according to the profitability of the commodities sold by the enterprises. In the context under consideration here, this means that the capitalist farm, leased from a landlord by a farmer who supervises the labourers who work it, is an enterprise whose continued existence depends on the profitability of the commodities that it sells." But it was as much a capitalist farm if the "labourers" were all members of the farmer's family as it was if they were all strangers working for wages; the key element was market-dominated production. This seems a logical modification of Marx's theory for an age in which a large percentage of tenants still ran family-operated farms, but taken at its most extreme, Tribe's model would make the slave-dependent plantations of the Americas quintessentially capitalist institutions, and push the horizon back two centuries before Tribe's own cut-off for agrarian capitalism.

102. Locke, *Two Treatises,* 322–23 (II.7.85).

103. Ibid., 289 (II.5.30), already cited.

104. See, for example, Macpherson, *Possessive Individualism,* 205, 215, 219.

105. Taking Keith Tribe's eighteenth-century Agrarian Capitalism and moving it back into the seventeenth century. For which, see Wood, *Locke,* 13, 26–29, 38–39, 47, 60–61. For Tribe's discussion of "Agrarian Capitalism," see Keith Tribe, *Land, Labour and Economic Discourse* (London: Routledge and Kegan Paul Ltd., 1978), 4, 25–28, 33, 54–56, 61, 66.

106. Wood suggested that Locke was actually generalizing the specific agricultural system with which he was most familiar, agrarian capitalism being general at the time only in certain sections of the country and not yet the dominant practice throughout. For which, see Wood, *Locke,* 45.

107. Tully, *Discourse on Property,* 138.

108. Contrast Locke, *Two Treatises,* 322–23 (II.7.85) with James Tully, *Discourse on Property,* 137–38.

109. Tully, *Discourse on Property,* 137. This is actually Macpherson's phrase (*Possessive Individualism,* 51–52).

110. For Locke's proposed reform of the poor laws, see John Marshall, *John Locke: Resistance, Religion and Responsibility* (Cambridge: Cambridge University Press, 1994),

324–25; Wood, *Locke*, 107–8, and Horne, *Property Rights*, 64–65. But the best way to understand Locke's stringent treatment of the poor is probably, as John Dunn did, through the lens of the calling. For which, see John Dunn, *The Political Thought of John Locke: An Historical Account of the Argument of the 'Two Treatises of Government'* (Cambridge: Cambridge University Press, 1969), 217, 226–27. See also Sreenivasan's parallel idea that "the production right is not to be identified with the consumption right. . . . [the consumption right] depends upon his *labouring*. . . . charity and inheritance apply *only* where a man is *unable* to labour." For which, see Gopal Sreenivasan, *The Limits of Lockean Rights in Property* (New York: Oxford University Press, 1995), 44.

111. Tully, *An Approach*, 123.

112. See Jeremy Boulton, "Wage Labour in Seventeenth-Century London," *Economic History Review* 49, no. 2 (May 1996): 270–71.

113. Pribham (*Economic Reasoning*, 40) notes the danger of cultural-stage centered reasoning when applied to the development of capitalism, "since stage analysis tends to dissect the continuous flow of economic developments and to telescope extended processes into ill-defined periods marked by specific characteristics."

114. Tully's own remark (*An Approach*, 78) that the texts of seventeenth-century political and economic thought (including Locke's) "were responses to problems thrown up by the emergence of capitalist relations" would seem to indicate that there is as great a risk in abandoning the framework as in using it (and risking more "Whig interpretions" of history).

115. Locke, *Essays on the Law of Nature*, trans. W. von Leyden, corrected reprint of the 1954 edition (Oxford: Clarendon, 1958), 211. Pagination note: in this edition, the Latin text appears on the even-numbered pages and the English translation on the odd.

116. Locke, *Two Treatises*, 290 (II.5.31).

117. This was also one of his longest held beliefs; for which, see the briefer but similar treatment in the *Law of Nature*, 137, 147.

118. John Locke, *An Essay Concerning Human Understanding* (1690), ed. Alexander Campbell Fraser (Oxford: Oxford University Press, 1894), 2:38 (I.1.1).

119. Ibid., 1:126 (II.1.7).

120. Ibid., 2:443 (IV.20.2).

121. John Locke, *The Reasonableness of Christianity: As Delivered in the Scriptures* (London, 1695), ed. George W. Ewing (Washington, DC: Regnery Gateway, 1965), 178–79.

122. See, for example, ibid., 2:270–71 (IV.7.4).

123. Locke, *Human Understanding*, 1:160–61 (II.7.1–4).

124. Ibid., 1:162 (II.7.5).

125. Locke, *Two Treatises*, 286 (II.5.25–26), 290 (II.5.31).

126. Which was why Locke wanted "*Propriety* and Possession, pleasing themselves with the Power which that seems to give, and the Right they thereby have, to dispose of them as they please" rooted out of children at an early age. For which, see John Locke, *Some Thoughts Concerning Education* (§103–105.2), in *The Works of John Locke. A New edition. Corrected* (London: Thomas Tegg, 1823; reprint, Aalen: Scientia Verlag, 1963), 9:93–94. Page numbers are to the reprint edition.

127. Locke, *Human Understanding*, 1:194 (II.10.3). See also Hans Aarsleff, "The State of Nature and the Nature of Man in John Locke," in Yolton, *Locke*, 111, on what seems to be "hedonism" in Locke as really being one of "two halves of a sphere"—the other being his "natural-law teaching"—because "pleasure and pain also come under the

wise dispensation of the Creator and law-maker, whose rewards and punishments they are."

128. Locke, *Human Understanding*, 1:347 (II.21.51).

129. Ibid., 1:303 (II.20.3).

130. Ibid., 1:334–35 (II.21.33–35).

131. Ibid., 1:343 (II.21.46).

132. Locke, *Concerning Education* (§33, §45.1), in *Works*, 9:27, 36.

133. Ibid., 9:15 (§14).

134. Ibid., 9:7 (§2).

135. Locke, *Human Understanding*, 2:233 (IV.4.8).

136. Marshall, *Locke*, xviii, 453, seems uncertain about this, first (xviii) implying an inability in Locke himself, but then (453) a general impossibility of achievement.

137. Locke, *Law of Nature*, 109. Nicholas Jolley offers an interesting view that might stand as a bridge between the *Law of Nature* and the *Essay on Human Understanding*. For Jolley, "Locke is a scientific realist for whom the independent existence of the physical world as a vast, law-governed machine is never seriously in question; it is an assumption which pervades the whole philosophy of the *Essay*." For which, see Nicholas Jolley, *Leibniz and Locke: A Study of the New Essays on Human Understanding* (Oxford: Clarendon, 1984), 4.

138. Locke, *Human Understanding*, 1:121 (II.1.1); similarly, ibid., 2:307.

139. See W. von Leyden's "Introduction" to *Essays on the Law of Nature*, 35. Letwin (*Origins*, 184–85) stressed an Aristotelian-Ciceronian origin for Locke's use of natural law. Marshall (*Locke*, 309–15) picked up on the Ciceronian influence with respect to Locke's ideas of "beneficence as well as justice" though there were strong areas of disagreement between the two men.

140. For Marshall, these men's works acted more as refracting mirrors that helped Locke sharpen his own positions than as direct influences; for which see Marshall, *Locke*, 201–4, 210–11.

141. See, for example, Dunn, *Political Thought*, 220, though he discusses only the Protestant aspect.

142. Tully, *An Approach*, 66.

143. Ibid., 103, 99.

144. Locke's connections to these three men and his reactions to their works can be found in Marshall, *Locke*, 7, 406, 409–10.

Chapter 10

1. As, for example, Lansdowne, *Correspondence*, 51, 321, and *Petty Papers* 2:39.

2. Malynes, *Lex Mercatoria*, 491.

3. Lansdowne, *Correspondence*, 295–96 (Petty to Southwell, 14 Oct. 1687). See also "The explication of 12 theological words (1686)," in *Petty Papers*, 1:165.

4. Compare, for example, the treatments of sense, memory, and speech in Hobbes, *Leviathan*, 85–86 (Chapter I), 89 (Chapter II), and 100 (Chapter IV), to Petty's definitions of the same in "A Dialogue between A and B," in Lansdowne, *Petty Papers*, 1:152, 155–57. See also the discussion of the relations between Petty and Hobbes in Aspromourgos, *Origins*, 54–56. See also Buck, "Seventeenth-Century," 78, on Petty's praise of "clarissimus Hobbes."

5. Hobbes, *Leviathan,* 110–11 (Chapter V).

6. Ibid., 112 (Chapter V). The attempt by Aspromourgos (*Classical Economics,* 67) to fuse Petty's and Hobbes's definitions into a single system of "empirically definite concepts and rigorous, deductive methods" seems ill-advised.

7. A parallel argument appeared in an unpublished "Scheme for a medical essay" in which Petty proposed "That as few as possible of insensible things, and such as cannot be examined by experiment, bee supposed." For which, see Lansdowne, *Petty Papers,* 2:168. Compare Thomas Sprat's characterization of the Royal Society as devoted to the investigation of "visible and sensible matter." For which, see Sprat, *History,* 238–39.

8. Compare Aspromourgos, *Classical Economics,* 17, 55–58. Aspromourgos took the position that while both Bacon and Hobbes were major influences on Petty, Hobbes's influence was the more formative of the two based on the connection between Petty's work and "the fundamental conviction of Hobbes's political theory that the purpose of theory is to determine the rational requirements for civil peace and material plenty" (17), and Petty's "demand for empirical 'data'" as a "corollary of Petty's repudiation of comparative and superlative words" (58). But the first criterion could be as well applied to Bacon's thought, while the second clearly pushed Hobbes's "deductive" concept of reason in a Baconian direction.

9. Petty, "Rules for the Dublin Society," in Lansdowne, *Petty Papers,* 2:88.

10. Petty, "Advertisements to the Dublin Society," in ibid., 2:90.

11. Ibid., 2:91.

12. Peter Robert Dear, *Mersenne and the Learning of the Schools* (Ithaca, NY: Cornell University Press, 1988), 6, 41; similarly 48, on Mersenne's *La verité des sciences contre les sceptiques ou Pyrrhoniens* (1625). Similarly, Popkin, *Scepticism,* 132, 137–38. I owe the suggestion of Mersenne as a source to James Jacob.

13. Descartes to Mersenne (April 15, 1630) quoted in Dear, *Mersenne,* 55.

14. Ibid., 68, 71.

15. Shapiro, *Probability and Certainty,* 22; also 238 on Petty's dictionary exercises in regard to this. The entire chapter "Language, Communication, and Literature" (227–66) shows the scope of this imperative extending far beyond the confines of its relationship to science and economics.

16. Bacon, *Advancement of Learning,* 272.

17. Petty, *Advice of W. P.,* "Epistle Dedicatory."

18. Hobbes, *Leviathan,* 116 (Chapter V).

19. Joseph Glanvill, *Scepsis Scientifica: or, Confest Ignorance, the way to Science; In an Essay of The Vanity of Dogmatizing, and Confident Opinion. With a Reply to the Exceptions of the Learned Thomas Albius* (London,1665), Dedication (a2, b1, reverse).

20. Allen G. Debus, *Science and Education in the Seventeenth Century: The Webster-Ward Debate* (London: Macdonald and Co. Publishers Ltd., 1970), 9, 16–17.

21. Bacon, *Advancement of Learning,* 184.

22. See Cope's and Jones's "Introduction" to Sprat's *History,* xxix.

23. Locke, *Human Understanding,* 2:126–35 (III.10.6–16).

24. Ibid., 2:128 (III.10.9).

25. Vaughn (*Locke,* 28–29) drew a nice parallel between Kepler's planetary laws, Boyle's work on the pressure and volume of gas, Newton's law of gravity, and Locke's price theory: all turn on a direct or inverse proportion.

26. Blount, *Glossographia* (1656), quoted in George Williamson, "The Restoration Revolt against Enthusiasm," *Studies in Philology* 30 (1933): 583.

27. Bacon, *De Augmentis* V.i, quoted in ibid., 573.

28. Williamson, "Restoration Revolt," 582–87.

29. Sprat, *History,* 62. See also ibid., III (against "luxury and redundance of *Speech*").

30. Ibid., 112–13.

31. See Stuart E. Prall, *The Agitation for Law Reform during the Puritan Revolution, 1640–1660* (The Hague: Martinus Nijhoff, 1966), 38, 54–56, 101.

32. Buck, "Seventeenth-Century Political Arithmetic," 67, 73–76.

33. Ibid., 78–80.

34. Locke, *Some Considerations,* 51–52.

35. Ibid., 32. Compare Malynes, *Canker,* 56, and Wilson, *Discourse,* 313.

36. Child, *New Discourse,* in *Works,* preface, already cited.

37. Ibid., 56, 136–37, 143–45, already cited.

Chapter 11

1. "Instructions to the Council of Trade, 1650," in Thirsk and Cooper, *Economic Documents,* 501.

2. "Instructions to the Council for Trade, September, 1668," in ibid., 527.

3. "The Commissioners of Trade and Plantations Report on the State of Trade, 1697," in ibid., 568.

4. *A Proclamation of his Majesty The King of Spaine. For the Conservation of the Contrabando. Revocation of the Permissions. Prohibition of the use of the Merchandizes, and Fruits of the Realms of France, England, and Portugal; and Reformation of Vestures: and Apparel, and other things. Published in Madrid, the 11th of September, Anno 1657. Translated out of Spanish* (London, 1657), 2.

5. Thomas Willsford, *The Scales of Commerce and Trade. Ballancing betwixt the Buyer & Seller, Artificer and Manufacture, Debitor and Creditor, the most general Questions, artificial Rules, and usefull conclusions incident to Traffique.* . . . (London, 1660), passim.

6. Perkins, *Works,* 474.

7. Ibid.

8. Ibid., 474, 475.

9. The first quotation is from S. E., *The Toutch-Stone of Money and Commerce* (London, 1659), 12, while the second is from Henry Parker, *Of a Free Trade* (London, 1648), sig. A2r, p. 2. Both are as quoted in Steve Pincus, "Neither Machiavellian Moment nor Possessive Individualism: Commercial Society and the Defenders of the English Commonwealth," *American Historical Review* 103, no. 3 (June 1998): 722. Pincus makes a strong case overall for a form of middle way, but he needs to refine it. According to his own definition of pro-commercial tradition (708), it "melds" a "commitment to the promotion of the common good" with "a commitment to commercialization," celebrating "neither possessive individualism nor the anti-commercialism of republican Sparta." This is not a wholehearted acceptance of "merchants, tradesmen, and citizens as the heart and soul of their new commercial society" as Pincus claims (722), nor do his examples illustrate such an acceptance. The most common definition of "Merchants" at the time was still that restricting the term to import-export dealers, and their accep-

tance in his own citations is limited to their ability to bring in bullion. Pincus does not account for what happened when these same merchants profited in periods of a negative trade balance.

10. Charles Davenant, *Balance of Power,* in *Works,* 3:315–16 (see the full citation in the chapter on Charles Davenant).

11. "The King's Answer to the Nineteen Propositions, 18 June 1642," in *The Stuart Constitution 1603–1688: Documents and Commentary,* ed. J. P. Kenyon (Cambridge: Cambridge University Press, 1966), 21.

12. Harrington, *Oceana,* in *Political Works,* 405.

13. Mayr, *Authority,* 148.

14. For the opinion that Harrington intended the Agrarian Law to equalize estates, see John F. H. New, "Harrington, a Realist?" in *Past and Present* 24 (April 1963): 79, and his "Communication: The Meaning of Harrington's Agrarian," *Past and Present* 25 (July 1963): 94–95. For the counterargument that Harrington meant inheritances to be passed on as unequally as possible, see C. B. Macpherson, "Harrington as Realist: A Rejoinder," *Past and Present* 24 (April 1963): 82.

15. Wren, *Considerations,* 84.

16. Ibid., 7.

17. Ibid., 8.

18. Macpherson, "Harrington's Opportunity State," 46. Kathleen Toth made a better case for "balance" as "preponderance" in Harrington's thought based on the section in which Harrington classified governments (as absolute monarchy, Gothic mixed-monarchy, or a commonwealth) according to who held the *preponderance* of both land and power. For which, see Toth, "Interpretation in Political Theory: The Case of Harrington," *Review of Politics* 37, no. 3 (July 1975): 331.

19. A. S. P. Woodhouse, ed., *Puritanism and Liberty, Being the Army Debates (1647–9) from the Clarke Manuscripts with Supplementary Documents,* 3d ed. (London: J. M. Dent and Sons, Ltd., 1986), 53, 56.

20. Ibid., 53–55, 58, 60, 66–67, running all of Ireton's replies into one.

21. *Chaos,* unpaged preface.

22. This is the basis of New's case, "Harrington," 79.

23. Jacob, "Restoration Ideologies," 27.

24. Ibid., 28.

25. *Usury Debate,* 1–2.

26. James Harrington, *The Oceana and Other Works of James Harrington, with an Account of his Life by James Toland* (London, 1771), facsimile reprint (Aalen: Scientia Verlag, 1963), 149–50. For the influence of Harvey on Harrington, see Cohn, "Harrington and Harvey," 199–204.

27. See the discussion in Levy, *Economic Ideas,* 135–38, of Athenian democracy in this regard. The idea of their use of the casting of lots as a means of approximating a median policy position had a rather interesting echo in Harrington's work. Though Harrington thought the lot inappropriately combined with annual election of their entire "senate" by the Athenians (*Oceana,* introduction, in *Oceana and Other Works,* 54) he did temper his method of progressive indirect elections with lot casting (ibid., 79, 83, 86) and approved their use by the Israelites for land distribution (*Prerogative of Popular Government,* II.3, in *Oceana and Other Works,* 321).

28. Malynes, *Center of the Circle,* "Epistle."

29. Fletcher, *Political Writings,* 5.

Chapter 12

1. Dudley, 4th Baron North, *Observations and Advises Oeconomical* (1669), preface, 18, quoted in Richard Grassby, *The English Gentleman in Trade: The Life and Works of Sir Dudley North, 1641–1691* (Oxford: Clarendon, 1994), 19. Unless otherwise noted this biographical outline has been greatly condensed from Grassby's work.

2. On his election as treasurer, see *Calendar of State Papers, Domestic Series: Reign of Charles II (vol. 10), 1667 and Addenda 1660–1670*, 410, 414.

3. Jones, *First Whigs*, 161–62, 191, 199–201.

4. The unfolding story can be followed in *Calendar of State Papers, Domestic Series: Reign of Charles II (vol. 23), 1682*, 189–90, 263–65, 280–81, 293–95, 381, 391, 394, 412, 430–31, 433, 448, 512; *Vol. 24, January 1–June 30, 1683*, 204–6, 214–15, 317.

5. According to his brother Roger, quoted in Letwin, *Scientific Economics*, 198. Spiegel (*Growth*, 167) believed North "was able to emancipate himself from the preconceptions and prejudices of his time" because of the "deficiencies of his formal education." But, as we have seen, a mercantile education was undergirt with the same worldview.

6. Grassby has an excellent chapter on the mix of sophistication and speculation in these markets; for which, see Grassby, *English Gentleman*, 38–58. On a commission agent's tasks, see also Roseveare, *Markets and Merchants*, 20–21.

7. Roseveare, *Markets and Merchants*, 221 (16 January 1668; from Thomas Death, Ephraim Skinner and Company to Sir John Lethieullier and Charles Marescoe)

8. Grassby, *English Gentleman*, 59–65, 69–70, 80.

9. Ibid., 90–92.

10. Ibid., 195–97. Grassby did conclude, however (195), that though Dudley North did not reject the Baconian method, he had a lifelong focus on "general principles" that predated his actual introduction by Roger to the work of Descartes.

11. See Grassby's notes to the unpublished works he transcribed in ibid., 308, 317, 321.

12. Letwin, *Scientific Economics*, 271–95 (appendix IV). Pribham (*Economic Reasoning*, 66–67), who did not seem to have read Letwin, based his assessment of Dudley North in large part on Roger North's work. Even when modern assessments of North's work are not so heavily based on passages written by Roger, they are colored by them. Roll (*Economic Thought*, 114) called North an "intransigent" free-trader who expressed, "for the first time, the view that [the]whole world was as much an economic unit as was a single nation," ignoring the classical and Scholastic tradition to this effect. How modern commentators react to North sometimes reveals as much about their attitudes toward laissez-faire capitalism as about North's theories. Spiegel (*Growth*, 167, 169) considered his views "so much ahead of his time that they could find a sympathetic response only in a later age, one that had discarded the ideas of the mercantilists." Routh (*Origin*, 46, 50), on the other hand, saw him as a coiner of "comforting" formulas "that gave instant absolution to the money-makers of their day."

13. The influence of the work on economic thought is another matter. Though the *Discourses* seem quickly to have vanished from view, Routh (*Origin*, 51) has pointed out two possible borrowings from the work before its rediscovery by James Mill: a passage from the "Preface" on the way individuals masked their private interests "under the covert of the Publick" was "reproduced by Boisguillbert (without acknowledgment) and

paraphrased (without acknowledgment) by Adam Smith." For the disappearance of the *Discourse* and its later rediscovery by Mill, see Letwin, *Scientific Economics,* 273–74.

14. North, *Discourses,* in Grassby, *English Gentleman,* 291.

15. Ibid., 292; also 295 (the denominational stamp confirmed weight and purity, but did not set value), 299 (on coins as more convenient counters than logs).

16. Ibid., 293.

17. Ibid., 293.

18. Ibid., 292.

19. Ibid., 292–93.

20. Vickers (*Theory of Money,* 95–97) pointed out that not only was North's "monetary *laissez-faire*" supply-driven, but that North concentrated "on the supply side of the successive economic relations . . . throughout his essay."

21. North, *Discourses,* in Grassby, *English Gentleman,* 293.

22. Ibid.

23. Ibid., 294.

24. Ibid., 295.

25. Ibid., 294.

26. Letwin, *Scientific Economics,* 206, 210, 217.

27. North, "Concerning the values of land and fall of rents," in Grassby, *English Gentleman,* 313.

28. North, "Some notes concerning the laws for the poor," in ibid., 317.

29. Ibid., 318.

30. North, "values of land," in ibid., 310. The policy of free movement was recommended in "laws for the poor," in ibid., 320.

31. North, "laws for the poor," in ibid., 320.

32. North, "values of land," in ibid., 314, 315.

33. Ibid., 312.

34. Ibid., 314.

35. Ibid., 315.

36. Ibid., 316.

37. Ibid., 308, 309. This was just the argument we saw Locke use to create an interest-rent par.

38. Ibid., 310–11. He also slipped from the price of money as interest to the value of money in exchange and back again in this argument, but we are not concerned here with his expertise so much as with his use of a certain kind of argument.

39. North, "values of land," in Grassby, *English Gentleman,* 308.

40. Ibid., 308, 311.

41. Ibid., 312. He also did not explain why he thought wages would increase simultaneously with population or explain how he thought such higher wages would affect a farmer's profit.

42. See Roger North, *A Discourse of the Poor* (posthumously published in 1753), 59, quoted in George D. Choksy, "Previously Undocumented Macroeconomics from the 1680s: The Analytical Arguments and Policy Recommendations of Sir Dudley North and Roger North," *History of Political Economy* 24, no. 2 (summer 1992): 523. Choksy's solution to the problem of determining each brother's contribution to Dudley's oeuvre is to treat everything written by either brother as by both, making his conclusions unsuitable for this study. The same condition applies to his conclusion that their work was simultaneously "bifurcated" and "holistic," in which apparent differences between

the brothers are resolved into different analytic *perspectives* (rather than opinions). For which, see Choksy, "The Bifurcated Economics of Sir Dudley North and Roger North: One Holistic Analytical Engine," *History of Political Economy* 27, no. 3 (fall 1995): 487, taking Roger's *Discourse of the Poor* as a planned second part of Dudley's *Discourses*. Letwin's opinion, that they were real differences of opinion, can be found in *Scientific Economics*, 282, and the table on page 293. I tend to agree with Letwin here.

43. North, *Discourses*, in Grassby, *English Merchant*, 297.

44. Vickers, *Theory of Money*, 103.

45. Compare Grassby, *English Gentleman*, 252n., to the effect that "The circular flow of money has been linked with the discovery of the circulation of the blood, but the concept is of great antiquity and it could just as easily be argued that William Harvey borrowed the idea from his numerous relations in the Levant Trade. It is important to distinguish between analogies and causes." I would counter that it is important to ask what caused the demonstrated analytical changes in the use of the analogy.

46. North, *Discourses*, in ibid., 296, 299.

47. Ibid., 296.

48. North, "A Representation intended to be layd before the parliament in the year 1683 concerning the bad condition of the mony current in England and the meanes to remedy it," in ibid., 306, 307.

49. Ibid., 299.

50. Ibid., 302–3 (Postscript). Letwin (*Scientific Economics*, 211), taking it that North meant war to stand in for "any circumstance which might interrupt the normal course of cash payments or increase the expectation of emergencies," decided that North realized that "two general factors determine the nation's demand for money," namely, "transactions demand and precautionary demand." Thus "the fact that North's categories can be translated so readily into the terms of modern theory is a measure of the advances he made in the substance of economic doctrine." There are two problems with this argument, the first being that the ease of translation is not sufficient evidence of a similarity of understanding (remember Locke's quantity theory of silver) and the second being that whether or not North used "war" the way Letwin assumed he did can neither be proved nor disproved from the text.

51. North, *Discourses*, in Grassby, *English Gentleman*, 303 (Postscript): these are the two famous "buckets."

52. Ibid. In the bucket analogy, North claimed any "overplus" of money would be melted down to supply the domestic demand for plate or "for Transportation," but never asked if foreign trade demands could themselves bring the money supply down below the equilibrium point, or, for that matter, how the coin lost to transportation might be replaced. North seems always to treat the sum total of England's coin and plate as a virtual constant. On foreign and domestic trade as "both being connected together" (without any explanation of how), see ibid., 302.

53. Ibid.

54. Ibid., 303.

55. Ibid., 296.

56. Ibid., 298.

57. North, "A Representation," in Grassby, *English Gentleman*, 307. Grassby (ibid., 243) is big on the demand side of this characterization: "In Dudley's theory, consumption was king and the economy was pulled by demand rather than pushed by supply, as riches were tossed from hand to hand" (though North had taken an opposite view

when it came to interest rates). What Letwin (*Scientific Economics*, 213–14) more wisely saw in North's attempt to explain the mechanics of coin-plate equilibrium was the then still unique combination of equilibrium theory (as incomplete as it was) and laissez-faire, as the first need not necessarily lead to the other, and the second may be made on some basis other than the first.

58. North, *Discourses*, in Grassby, *English Gentleman*, 297–98.

59. North, *Discourses*, in Grassby, *English Gentleman*, 303 (Postscript), concerning a proposed law to fix the price of bullion at 5*s.* per ounce, while turning each ounce of bullion into 5*s. 4d.* or 5*s. 6d.* in coins to force the melting down of plate stocks and relieve the coin shortage.

60. Ibid., 300. Compare Appleby, *Economic Thought*, 256, 259, 262–63. Appleby generally considered Dudley North and Nicholas Barbon as "optimists" (256) and "men who wished to widen the ambit of economic freedom. . . . revealing the socially radical force of the free market (262–63)," thus as part of a group in opposition to oligarchic balance-of-trade supporters such as John Locke. However, Appleby also said of this group opposing Locke that they were "advocates of free trade and the devaluation of the shilling" (259). North, however, did not favor devaluation but joined Locke in favoring recoining at the higher standard (and for the same reasons). North also, like Locke, favored a higher interest rate, tied to the land values whether set by the market (in theory) or by the state (in practice).

61. North, *Discourses*, in Grassby, *English Gentleman*, 300–301; similarly, "A Representation," in ibid., 305.

62. Ibid., 304.

63. North, *Discourses*, in ibid., 300. This was an overly conservative estimate; for the actual loss to the money supply, see the chapter on John Locke.

64. A variation on this argument in the unpublished "Representation" shows North's (perhaps Roger's) political editing skills. In the unpublished piece North claimed the burden would fall most on "the Moneyed Men," those "best able to bear it." Since, as we have seen in Locke's work, "Moneyed Men" was a term used for the landed gentry, the contortions of the published version (about the gentry, their farmers, and merchants with or without stock) may be more the result of a political ploy than of an economic confusion. For which, see "A Representation," in Grassby, *English Gentleman*, 305. McNally (*Political Economy*, 64–65) picked up on the "conscious appeal" to the "landed interests" in the work both of Barbon and North (despite their differences on the interest rate), considering the fact that they felt "compelled" to do so to be "most significant" for his own "Agrarian Capitalism" thesis.

65. North, *Discourses*, in Grassby, *English Gentleman*, 300–301.

66. Ibid., 300.

67. Ibid., 303 (Postscript).

68. North, "A Representation," in ibid., 307.

69. Vickers argued for North as essentially (if imperfectly) a cartalist, because he concentrated on the "functional significance of money rather than on the question of the form of money." For which, see Vickers, *Theory of Money*, 101–2. But would any true cartalist argue for a revaluation at an abandoned de jure standard (with its concomitant reduction of the money supply) rather than for the retention of a current de facto standard?

70. Grassby, *English Gentleman*, 251.

71. Ibid., 82.

72. Ibid., 100–101, 103, 264–65.

73. Ibid., 112.

74. Grassby, *Business Community*, 181, 186–89. For other examples, see Roseveare, *Markets and Merchants*, 23.

75. Grassby, *Business Community*, 185.

Chapter 13

This chapter first appeared, in a slightly different form, in the *History of Political Economy* 32, no. 1 (spring 2000).

1. Unless otherwise noted, this biographical study is taken from the article in the *Dictionary of National Biography (D.N.B)*, CD-ROM (Version 1).

2. Praisegod Barbon headed a Baptist splinter group that accepted infant baptism as scripturally warranted and published *A Discourse tending to prove Baptisme in or under the Defection of Ant-Christ, to be the Ordinance of Jesus Christ. . . .* (1642). For which, see the article on Praisegod Barbon in the *D.N.B.*

3. Reynolds, *Wells Cathedral,* 67; quoted in *D.N.B.*

4. See *Calendar of State Papers, Domestic Series: Reign of James II (vol. 23), 1682,* 71.

5. *Calendar of State Papers, Domestic Series: Reign of William II and Mary III (vol. 6), 1 July 1695–31 December 1695 and Addenda, 1689–1695,* 296. This appears to be the "Water-works" referred to in Barbon's 1694 broadside advertisement for his insurance company; for which, see *An Advertisement. Being A Proposal by Dr. Barbon and Partners for Insuring Houses and Goods from Fire, by A Water-Work, And to serve the Insured Houses and others with Water, at a Cheaper Rate, in the Price of the Water, and Insurance* (London, 1694), single sheet. The "Water-work" was also designed to serve the purpose of extinguishing fires.

6. Ibid.

7. *Calendar of State Papers, Domestic Series: Reign of James II (vol. 3), 1687–1689,* 137. The Friendly Society had been founded by William Hale and Henry Spelman in 1684 and insured about 1,000 homes to Barbon's 4,000 by the time of the restraint order. On this, see Letwin, *Scientific Economics,* 57–58.

8. See Horsefield, *British Monetary Experiments,* 197–98. According to Horsefield, the opening of the subscriptions on May 29, 1695, gave the Barbon-Asgill venture priority over two other banks (those of Chamberlen and John Briscoe) started the same year. It was also a good deal for its customers: paying 2 percent on deposits and charging only 3.5 percent on mortgages when the legal rate was still 6 percent.

9. Ibid., 206–7.

10. Ibid., 208–9.

11. Nicholas Barbon, *A Discourse Concerning Coining the New Money lighter. In Answer to Mr. Lock's Considerations about raising the Value of Money* (London, 1696), 12.

12. Nicholas Barbon, *A Discourse of Trade* (London, 1690), ed. by Jacob H. Hollander (Baltimore: Lord Baltimore, 1905), 16–17; and *New Money Lighter,* 61, 71–72, 75, 80.

13. Barbon, *New Money Lighter,* 30.

14. Barbon, *Discourse of Trade,* 16–17.

15. Ibid.

16. Vickers, *Theory of Money,* 87. Although, as Vickers also pointed out (81–82), Barbon "failed to see completely the logic of his attitudes" and "press" the argument "to the point of advocating a paper currency."

17. Barbon, *New Money Lighter,* 71. Barbon did argue (87) that "if the lightness or Heaviness of the Money had any influence over the Price of Commodities, then all sorts of Commodities ought to be cheap when the Money is Heavy, and dear when the Money is Light," which was manifestly not the case, but this was an argument against the *weight* of the coin being the determining variable, and not an argument against the *quantity* of the coin in circulation fulfilling that role.

18. Viner, *International Trade,* 37.

19. Nicholas Barbon, *An Apology for the Builder: Or a Discourse shewing the Cause and Effects of the Increase of Building* (London, 1685), 30.

20. Barbon, *Discourse of Trade,* 18–19. Also *New Money Lighter* (unpaged preface): "Nothing can be of greater Advantage to Banks than scarcity of Money, when men will be glad to take a Bank-Note for want of it." But note Vickers (*Theory of Money,* 81) that Barbon, unlike Lowndes, does not address the issue of an optimal proportion between the relative quantity of the two.

21. Barbon, *Discourse of Trade,* 16–17.

22. Ibid., 15. Hutchison (*Before Adam Smith,* 75) rightly considered this to be an implicit recognition of "the idea of diminishing utility."

23. Barbon, *New Money Lighter,* 6.

24. Ibid., 43.

25. Ibid., 7. Here discussing why a nettle recognized as useful in stanching bleeding was a "Weed of no Value" in England from its "plenty." This was yet another variation on the diamond-water value paradox.

26. Ibid., 4–5.

27. See Bowley, "Seventeenth-Century," 127–29, for Barbon's place in a chain of argument going back through the century to Malynes, Misselden, and Mun.

28. Child, *New Discourse,* in *Works,* 22.

29. Barbon, *Discourse of Trade,* 20.

30. Ibid., 20. As a component of production, this was interest as a price of goods produced, rather than as the price of *capital goods,* as Schumpeter (*Economic Analysis,* 330) would have it. But while Letwin (*Scientific Economics,* 67) was correct to say Schumpeter went too far in this regard, he himself went too far in trying to disparage Barbon's overall achievement. Making interest one cost even of "a supply of processed commodities" (in Letwin's phrase) was still a startling departure from the general trend of the century's thought. Hutchison (*Before Adam Smith,* 75) reasserts the importance of the introduction of a "real" theory of interest.

31. Barbon, *Discourse of Trade,* 38.

32. Petty, "An Explication," in Lansdowne, *Petty Papers,* 1:210, 214, already cited. Concerning the broad acceptance of this identity of wealth and precious metals, see Viner, *International Trade,* 17–19, 27–28.

33. Petty, *Political Arithmetick,* in Hull, *Economic Writings,* 1:295.

34. See Barbon, *Apology for the Builder,* 27; although he (or his printer) mistakenly referred to him as Sir William Petit, it is clear that Petty was meant.

35. Barbon, *New Money Lighter,* 48.

36. Barbon, *Discourse of Trade,* 22.

37. Barbon, *New Money Lighter,* 41.

38. Barbon, *Discourse of Trade*, 23. This, as Viner (*International Trade*, 52) claimed and Bowley (*Economic Thought*, 32) reaffirmed, can be seen as the beginning of a replacement of balance of trade theory by a balance of employment theory.

39. Barbon, *Discourse of Trade*, 9–10.

40. Ibid., 11. Wiles, however, takes this as indicating both an objective of and a belief in the possibility of forever sustained economic growth. For which, see Richard C. Wiles, "The Development of Mercantilist Economic Thought," in S. Todd Lowry, editor, *Pre-Classical Economic Thought: From the Greeks to the Scottish Enlightenment* (Boston: Kluwer Academic Publishers, 1987), 155.

41. Barbon, *New Money Lighter*, 35–53.

42. Ibid., 40.

43. Ibid., 47.

44. Ibid., 48.

45. Barbon, *Discourse of Trade*, 14.

46. Hobbes, *Leviathan*, 130 (Chapter VII), 160 (Chapter XI) .

47. Hobbes, *Leviathan*, 119–20 (Chapter VI).

48. Barbon, *Discourse of Trade*, 32–33.

49. For an analysis of Aristotle's views on limited and unlimited needs (*Politics* VII, 1323), see Lowry, *Archaeology*, 219–21, though it cannot be established whether Hobbes or Barbon ever interpreted Aristotle in this fashion.

50. Barbon, *Discourse of Trade*, 32–33. The "perpetual spring" was Barbon's take on Hobbes's perpetually impelled human being filtered through ubiquitous clock metaphors of the age.

51. Barbon, *Apology for the Builder*, 33. Tyler Cowen wisely took Barbon's concept of "public" benefit to be "linked much closer to the well-being of the *state* [emphasis added] than would the concept of the classical school." For which, see Tyler Cowen, "Nicholas Barbon and the Origins of Economic Liberalism," *Research in the History of Economic Thought and Methodology* 4 (1986): 69–71.

52. Barbon, *Discourse of Trade*, 35.

53. Ibid., 37.

54. According to Barbon, trade would "continue Open, and Free" in this case, for which, see *Discourse of Trade*, 37–38. Cowen ("Barbon," 76) thought the free-trade rhetoric in Tory writers was as much, if not more, the result of opposition to "Whig" policies than to policies that were "protectionist."

55. Barbon, *New Money Lighter*, 42. But Barbon failed to ask if such extremely high duties might trigger the same retaliatory measures as would outright prohibitions. See, for example, his *Discourse of Trade*, 78: "If the bringing in of foreign goods, should hinder the making and consuming of the native, which will very seldom happen; this disadvantage is not to be remedied by a prohibition of those goods; but by laying on so great duties upon them, that they may always be dearer than those of our country make: the dearness will hinder the consumption of them." Irwin (*Against the Tide*, 52) used this passage to prove that Barbon's thought was ultimately "incompatible with the free trade position."

56. Barbon, *Discourse of Trade*, 10.

57. Ibid., 10–11.

58. Barbon, *Apology for the Builder*, 13.

59. Xenophon's *Ways and Means* was a possible, but not as likely source. Xenophon's claim (IV.11) that the Athenian silver mines would never give out (οὔτε

ἐπιλειψούσης ποτε) was of a different order, being a judgment that, given the extent
of the presumably ore-rich hills surrounding terrain already worked over several generations (IV.2–3), there was no reason to imagine the ore would give out in the foreseeable
future. No claim was made for any generalized infinite supply of silver in the earth or of
an infinite supply of the copper or gold whose prices relative to silver were discussed in
some detail (IV.6–10) in this piece.

60. Arthur O. Lovejoy, *The Great Chain of Being: A Study of the History of an Idea*
(Cambridge, MA: Harvard University Press, 1936), 64.

61. Lovejoy, *Great Chain*, 67 (as used by Pseudo-Dionysius).

62. Lovejoy, *Great Chain*, 124–25, 130.

63. Charles Webster, *From Paracelsus to Newton: Magic and the Making of Modern Science* (Cambridge: Cambridge University Press, 1982; reprint, New York: Barnes
and Noble, 1996), 93 (page references are to reprint edition).

64. Compare Bernard le Bovier de Fontenelle, *Conversations on the plurality of
Worlds*, trans. H. A. Hargreaves (Berkeley: University of California Press, 1990), 44:
"there are as many species of invisible animals as visible. We see from the elephant down
to the mite; there our sight ends. But beyond the mite [is] an infinite multitude of animal beings for which the mite is an elephant."

65. Lovejoy, *Great Chain*, 25.

66. Webster, *Paracelsus to Newton*, 93.

67. Robert Boyle, *Tracts containing I. Suspicions about some Hidden Qualities of the
Air; with an Appendix touching Celestial Magnets, and some other Particulars. II. Animad-
versions upon Mr. Hobbes's Problemata de Vacuo. III. A Discourse of the Cause of Attraction
by Suction*, in *The Works of the Honourable Robert Boyle. In Six Volumes. To which is prefixed
The life of the Author*, new edition, ed. Thomas Birch (London: W. Johnston, S. Crowder et al., 1772), facsimile reprint (Hildesheim: George Olms Verlagsbuchhandlung,
1966), 4:79–84.

68. Frances A. Yates, *Giordano Bruno and the Hermetic Tradition* (Chicago: University of Chicago Press, 1964), 244–46.

69. Gabriel Plattes, *A Discovery of Infinite Treasure, Hidden Since The Worlds
Beginning. Whereunto all men, of what degree soever, are friendly invited to be sharers with
the Discoverer* (London, 1638), 79. Similarly, ibid., 87: "for what am I but a piece of earth
quickened and animated by the universall soule of the world?" This source was suggested to me by James Jacob.

70. Plattes, *Infinite Treasure*, 19, and "Epistle Dedicatorie" (a); but note, ibid., 19,
that may or may not imply that some minerals were not infinitely renewable: "limestone
and chalk doth fatten ground . . . [and so] are farre more worth then any Gold or Silver
mine; being not onely infinite, and not to be exhausted by time: but also the profit
thereof not to be diminished through the multitude of sharers; which inconvenience all
other Treasures are subject to." The treatment of gold by Plattes in *A Discovery of Subterraneall Treasure* would imply that it was infinitely renewable, however, though it
would not "putrifie" and turn into a different metal because of its "ecellent composition."
For which, see Gabriel Plattes, *A Discovery of Subterraneall Treasure, viz. Of all manner
of Mines and Mineralls, from the Golde to the Coale; with Plaine Directions and Rules for the
finding of them in all Kingdomes and Countries* (London, 1639), 36–37. References to the
"generation" of metals from the earth's "womb" are scattered throughout the work. See,
for example, ibid., 1, 2, 4, 7.

71. Plattes, *Infinite Treasure*, 77–79.

72. He is not on any of the lists of Royal Society Fellows reproduced in appendix IV of Thomas Thomson's *History of the Royal Society, from its Institution to the end of the Eighteenth Century* (London: Robert Baldwin, 1812), the most complete of the early listings.

73. For which, see *The Diary of Robert Hooke M. A., M. D., F. R. S., 1672–1680*, ed. Henry Robinson and Walter Adams (London: Taylor and Francis, 1935) 14 (23 Nov. 1672) and 324 (26 and 30 Oct. 1677).

74. See Barbon, *Discourse of Trade*, 42 (editor's note 7).

75. On Graunt's *Observations on the Bills of Mortality*, see Barbon, *Apology for the Builder*, 18–19, 27; Barbon's only criticism of Graunt's work was that his calculations of London's growth were too low.

76. For a multipage summation of Hale's argument studded with lengthy quotations, see Barbon's *Apology for the Builder*, 7ff. Hale's book is also referred to in Barbon's *Discourse of Trade*, 25. Hale was an important authority for Barbon.

77. *Philosophical Transactions*, abridged, ii.134; quoted in *D.N.B.*

78. *O.E.D.* (1933), 5:264.

79. *O.E.D.* (1933), 5:262.

80. Koyré, *Closed World*, 58 (on Kepler's rejection of an infinite universe on these grounds), 106, 124 (on Descartes's rejection of the term on the same grounds). Note, ibid., 42–43, 137, on the ability of Giordano Bruno and Henry More to accept an infinite universe through their adhesion, respectively, to hermetic plentitude and Platonism.

81. *O.E.D.* (1933), 5:262 (Addison, 1709, *Tattler* no. 119, ¶2). This is technically later than Barbon's writings, but Berkeley did attack Halley for just such a pronouncement; for which see the article on Edmund Halley in the *D.N.B.*

82. George (Bishop) Berkeley, *Philosophical Works*, ed. M. R. Ayers (London: J. M. Dent and Sons Ltd., 1989), 118.

83. See David M. Levy, "Bishop Berkeley Exorcises the Infinite: Fuzzy Consequences of Strict Finitism," *Hume Studies* 18, no. 2 (Nov. 1992), 512, 514. However, leaving aside any consideration of the problems in Berkeley's epistemological system, one still has to keep in mind that Berkeley's objections were part of a larger, lifelong effort to refute atheistical materialism, which he saw as rooted in the idea of matter itself ("there is not any other substance than *spirit*"; the *"real things"* we see are only "ideas imprinted on the senses by the Author of Nature," etc.). For which, see Berkeley, *Philosophical Works*, 79, 86.

84. For this and the following paragraph, see Lovejoy, *Great Chain*, 64, 67, 124–25, 130 already cited, but also ibid., 49–50, 54–55, for its origins in the thought of Plato and Aristotle.

85. Robert Boyle, *Works* (London, 1744), 1:441; quoted in Jacob, "Political Economy," 522.

86. Jacob, "Political Economy," 523.

87. Jacob, "Restoration Ideologies," 26, 28.

88. Barbon, *Apology for the Builder*, 6.

89. Ibid., 19–20.

90. Barbon, *New Money Lighter*, 49. Thus there would seem to be a problem here with Appleby's contention (*Economic Thought*, 176) that "Barbon laid bare the 'invisible hand of the market' when he explained that it is the trader who takes care to provide a sufficient quantity of the goods for man's needs. And how does he find out how much to provide? From the market." Barbon's examples of overproduction were

chosen by Eli Heckscher to illustrate his "fear of goods" thesis and its persistence even up to the "threshold of *laissez-faire*." For which, see Eli Heckscher, *Mercantilism*, revised (2d) ed., ed. E. F. Söderlund, trans. Mendel Shapiro (London: George Allen and Unwin, 1955), 2:115; see also ibid., 2:57.

91. Barbon, *Apology for the Builder*, 24.

92. Ibid., 25.

93. Vickers, *Theory of Money*, 86n.

Chapter 14

1. John Brewer's argument hinged on "three features of the English state," namely, "early centralization, limited participation in European War and the [relative] absence of venality" rather than on its constitutional struggles as causing England to diverge from the Continental model, but he also included a discussion of the effects of country ideology in channeling *how* the government expanded even if it failed to altogether stop that expansion. For which, see John Brewer, *The Sinews of Power: War, Money and the English State, 1688–1783* (Cambridge, MA: Harvard University Press, 1990), 21, 155–61.

2. Berkeley, *Philosophical Works*, 69, 78, 82, 86, 108–9.

3. Exchequer Bills (first issued under an act of April 27, 1696) became legal tender in 1697; Treasury and Exchequer Orders of repayment (Tallies) were not legal tender but, being assignable, did circulate. The creation of a "credit currency" was part of the original intention of the formation of the Bank of England. For which see Abbott Payson Usher's "Introduction" to *Two Manuscripts by Charles Davenant* (Baltimore: Johns Hopkins Press, 1942), vii–ix; and Feavearyear, *Pound Sterling*, 125.

4. Peter George Michael Dickson, *The Financial Revolution in England: A Study in the Development of Public Credit, 1688–1756* (London: Macmillan, 1967), 46. Military spending amounted to anywhere from 67 to 79 percent of this budget; for which, see O'Brien, "Political Economy," 2. Brewer (*Sinews of Power*, 40) gives 74 percent for 1689–97 (also known as the Nine Years' War) and 66 percent for 1702–13 (War of the Spanish Succession) so there was little relief in sight the entire period of Davenant's activity.

5. Dickson, *Financial Revolution*, 53. The extent to which the English copied Dutch models in this, in an unsuccessful 1692 proposal for a bank currency and in the 1643 excise itself, is discussed in ibid., 42, 51–52. The Tontine was so named because the idea behind it was usually attributed to Lorenzo Tonti (1630–1695), adviser to Cardinal Mazarin. The last subscriber to the 1692 tontine died in 1783, receiving an annual pension of £1,000 on an initial investment of £100. For which, see Wilson, *England's Apprenticeship*, 218.

6. 5 and 6 William III and Mary II, c.20. See Dickson, *Financial Revolution*, 53–54. The loan was to be secured by revenues brought in from excises on alcohol and a tonnage grant authorized in the act.

7. Ibid., 54–56.

8. Wilson, *England's Apprenticeship*, 313; and O'Brien, "Political Economy," 2. Brewer (*Sinews of Power*, 30, 41) gives the debt as £13.1 million in 1702 and £36.2 million in 1713. He also takes national income to be £59.8 million in 1710, which would give us a

national debt at somewhere between 21.9 percent and 60.5 percent of the national income.

9. Dickson, *Financial Revolution,* 59, 62.

10. Ibid., 55–56. He has an excellent summary (56) of the long association of public banks with republics in the popular mind, viz., Harrington's "Where there is a Bank, ten to one there is a Commonwealth" (*The Prerogative of popular Government,* 1658), quoted in ibid., 56.

11. Ibid., 56–57. The two companies were merged in 1709 as the United East India Company, a move made easier no doubt by the additional £1.2 million they had agreed to lend the government in 1708.

12. Brewer, *Sinews of Power,* 89. These numbers were also high for Europe itself: by 1725 the average Englishman was paying a bit more than twice as much per year in taxes as was the average Frenchman.

13. Ibid., 31–32, 34, 37, 66.

14. Dickson, *Financial Revolution,* 255 (table 31).

15. Ibid., 258. As Dickson pointed out, only the Bank recorded the occupations of its subscribers, so this was a list gathered from the smaller shareholders of the more aristocratic institution; a list gathered from the Tontine purchasers might even reach farther down the social scale. As to the peerage, Dickson found 2 peers and 42 MPs ("several of whom were baronets") among the Tontine subscribers, and only 9 peers and 30 MPs on the 1694 Bank lists; for which, see ibid.

16. Ibid., 256.

17. Ibid., 261, 268. Peers and MPs still lagged behind, making up only 0.1 percent and 3.5 percent respectively of the 1707 Annuity subscribers, 0.3 percent and 1.5 percent of the Bank stockholders in 1709, and 0.3 percent and 1.9 percent of the East India stockholders in 1709. For which, see ibid., 266. The dollar value of the stock they held was only slightly greater than their numbers among Bank shareholders but a bit less proportionate for those in East India stock.

18. Ibid., 487–88 (the earliest surviving issue of Castaing's is from 1698 though Dickson thinks there might have been earlier ones), 490–91 (Jonathan's and Garraway's coffeehouses had price quotes by 1692 at the latest), 494–95 (brokers could not deal on their own behalf, jobbers could; a "refusal" was the right to buy at a future date, while the "put" was the right to sell at a future date).

19. Unless otherwise noted this account of Davenant's life is taken from the *Dictionary of National Biography,* CD-ROM (Version 1). Exactly where Davenant managed to get the degree is not known.

20. See *Calendar of State Papers, Domestic Series: Reign of Charles II (vol. 21), 1679–1680,* 371.

21. See *Calendar of State Papers, Domestic Series: Reign of Charles II (vol. 25), July 1–September 30, 1683,* 109 (claiming Monmouth was hidden either in the theater owned by Davenant or in another owned by one Betterton).

22. See, for example, Charles Davenant, *The true Picture of A Modern Whig, set forth in a dialogue between Mr. Whiglove and Mr. Double, two under-spur-leathers to the late Ministry* (London, 1701), in *The Political and Commercial Works Of that celebrated Writer Charles D'Avenant, LL. D. Relating to the Trade and Revenue of England. The Plantation Trade. The East-India Trade, And African Trade,* ed. Sir Charles Whitworth (London, 1771); facsimile reprint (Farnborough, UK: Gregg Press Limited, 1967), 4:128, 137. And *Tom Double Returned out of the Country: Or, The True Picture of a Modern Whig,*

set forth in a Second Dialogue between Mr. Whiglove and Mr. Double, At the Rummer Tavern in Queen-Street (London, 1702), in ibid., 4:191, 216–17.

23. See, for example, Davenant, *An Essay upon the Balance of Power* (London, 1701), in *Works*, 3:328–29; *An Essay Upon the Right of Making War, Peace, and Alliances* (London, 1701), in ibid., 3:365–67; and *An Essay upon Universal Monarchy* (London, 1701), in ibid., 4:25.

24. *Calendar of State Papers, Domestic Series: Reigns of William III and Mary II (vol. 6), July 1–December 31, 1695 and Addenda 1689–1695*, 71.

25. He had earlier sat for St. Ives in Cornwall in the first Parliament of James II.

26. Davenant, *Essays upon Peace at Home, and War Abroad* (London, 1704), in *Works*, 4:317.

27. This was essentially the position of D. Waddell, who attempted to trace every change in tone in Davenant's works to his hopes of or disappointment in office and the rise and fall of Montagu and the Junto, but overlooked the real continuity in his thought. For Waddell's thesis, see his "Charles Davenant (1656–1714)—A Biographical Sketch," *Economic History Review*, 2d ser., 11, no. 2 (Dec. 1958): 279–88.

28. Davenant, *Discourses on the Public Revenues, and on the Trade of England. In Two Parts* (London, 1698), in *Works*, 2:53.

29. Davenant, *An Essay upon Ways and Means of supplying the war* (London, 1695), in *Works*, 1:4, 11; *On the Public Revenues*, in ibid., 2:24; and *Peace at Home*, in ibid., 5:17. Similarly, *An Essay upon the Probable Methods of making a People Gainers in the Balance of Trade* (London, 1699), in ibid., 2:300. And particularly, *On the Public Revenues*, in ibid., 2:72: "Machiavel says, That to render a commonwealth long-lived, it is necessary to correct it often, and reduce it towards its first principles." The idea of the involvement of "specialization" is taken from Pocock. For which, see Pocock, *Machiavellian Moment*, 430 ("The danger of luxury [is that] it leads to choice and consequently to specialization"), 431 ("'Luxury,' then, is shorthand for culture, leisure, and choice").

30. Davenant, *On the Public Revenues*, in *Works*, 2:52.

31. Davenant, *Probable Methods*, in ibid., 2:314.

32. Pocock, *Machiavellian Moment*, viii.

33. Davenant, *Peace at Home*, in *Works*, 4:289–92, 389; *Ways and Means*, in ibid., 1:10; and *On the Public Revenues*, in ibid., 2:54.

34. Davenant, *Probable Methods*, in ibid., 2:185.

35. Pocock, *Machiavellian Moment*, viii.

36. O'Brien, "Political Economy," 15.

37. Estimates of the portion of the total population (not work force) "engaged in agriculture" in 1700 range from as high as 55 percent to as low as 42 percent; for which see, Mark Overton, *Agricultural Revolution in England: The Transformation of the Agrarian Economy, 1500–1850* (Cambridge: Cambridge University Press, 1996), 82. The higher number seems the more likely in this case, and contemporary observers would have probably thought it higher than that.

38. Davenant, *Ways and Means*, in *Works*, 1:16; and compare *Probable Methods*, in ibid., 2:275: "if trade cannot be made subservient to the nation's safety, it ought to be no more encouraged here than it was in Sparta."

39. Davenant, *Ways and Means*, in ibid., 1:13.

40. Ibid., 1:30.

41. Ibid., 1:16.

42. Davenant, *On the East-India Trade*, in ibid., 1:90, 94.

43. Davenant, *On the Public Revenues*, in ibid., 1:442, 447.

44. Ibid., 1:448. This passage was taken almost word for word from his unpublished essay of July 15, 1696, "A Memorial concerning Creditt (July 15, 1696)," in *Two Manuscripts*, 79.

45. Davenant, *On the Public Revenues*, in *Works*, 1:151. This passage was also taken almost word-for-word from Davenant's "Memorial concerning Creditt"; for which, see *Two Manuscripts*, 75.

46. Davenant, *On the Public Revenues*, in *Works*, 1:152–53, 168–69.

47. Ibid., 1:353.

48. Davenant, *Probable Methods*, in ibid., 2:291.

49. Davenant, *On the Public Revenues*, in ibid., 1:405–6.

50. Davenant, *Ways and Means*, in ibid., 1:6–7; and *On the Public Revenues*, in ibid., 1:419–20 (similarly, 422). Other examples (some with extended quotations from Richelieu's *Testament Politique*) can be found in *An Essay on the East India Trade* (London, 1697), in ibid., 1:36; *Probable Means*, in ibid., 2:269–61, 291; and *Universal Monarchy*, in ibid., 4:25. In fact, by simple bulk, there was far more reliance on Richelieu in Davenant's work than on Machiavelli. Gunn suggested Tacitus as the main source of what he took to be Davenant's neoclassical republicanism, claiming all of Davenant's work from 1698 on "bore the mark of Tacitus's description of Rome's loss of liberty" based on "a major new translation of Tacitus" appearing in 1698. For which, see J. A. W. Gunn, *Beyond Liberty and Property: The Process of Self-Recognition in Eighteenth-Century Political Thought* (Kingston and Montreal: McGill-Queen's University Press, 1983), 15. But Gunn seems not to have noticed these antirepublican passages in Davenant's thought.

51. On trade councils, see Davenant, *On the Public Revenues*, in *Works*, 1:425–26. In the same essay, Davenant quoted Sir Josiah Child's recommendations of such councils at some length; for which, see ibid., 1:449, 452. See also "A Memorial Concerning the Coyn of England (November 1695)," in *Two Manuscripts*, 52–53 (proposing the council be made up of retired merchants—as they would no longer have private interests to favor over public ones—but led by government ministers). On tax commissioners, see *Ways and Means*, in *Works*, 1:56.

52. Colbert inherited the system of *hôpitaux* begun under Mazarin's and Fouquet's ministries. The *hôpitaux* were modeled on the Elizabethan workhouse and housed married as well as unmarried indigent, setting them to work in lace, silk, and ribbon manufacture (predominantly, though each *hôpital* had its specialty). As developed by Colbert they continued to be much closer to factories than educational institutions, and one or two became more houses of correction than anything else. Colbert did encourage some educational projects, such as sending older boys to a special institution set up by the French government in the Levant to learn the languages necessary for doing business there, but these were separate from the *hôpitaux*. For which, see Charles Woolsey Cole, *Colbert and a Century of French Mercantilism* (New York: Columbia University Press, 1939), 1:266, 270, 272, 275, 351, 397; 2:220, 236.

53. As, for example, in Davenant, *On the East-India Trade*, in *Works*, 1:98 (against import prohibitions). Heckscher (*Mercantilism*, 2:115) saw Davenant as "already influenced by *laissez-faire* to far greater extent than most writers of the end of the 17th century." Hutchison remarked (*Before Adam Smith*, 50, 53) on the "notably free-trade stance" of Davenant's *Essay on the East-India Trade*, even if tempered by the "'mercantilist' inclinations" of his praise of Colbert. Gunn (*Politics*, 241–42) considered Dav-

enant's free-trader reputation ultimately "merited by his writings" despite his overall "pattern of vacillation."

54. See Davenant, *Ways and Means*, in *Works*, 1:64, in which he proposed a law of assize to increase the weight of loaves of bread as the market price of the wheat crop fell. He claimed it would "augment consumption among the common people," who "would consume more, if they might have more for the same money." Davenant did drop the idea of assizes three years later as "impracticable" but that was in the context of their ability to prevent "the general fraud of retailers," and because they might be "a bar to industry" (in the sense of worker industriousness), not as price controls "for the public advantage." For this later position, see *On the Public Revenues*, in ibid., 1:286–87.

55. Ibid., 1:128. Petty's position was acknowledged by Davenant on the same page: "the application of it to the particular objects of revenue and trades, is what Sir William Petty first began." As to a greater continuing influence of this school than had earlier been supposed in eighteenth-century England, see Julian Hoppit, "Political Arithmetic in Eighteenth-Century England," *Economic History Review* 49, no. 3 (Aug. 1996): 516–40. For the purposes of our century, note the statistics compiled by Sir Peter Pett (1681) and John Houghton (in 1683 and 1693), discussed in ibid., 518.

56. Pocock, *Machiavellian Moment*, 425. Aspromourgos (*Classical Economics*, 163) felt Davenant's work represented an emasculation of Petty's ideas because of Davenant's restriction of them to "merely public finance," and he thought them of little value as analysis once stripped of Gregory King's data.

57. Davenant, *On the Public Revenues*, in *Works*, 1:251–52.

58. Davenant, *On the East-India Trade*, in ibid., 1:102. He repeats this refrain at least two or three times per essay. For some examples, see Davenant, *Ways and Means*, in ibid., 1:16; *On the East-India Trade*, in ibid., 1:86, 88; *On the Public Revenues*, in ibid., 2:17–18; *A Report to the honourable The Commissioners For putting in Execution the Act, intituled An Act for the taking, examining, and stating the publick Accounts of the Kingdom* (London, 1712), in ibid., 5:391, 461–62 (with praise for Thomas Mun's work on this score); and "Memorial Concerning the Coyn, " in *Two Manuscripts*, 12. See also Endres, "Numerical Data," 256–68, on effect of Davenant's bullionism on his data evaluation.

59. Davenant, *Probable Methods*, in *Works*, 2:261.

60. Davenant, *Ways and Means*, in ibid., 1:13.

61. See, for example, Davenant, *Probable Methods*, in ibid., 2:226; and *On the Public Revenues*, in ibid., 1:385.

62. Davenant, *Peace at Home*, in ibid., 4:388.

63. Davenant, *Balance of Power*, in ibid., 3:315–16.

64. Davenant, *On the Public Revenues*, in ibid., 1:396–97, 2:8–10.

65. Davenant, *Probable Methods*, in ibid., 2:237, 252 (citing Petty's data to prove the benefits England reaped from Irish trade), 255.

66. Davenant, *On the East-India Trade*, in ibid., 1:98.

67. Ibid., 1:81, 1:92.

68. Davenant, *Report to the honourable The Commissioners*, in ibid., 5:351.

69. Ibid., 5:378.

70. *Britannia Languens*, 51–54.

71. Davenant, *Reflections upon the Constitution and management of the Trade to Africa, through The whole Course and Progress thereof, from the Beginning of the last Century, to this Time. Herein The nature and uncommon Circumstances of that Trade are particularly considered, and all the Arguments urged alternately by the two contending Parties here,*

touching the different Methods now proposed by them, for carrying on the same to a national Advantage, impartially stated and considered. By which A clear View is given of such a Constitution, as (if established by Act of Parliament) would, in all Probability, render the African Trade a permanent, creditable, and advantageous Trade to Britain (London, 1709), in *Works*, 5:130–43, 148. Dutch interlopers concerned him as much if not more than domestic ones; hence his citation (143) of Josiah Child's complaints on this score.

72. Davenant, *On the Public Revenues*, in ibid., 2:38.

73. Davenant, "Memorial Concerning the Coyn," in *Two Manuscripts*, 50.

74. Davenant, *On the Public Revenues*, in *Works*, 1:385.

75. Davenant, *Ways and Means*, in ibid., 1:16.

76. Davenant, *On the Public Revenues*, in ibid., 1:288. In the same work (1:154), he proposed the formation of a sinking fund to bring debt levels down gradually.

77. Davenant, *On the Public Revenues*, in ibid., 1:293. He also suggested all banks should be "incorporated with the State" so they did not develop a "Separate Interest." For which, see "Memorial Concerning the Coyn," in *Two Manuscripts*, 61.

78. Davenant, "Memorial Concerning the Coyn," in *Two Manuscripts*, 8 (with a bit of Galen's influence remaining). See similarly, *Probable Methods*, in *Works*, 2:237; *On the Public Revenues*, in ibid., 1.388; and *Ways and Means*, in ibid., 1:16.

79. Davenant, *Probable Methods*, in ibid., 2:264.

80. John Houghton (d. 1705), *A collection of letters for the improvement of husbandry and trade* (2 vols., London, 1681–83), 2:121, 132, 134–35, 138–39, cited in Jacob, "Restoration Ideologies," 31.

81. Davenant, *On the Public Revenues*, in *Works*, 1:252 (mislabeled 242).

82. O'Brien, "Political Economy," 3. These numbers should be used merely to chart the approximate change as it is not clear to what extent the figures presented as "National Income" are net of any of the taxes.

83. Davenant, *Ways and Means*, in *Works*, 1:79.

84. Ibid., 1:26–27, 29.

85. Davenant, *Ways and Means*, in *Works*, 1:31. For the trade wars set off by high duties and import prohibitions, see also *Report to the honourable the Commissioners*, in ibid., 5:379 (citing Thomas Mun on their inefficacy), 387 (approving of their use in retaliation, however), 391 (recommending only "moderate duties").

86. Davenant, *Ways and Means*, in ibid., 1:70–71.

87. Ibid., 1:63, 66.

88. Davenant, *On the Public Revenues*, in ibid., 1:202, 215, but see ibid., 220, to the effect that farming was only appropriate for excises on domestic goods as tax-farmers could use their knowledge to load up on imports when profitable.

89. Ibid., 1:224 (mislabeled 124).

90. Davenant, *Probable Methods*, in ibid., 2:199.

91. Davenant, "Memorial Concerning the Coyn," in *Two Manuscripts*, 53.

92. Davenant, *On the East-India Trade*, in *Works*, 1:99, 114.

93. Davenant, *Report to the honourable the Commissioners*, in ibid., 5:379.

94. Davenant, *On the Public Revenues*, in ibid., 2:42. On the power of the "example of the great ones," see ibid., 1:298, 300; *Probable Methods*, in ibid., 2:22; and *Report to the honourable the Commissioners*, in ibid., 5:379.

95. See Davenant, *Probable Methods*, in ibid., 2:307, quoting from *Leviathan* (Chapter 3) to the effect that those with the most experience in a field are its best policymakers (predictors).

96. Davenant, *Universal Monarchy*, in ibid., 4:3.

97. As, for example, Appleby, *Economic Thought*, 187; she termed this the century's "pithiest expression" of the "theory of interchangeable participants."

98. The first person to notice Hobbes's role in this seems to have been James Bonar, who called Hobbes's conception of human equality an "anticipation of a later economical hypothesis" though not "turned to special economical account by Hobbes himself." For which, see Bonar, *Philosophy and Political Economy in Some of Their Historical Relations*, facsimile reprint of the 3d ed. of 1922 (New York: A. M. Kelley, 1966), 82.

99. Davenant, "Memorial Concerning the Coyn," in *Two Manuscripts*, 19–21.

100. See James R. Jacob and Timothy Raylor, "Opera and Obedience: Thomas Hobbes and *A Proposition for Advancement of Moralitie* by Sir William Davenant," *The Seventeenth Century* 6, no. 2 (autumn 1991): 205–6, 211–12, 215, 218 (the reference is to Hobbes's plan for sabbath-centered adult civic education, in *Leviathan,* Chapter 30).

101. See Davenant, *On the Public Revenues*, in *Works*, 2:216–20, 222.

102. Davenant, *Ways and Means*, in ibid., 1:62.

103. Ibid., 1:356–57, 373, 382, 447.

104. Davenant did recognize the functional element. He wrote at one point of money as "at bottom no more than the counters with which men, in their dealings, have been accustomed to reckon." For which, see ibid., 1:355. He just thought its real component was more important.

105. Davenant, "Memorial Concerning the Coyn," in *Two Manuscripts*, 12–15. Unlike Locke, however, Davenant did not set up differing rules for silver and gold; he considered them interchangeable. On gold and silver as the "measure of trade," see also *On the Public Revenues*, in *Works*, 1:160.

106. Davenant, "Memorial Concerning the Coyn," in *Two Manuscripts*, 29, 17. Davenant does not put forward any specific proposals for reforming the coin in this piece, but suggests instead more attention be paid to the balance of trade as a long-term solution. His reason for this would seem to be a rationale for not recoining at the higher standard, despite his ideas on purity, because he supposed that the shrinkage in the coin supply caused by such a recoinage could not be made up either by melting down existing stocks of plate or stretching the amount of credit currently at large. For this, see ibid., 36–38.

107. Davenant, "Memorial concerning Creditt," in ibid., 103.

108. Davenant, *On the Public Revenues*, in *Works*, 2:105–6, 1:382.

109. Davenant, "Memorial Concerning the Coyn," in *Two Manuscripts*, 25–26.

110. Davenant, "Memorial concerning Creditt," in ibid., 68.

111. Coleman was generally correct to assume that such an emphasis on population on Davenant's part was less the result of some labor theory of value than of a practical recognition that in his day, except in a few industries "such as iron smelting or paper making" that used "heavy fixed capital equipment," labor "was easily the most important factor of production." The only way to raise output was to employ more hands. For which, see D. C. Coleman, "Labour in the English Economy of the Seventeenth Century," *Economic History Review*, 2d ser., 8, no. 3 (April 1956): 287. We have seen this same insight in all of the writers in this study.

112. Davenant, *Probable Methods*, in *Works*, 2:186–87, 191. Similarly, *Ways and Means*, in ibid., 1:73. He did believe there were upper limits to such growth, but as well as believing that England could hold twice as many as at present, he seems to have

thought of those limits as flexible, with trade supplying what the natural product could not. For this, see *On the Public Revenues*, in ibid., 2:110.

113. Davenant, *Probable Methods*, in ibid., 2:203.

114. This account of King's life is taken from the *Dictionary of National Biography*, CD-ROM (Version 1).

115. Though extracts from the piece were used by Charles Davenant and published in his works, King's treatise was not published until 1801, when George Chalmers included it in his *Estimate of the Comparative Strength of Great Britain*.

116. The data following come from King's table as reproduced by Davenant. For which, see *Probable Methods*, in *Works* 2:184 (the table), 2:173, 197–98, 202 (Davenant's summaries). Davenant made similar demographic divisions based on hearth money receipts in *Ways and Means*, in ibid., 1:19. There are some discrepancies between King's and Davenant's figures. Both came up with a total population of 5,500,520, but using slightly different figures for the number of families in each category and in some of their annual incomes, Davenant managed to increase King's net annual income from £1,825,100 to £2,401,200. It is possible, of course, that Davenant had access to an earlier version of the manuscript or even to King's notebooks. The final version of King's figures can be found in *Two Tracts by Gregory King*, ed. George E. Barnett (Baltimore: Johns Hopkins Press, 1936), 31.

117. Davenant, *Probable Methods*, in *Works*, 2:202.

118. Davenant, *Probable Methods*, in *Works*, 2:204, 207–11. Similarly, *Ways and Means*, in ibid., 1:71–72. On the existing laws as encouraging beggary, see especially *On the East-India Trade*, in ibid., 1:100.

119. Davenant, *On the Public Revenues*, in ibid., 1:229.

120. Davenant, *Probable Methods*, in ibid., 2:224 (the quotation and the table).

121. See G. Heberton Evans, Jr., "The Law of Demand—The Roles of Gregory King and Charles Davenant," *Quarterly Journal of Economics* 81, no. 3 (August 1967): 483–92, which reproduces the pertinent pages of King's journal. Evans (492) took Davenant as the major author.

122. Hutchison, *Before Adam Smith*, 48.

123. A good summary of Jevons's work can be found in Stephen M. Stigler, "Jevons on the King-Davenant Law of Demand: A Simple Resolution of a Historical Puzzle," *History of Political Economy* 26, no. 2 (summer 1994): 185–91. Stigler aimed to show that Jevons had used a simpler mathematical solution than the nonlinear least squares (a method based on the calculus of probabilities) proposed by Aldrich. John Creedy believed Gregory King had used the method ("based on the factorial expansion of a polynomial") devised by James Gregory (in 1670) and developed and popularized by Sir Isaac Newton (in 1687). For Creedy's thesis, see "On the King-Davenant 'Law' of Demand," *Scottish Journal of Political Economy* 33, no. 3 (August 1986): 193–212 (especially the conclusion, 209).

124. Davenant, "Memorial Concerning the Coyn," in *Two Manuscripts*, 7. Similarly, *On the Public Revenues*, in *Works*, 1:355.

125. Davenant, "Memorial Concerning the Coyn," in *Two Manuscripts*, 7.

126. Davenant, *On the Public Revenues*, in *Works*, 1:160.

127. Davenant, "Memorial Concerning the Coyn," in *Two Manuscripts*, 19–21, already cited.

128. Locke, *Some Considerations*, in *Several Papers*, 6, 4, already cited.

129. Davenant, *On the Public Revenues*, in *Works* 1:151, already cited.

130. Or, more exactly, whether all the links between the idea (taken from Hobbes) of self-preservation that Davenant seems to have believed to be its root and those mutable tastes could ever be discovered.

131. See the data referenced in notes 38 and 39 of this chapter.

132. Pocock, *Machiavellian Moment*, 450. Pocock saw Davenant's "attitude toward trade" as "at bottom as morally ambivalent as Machiavelli's toward *virtù.*" For which, see ibid., 442. With that as it stands, there can be no quarrel.

Conclusion

1. Max Beer, *An Inquiry into Physiocracy* (London: George Allen and Unwin, Ltd., 1939), 74; H. T. Dickinson, *Liberty and Property: Political Ideology in Eighteenth-Century Britain* (New York: Holmes and Meier, Publishers, 1977), 68, 86; Johnson, *Predecessors*, 45; Vilar, *Gold and Money*, 224; Wiles, "Development," in Lowry, *Pre-Classical*, 155; Roll, *Economic Thought*, 58, 72, 101; and Vickers, *Theory of Money*, 75.

2. Smith, *Wealth of Nations*, 1.449 (IV. introduction).

3. Ibid., 1.450 (IV.i), 1.456 (IV.i), 2.146 (IV.vii.iii), 2.179–80 (IV.viii).

4. Gustav Schmoller, *The Mercantilist System and its Historical Significance, Illustrated chiefly from Prussian History; being a chapter from the Studien über die wirtschaftliche Politik Friedrich des Grossens* (1884), trans. W. J. Ashley (New York: P. Smith, 1931), 51.

5. Bonar, *Philosophy*, 69.

6. Heckscher, *Mercantilism*, 2.25, 114, 363.

7. Rothbard, *Economic Thought*, 21.

8. Ibid., 214.

9. Mark Perlman and Charles R. McCann Jr., *The Pillars of Economic Understanding: Ideas and Traditions* (Ann Arbor: University of Michigan Press, 1998), 75, 85, 92.

10. Ibid., 81, 83.

11. See Viner's essay in Coleman, *Revisions*, 71. He also suggested (64) that historians who favored the power thesis "seem to have been themselves sympathetic to the subordination of the individual to the state." Heckscher's defense can be found in ibid., 25–26.

12. William Dyer Grampp, *Economic Liberalism* (New York: Random House, 1965), 48–49, 52, 56.

13. Ibid., 55–56.

14. Wiles, "Development," in Lowry, *Pre-Classical*, 154–55.

15. Ekelund and Tollison, *Mercantilism*, 5, 18–19.

16. Ibid., 155.

17. As John Brewer seemed to think. For which, see his *Sinews of Power*, 169.

18. This is a point well-made by Joyce Appleby, in her *Economic Thought*, 10, 26–30, but one that actually works against her thesis that there was no consciously pursued mercantilism in England until the end of the seventeenth century. D. C. Coleman explained the problem with Appleby's chronology thus: "At the time when Mrs. Appleby has mercantilism beginning in England [1696–1713], most branches of English trade (with the notable exception of that to the East) had been freed from the control of monopolistic companies. Conversely, in the later sixteenth century, when most of En-

glish overseas trade was controlled by such companies, England was, apparently, barely emergent from a subsistence economy with mercantilism hardly a cloud on the horizon." For which, see D. C. Coleman, "Mercantilism Revisited," *Historical Journal* 23, no. 4 (Dec. 1980): 780.

Bibliography

Primary Sources

Acts of the Privy Council of England. London, HMSO.
Calendar of State Papers, Colonial. London, HMSO.
Calendar of State Papers, Domestic. London, HMSO.
Calendar of State Papers, Foreign. London, HMSO.
A Collection of the State Papers of John Thurloe. London, 1742.
Historical Manuscripts Commission: Calendar of the Manuscripts of the Most Hon. the Marquis of Salisbury, K.G. preserved at Hatfield House, Hertfordshire. Parts IV–IX. London: HMSO, 1892–1902.
Royal Commission on Historical Manuscripts. Third Report. London: HMSO, 1872. Eighth Report, Part 1. London: HMSO, 1881.

[Anonymous]. *Britannia Languens, or A Discourse of Trade: shewing The grounds and Reasons of the Increase and Decay of Land-Rents, National Wealth and Strength. With Application to the late and present State and Condition of England, France, and the United Provinces.* London, 1680.
[Anonymous]. *Chaos: Or, a Discourse, wherein Is presented to the view of the Magistrate, and all others who shall peruse the same, a Frame of Government by way of a Republique, wherein is little or no danger of miscarriage, if prudently attempted, and thoroughly prosecuted by Authority. Wherein is no difficulty in the Practice, nor obscurity in the Method; But all things plain and easie to the meanest capacity. Here's no hard or strange Names, or unknown Titles (to amaze the hearers) used, and yet here's a full and absolute Power derivative insensibly from the whole, and yet practically conveyed to the best men; wherein if any endeavour a breach, he shall break himself: and if it must be so, that Cats shall provide Supper, here they shall so it suitable to the best Palate, and easie to digest.* London, 1659.
[Anonymous]. *England's Great Happiness; or a dialogue between Content and Complaint. Wherein Is demonstrated that a great part of our Complaints are causeless. And we have more Wealth now, than ever we had at any time before the Restauration of his sacred Majestie. By a real and hearty Lover of his King and Countrey.* London, 1677.
[Anonymous]. *Interest of Money Mistaken. Or A Treatise, Proving, that the Abatement of Interest is the Effect And not the Cause Of the Riches of a Nation, and that Six Per Cent. Is a Proportionable Interest to the present condition of this Kingdom.* London, 1668.
Bacon, Francis (1587–1657). *Essays and New Atlantis.* New York: Walter J. Black, 1942.

345

————. "A Letter of Advice, written by Sir Francis Bacon to the Duke of Buckingham, when he became Favorite to king James I." Vol. 13. *The Works of Francis Bacon.* Edited by James Spedding, Robert Leslie Ellis, and Douglas Denon Heath. London: Longman and Company Ltd., 1857–1874; facsimile reprint, New York: Garrett, 1968.

————. *Selected Writings of Francis Bacon.* Edited by Hugh G. Dick. New York: Random House, 1955.

Barbon, Nicholas (1637–1698). *An Advertisement. Being a Proposal by Dr. Barbon and Partners for Insuring Houses and Goods from Fire, by A Water-Work, And to serve the Insured Houses and others with Water, at a Cheaper rate, in the Price of the Water, and Insurance.* London, 1694.

————. *An Apology for the Builder: or a Discourse shewing the Cause and Effects of the Increase of Building.* London, 1685.

————. *A Discourse Concerning Coining the New Money Lighter. In Answer to Mr. Lock's Considerations about raising the Value of Money.* London, 1696.

————. *A Discourse of Trade* (London, 1690). Edited by Jacob H. Hollander. Baltimore: Lord Baltimore, 1905.

Baxter, Richard (1615–1691). *A Holy Commonwealth, or Political Aphorisms, Opening The true Principles of Government: For The Healing of the Mistakes, Resolving the Doubts, that most endanger and trouble England at this time: (if there may be hope.) And directing the Desires of Sober Christians that long to see the Kingdoms of this world, become the Kingdoms of the Lord, and of his Christ.* London, 1659.

Berkeley, George (1685–1753). *A treatise Concerning the Principles of Human Knowledge. Wherein the Chief Causes of Error and Difficulty in the Sciences, with the Grounds of Scepticism, Atheism, and Irreligion, are inquired into.* Rev. ed. of 1734. *Philosophical Works, including the Works on Vision.* Edited by M. R. Ayers. London: J. M. Dent and Sons Ltd., 1989.

Bland, A. E., P. A. Brown, and R. H. Tawney, eds. *English Economic History: Select Documents.* London: G. Bell and Sons, Ltd., 1914.

Bodin, Jean (1529/30–1596). *The Response of Jean Bodin to the Paradoxes of Malestroit, and the Paradoxes.* Translated by George Albert Moore. Washington, DC: Country Dollar, 1947.

Boyle, Robert (1627–1691). *The Origins of Forms and Qualities According to the Corpuscular Philosophy* (1666). In *Selected Philosophical Papers of Robert Boyle.* Edited by M. A. Stewart. Manchester: Manchester University Press, 1979.

————. *The Works of the Honourable Robert Boyle. In Six volumes. To which is prefixed The Life of the Author.* Edited by Thomas Birch. New edition. London: W. Johnston, S. Crowder, et al., 1772; facsimile reprint, Hildesheim: Georg Olms Verlagsbuchhandlung, 1966.

Burton, Robert (1577–1639). *The Anatomy of Melancholy* (1621). 3 vols. Edited by Holbrook Jackson. London: J. M. Dent and Sons Ltd., 1932.

Carlyle, Thomas (1795–1881). *Selected Writings.* Edited by Alan Shelston. London: Penguin, 1971.

Child, Sir Josiah (1630–1699). *Sir Josiah Child: Selected Works, 1668–1697.* Farnborough, UK: Gregg, 1968.

Coke, Roger (fl. 1671–1696). *Treatise wherein is demonstrated that the Church and State of England are in equal danger with the Trade of it.* London, 1671.

Cromwell, Oliver (1599–1658). *Speeches of Oliver Cromwell.* Edited by Ivan Roots. London: J. M. Dent and Sons Ltd., 1989.

Culpeper, Sir Thomas, Sr. (1578–1662). *A Tract against Usurie, Presented to the High Court of Parliament* (London, 1621). In *Sir Josiah Child: Selected Works, 1668–1697.* Farnborough, UK: Gregg, 1968.

Davenant, Charles (1656–1714). *The Political and Commercial Works Of that celebrated Writer Charles D'Avenant, LL. D. Relating to the Trade and Revenue of England, The Plantation Trade, the East-India Trade, And African Trade* (1771). Edited by Sir Charles Whitworth. 5 vols. Facsimile reprint. Farnborough, UK: Gregg, 1967.

———. *Two Manuscripts: 1. A Memorial Concerning the Coyn of England (November, 1695), and 2. A memoriall concerning Creditt (July 15, 1696).* Edited by Abbott Payson Usher. Baltimore: Johns Hopkins Press, 1942.

Descartes, René (1596–1650). *The Philosophical Writings of Descartes.* 3 vols. Translated by John Cottingham, Robert Stonehoff, Dugald Murdoch, and Anthony Kenny. Cambridge: Cambridge University Press, 1985–91.

Dury, John (1596–1680). For Dury's works, see *Samuel Hartlib and the Advancement of Learning.* Edited by Charles Webster. Cambridge: Cambridge University Press, 1970.

Elyot, Sir Thomas (ca. 1490–1546). *The Book Named the Governor* (London, 1531). Edited by S. E. Lehmberg. 2d ed. London: J. M. Dent and Sons Ltd., 1962.

Evelyn, John (1620–1706). *The Diary of John Evelyn.* 6 vols. Edited by E. S. de Beer. Oxford: Clarendon, 1955.

Ferguson, Adam (1723–1816). *An Essay on the History of Civil Society* (1767). Edited by Duncan Forbes. Edinburgh: Edinburgh University Press, 1966.

Fletcher, Andrew (1653–1716). *Andrew Fletcher of Saltoun: Selected Political Writings and Speeches.* Edited by David Daiches. Edinburgh: Scottish Academic, 1979.

Fontenelle, Bernard le Bovier de (1657–1757). *Conversations on the Plurality of Worlds* (1686). Translated by H. A. Hargreaves. Berkeley: University of California Press, 1990.

Forset, Edward (1553?–1630). *A Comparative discourse of the Bodies natural and Politique. Wherein out of the principles of nature, is set forth the true forme of a Commonweale, with the dutie of Subjects, and the right of the Soveraigne: together with many good points of Politicall learning, mentioned in a brief after the Preface.* London, 1606.

Fortescue, Sir John (1385/95–1479). *De Laudibus Legum Anglie.* Edited and translated by S. B. Chrimes. Cambridge: Cambridge University Press, 1942.

Fortrey, Samuel (1622–1681). *Englands Interest and Improvement. Consisting in the Increase of the Store, and Trade of this Kingdom* (London, 1673). In *Early English Tracts on Commerce [A Select Collection of Early English Tracts on Commerce, from the Originals of Mun, Roberts, North, and Others].* Edited by John Ramsay McCulloch. Cambridge: Cambridge University Press, 1954.

Galen (ca. 129–ca. 200). *Galen on Respiration and the Arteries [De usus respirationis, An in arteriis natura sanguis contineatur, De usu pulsuum, De causis respirationis].* Edited and translated by David J. Furley and J. S. Wilkie. Princeton, NJ: Princeton University Press, 1984.

Glanvill, Joseph (1636–1680). *Scepsis Scientifica: or, Confest Ignorance, the way to Science; In an Essay of The Vanity of Dogmatizing, and Confident Opinion. With A Reply to the Exceptions Of the Learned Thomas Albius.* London, 1665.

Godwin, William (1756–1836). *Poetical Justice.* 3d ed. 3 vols. Edited by F. E. L. Priestley. Toronto: University of Toronto Press, 1969.

Gresham, Sir Thomas (1519?–1579). *Gresham on Foreign Exchange: An Essay on Early English Mercantilism with the Text of Sir Thomas Gresham's Memorandum for the Understanding of the Exchange.* Edited by Raymond de Roover. Cambridge, MA: Harvard University Press, 1949.

Grotius, Hugo (1583–1645). *Mare Liberum sive de ivre quod batavis competit ad indicana commercia, dissertatio* (1608). Edited by James Brown Scott. Translated by Ralph van Deman Magoffin. New York: Oxford University Press, 1916; reprint, New York: Arno, 1972.

Harrington, James (1611–1677). *The Oceana and Other Works of James Harrington, with an account of his life by John Toland* (London, 1771). Facsimile reprint. Aalen, Germany: Scientia Verlag, 1963.

———. *The Political Works of James Harrington.* Edited by J. G. A. Pocock. Cambridge: Cambridge University Press, 1977.

Hartlib, Samuel (1600–1662). *Londons Charitie inlarged. Stilling The Orphans Cry. By The Liberality of the Parliament, in granting two Houses by Act, and giving a thousand pound towards the work for the imployment of the Poor, and education of poor children, who many of them are destroyed in their youth for want of being under a good Government and education, whereby they may be made servicable for God, and the Commonwealth, Also This good work is much encouraged by the liberall Contributions of many well-affected Citizens of London, for the better carrying it on for the glory of God, the honor of the Nation, and comfort of the helples Poor. With A Platform, how many Officers needfull to govern 100 children in a Work-house, with Laws and Orders for the Schoolmaster to read to the children once a day for a time, afterwards twice a month, whereby they may be kept under a godly and civill Government, to the great joy of good peopl. With other Observations worthy the reading.* London, 1650.

———. *Samuel Hartlib his Legacy of Husbandry. Wherein are bequeathed to the Commonwealth of England, not onely Braband, and Flanders, but also many more Outlandish and Domestick Experiments and Secrets (of Gabriel Plats and others) never heretofore divulged in reference to Universal Husbandry. With a Table shewing the general Contents or Sections of the several Augmentations and enriching Enlargements of this Third Edition.* London, 1655.

———. *Samuel Hartlib (1600–1662) and the Advancement of Learning.* Edited by Charles Webster. Cambridge: Cambridge University Press, 1970.

Harvey, William (1578–1657). *The Circulation of the Blood and Other Writings.* Translated by Kenneth J. Franklin. Introduction by Dr. Andrew Wear. London: J. M. Dent and Sons Ltd., 1990.

Hobbes, Thomas (1588–1679). *Leviathan, or The Matter, Forme, & Power of a Commonwealth Ecclesiastical and Civill* (London, 1651). Edited by C. B. Macpherson. London: Penguin Books Ltd., 1985.

———. *Man and Citizen (De Homine and De Cive)* (1658 and 1651). *De Homine* translated by Charles T. Wood, T. S. K. Scott-Craig, and Bernard Gert; *De Cive* translated by Thomas Hobbes (*Philosophical Rudiments Concerning Government and Society*). Edited by Bernard Gert. Indianapolis: Hackett Publishing Company, 1991.

Hooke, Robert (1635–1703). *The Diary of Robert Hooke, M.A., M.D., F.R.S., 1672–1680.*

Edited by Henry Robinson and Walter Adams. With a foreword by Sir Frederick Gowland Hopkins. London: Taylor and Francis, 1935.

Hooker, Richard (1554–1600). *The Works of that Learned and Judicious Divine, Mr. Richard Hooker: with an account of his life and death by Isaac Walton.* 2 vols. Oxford: Clarendon, 1890.

James I (1566–1625). *The Political Works of James I.* Reprinted from the edition of 1616. Edited by Charles Howard McIlwain. Cambridge, MA: Harvard University Press, 1918.

Kenyon, J. P., ed. *The Stuart Constitution, 1603–1688: Documents and Commentary.* Cambridge: Cambridge University Press, 1966.

King, Gregory (1648–1712). *Natural and Political Observations and Conclusions upon the State and Condition of England.* In *The Earliest Classics.* Edited by Peter Laslett. London: Gregg International Publishers Ltd., 1973.

———. *Two Tracts: (a) Natural and Political Observations and Conclusions upon the State and Condition of England, and (b) Of the Naval Trade of England A o 1688 and the National Profit then arising thereby.* Edited by George E. Barnett. Baltimore: Johns Hopkins University Press, 1936.

Kirk, R. E. G., and Ernest F. Kirk, eds. *Returns of Aliens Dwelling in the City and Suburbs of London: from the Reign of Henry VIII to that of James I (Part I: 1525–1571 and Part II: 1571–1597).* Aberdeen: Huguenot Society of London, 1900, 1902.

Laud, William (1573–1645). *The Works of William Laud, D. D.* Edited by William Scott. London, 1847.

Lever, Thomas (1521–1577). *Sermons* (1550). *English Reprints* VI. Edited by Edward Arber. New York: AMS, 1966.

Locke, John (1632–1704). *An Essay Concerning Human Understanding* (London, 1690). 2 vols. Edited by Alexander Campbell Fraser. Oxford: Oxford University Press, 1894; reprint, New York: Dover, 1959.

———. *Essays on the Law of Nature.* Edited by W. von Leyden. Oxford: Clarendon, 1958.

———. *Further Considerations concerning Raising the Value of Money. Wherein Mr. Lowndes Arguments for it in his late Report concerning An Essay for the Amendment of the Silver Coins, are particularly Examined.* 2d ed. London, 1696.

———. *A Letter Concerning Toleration* (London, 1690). Buffalo: Prometheus Books, 1990.

———. *Locke on Money.* 2 vols. Edited by Patrick Hyde Kelly. Oxford: Clarendon, 1991.

———. *The Reasonableness of Christianity: As Delivered in the Scriptures* (London, 1695). Edited by George W. Ewing. Washington, DC: Regnery Gateway, 1965.

———. *Short Observations on a Printed Paper, Intituled, For encouraging the Coining Silver Money in England, and after for keeping it here.* London, 1695.

———. *Some Considerations of the Consequences of the Lowering of Interest, and Raising the Value of Money. In a Letter sent to a Member of Parliament.* 2d ed. London, 1691.

———. "Some of the Consequences that are like to follow upon Lessening of Interest to 4 Percent." Unpublished manuscript in William Letwin, *The Origins of Scientific Economics.* London: Methuen and Company Ltd., 1963.

———. *Some Thoughts Concerning Education* (London, 1693). In *The Works of John Locke.* A New edition, Corrected, Volume 9. London: Thomas Tegg, 1823; reprint, Aalen: Scientia Verlag, 1963.

———. *Two Treatises of Government: In the Former, The False Principles and Foundation of Sir Robert Filmer, And his Followers, are Detected and Over-thrown. The Latter is an Essay concerning The True Original, Extent, and End of Civil Government* (London, 1698; originally 1690). Edited by Peter Laslett. Cambridge: Cambridge University Press, 1988.

[Lowndes, William (1652–1724)]. *A Further Essay for the Amendment of the Gold and Silver Coins. With the Opinion of Mr. Gerrard de Malynes, who was an Eminent Merchant in the Reign of Queen Elizabeth, concerning the Standard of England.* London, 1695.

Machiavelli, Niccolò (1469–1527). *The Prince and the Discourses.* Edited by Max Lerner. New York: Random House (Modern Library), 1950.

Malynes, Gerard de (fl. 1586–1641). *The Center of the Circle of Commerce. Or, a Refutation of a Treatise, Intituled "The Circle of Commerce, or the Ballance of Trade," lately published by E. M.* London, 1623.

———. *Consuetudo, Vel Lex Mercatoria, or The Ancient Law-Merchant. Divided into three Parts: According to the Essentiall Parts of Trafficke. Necessarie for all Statesmen, Judges, Magistrates, Temporall and Civile Lawyers, Mint-men, Merchants, Marriners, and all others negotiating in all places of the World.* London, 1622.

———. *Englands View, in the Unmasking of Two Paradoxes: With a replication unto the answer of Maister John Bodine.* London, 1603.

———. *An Essay on the Fishing Trade* (Chapter 47 of *Lex Mercatoria*). Edinburgh: Privately printed by William Adams, Jr., 1720.

———. *The Maintenance of Free Trade, According to the Three Essentiall Parts of Traffique; Namely, Commodities, Moneys, and Exchanges of Moneys, by Bills of Exchanges for other Countries. Or, An answer to a Treatise of Free Trade, or the meanes to make Trade flourish, lately Published.* London, 1622.

———. *Saint George for England, Allegorically described.* London, 1601.

———. *A Treatise on the Canker of Englands Common Wealth. Divided into three parts: Wherein the Author imitating the rule of good Phisitions, First, declareth the disease. Secondarily, sheweth the efficient cause thereof. Lastly, a remedy for the same.* London, 1601.

Manley, Thomas (1628–1690). *Usury at Six per Cent examined, and Found unjustly charged by Sir Thomas Culpepper, and J.C. with many Crimes and Oppressions, whereof 'tis altogether innocent. Wherein is shewed, The necessity of retrenching our Luxury, and vain consumption of Forraign Commodities, imported by English Money: Also The reducing the Wages of Servants, Labourers, and Workmen of all sorts, which raiseth the value of our Manufactures, 15. or 20. per Cent. dearer than our Neighbours do afford them, by reason of their cheap wages: Wherein likewise is hinted, Some of the many mischiefs that will ensue upon retrenching Usury; Humbly Presented to the High Court of Parliament Now Sitting.* London, 1669.

[Milles, Thomas (d. 1627)]. *The Customers Apology. That is to say, A generall Answere to Informers of all sortes, and their injurious complaints, against the honest reputation of the Collectors of her Majesties Custome specially in the Out-Portes of this Realme. Written onely For Understanding Readers and Wise in highest Authoritie, to Reade and disceren by. Alwaies provided, In reading Reade all, or nothing at all.* London, 1599.

———. *The Customers Replie. or Second Apologie. That is to say, An Aunswer to a confused Treatise of Publicke Commerce, printed and dispersed at Midlebourghe and London, in favour of the private Society of Merchants-Adventurers. By a more serious Discourse of Exchange in Merchandise, and Merchandising Exchange. Written for understanding*

Readers onely, in favour of all loyall Merchants, and for the advancing of Traffick in England. London, 1604.

Misselden, Edward (fl. 1608–1654). *The Circle Of Commerce. Or The Ballance Of Trade, in defence of free Trade: Opposed To Malynes Little Fish and his Great Whale, and poized against them in the Scale. Wherein also, Exchanges in generall are considered: and therein the whole Trade of this Kingdome with forraine Countries, is digested into a Ballance of Trade, for the benefite of the Publique. Necessary for the present and future times.* London, 1623.

———. *Free Trade. Or, The Meanes To Make Trade Florish. Wherein, The Causes of the Decay of Trade in this Kingdome, are discovered: And the Remedies also to remoove the same, are represented. The second Edition with some Additions.* London, 1622.

More, Sir Thomas (1478–1535). *Utopia.* Translated by Paul Turner. London: Penguin Books Ltd., 1965.

Mun, Thomas (1571–1641). *A Discourse of Trade, From England unto the East-Indies: Answering to diverse Objections which are usually made against the same.* London, 1621.

———. *Englands Treasure by Forraign Trade. Or, The Ballance of our Forraign Trade Is The Rule of our Treasure* (London, 1664). Reprint. Fairfield, NJ: Augustus M. Kelley, 1986.

Nicholas of Cusa (1401–1464). *Nicholas of Cusa On Learned Ignorance: A Translation and an Appraisal of De Docta Ignorantia.* Edited and translated by Jasper Hopkins. 2d ed. Minneapolis: Arthur J. Banning, 1985.

North, Sir Dudley (1641–1695). *Discourses upon Trade* (1691) and several unpublished papers. In Richard Grassby, *The English Gentleman in Trade: The Life and Works of Sir Dudley North, 1641–1691.* Oxford: Clarendon, 1994.

Pacioli, Luca (d. ca. 1514). *Paciolo on Accounting.* Translated by R. Gene Brown and Kenneth S. Johnston. Introduction by Alvin R. Johnston. New York: McGraw-Hill Book Company, 1963.

Page, William, ed. *Letters of Denization and Acts of Naturalization for Aliens in England, 1509–1603.* Lymington: Huguenot Society of London, 1893.

Paracelsus (1493–1541). *Selected Writings.* Translated by Norbert Guterman. Princeton, NJ: Princeton University Press, 1979.

Pepys, Samuel (1633–1703). *The Diary of Samuel Pepys.* 9 vols. Edited by Henry B. Wheatley. London: Macmillan and Company Ltd., 1918.

Perkins, William (1558–1602). *The Work of William Perkins.* Edited by Ian Breward. Appleford, UK: Sutton Courtenay, 1970.

Petty, Sir William (1623–1687). *The Advice of W. P. to Mr. Samuel Hartlib, For The Advancement of some particular Parts of Learning.* London, 1648.

———. *The Economic Writings of Sir William Petty; together with the Observations Upon the Bills of Mortality, more probably by Captain John Graunt* (1662 et seq.). Edited by Charles Henry Hull. 2 vols. bound as one. Cambridge: Cambridge University Press, 1899; reprint, Fairfield, NJ: Augustus M. Kelley, 1986.

———. *The History of the Survey of Ireland commonly called the Down Survey by Doctor William Petty, A. D. 1655–1656.* Edited by Thomas Aiskew Larcom. Dublin: Irish Archaeological Society, 1851; reprint, New York: Augustus M. Kelley, 1967.

———. "Petty contra Hobbes: A Previously Untranslated Manuscript." Translated and edited by Frank Amati and Tony Aspromourgos. *Journal of the History of Ideas* 46, no. 1 (Jan. 1985): 127–32.

————. *The Petty Papers: Some Unpublished Papers of Sir William Petty, Edited from the Boxwood Papers of the Marquis of Lansdowne.* 2 vols. bound as one. London: Constable and Company Ltd., 1927; reprint, New York: Augustus M. Kelley, 1967.

————. *The Petty-Southwell Correspondence, 1676–1687; Edited from the Boxwood Papers of the Marquis of Lansdowne.* London: Constable and Company Ltd., 1928; reprint, New York: Augustus M. Kelley, 1967.

————. "Sir William Petty: An Unpublished Manuscript." Edited by Shichiro Matsukawa. *Hitotsubashi Journal of Economics* 17, no. 2 (Feb. 1977): 33–50.

[Philip IV (1605–1665)]. *A Proclamation of his Majesty The King of Spaine. For the Conservation of the Contrabando. Revocation of the Permissions. Prohibition of the use of the Merchandizes, and Fruits of the Realms of France, England, and Portugal; and Reformation of Vestures: and Apparel, and other things. Published in Madrid, the 11th of September, Anno. 1657. Translated out of Spanish.* London, 1657.

Pico Della Mirandola, Giovanni (1463–1494). *Pico Della Mirandola On the Dignity of Man.* Translated by Charles Glenn Wallis. Indianapolis: Hackett Publishing Company, 1998.

[Plattes, Gabriel (fl. 1638)]. *A description of the Famous Kingdome of Macaria; shewing its Excellent Government: wherein The Inhabitants live in great Prosperity, Health, and Happinesse; the King obeyed, the Nobles honoured; and all good men respected, Vice punished, and vertue rewarded. An Example to other Nations. In a Dialogue between a Schollar and a Traveller* (London, 1641). In *Samuel Hartlib and the Advancement of Learning.* Edited by Charles Webster. Cambridge: Cambridge University Press, 1979.

————. *A Discovery of Infinite Treasure Hidden since the Worlds Beginning. Wherein all men, of what degree soever, are friendly invited to be sharers with the Discoverer.* London, 1638.

————. *A Discovery of Subterraneall Treasure, viz. Of all manner of mines and Mineralls, from the Golde to the Coale; with Plaine Directions and Rules for the finding of them in all Kingdomes and Countries.* London, 1639.

Plutarch (fl. 50–120). *Plutarch's Lives.* Dr. Dryden's translation revised by A. H. Gough. New York: Hearst's International Library Co., 1914.

Roberts, Lewes (1596–1640). *The Merchants Mappe of Commerce. Wherein the Universal Manner and Matter of Trade is compendiously handled. The Standard and Current Coines of sundry Princes, Observed. The Reall and Imaginary Coines of Accompts and Exchanges, Expressed. The Naturall and Artificiall Commodities of all Countries for Transportation Declared. The Weights and Measures of all eminent Cities and Townes of Traffique Collected and Reduced into one another; and all to the Meridian of Commerce practised in the famous Citie of London.* London, 1638.

Robinson, Henry (1605?–1664?). *Englands Safety in Trades Encrease. Most humbly Presented to the High Court of Parliament.* London, 1641.

Scaliger, Joseph Juste (1540–1609). *The Autobiography of Joseph Scaliger with Autobiographical Selections from his Letters, his Testament, and the Funeral Orations by Daniel Heinsius and Dominicus Baudius.* Translated by George W. Robinson. Cambridge, MA: Harvard University Press, 1927.

Scott, Walter, ed. *Hermetica: the Ancient Greek and Latin Writings which contain Religious or Philosophic Teachings Ascribed to Hermes Trismegistus.* Boston: Shambhala Publications, 1993.

Seneca (ca. 5–65). *Naturales Questiones.* Translated by Thomas H. Corcoran. Cambridge, MA: Harvard University Press/Loeb Classical Library, 1971.

Serra, Antonio (fl. 1613). *A Brief Treatise on the Causes which can make Gold and Silver Plentiful in Kingdoms where there are no Mines* (1613). In *Early Economic Thought: Selections from Economic Literature Prior to Adam Smith.* Edited by Arthur Eli Monroe. Cambridge, MA: Harvard University Press, 1930.

Smith, Adam (1723–1790). *An Inquiry into the Nature and Causes of the Wealth of Nations* (1776). 2 vols. bound as one. Edited by Edwin Canaan. Chicago: University of Chicago Press, 1976.

[Smith, Sir Thomas?/John Hales?]. *A Discourse of the Common Weal of this Realm of England* (London, 1581). Edited by Mary Dewar. Charlottesville: University Press of Virginia, for the Folger Shakespeare Library, 1969.

Sprat, Thomas (1635–1713). *The History of the Royal Society of London, For the Improving of Natural Knowledge* (London, 1667). Edited by Jackson I. Cope and Harold Whitmore Jones. St Louis: Washington University Press, 1958.

Starkey, Thomas (ca. 1495/9–1538). *A Dialogue between Reginald Pole and Thomas Lupset.* Edited by Kathleen M. Burton. London: Chatto and Windus, 1948.

Tawney, Richard Henry, and Eileen Power, eds. *Tudor Economic Documents: Being Select Documents Illustrating the Economic and Social History of Tudor England.* 3 vols. London: Longmans, Green and Co. Ltd., 1924.

Temple, Sir William (1628–1699). *Observations upon the United Provinces of the Netherlands* (1672). Edited by Sir George N. Clark. Oxford: Clarendon, 1972.

Thirsk, Joan, and J. P. Cooper, eds. *Seventeenth-Century Economic Documents.* Oxford: Clarendon, 1972.

The Usury Debate in the Seventeenth Century: Three Arguments. New York: Arno, 1972.

Violet, Thomas (fl. 1634–1662). *An Appeal to Caesar: wherein Gold and Silver is Proved to be the Kings Majesties Royal Commodity. Which By the Lawes of the Kingdom, no Person of what Degree soever, but the kings Majestie, and his Privy Councel, can give License to transport either Gold or Silver to any Person, after it is Landed in any part of the kingdome of England. That this Great and Sacred Trust cannot be changed into the Hands of any Person, Persons, or Corporations whatsoever, without changing or diminishing the Sacred Power of his Majestie, it being against his Crown and Dignity. Humbly Presented to his Most Sacred Majestie, and his Most Honourable Privy Councel, in opposition to some Merchants, who are Endeavouring, upon feigned Prentences, to dispossesse his Majestie of this royal Trust, and to have it Confirmed by Act of Parliament, to Transport at the Merchants pleasure, Forreign Bullion and Coine freely, after it is Imported into the Kingdom and make it a Free merchandize for their private profit, to the Damage of the whole Kingdom in general.* London, 1660.

Weston, Sir Richard (1579?–1652). *A Discourse of Husbandry used in Brabant and Flanders, shewing The wonderfull improvement of Land there; and serving as a pattern for our practice in this Commonwealth.* London, 1650.

Wilkins, John (1614–1672; Bishop of Chester). *The Mathematical and Philosophical Works of the Right Rev. John Wilkins, Late Lord Bishop of Chester. To which is prefixed the Author's Life, and an account of his Works* (London, 1708). Facsimile reprint of both volumes bound as one. London: Frank Cass and Company Ltd., 1970.

Willsford, Thomas (fl. 1660). *The Scales of Commerce and Trade. Ballancing betwixt the Buyer & Seller, Artificer and Manufacture, Debitor and Creditor, the most general Questions, artifical Rules, and usefull conclusions incident to Traffique: Comprehended in Two Books. The first states and ponderates to Equity & Custome, all usuall Rules, legall bargains and Contracts, in Wholesale or Retail, with Factorage, Returns, & Exchanges of Forreign Coyn, of Interest-Mony, both Simple and Compounded, with Solutions from naturall and Artificall Arithmetick. The second Book treats of Geometricall Problems and Arithmeticall Solutions, in dimensions of lines, Superficies and Bodies, both solid and concave, viz. Land, Wainscot, Hangings, Board, timber, Stone, gaging of Casks, Military Propositions, Merchants Accounts by Debitor and Creditor: Architectonice, or the Art of Building, discovered.* London, 1660.

Wilson, Thomas (1525?–1581). *A Discourse uppon Usurye, By waye of Dialogue and oracions, for the better varietye and more delite of all those that shall reade thys treatise* (1572). Edited by R. H. Tawney. London: G. Bell and Sons, Ltd., 1925.

Wither, William (fl. 1660). *Proposals to the Officers of the Army, And to the City of London for The taking off all Excise, Taxes, and Custom: with a Perfect Unity of the Army, City, and Commons of England, for a Free Parliament, And a firm Peace, throughout the Three Nations.* London, 1660.

Woodhouse, A. S. P., ed. *Puritanism and Liberty, Being the Army Debates (1647–1649) from the Clarke Manuscripts with Supplementary Documents.* 3d ed. London: J. M. Dent and Sons Ltd. 1986.

Wren, Matthew (1629–1672). *Considerations on Mr. Harrington's Common-wealth of Oceana: Restrained to the first part of the Preliminaries.* London, 1657.

Secondary Sources

Allen, Robert C. "The Price of Freehold Land and the Interest Rate in the Seventeenth and Eighteenth Centuries." *Economic History Review,* 2d ser., 41, no. 1 (Feb. 1988): 33–50.

Appleby, Joyce Oldham. *Economic Thought and Ideology in Seventeenth-Century England.* Princeton, NJ: Princeton University Press, 1978.

———. "Ideology and Theory: The Tension between Political and Economic Liberalism in Seventeenth-Century England." *American Historical Review* 81, no. 4 (Oct. 1976): 499–515.

———. *Liberalism and Republicanism in the Historical Imagination.* Cambridge, MA: Harvard University Press, 1992.

———. "Locke, Liberalism and the Natural Law of Money." *Past and Present* 71 (May 1976): 43–69.

Arneil, Barbara. *John Locke and America: The Defence of English Colonialism.* Oxford: Clarendon, 1996.

———. "Trade, Plantations, and Property: John Locke and the Economic Defense of Colonialism." *Journal of the History of Ideas* 55, no. 4 (Oct. 1994): 591–609.

Ashley, Maurice. *Financial and Commercial Policy under the Cromwellian Protectorate.* 2d ed. London: Frank Cass and Company Ltd., 1962.

Ashton, Robert. "Deficit Finance in the Reign of James I." *Economic History Review,* 2d ser., 10, no. 1 (Aug. 1957): 15–29.

———. "Jacobean Free Trade Again." *Past and Present* 43 (May 1969): 151–57.

———. "The Parliamentary Agitation for Free Trade in the Opening Years of the Reign of James I." *Past and Present* 38 (Dec. 1967): 40–55.

Aspromourgos, Tony. *On the Origins of Classical Economics: Distribution and Value from William Petty to Adam Smith.* London: Routledge, 1996.

Aubrey, John. *Brief Lives.* Edited by Oliver Lawson Dick. Ann Arbor: University of Michigan Press, 1957.

Barnard, Toby Christopher. *Cromwellian Ireland: English Government and Reform in Ireland, 1649–1660.* London: Oxford University Press, 1975.

Beer, Max. *Early British Economics, from the XIIIth to the Middle of the XVIIIth Century.* London: George Allen and Unwin Ltd., 1938.

———. *An Inquiry into Physiocracy.* London: George Allen and Unwin Ltd., 1939.

Berlin, Sir Isaiah. "Hobbes, Locke and Professor Macpherson." *Political Quarterly* 35, no. 4 (Oct. 1964): 444–68.

Berns, Laurence. "Thomas Hobbes." In *History of Political Philosophy.* 3d ed. Edited by Leo Strauss and Joseph Cropsey. Chicago: University of Chicago Press, 1987.

Blaug, Mark. *Economic Theory in Retrospect.* Rev. ed. Homewood, IL: R. D. Irwin, 1968.

Bonar, James. *Philosophy and Political Economy in Some of Their Historical Relations.* Facsimile reprint of the 3d ed. of 1922. New York: A. M. Kelley, 1966.

Bottigheimer, Karl S. *English Money and Irish Land: The "Adventurers" in the Cromwellian Settlement of Ireland.* Oxford: Clarendon, 1971.

Boulton, Jeremy. "Wage Labour in Seventeenth-Century London." *Economic History Review* 49, no. 2 (May 1996): 268–90.

Bowley, Marian. "Some Seventeenth-Century Contributions to the Theory of Value." *Economica,* n.s., 30, no. 118 (May 1963): 122–39.

———. *Studies in the History of Economic Thought before 1870.* London: Macmillan Press Ltd., 1973.

Brems, Hans. "Cantillon versus Marx: The Land Theory and the Labor Theory of Value." *History of Political Economy* 10 (winter 1978): 669–78.

———. *Pioneering Economic Theory, 1630–1980: A Mathematical Restatement.* Baltimore: Johns Hopkins University Press, 1986.

Brenner, Robert. "The Civil War Politics of London's Merchant Community." *Past and Present* 58 (Feb. 1973): 53–107.

———. *Merchants and Revolution: Commercial Change, Political Conflict, and London's Overseas Traders, 1550–1653.* Princeton, NJ: Princeton University Press, 1993.

Brewer, Anthony. "Petty and Cantillon." *History of Political Economy* 24, no. 3 (fall 1992): 711–28.

Brewer, John. *The Sinews of Power: War, Money and the English State, 1688–1783.* Cambridge, MA: Harvard University Press, 1990.

Brown, Keith C., ed. *Hobbes Studies.* Oxford: Basil Blackwell, 1965.

Buck, Peter. "Seventeenth-Century Political Arithmetic: Civil Strife and Vital Statistics." *Isis* 68, no. 241 (Mar. 1977): 67–87.

Burke, Peter. *Popular Culture in Early Modern Europe.* New York: Harper and Row, 1978.

Chalk, A. F. "Natural Law and the Rise of Economic Individualism in England." *Journal of Political Economy* 59, no. 4 (Aug. 1951): 332–49.

Challis, C. E. *The Tudor Coinage.* Manchester: Manchester University Press, 1978.

Chancey, Karen. "The Amboyna Massacre in English Politics, 1624–1632." *Albion* 30, no. 4 (winter 1998): 583–98.

Charlton, Kenneth. *Education in Renaissance England.* London: Routledge and Kegan Paul, 1965.

Chaudhuri, K. N. *The English East India Company: The Study of an Early Joint-Stock Company, 1600–1640.* London: Frank Cass and Co. Ltd., 1965.

Choksy, George D. "The Bifurcated Economics of Sir Dudley North and Roger North: One Holitistic Analytical Engine." *History of Political Economy* 27, no. 3 (fall 1995): 477–92.

———. "Previously Undocumented Macroeconomics from the 1680s: The Analytical Arguments and Policy Recommendations of Sir Dudley North and Roger North." *History of Political Economy* 24, no. 2 (summer 1992): 515–32.

Christensen, Paul P. "Hobbes and the Physiological Origins of Economic Science." *History of Political Economy* 21, no. 4 (winter 1989): 689–709.

Cohen, I. Bernard. "Harrington and Harvey: A Theory of the State based on the New Physiology." *Journal of the History of Ideas* 55, no. 2 (Apr. 1994): 187–210.

Cole, Charles Woolsey. *Colbert and a Century of French Mercantilism.* 2 vols. New York: Columbia University Press, 1939.

Coleman, D. C. "Labour in the English Economy of the Seventeenth Century." *Economic History Review,* 2d ser., 8, no. 3 (Apr. 1956): 280–95.

———. "Mercantilism Revisited." *Historical Journal* 23, no. 4 (Dec. 1985): 773–91.

———. "Review of *Economic Thought and Ideology.*" *Journal of Modern History* 53, no. 1 (Mar. 1981): 105–6.

———, ed. *Revisions in Mercantilism.* London: Methuen and Co. Ltd., 1969.

Collins, Stephen L. *From Divine Cosmos to Sovereign State: An Intellectual History of Consciousness and the Idea of Order in Renaissance England.* New York: Oxford University Press, 1989.

Cowen, Tyler. "Nicholas Barbon and the Origins of Economic Liberalism." *Research in the History of Economic Thought and Methodology* 4 (1986): 67–83.

Cranston, Maurice William. *John Locke: A Biography.* Toronto: Longmans, Green and Co. Ltd., 1957.

Creedy, John. "On the King-Davenant 'Law' of Demand." *Scottish Journal of Political Economy* 33, no. 3 (Aug. 1986): 193–212.

Davies, K. G. "Joint-Stock Investment in the Later Seventeenth Century." *Economic History Review,* 2d ser., 4, no. 3 (1952): 283–301.

Davis, Ralph. "English Foreign Trade, 1660–1700." *Economic History Review,* 2d ser., 7, no. 2 (Dec. 1954): 150–66.

———. *The Rise of the Atlantic Economies.* Ithaca, NY: Cornell University Press, 1973.

De Roover, Raymond. *Business, Banking, and Economic Thought in Late Medieval and Early Modern Europe.* Edited by Julius Kirshner. Chicago: University of Chicago Press. 1974.

———. *Gresham on Foreign Exchange: An Essay on Early English Mercantilism with the Text of Sir Thomas Gresham's Memorandum for the Understanding of the Exchange.* Cambridge, MA: Harvard University Press, 1949.

———. "Thomas Mun in Italy." *Bulletin of the Institute of Historical Research* 30 (1957): 80–85.

De Vries, Jan. *The Economy of Europe in an Age of Crisis, 1600–1750.* Cambridge: Cambridge University Press, 1976.

Dear, Peter Robert. *Mersenne and the Learning of the Schools.* Ithaca, NY: Cornell University Press, 1988.

Debus, Allen G. *Science and Education in the Seventeenth Century: The Webster-Ward Debate.* London: Macdonald and Co. (Publishers Ltd., 1970.

Dickinson, H. T. *Liberty and Property: Political Ideology in Eighteenth-Century Britain.* New York: Holmes and Meier, 1977.

Dickson, Peter George Michael. *The Financial Revolution in England: A Study in the Development of Public Credit, 1688–1756.* London: Macmillan,1967.

Dobb, Maurice Herbert. *Studies in the Development of Capitalism.* Rev. ed. New York: International, 1963.

Dunn, John. *The Political Thought of John Locke: An Historical Account of the Argument of the Two Treatises of Government.* Cambridge: Cambridge University Press, 1969.

Durkheim, Émile. *The Division of Labor in Society* (1893). Translated by George Simpson. New York: Macmillan/Free Press, 1933.

Eagly, Robert V. *The Structure of Classical Economic Theory.* New York: Oxford University Press, 1974.

———, ed. *Events, Ideology, and Economic Theory: The Determinants of Progress in the Development of Economic Analysis.* Detroit: Wayne State University Press, 1968.

Ekelund, Robert Burton, Jr., and Robert D. Tollison. *Mercantilism as a Rent-Seeking Society: Economic Regulation in Historical Perspective.* College Station: Texas A&M University Press, 1981.

Elliot, J. H. *Imperial Spain, 1469–1716.* London: Edward Arnold, 1963; reprint, London: Penguin Books Ltd., 1990.

Endres, A. M. "The Functions of Numerical Data in the Writings of Graunt, Petty and Davenant." *History of Political Economy* 17, no. 2 (summer 1985): 245–64.

Evans, G. Heberton, Jr. "The Law of Demand: The Roles of Gregory King and Charles Davenant." *Quarterly Journal of Economics* 81, no. 3 (Aug. 1967): 483–92.

Feavearyear, Sir Albert. *The Pound Sterling: A History of English Money.* 2d ed. Revised by E. Victor Morgan. Oxford: Clarendon, 1963.

Finley, M. I. "Aristotle and Economic Analysis." *Past and Present* 47 (May 1970): 3–25.

Friis, Astrid. *Alderman Cockayne's Project and the Cloth Trade.* Copenhagen: Levin & Munksgaard, 1927.

Furniss, Edgar Stephenson. *The Position of the Laborer in a System of Nationalism: A Study in the Labor Theories of the Later English Mercantilists.* Boston: Houghton Mifflin, 1920.

Ginzburg, Carlo. "High and Low: The Theme of Forbidden Knowledge in the Sixteenth and Seventeenth Centuries." *Past and Present* 73 (Nov. 1976): 28–41.

Gould, J. D. "The Trade Depression of the Early 1620s." *Economic History Review,* 2d ser., 7, no. 1 (Aug. 1954): 86–98.

Grampp, William Dyer. *Economic Liberalism.* 2 vols. New York: Random House, 1965.

Grassby, Richard. *The Business Community of Seventeenth-Century England.* Cambridge: Cambridge University Press, 1995.

———. *The English Gentleman in Trade: The Life and Works of Sir Dudley North, 1641–1691.* Oxford: Clarendon, 1994.

Greaves, Richard L. *The Puritan Revolution and Educational Thought: Background for Reform.* New Brunswick, NJ: Rutgers University Press, 1969.

Grell, Ole Peter. *Dutch Calvinists in Early Stuart London: The Dutch Church in Austin Friars, 1603–1642.* Leiden: E. J. Brill, 1989.

Gunn, J. A. W. *Beyond Liberty and Property: The Process of Self-Recognition in Eighteenth-Century Political Thought.* Kingston: McGill-Queen's University Press, 1983.

————. *Politics and the Public Interest in the Seventeenth Century.* London: Routledge and Kegan Paul, 1969.

Hadden, Richard W. *On the Shoulders of Merchants: Exchange and the Mathematical Conception of Nature in Early Modern Europe.* Albany: State University of New York Press, 1994.

Hamilton, E. J. "Import of American Gold and Silver into Spain, 1503–1660." *Quarterly Journal of Economics* 43, no. 3 (May 1929): 436–72.

Heckscher, Eli. *Mercantilism.* Revised (2d) ed. Edited by E. F. Söderlund. Translated by Mendel Shapiro. 2 vols. London: George Allen and Unwin, 1955.

Hill, Christopher. "William Harvey and the Idea of Monarchy." *Past and Present* 27 (Apr. 1964): 54–72.

————. "William Harvey (No Parliamentarian, No Heretic) and the Idea of Monarchy." *Past and Present* 31 (July 1965): 97–103.

Hilton, R. H. "Capitalism: What's in a Name?" *Past and Present* 1 (Feb. 1952): 32–43.

Hinton, R. W. K. *The Eastland Trade and the Common Weal in the Seventeenth Century.* Cambridge: Cambridge University Press, 1959; reprint, Hamden, CT: Archon Books, 1975.

————. "The Mercantile System in the Time of Thomas Mun." *Economic History Review*, 2d ser., 7, no. 3 (Apr. 1955): 277–90.

Hirschman, Albert O. *The Passions and the Interests: Political Arguments for Capitalism before Its Triumph.* Princeton, NJ: Princeton University Press, 1977.

Hoppit, Julian. "Political Arithmetic in Eighteenth-Century England." *Economic History Review* 49, no. 3 (Aug. 1996): 516–40.

Horne, Thomas A. *Property Rights and Poverty: Political Argument in Britain, 1605–1834.* Chapel Hill: University of North Carolina Press, 1990.

Horowitz, Henry. "The East India Trade, the Politicans, and the Constitution: 1689–1702." *Journal of British Studies* 17, no. 2 (spring 1978): 1–18.

Horsefield, J. Keith. *British Monetary Experiments, 1650–1710.* London: G. Bell and Sons Ltd., 1960.

Hoskins, W. G. *The Age of Plunder: King Henry's England, 1500–1547.* London: Longman, 1976.

Hueckel, Glenn. "Sir William Petty on Value: A Reconsideration." *Research in the History of Economic Thought and Methodology* 4 (1986): 37–66.

Hutchison, Terence Wilmot. *Before Adam Smith: The Emergence of Political Economy, 1662–1776.* London: Basil Blackwell Ltd., 1988.

————. *On Revolutions and Progress in Economic Knowledge.* Cambridge University Press, 1978.

Irwin, Douglas A. *Against the Tide: An Intellectual History of Free Trade.* Princeton, NJ: Princeton University Press, 1996.

Israel, Jonathan I. *The Dutch Republic: Its Rise, Greatness, and Fall, 1477–1806.* Oxford: Clarendon, 1995.

Jacob, James R. "The Political Economy of Science in Seventeenth-Century England." *Social Research* 59, no. 3 (fall 1992): 505–32.

————. "Restoration Ideologies and the Royal Society." *History of Science* 18 (1980): 25–38.

————, and Timothy Raylor. "Opera and Obediences: Thomas Hobbes and *A Proposition for Advancement of Moralitie* by Sir William Davenant." *The Seventeenth Century* 6, no. 2 (autumn 1991): 205–50.

Johnson, E. A. J. "Gerard de Malynes and the Theory of the Foreign Exchanges." *American Economic Review* 13 (1933): 442–54.

———. *Predecessors of Adam Smith: The Growth of British Economic Thought.* New York: Prentice-Hall, 1937.

Jolley, Nicholas. *Leibniz and Locke: A Study of the New Essays on Human Understanding.* Oxford: Clarendon, 1984.

Jones, J. R. *The First Whigs: The Politics of the Exclusion Crisis, 1678–1683.* London: Oxford University Press, 1961.

Kearney, H. F. "Puritanism, Capitalism and the Scientific Revolution." *Past and Present* 28 (July 1964): 81–101.

Kenyon, John Philipps. *Robert Spencer, Earl of Sunderland, 1641–1702.* London: Longmans Green, 1958.

Keohane, Nannerl O. *Philosophy and the State in France: The Renaissance to the Enlightenment.* Princeton: Princeton University Press, 1980.

Kerridge, Eric. "The Movement of Rent, 1540–1640." *Economic History Review,* 2d ser., 6, no. 1 (Aug. 1953): 16–34.

Keynes, John Maynard. "Notes on Mercantilism, the Usury Laws, Stamped Money and Theories of Underconsumption." In *The General Theory of Employment, Interest and Money* (1936). *Collected Writings,* vol. 7. London: Macmillan Press Ltd., 1973.

Koyré, Alexandre. *From the Closed World to the Infinite Universe.* Baltimore: Johns Hopkins University Press, 1957.

Krailsheimer, A. J. *Studies in Self-Interest, From Descartes to La Bruyère.* Oxford: Clarendon, 1962.

Kuhn, Thomas S. *The Structure of Scientific Revolutions.* 2d ed. Chicago: University of Chicago Press, 1970.

Langholm, Odd. "Economic Freedom in Scholastic Thought." *History of Political Economy* 14, no. 2 (summer 1982): 260–83.

———. *Wealth and Money in the Aristotelian Tradition: A Study in Scholastic Economic Sources.* Bergen: Universitetsforlaget, 1983.

Leigh, A. H. "John Locke and the Quantity Theory of Money." *History of Political Economy* 6, no. 2 (summer 1974): 200–234.

Letwin, William. *The Origins of Scientific Economics.* London: Methuen and Company Ltd., 1963.

———. *Sir Josiah Child, Merchant Economist.* Boston: Harvard Graduate School of Business Administration, 1959.

Levy, David M. "Bishop Berkeley Exorcises the Infinite: Fuzzy Consequences of Strict Finitism." *Hume Studies* 18, no. 2 (Nov. 1992): 511–36.

———. *The Economic Ideas of Ordinary People: From Preferences to Trade.* London: Routledge, 1992.

Lovejoy, Arthur O. *The Great Chain of Being: A Study of the History of an Idea.* Cambridge, MA: Harvard University Press, 1936.

Lowry, S. Todd. *The Archaeology of Economic Ideas: The Classical Greek Tradition.* Durham, NC: Duke University Press, 1987.

———, ed. *Pre-Classical Economic Thought: From the Greeks to the Scottish Enlightenment.* Boston: Kluwer Academic Publishers, 1987.

Macfarlane, Alan. *The Origins of English Individualism: The Family, Property, and Social Transition.* London: Basil Blackwell, 1978.

Macpherson, C. B. "Harrington as Realist: A Rejoiner." *Past and Present* 24 (Apr. 1963): 82–85.

———. "Harrington's 'Opportunity State.'" *Past and Present* 17 (Apr. 1960): 45–69.

———. *The Political Theory of Possessive Individualism: Hobbes to Locke.* Corrected Reprint. Oxford: Clarendon, 1964.

———. "Scholars and Spectres: A Rejoinder to Viner." *Canadian Journal of Economics and Political Science* 29, no. 4 (Nov. 1963): 559–62.

Marshall, John. *John Locke: Resistance, Religion and Responsibility.* Cambridge: Cambridge University Press, 1994.

Martin, Julian. *Francis Bacon, the State, and the Reform of Natural Philosophy.* Cambridge: Cambridge University Press, 1992.

Marx, Karl. *Capital: A Critique of Political Economy. Volume 1: The Process of Capitalist Production.* Edited by Friedrich Engels. Translated by Samuel Moore and Edward Aveling. New York: International, 1967.

———. *A Contribution to the Critique of Political Economy.* Translated by W. Ryazanskaya. Edited by Maurice H. Dobb. New York: International, 1970.

———. *Theories of Surplus Value.* 3 vols. Translated by Emile Burns. Edited by S. Ryazanskaya. Moscow: Progress Publishers, 1963.

Mayhew, N. J. "Population, Money Supply, and the Velocity of Circulation in England, 1300–1700." *Economic History Review,* 2d ser., 48, no. 2 (May 1995): 238–57.

———. "Silver, Not Sterling: A Reply to Prof. Miskimin." *Economic History Review* 49, no. 2 (May 1996): 361.

Mayr, Otto. *Authority, Liberty and Automatic Machinery in Early Modern Europe.* Baltimore: Johns Hopkins University Press, 1986.

McNally, David. *Political Economy and the Rise of Capitalism: A Reinterpretation.* Berkeley: University of California Press, 1988.

Meek, Ronald L. *Studies in the Labour Theory of Value.* London: Lawrence and Wishart, 1956.

Muchmore, Lynn. "Gerrard de Malynes and Mercantile Economics." *History of Political Economy* 1, no. 3 (fall 1969): 336–58.

Mulligan, Lotte. "Robert Boyle, 'Right Reason,' and the Meaning of Metaphor." *Journal of the History of Ideas* 55, no. 2 (Apr. 1994): 235–57.

Myers, Milton. "Philosophical Anticipations of Laissez-Faire." *History of Political Economy* 4, no. 1 (spring 1972): 163–75.

———. *The Soul of Modern Economic Man: Ideas of Self-Interest, Thomas Hobbes to Adam Smith.* Chicago: University of Chicago Press, 1983.

Neale, J. E. *Elizabeth I and Her Parliaments, 1584–1604.* New York: St. Martin's, 1958.

New, John F. H. "Harrington, a Realist?" *Past and Present* 24 (Apr. 1963): 75–81.

———. "The Meaning of Harrington's Agrarian." *Past and Present* 25 (July 1963): 94–95.

O'Brien, Patrick K. "The Political Economy of British Taxation, 1660–1815." *Economic History Review,* 2d ser., 41, no. 1 (Feb. 1988): 1–32.

Officer, Lawrence H. "The Purchasing Power-Parity-Theory of Gerrard de Malynes." *History of Political Economy* 14, no. 2 (summer 1982): 256–59.

Oldys, Sir William. *The British Librarian: Exhibiting a Compendious Review or Abstract of our most Scarce, Useful, and Valuable Books in all Sciences as well in Manuscript as in Print: With many Characters, Historical and Critical, of the Authors, their Antago-*

nists, Etc. In a Manner never before attempted, and Useful to all Readers. With a Complete Index to the Volume. London: Printed for T. Osborne, in Gray's Inn, 1738.

Olson, Richard. *The Emergence of the Social Sciences, 1642–1792.* New York: Twayne, 1993.

Overton, Mark. *Agricultural Revolution in England: The Transformation of the Agrarian Economy, 1500–1800.* Cambridge: Cambridge University Press, 1996.

Pack, Spencer J. *Capitalism as a Moral System: Adam Smith's Critique of the Market Economy.* Brookfield, VT: Edward Elgar, 1991.

Palliser, D. M. *The Age of Elizabeth: England under the Later Tudors, 1547–1603.* London: Longman Group UK Ltd., 1983.

Pauling, N. G. "The Employment Problem in Pre-Classical English Economic Thought." *Economic Record* 27, no. 52 (June 1951): 52–65.

Perlman, Mark, and Charles R. McCann Jr. *Pillars of Economic Understanding: Ideas and Traditions.* Ann Arbor: University of Michigan Press, 1998.

Phelps Brown, E. H., and Shiela V. Hopkins. "Seven Centuries of the Prices of Consumables, Compared with Builders' Wage-Rates." *Economica,* n.s., 23, no. 92 (Nov. 1956): 296–314.

Pincus, Steve. "Neither Machiavellian Moment nor Possessive Individualism: Commercial Society and the Defenders of the English Commonwealth." *American Historical Review* 103, no. 3 (June 1998): 705–36.

Pocock, J. G. A. *The Machiavellian Moment: Florentine Political Thought and the Atlantic Republican Tradition.* Princeton, NJ: Princeton University Press, 1975.

———. "To Market, to Market: Economic Thought in Early Modern England." *Journal of Interdisciplinary History* 10, no. 2 (autumn 1979): 303–9.

Popkin, Richard H. *The History of Scepticism from Erasmus to Descartes.* Assen, The Netherlands: Koninklijke Van Gorcum & Comp. N.V., 1960.

Prall, Stuart E. *The Agitation for Law Reform during the Puritan Revolution, 1640–1660.* The Hague: Martinus Nijhoff, 1966.

Pribham, Karl. *A History of Economic Reasoning.* Baltimore: Johns Hopkins University Press, 1983.

Priestley, Margaret. "London Merchants and Opposition Politics in Charles II's Reign." *Bulletin of the Institute of Historical Research* 29 (1956): 205–19.

Quinn, Stephen. "Gold, Silver, and the Glorious Revolution: Arbitrage between Bills of Exchange and Bullion." *Economic History Review* 49, no. 3 (Aug. 1996): 473–90.

Rabb, Theodore K. "Free Trade and the Gentry in the Parliament of 1604. *Past and Present* 40 (July 1968): 165–73.

———. "Investment in English Overseas Enterprise, 1575–1630." *Economic History Review,* 2d ser., 19, no. 1 (Apr. 1966): 70–81.

———. "Sir Edwin Sandys and the Parliament of 1604." *American Historical Review* 69, no. 3 (Apr. 1964): 646–70.

———. *The Struggle for Stability in Early Modern Europe.* New York: Oxford University Press, 1975.

———, and Jerrold E. Siegel, eds. *Action and Conviction in Early Modern Europe: Essays in Memory of E.H. Harbison.* Princeton, NJ: Princeton University Press, 1969.

Roll, Sir Eric. *A History of Economic Thought.* 3d ed. Englewood Cliffs, NJ: Prentice-Hall, 1956.

Roncaglia, Alessandro. *Petty: The Origins of Political Economy.* Translated by Isabella Cerubini. Armonk, NY: M. E. Sharpe, 1985.

Roseveare, Henry, ed. *Markets and Merchants of the Late Seventeenth Century: The Marescoe-David Letters, 1668–1680.* Oxford: Oxford University Press, 1987.

Rothbard, Murray N. *Economic Thought before Adam Smith: An Austrian Perspective on the History of Economic Thought.* Vol. 1. Aldershot: Edward Elgar Publishing Ltd., 1995.

Routh, Guy. *The Origin of Economic Ideas.* London: Macmillan Press Ltd., 1975.

Sacksteder, William. "Speaking about Mind: Endeavor in Hobbes." *Philosophical Forum* 11, no. 1 (fall 1979): 65–79.

Sandison, Helen E. "An Elizabethan Economist's Method of Literary Composition." *Huntington Library Quarterly* 6, no. 2 (Feb. 1943): 205–11.

Schmitt, Charles B., Quentin Skinner, et al. *The Cambridge History of Renaissance Philosophy.* Cambridge: Cambridge University Press, 1988.

Schmoller, Gustav. *The Mercantilist System and its Historical Significance, Illustrated chiefly from Prussian History; being a chapter from the Studien über die Wirtschaftliche Politik Friedrich des Grossens* (1884). Translated by W. J. Ashley. New York: P. Smith, 1931.

Schumpeter, Joseph A. *Economic Doctrine and Method: An Historical Sketch.* Translated by R. Atis. New York: Oxford University Press, 1954.

———. *History of Economic Analysis.* Edited by Elizabeth Boody Schumpeter. New York: Oxford University Press, 1954.

Shapiro, Barbara J. *Probability and Certainty in Seventeenth-Century England: A Study of the Relationships between Natural Science, Religion, History, Law, and Literature.* Princeton, NJ: Princeton University Press, 1983.

Spengler, Joseph John, and William R. Allen, eds. *Essays in Economic Thought: Aristotle to Marshall.* Chicago: Rand McNally, 1960.

Spiegel, Henry William. *The Growth of Economic Thought,* 3d ed. Durham, NC: Duke University Press, 1991.

Sreenivasan, Govind. "The Land-Family Bond at Earls Colne (Essex), 1550–1650." *Past and Present* 131 (May 1991): 3–37.

———. *The Limits of Lockean Rights in Property.* New York: Oxford University Press, 1995.

Stigler, Stephen M. "Jevons on the King-Davenant Law of Demand: A Simple Resolution of a Historical Puzzle." *History of Political Economy* 26, no. 2 (summer 1994): 185–91.

Stone, Lawrence. *An Elizabethan: Sir Horatio Palavicino.* Oxford: Clarendon, 1956.

———. "Social Mobility in England, 1500–1700." *Past and Present* 33 (Apr. 1966): 16–55.

——— and Jeanne C. Fawtier Stone. *An Open Elite? England, 1540–1880.* Abridged edition. Oxford: Oxford University Press, 1986.

Strauss, Erich. *Sir William Petty, Portrait of a Genius.* Glencoe, IL: Free Press, 1954.

Stubbs, Mayling. "John Beale, Philosophical Gardener of Herefordshire. Part II: The Improvement of Agriculture and Trade in the Royal Society (1663–1683)." *Annals of Science* 46, no. 4 (Jul. 1989): 323–63.

Supple, B. E. *Commercial Crisis and Change in England, 1600–1642: A Study in the Instability of a Mercantile Economy.* Cambridge: Cambridge University Press, 1959.

———. "Currency and Commerce in the Early Seventeenth Century." *Economic History Review,* 2d ser., 10, no. 2 (Dec. 1957): 239–55.

———. "Thomas Mun and the Commercial Crisis, 1623." *Bulletin of the Institute of Historical Research* 27 (1954): 91–94.

Suviranta, Bruno. *The Theory of the Balance of Trade in England: A Study in Mercantilism.* Helsingors: privately printed, 1923; facsimile reprint, New York: A. M. Kelley, 1967.

Tawney, Richard Henry. *Religion and the Rise of Capitalism: A Historical Study.* New York: Harcourt, Brace and World, 1926; reprint, Gloucester, MA: Peter Smith, 1962.

Thirsk, Joan. *Economic Policy and Projects: The Development of a Consumer Society in Early Modern England.* Oxford: Clarendon, 1978.

Thompson, E. P. "The Moral Economy of the English Crowd in the Eighteenth Century." *Past and Present* 50 (Feb. 1971): 76–136.

Thomson, Thomas. *History of the Royal Society, from its Institution to the end of the Eighteenth Century.* London: Robert Baldwin, 1812.

Tillyard, Eustace Mandeville Wetenhall. *The Elizabethan World Picture: A Study of the Idea of Order in the Age of Shakespeare, Donne and Milton.* Paperback ed. New York: Vintage Books/Random House [no date].

Todd, Margo. *Christian Humanism and the Puritan Social Order.* Cambridge: Cambridge University Press, 1987.

Tomlinson, Howard. "Financial and Administrative Developments in England, 1660–1688." In *The Restored Monarchy, 1660–1688.* Edited by J. R. Jones. Totowa, NJ: Rowman and Littlefield, 1979.

Toth, Kathleen. "Interpretation in Political Theory: The Case of Harrington." *Review of Politics* 37, no. 3 (July 1975): 317–39.

Toulmin, Stephen. *Cosmopolis: The Hidden Agenda of Modernity.* Chicago: University of Chicago Press, 1992.

Trevor-Roper, Hugh. *Renaissance Essays.* Chicago: University of Chicago Press, 1985.

Tribe, Keith. *Genealogies of Capitalism.* Atlantic Highlands, NJ: Humanities Press, 1981.

———. *Land, Labour, and Economic Discourse.* London: Routledge and Kegan Paul, 1978.

Tuck, Richard. *Hobbes.* Oxford and New York: Oxford University Press, 1989.

Tucker, G. S. L. *Progress and Profits in British Economic Thought, 1650–1850.* Cambridge: Cambridge University Press, 1960.

Tully, James. *An Approach to Political Philosophy: Locke in Contexts.* Cambridge: Cambridge University Press, 1993.

———. *A Discourse on Property: John Locke and His Adversaries.* Cambridge: Cambridge University Press, 1980.

Vaughn, Karen Iversen. *John Locke, Economist and Social Scientist.* Chicago: University of Chicago Press, 1980.

Venn, John, and J. A. Venn. *Alumni Cantabrigienses: a biographical list of all known students, graduates and holders of office at the University of Cambridge from the earliest times to 1900. Part One: From the Earliest Times to 1751.* Vol. 3. Cambridge: Cambridge University Press, 1924.

Vickers, Douglas. *Studies in the Theory of Money, 1690–1776.* Philadelphia: Chilton, 1959.

Vilar, Pierre. *A History of Gold and Money, 1450–1920.* Translated by Judith White. London: N.L.B., 1976.

Viner, Jacob. *Essays in the Intellectual History of Economics.* Edited by Douglas A. Irwin. Princeton, NJ: Princeton University Press, 1991.

———. "'Possessive Individualism' as Original Sin." *Canadian Journal of Economics and Political Science* 29, no. 4 (Nov. 1963): 548–66.

————. "The Perils of Reviewing: A Counter-rejoinder." *Canadian Journal of Economics and Political Science* 29, no. 4 (Nov. 1963): 562–66.

————. "Religious Thought and Economic Society: Four Chapters of an Unfinished Work by Jacob Viner." Edited by Jacques Melitz and Donald Winch. *History of Political Economy* 10, no. 1 (spring 1978): 1–192.

————. *Studies in the Theory of International Trade and Economic Theory.* Glencoe, IL: Free Press, 1952.

Waddell, D. "Charles Davenant (1658–1714): A Biographical Sketch." *Economic History Review,* 2d ser., 11, no. 2 (Dec. 1958): 279–88.

Walzer, Michael. *The Revolution of the Saints: A Study in the Origins of Radical Politics.* New York: Athenaeum, 1969.

Weber, Max. *The Protestant Ethic and the Spirit of Capitalism.* Edited by Anthony Giddens. Translated by Talcott Parsons. New York: Charles Scribner's Sons, 1976.

Webster, Charles. "The Authorship and Significance of *Macaria.*" *Past and Present* 56 (Aug. 1972): 34–48.

————. *From Paracelsus to Newton: Magic and the Making of Modern Science.* Cambridge: Cambridge University Press, 1982; reprint, New York: Barnes and Noble, 1996.

————. *The Great Instauration: Science, Medicine and Reform, 1626–1660.* New York: Holmes and Meier, 1976.

Westfall, Richard S. *The Construction of Modern Science: Mechanisms and Mechanics.* New York: John Wiley and Sons, 1971.

White, Harold Ogden. *Plagiarism and Imitation during the English Renaissance: A Study in Critical Distinctions.* Cambridge, MA: Harvard University Press, 1935.

Whitteridge, Gweneth. "William Harvey: A Royalist and No Parliamentarian." *Past and Present* 30 (April, 1965): 104–9.

Williamson, George. "The Restoration Revolt against Enthusiasm." *Studies in Philology* 30 (1933): 571–603.

Wilson, Charles Henry. *Economic History and the Historian: Collected Essays.* London: Weidenfeld and Nicolson, 1969.

————. *England's Apprenticeship, 1603–1763.* London: Longmans, 1965.

Winch, Donald. "Economic Liberalism as Ideology: The Appleby Version." *Economic History Review,* 2d ser., 38 (May 1985): 287–97.

Wood, Neal. *John Locke and Agrarian Capitalism.* Berkeley: University of California Press, 1984.

Wrigley, E. A., and R. S. Schofield. *The Population History of England, 1541–1871: A Reconstruction.* Cambridge, MA: Harvard University Press, 1981.

Yates, Frances A. *Giordano Bruno and the Hermetic Tradition.* Chicago: University of Chicago Press, 1964.

Yolton, John W., ed. *John Locke: Problems and Perspectives.* Cambridge: Cambridge University Press, 1969.

Index

Cadmus, 56

Caen, 108

Caesar, Julius, 79

Caesar, Sir Julius, 64

Calais (as "Calis"), 27

calendar systems, 30, 275

Calvinism, 12, 253, 271. *See also* Protestantism

Cambridge. *See* Oxford and Cambridge, colleges of

Campanella, Thomas, 214

Cantillon, Richard, 317

Canute II (the Great), 276

capitalism, 4, 11, 17–18, 20, 47, 161, 162–65, 170, 226, 246, 248, 253, 255, 319, 320 (*see also* agrarian capitalism; wage-labor); capitalist *Geist*, 11–12, 15–25, 132, 175, 203, 265, 271

Carleton, Sir Dudley (first Viscount Dorchester), 55–56

Carlyle, Thomas, 19

Carolinas, Lords Proprietors of, 148

Carroll, Lewis, 263

carrying trade, attitudes toward, in trade balance theory, 85, 92, 180, 312

cartography, use of, in economic tracts, 32–33

Casaubon, Meric, 174

Cassandra, 219

Castaing, John, 222, 335

Castile, 128

Catalonian Revolt, 253

Catholicism, 4, 22, 150, 213, 253, 255

Cato, Marcus Porcius (the elder), 15, 30, 57, 91, 155, 173, 212, 224, 271, 276, 279, 294

Cavendish, Thomas, 32

Cecil, Robert, 27

Challis, C. E., 279, 283

Chalmers, George, 341

Chamberlen, Hugh (the elder), 302, 329

Chamberlin, Edward Hastings, 288

Chancery Lane, 205

Chancey, Karen, 284

chaos, fear of, 2, 23, 24, 39, 67, 97, 250. See also *logos*

Charles I (king of England), 56, 64, 79, 101, 102, 108, 114, 130, 181, 284, 298

Charles II (king of England), 6, 109, 114,

127, 131, 132, 148, 187, 188, 300, 308

Chaucer, Geoffrey, 32, 276

Chaudhuri, K. N., 294

Child, Sir Josiah, 1, 3, 5, 6, 9, 101–2, 106, 113, 130–46, 148, 149, 156, 163, 175, 176, 187, 191, 205, 208, 210, 223, 247, 256, 258, 259, 261, 307–13, 337, 339

Choksy, George D., 326–27

Christendom, 15, 30, 34, 48, 69, 72, 73, 82, 288, 289, 290

Christianity, 35, 180, 255, 282, 295. *See also* *specific branches and sects of Christianity*

Churchill, John. *See* Marlborough, first duke of

Cicero, Marcus Tullius, 30, 33, 57, 253, 288, 321

cities as the heart (circulating pump) of the society, 207

Civil War, American, 67

Civil War, English. *See* English Revolution and Civil War (or Royalists and Parliamentarians)

Clarendon, first earl of (Edward Hyde), 128

classical economics, 107, 263, 290

Cleves, 53

Clitherow, Sir Christopher, 291

Cockayne, William (Alderman), 27, 46, 54, 63, 280, 283

Cohen, I. Bernard, 297, 300, 324

coins: clipping and culling of, 71, 85, 150, 151, 155, 194, 198, 201, 207, 257, 258; data on metal content, 314–15; data on supply, 53, 155, 201, 257; devaluation through debasement or depreciation, 42, 52, 68, 75, 87, 93, 149, 151, 154, 206–7, 239, 257–58, 328, 330; gold and silver, special qualities of, 43, 120, 150, 190, 239; hoarding, 71, 85, 113, 198–200, 201–2, 211, 257, 261; milled versus hammered, 150, 201, 257–58; recoinage of 1561, 26, 42, 53, 75; recoinage of 1696, 132, 149, 150–51, 154–55, 201, 206, 219, 220, 223, 236, 257–58, 340; troy weight versus avoirdupois, 41–42, 279. *See also* exchange, rates and gold-silver pars; money, metallism

Coke, Roger, 74